MW00652167

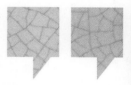

Janet Koplos

WHAT MAKES A
POTTER

Functional Pottery in America Today

SCHIFFER
PUBLISHING
4880 Lower Valley Road · Atglen, PA 19310

In memory of Warren MacKenzie (1924–2018),
indefatigable promoter of the philosophical, emotional,
and practical values of functional pottery.

Copyright © 2019 by Janet Koplos

Library of Congress Control Number:
2019936081

All rights reserved. No part of this work may
be reproduced or used in any form or by any
means—graphic, electronic, or mechanical,
including photocopying or information
storage and retrieval systems—without
written permission from the publisher.

The scanning, uploading, and distribution of
this book or any part thereof via the Internet
or any other means without the permission
of the publisher is illegal and punishable by
law. Please purchase only authorized editions
and do not participate in or encourage the
electronic piracy of copyrighted materials.

"Schiffer," "Schiffer Publishing, Ltd.," and
the pen and inkwell logo are registered
trademarks of Schiffer Publishing, Ltd.

Research for this book was supported by a
Craft Research Fund grant from the Center
for Craft, Asheville, NC.

 Center for Craft

Designed by Brenda McCallum

Type set in Faktos/Helvetica/Times

ISBN: 978-0-7643-5811-1
Printed in China
Published by Schiffer Publishing, Ltd.
4880 Lower Valley Road
Atglen, PA 19310
Phone: (610) 593-1777; Fax: (610) 593-2002
E-mail: Info@schifferbooks.com
Web: www.schifferbooks.com

For our complete selection of fine books
on this and related subjects, please visit our
website at www.schifferbooks.com. You may
also write for a free catalog.

Schiffer Publishing's titles are available at
special discounts for bulk purchases for sales
promotions or premiums. Special editions,
including personalized covers, corporate
imprints, and excerpts, can be created in
large quantities for special needs. For more
information, contact the publisher.

We are always looking for people to write
books on new and related subjects. If you
have an idea for a book, please contact us at
proposals@schifferbooks.com.

Other Schiffer Books on Related Subjects:

The Ceramics Studio Guide: What Potters Should Know,
Jeff Zamek, ISBN 978-0-7643-5648-3

William Daley: Ceramic Artist, Ruth Fine, ISBN 978-0-7643-4523-4

CONTENTS

POTTERY PERSISTS

At the University of Minnesota, as I was wrapping up my off-and-on undergraduate education, I began to write for the campus newspaper. My first published interview was with a professor who had talked with a class I was enrolled in. His name was Warren MacKenzie. If you know the world of studio (individual) pottery, that's a punch line. Fortuitously, I interviewed the most legendary and influential maker of pottery in the US in the second half of the 20th century—the only person I'm aware of who can be credited with single-handedly shaping a multigenerational community of ceramics makers and appreciators. Thus was I introduced to a creative field that has been one of the great pleasures of my life ever since.

Pottery is an ancient activity that has always been associated with both utility and aesthetic appreciation. It connects to human history in nearly all cultures and has always included domestic service items from teapots to dinner plates AND decorative objects AND symbolic objects—the basins and goblets of Christian ritual, for example. Ceramics was at the leading edge of industrialization in England and has been produced by American businesses large and small. Pottery has taken an alternative role in various periods of American history—as a creative way to make a living during the Great Depression, as support for a counterculture lifestyle during the rebellious '60s, and more recently as a tangible, tactile revitalization in an increasingly virtual era. Today, pottery is a linking field that joins art, craft, and design.

Contemporary pottery is a choice more than a necessity. It was an unexpected discovery for most current makers. Only in communities of the Appalachian Southeast and the Native American Southwest is there still a tradition of multiple generations of families producing pottery. But even where the tradition has been lost, pottery persists. There are many reasons for that. For one thing, it's a satisfying activity that gives physical pleasure through motion, rhythm, touch, and even odor during the making process, to say nothing of the visual satisfactions of the finished work. For the makers, that is a rich combination. It requires physical skills, scientific knowledge, and creative thought.

For the buyers and users of pottery, it is also physically rewarding. All ceramic objects, manufactured or handmade, offer the gratifications of form, color, pattern, and smooth, seductive glossiness, but studio pottery, being handmade by individuals, adds to that the human appeal of personality and uniqueness. Pots reflect the individual who made them as well as the buyer who responded to their subtle features. Buyers of pottery can look at a row of dishes and choose the one that distinguishes itself through a slightly different curve or shading. Users of pottery have their favorite bowls, or the particular mug whose handle width, or thickness of rim, or stability of base make it a must every morning.

The experience of using handmade pottery involves memory of—or imaginative projection into—the processes that formed it. It allows a relationship between the user and the maker invoked by the sensations of touch, a pleasure and a need apparently not eliminated by the inexpensiveness and convenience of mechanical production and wondrous new artificial materials.

Pottery is also—and this is a huge bonus—an affordable art. While it is not as cheap as mass-produced china made at slave-labor wages and imported vast distances using fossil fuels that damage the environment—costs that we forget to calculate—it is inexpensive in relation to other art forms. Compared

with a sculpture or a painting, a pot, which is an individually made, unique object, is a bargain that anyone with a modest disposable income can afford. It is no less rewarding of attention than a painting, but it tells its story in different ways.

Since that fateful meeting with Warren MacKenzie, I have been a casual collector of ceramics, but not of museum pieces. My collection goes into my kitchen cabinets and is pulled out for breakfast, lunch, and dinner. On occasion, one is lost to breakage, but that is not a staggering expense, although sometimes it is a considerable emotional loss. My cupboards, like those of any pottery aficionado, are a storehouse of personalities and stories, ideas and feelings, skills and surprises, all communicated by the pots.

The visual richness of this work may compare with that of other art forms, but there are several important differences in addition to cost. For one, pottery has traditionally been abstract rather than representational. It is understood and appreciated in formal terms of color, line, symmetry, etc. For

OPPOSITE PAGE: Noah Riedel. Banana frame, 2015. Stoneware with terra sigillata, 19" × 11" × 6".

ABOVE: Betsy Williams. "Rosa Parks' Dress," 2018. Stoneware with white slip, hand painted with underglaze oxides, electric fired to cone 6, each 4.25" dia.

another, visual aspects are not the whole effect. Pottery is tactile, and, because it's meant to be used, handling it offers another realm of sensory experience. The artist Robert Rauschenberg famously spoke of the gap between art and life, but in pottery there is no such gap. In addition, ceramics has its own history and to some degree its own language, although many art terms are shared with other mediums. Pottery as an aesthetic field has tended to be less theoretical and less verbalized than other art genres.

In the last few decades, crafts have increasingly become academicized. Subject to expectations that ceramics coincide with the goals and practices of other mediums in college coursework, pottery seemed to fall into an unprivileged position, often disregarded by professors and offered in fewer art departments. Yet again, pottery persists. Several regions of the country, in addition to MacKenzie's Upper Midwest, have become centers of handmade pottery production. North Carolina, Montana, and Maine are particular hothouses. In 2011, the Center for Crafts, Creativity and Design (now the Center for Crafts), then a part of the University of North Carolina system, awarded me a research grant that allowed me to travel to these regions to interview potters in their studios. Others I caught on their travels to places accessible to me. There remain others I would have loved to talk with but could not. There will always be others, because the field grows constantly and it can be decidedly local in emphasis.

Over several years, I talked with 160 potters, most often recording the conversations in digital files. The stories they told of their beginnings, their discovery of clay, and the development of a personal aesthetic were remarkable. For example, when I asked Matt Kelleher how he knew about handmade pottery, he gave a surprising answer: Rendezvous. His father, who worked at a John Deere manufacturing plant in Iowa, where Kelleher was born, was a history buff, and the family participated in Rendezvous, which are like Civil War reenactments but set in the 1820s mountain-man era. Everyone dresses in handmade clothes, and Kelleher wore buckskin pants that his dad had made. *The only modern thing was the cooler*, he told me. At their camps, set in farm fields or along a river, everyone would barter. In this setting, they used handmade pottery.

I couldn't make this up! Kelleher is now a professor at Alfred University, perhaps the leading ceramic program in the nation, and he says those pots would not please him now. But he thinks a great thing about it all was *challenging people to work with their hands*.

Of course, the stories of 160 people would make an impossibly large tome; his interview, like those of other fascinating people, had to be left out of this book.

But certainly, if anyone imagines that all potters are alike, they're wrong. The makers profiled here, although they largely concentrate on dishes for the table, come from different places geographically, culturally, economically, intellectually, and emotionally. Some embraced the profession as if it were predestined; others struggled to find their niche and their voice against great odds or even family opposition. All were driven by a conviction of the meaning and value of such work, convinced that their production was not just a business but something that made the world a better place.

The interviews included here are like a book of short stories that a reader can dip into and identify with. Some potters are profiled at length and some more briefly. All of the interviews—even those that with great sorrow I had to leave out—are available in full as recordings or transcriptions through the Archives of American Art, Smithsonian Institution, Washington, DC. Most transcriptions were funded by the Center for Crafts grant and made use of the skill and intelligence of Emily DuBois, herself a textile artist. A few were transcribed by volunteers convinced that the rewards of this work should be shared with a larger public. In the words of the potters you will meet in these pages, the philosophy and aesthetics of the age-old art form are made new for our time. ■

CHAPTER ONE

CURRENT CONDITIONS

Two big, world-changing events in pre-modern and modern times shaped the position of pottery in 21st-century culture. One was the Industrial Revolution. Industrialized rather than workshop production of ceramics was a central part of that revolution in the Staffordshire district of England starting in the 18th century. The most famous name in that process was Josiah Wedgwood, who started as an uneducated apprentice in his family's pottery workshop and ended up leading the change in methods, materials, and distribution of the pottery industry.

The Industrial Revolution had some favorable aspects, including an increase in the standard of living and more choice in goods for the majority of the population. The unfavorable aspects included a decrease in quality when manufacturers were concerned only with the largest profit, and a decrease in work satisfaction when labor was no longer creative. Labor was, in fact, split into repetitive and unsatisfying tasks that, the social critic John Ruskin observed, turned men into machines.[1] Ruskin's follower William Morris led a movement of educated men and women toward handmaking. In Morris's time, crafts were taken up by artists and architects as a rejection of the industrial value system.

Handmade pottery has never been totally absent since then.

The other pivot point was the aftermath of World War II. In America, when the veterans came home and went to college on the GI Bill, thousands of them chose the arts. Art departments and art schools burgeoned, and more teachers were needed in ceramics, as in many other mediums. Fewer people learned through old-fashioned apprenticeships.

An important line of information about pottery came through Bernard Leach, an Englishman who lived in Japan early in the 20th century and learned to make pottery there. He eventually became a conduit for information about Eastern aesthetic standards through the publication of *A Potter's Book* (1940), through two tours through America in the 1950s, and through apprenticeships at his Cornwall pottery (see chapter 12).

Various types of works can be included under the broad heading of "ceramics." Utilitarian pottery and decorative objects such as figurines were at first central to the new, modern American potters of the 1950s, along with pottery-like forms that were rendered nonfunctional by their large size or complicated structure. This has come to be called the "vessel" category. Sculpture —ceramic objects with little or no resemblance to pottery forms— became a serious new option, exemplified by the work of Peter Voulkos, John Mason, Daniel Rhodes, and others. The term "potter" is sometimes loosely applied to anyone working in clay, but more accurately, as used here, a potter is someone who makes utilitarian work.

Functional pottery filled the art fairs and offered a practical alternative means of support to those who wanted to live outside convention, while at the same time ceramics was becoming entrenched in academia. By the end of the 20th century, utilitarian pottery was a minority interest in the ceramics field, an underdog having to defend itself, especially in academia, as still relevant to modern times and economically sustainable. However, most ceramists make at least a little functional work—for their own use or as gifts or for fundraisers.

But in the 21st century, it's possible to assert

that pottery not only is continuing but is finding new expression and new passion in the work of a younger generation. There are multiple communities of potters and innumerable motivations pushing their work. There is no "typical" potter: each, as this book will show, has a unique story full of twists and turns. The only constants in these stories are that people fall in love with the material (malleable, sensual, responsive) or the processes (the rhythm of throwing on the wheel or the cycle of activities from preparing to shaping to drying to decorating to firing to preparing again). This is not entirely different from other art mediums—there are painters intoxicated by the smell and spreadability of their oils whose works express the fluidity and color possibilities of their chosen substance, for example—but this love of matter is a defining factor in clay.

Garth Clark, who may have written more on contemporary ceramics than anyone else in America today, offers a way to sort out current conditions in pottery—at least as he saw it in 1987. He wrote,

American ceramists who are strongly involved with utility tend to fall into three general groups, the purists, the symbolists and the stylists. The first group is the die-hard functionalists that have emerged from the British influence of Bernard Leach and [his student] Michael Cardew. They are in a strange way, despite their seemingly anachronistic stance, closer to the ideals of modernism than many more aggressively modern ceramists. The second group, the symbolists, are not true functionalists at all. They use the functional associations of pottery as a means of gaining access to a viewer's emotions, establishing a position of irony or making a statement on scale.

The third category is that of the stylists—an uneasy word in the semantic minefield of contemporary crafts for it is not generally seen to be flattering. Style is the visual sword of the Applied Arts. Stylists are not avant-garde even though their work might be innovative in a certain sense. They tend to reflect what is current in a culture's tastes, concerns and values. While the stylist might well use the fine arts as a source, they are spiritually closer to the world of design.[2]

This book might seem to favor those in the first category. Certainly a number of potters who apprenticed with Leach, and the next generation who studied with those individuals, populate these pages. But the situation has fractured into multiple branches since Clark wrote.

Two new approaches stand out and sharply contrast with postwar styles. One consists of pots made to be suitable surfaces for drawing and thus embellished with animals, human figures, or evocative scenes. Another is pots (usually cast rather than wheel-thrown) that resemble industrial design in their clarity of form and surface, although they are unique or at most limited editions, rather than mass produced.

Stylistically, there are also potters engrossed in patterning for its own sake. Some make reference to the decorative arts of cultures distant in space or in time; others find inspiration in the patterns of nature. Another subset puts the emphasis on form and material rather than applied surface ornamentation. They may do this because they find the unadorned material beautiful in itself, or because they like the feeling of collaboration with material and process, rather than the imposition of one's will upon it.

Another subset of pottery makers looks for new forms, other than the conventional bowls, jars, pitchers, and the like. Sometimes the object is still a bowl, but triangular or otherwise unusual in form. Many potters are expanding into unexpected purposes, from the heightened specificity of an asparagus server or a cracker dish to forms that are more familiar in other materials, such as juicers or spoons or spreading knives.

This book examines the range and considers the aesthetic qualities of contemporary American pottery. But more, by presenting the stories of the individuals who are following this new-old path, it teases out the philosophy that justifies handmaking in the postindustrial age. Studio pottery claims a lesser efficiency, perhaps, but a greater personal satisfaction. ■

1. John Ruskin, *The Stones of Venice*, vol. 2 (New York: E. P. Dutton, 1907), 176–77.
2. Garth Clark, "The Purist, the Symbolist, the Stylist," in *Functional Glamour: Utility in Contemporary American Ceramics*, ed. Yvonne Joris (Hertogenbosch, The Netherlands: Museum Het Kruithuis, 1987), 8.

CHAPTER TWO

WHY HANDMADE POTS?

Why is it that through the ups and down of aesthetic preferences, through mass-production undercutting of its practical justification, through the shifting market favoring branding and image uniformity, through the introduction of new technologies, there is still a desire by some people to make, and by others to buy, handmade functional pottery? In the Western world, no one has absolutely *needed* it for centuries, so there have to be other justifications. Pottery is a choice, and thus it always involves meaning.

The British art historian Philip Rawson, in his superb book *Ceramics*, noted that pottery has been used for goddess figurines, writing tablets, sculptures, electrical insulators, clothing storage, burial containers, and more. "But the constant relationship with food has probably played the most vital part in endowing pots with their special symbolic qualities."[1] And that remains a value. Even now, when sociologists worry about the disappearance of the family dinner as a time of intimacy and community, pottery is pulled out for holiday meals and given as wedding presents because it symbolizes that gathering and sharing.

But can't that sharing be just as easily symbolized by a manufactured object? It would seem so, and that's what store wedding registries are all about. The bridal couple can make a choice of style of commercial objects, devising a boundary within which gifts sure to be appreciated can be selected by any friend or relative. A small number of potters making utilitarian wares have adopted this marketing approach. Online purchasing, common for every kind of merchandise nowadays, has extended into handmade goods, notably through the website Etsy, while some makers have set up a sales capacity on their personal websites. They are addressing the conventional, expected pattern of buying and are responding to public preferences. Such behavior could be considered humane, adaptive, generous. Or it could be considered an example of yielding to a less-than-ideal means of experiencing clay just because it's the ordinary one now. It seems counterintuitive that something so tactile could be purchased without direct contact, but it happens.

Touch, in fact, comes up again and again in potters' explanations of what attracts them to clay. Just touch. The contact with the real: rough or silky or pebbled or ridged or glossy it might be, but in every case, it involves information and gratification through the fingertips. Visual art must be visual, of course, but ceramics benefits from the fact that the fingers are filled with sense receptors and can pick up information that the eyes cannot. Thus pots offer another dimension of response to artworks.

While the new outreach efforts do not allow touch until the merchandise is received, older marketing methods such as craft fairs, shops, galleries, and studio sales continue to be effective ways for people to buy handmade special dishes for the table. Before that, the source was the village local potter or an itinerant distributor, serving community needs.

But still, why pots?

Makers would answer the question in various ways. The majority of artists profiled in this book went to art school. A few had already discovered clay before that, but many stumbled across it in college and experienced an epiphany. These tend to be the most self-conscious potters, the ones who worry about it having more than a merely practical purpose. Some see it as a philosophy, some as a personal expression.

A few started as hobbyists and got serious, and

others looked into pottery simply as an enjoyable business. Hardly any studio potters were brought to clay by their parents' work, yet attraction to the continuity of tradition has influenced pottery being made today, and a considerable number of studio potters have chosen to settle in North Carolina to learn from the traditional work there, inspired by such forms as large storage jars and such techniques as wood-firing in a traditional groundhog kiln.

And what of the buyers of pottery?

Some people, exposed to craft sales on Mother's Day or pleasant summer weekends or when casually shopping during vacations, may randomly acquire a piece of pottery, sometimes marked with the place name, as a souvenir. But there comes a time, a point at which the offhand buyer becomes a more regular consumer of pottery and seeks out opportunities to buy.

I've frequently told the story of my older daughter accompanying me to a studio sale of the work of four potters, responding to a simple bowl by the Saint Paul, Minnesota, artist Jason Trebs but flinching at the price. She was instinctively comparing it to a manufactured object that might perform the same function, perhaps a plastic bowl stamped out in China and sold at Walmart or Pottery Barn. But that's apples to oranges. I launched into a defense: this was not mass-produced by a machine or made by an uneducated laborer in prescribed and repetitious effort, but by someone who went to school to study art, apprenticed, worked on his own to develop skills and a distinctive style, rented a studio space, purchased equipment and materials, devised a marketing plan. It was not and could not be the cheapest way to address any given function.

My ultimate answer to her doubt was to buy the bowl for her (and one for me). It became a kitchen accouterment, usually filled with fruit. It was not the star attraction of an event, but a cordial serving item, contributing to the sense of warmth, comfort, and plenty in a casual family environment. And she repeatedly told me, "I love that bowl!" She succumbed to the lure, and the reward, of the pottery object and from that point began to practice the same modest acquisition policy that has filled my cupboards. And—what luck!—as her husband became increasingly enamored of cooking, a growing selection of dishes gave him creative scope for presentation of food. Essentially it is the personality or power of the object that is persuasive.

Use is not just the practical aspect of pottery but an essential part of its value and justification. The potter Mark Hewitt, for example, has written of the humble mug that "by picking it up you have color in your hand, the electricity of texture against your lips, and the muscular instruction of balance in your mind. . . . A mug also has a therapeutic value in use, for it provides familiarity, consolation, comfort, and security. A mug is among the most intimate of pots."[2] If this is not a generally understood proposition in America, maybe part of the reason is our way of eating, which is not direct but makes use of metal tools. Potter Randy Johnston said, in an interview for this book, *part of the difference between people in the East like China and Japan and Korea using tableware and people in the United States using tableware is that you would rarely see a person in America in a kind of formal setting, picking up your soup bowl and drinking from it. Yet to hold a bowl of soup or a bowl of chili in your hand is a delightful experience. Number one on a cold day and it has a different physical proximity to your body, to your mouth, than if it's formally sitting on a table.* We Americans pick up dishes only to drink, but pottery encourages a more varied experience.

Studio pottery like this—for the kitchen, for the table—is not (usually) placed on a pedestal and spotlighted in a gallery or museum. But it is as much a unique object as any sculpture. Some degree of surprise is present in every handmade object, which encourages us to pay attention. The size, weight, color, or peculiarities of form, perhaps even a blemish that draws the eye or a deviation in the pot wall that gives a distinctive purchase to your hand as you hold it—details large and small—particularize and enrich the experience of every piece of pottery.

Opening a cupboard door on a collection of functional pots offers a selection of friends. It is strikingly unlike opening the cabinet to a stack of identical manufactured dishes that offer beauty and utility but nothing to distinguish one from the other. Potter Todd Piker noted that industry teaches us that perfect, consistent form and surface are desirable. *Well industry needed that sensibility. It couldn't have a populace that wanted a different one of everything; it didn't work.* Industry inured us to simply grabbing the top plate and hardly looking at it. That suits industrial food.

But what if you are using fresh local ingredients, cooking from scratch, and arranging the results on the plate with the same care and attention with which the potters make them? It's no surprise that many locavore restaurants have turned to locally made pottery in the last few years.

Every pot is distinctive and each has ideal partners. So going to the cupboard is not just choosing a tool according to form and size. It's like getting dressed, choosing by mood as well as fit. This fact makes every use—whether of a cereal bowl or a platter for the Thanksgiving turkey—a moment to be lived and enjoyed. It is also, in a sense, an on-call performance in which we are the producers.

Randy Johnston said that the plates he and his family use for food *are very, very important to us, and they function beyond just holding a croissant or a cookie or olives. There's a communication that's going on from the maker to the user. And we complete that process by using it for food. We'll hear back from buyers how much better the food tasted off the pots.* [Laughter] *I don't know if they're just pandering, but I think it's true. We've had other people come back and say, "You know, after I've used handmade pots I can't go back to the kinds of dishes that I was using." I truly believe that pots have the ability to transcend time and culture. And that's one of the things I love about using pots on a daily basis in the home.*

And what if the pot *were* on a pedestal and spotlighted? The visually apprehensible tactile range of the surface, along with its three-dimensional nature as an object, can keep viewers moving around a pot. Formal aspects can be satisfying enough in themselves: human beings seem to respond both instinctively and culturally to these visual and physical experiences. But humans are also meaning-makers, and every quality can be interpreted for suggested or specified meaning. Placing a pot on a pedestal encourages such musings.

The association of a vessel to the body is long established. It is conveyed in verticality and stance, sometimes in proportion, and most of all in the metaphors by which the parts of a pot are named. These could all as easily have other names, but the fact that body terms are commonplace shows the deep urge of people to find themselves, find the familiar, in their surroundings. It also demonstrates, clearly, the longtime, intimate association of people and pots.

Thinking of utilitarian pottery on a pedestal may help us focus on it and really see it. But mindful use itself may do the same. The Japanese tea ceremony, begun centuries ago as a spiritual observance, subsequently became equally an occasion for appreciation of hospitality, aesthetic environment, and the ritualized pleasures of using the implements of making and drinking tea. With thought, any meal could be the same, and the intentionality and variety of handmade pottery suit the effort to focus on the experience of a moment and the particularities of an event.

It's important to realize that the current privileging of a political, social, or psychological meaning that can be encapsulated in a few words is just one choice among many values for an artwork. According to the aesthetic anthropologist Jacques Maquet, it is just the current Euro-American preference. He writes that if all cultures in all times are surveyed, it is the formal qualities that make something art.[3]

The participatory act of using rather than the more passive act of looking might, in fact, *be* the sociological or psychological message; asserting this independent path has a "political" aspect because it resists routine and ordinary obliviousness. The option to handle pottery distinguishes it from other arts.

In addition, sometimes the very fact of craft skills and processes is a "message." Sometimes the amount of labor in craft has been questioned, particularly when midcentury conceptual art asserted that the idea was the only important thing. But apparently that answer was not sufficient. Today the amount of labor-focused work in installation, painting, and other genres, to say nothing of crafts, suggests that engagement in the task of making is something that's valuable in itself. Psychologist Mihaly Csikszentmihalyi has argued that to be engaged in a task that requires all one's attention but is not so difficult that it's frustrating is the most satisfying human activity.[4]

And if this might seem merely therapeutic or hedonistic, a number of thinkers have identified the hands as information-gathering tools that furnish the facts for broader issues. Potter Rob Barnard wrote more than a decade ago, "It is the physical senses that inform the spiritual: by this I mean physical senses are the route by which we begin to understand the nature of being."[5] In *The Craftsman*, sociologist Richard Sennett repeatedly argues that making is thinking.[6] In *Shop Class as Soulcraft*, Matthew B. Crawford—both a PhD in political philosophy and a motorcycle repairman—argues for the intellectual value of concrete knowledge.[7] All these theses attempt to reengage the tangible elements of the real world, which crafts in general have never devalued.

Still another realm in which pottery has meaning for the maker and the user is in its allusions to other times and other cultures. In medieval Japan, shoguns were so desirous of Korean potters' skills that they invaded that country and kidnapped potters. Local conditions defined the character of a nation's or a region's pottery, but then people from elsewhere wanted it too. Even if we might not applaud greed of this sort, simple appreciation is extremely widespread, and potters themselves often become obsessed with historical forms. Ceramics history speaks of beauty, power, economics, and more.

Still, the question of "why pots" is not completely answered by these visual and physical attractions and the capacity of meaning. Perhaps it can only be answered in the stories of the makers. ∎

1. Philip Rawson, *Ceramics* (Oxford: Oxford University Press, 1971), 3.
2. Mark Hewitt and Nancy Sweezy, *The Potter's Eye: Art and Tradition in North Carolina Pottery* (Chapel Hill: University of North Carolina Press, 2005), 49.
3. Jacques Maquet, *Introduction to Aesthetic Anthropology*, McCaleb Module in Anthropology (Reading, MA: Addison-Wesley, 1971), passim.
4. Mihaly Csikszentmihalyi, *Flow: The Psychology of Optimal Experience* (New York: HarperCollins, 1990), passim.
5. Rob Barnard, "A New Use for Function," in *The Body Politic: The Role of the Body and Contemporary Craft*, ed. Julian Stair (London: Crafts Council, 2000), 71.
6. Richard Sennett, *The Craftsman* (New Haven, CT: Yale University Press, 2008), passim.
7. Matthew B. Crawford, *Shop Class as Soulcraft* (New York: Penguin, 2009), passim.

CHAPTER THREE

HOW TO READ A POT

I f pottery is as visually abstract as a painting might be, and if it is to be understood through its formal elements of shape, color, texture, and the like, how does a person read those qualities? How can the pots illustrated in this book be appreciated and understood?

The best advice about critical writing that I ever got was from Shirley Johnson, an English professor turned potter. I was new to art writing then, and I needed to write about a show at the Rochester (Minnesota) Art Center. I had no idea what to say. Shirley said, "Well, what do you see?" I started, haltingly, saying the obvious: that it was ceramic, it was on the wall, it was multipart, it didn't have much color, and so on. I wrote up the show—not expertly, but at least sensibly. I later realized what good advice that was: not what the artist claims in a printed artist's statement, not what someone else says or writes about it, not what the press release says, but what you see. Careful looking is the essence.

This same advice could benefit anyone looking at or thinking about pottery. Start with what you see. In any field, knowledge is an advantage, deepening the appreciation of the work and furnishing a more specific vocabulary. But visual art must start with what is visually expressed. That's as true of a pot as of a painting.

So let's look at two forms as samples, a bowl and a vase. The bowl is the simpler of the two, a container recognizably related to the cupping of two hands. We know from everyday life experience that it can vary enormously in height and width, and that it is usually approximately round. The roundness can be squared off or pushed into an oval, a triangle, or any other geometric configuration. The walls can be thick, thin, or graduated from top to bottom. Walls may rise straight from a small base to a wider rim (making the profile of the bowl triangular and its form conical), or it may swell and recede—low, high, or in the middle.

The rim may turn inward or outward, be wide or cropped off. The opening will always be wide enough to allow easy access to the interior. Depending on the height and angle of the wall, the bowl form offers a range of exposure from predominantly interior to predominantly exterior, or both may be seen equally. Each of these aspects can convey a subjective, yet often shared, visual or emotional quality. For example: a wide, low bowl might be read as generous or relaxed while a smaller one feels precious and one with a bulging wall may seem sensuous. Lobed bowls, with their multiple curves, can seem fleshy to the point of erotic. A thin wall may seem tautly stretched, hovering momentarily, in danger of explosion or collapse. The width of the bowl's base can convey a feeling of stability or one of precariousness. Or it can be largely unnoticeable, secretively concealed by a low curve in the profile. All these characteristics and emotional associations are products of the form alone.

A vase is a more complex object, and its verticality gives it a suggestion of posture. Coinciding with that association, it offers the most extensive metaphors for aspects of the human body. A vocabulary of pottery that is familiar to most people calls the base a foot and the rim a mouth or lip. Vases also have necks, shoulders, waists, or bellies. More often than not, the vase form is linked to the female body. Vases emphasize the outside surface of the pot, offering only a glimpse of the inside at the mouth. But the contours themselves "speak about the space inside, expressing a dialogue with that space."[1] The inside/outside dynamic, along with the interior volume, is in fact a defining aesthetic of pottery, and a source of emotional associations such as swelling, thrusting, enfolding, closing, opening (the list is Garth Clark's[2]). Artist and teacher Richard Zakin has written, "For the ceramist, form is a shell or wall and volume is the space created and surrounded by that shell."[3]

Form often denotes time. Piercing, for example, or merely a visible seam, may make the viewer/user conscious of the process of construction and that the pot came into existence by the action of hands, over a period of time. Probably the most characteristic and distinctive evidence of pottery process is throwing rings, the mark of the potter's hand or tool spiraling up from the base. Throwing rings may be fine and tight, loose and ragged, or anything in between. They offer an opportunity for users to lay their hands in the place where the maker's hand was, offering time-travel bonding.

Classic vase forms can usually be identified by profile (the silhouette in rotation, assuming that the pottery wall around the central volume of space is uniform). Even when pots are not axially symmetrical, such as teapots that are assembled of many parts, they are often bilaterally symmetrical. Splitting the teapot from spout to handle would result in two mirror-image parts. It can still be identified in profile. Profile is a defining, encompassing line, and line in a broader application is part of the dynamic that leads viewers' eyes around the form—particularly engaging in a three-dimensional object that necessitates "mobile, surveying attention," in Philip Rawson's words.[4]

Profile calls attention to the lower termination of the pot. A great many pots have a trimmed foot ring on the bottom. Others meet the table bluntly and flatly, but even those often have a tiny angled edge cut away at the bottom, which creates a shadow separating the pot from the supporting surface. The subtle effect of this is that the perusing eye is held within that boundary, so that the motion suggested by curves and lines is contained.[5] Unlike sculpture, pottery seldom directs the eye outward and seldom interacts with the surrounding space. Profile might be called the potter's conceptual understanding of the pot, since it can be seen only when one steps back from a pot or raises it up. The potter in the process of throwing feels the profile rather than sees

it. (Throwing "off the hump" is an uncommon technique in America in which a large mass of clay is centered on the wheel, and a succession of pieces are shaped from the top of the mass. The potter works higher, bends over less, and can see more of the profile.)

Handles, although they are functional only on a few types of pots (mugs and cups, pitchers, casseroles, sugars and creamers, etc.), add an interesting element of complexity and should not be ignored. Generally they are consistent with aspects of the pot such as weight and curvature. The most persuasive handles seem to complete some other curve of the pot, such as echoing the contour of the belly, so that the movement of the eye directed by the handle leads back into the pot's volume.[6] Spouts are even more restricted in occurrence but again are an opportunity for the potter to comment on the other parts of the pot. Spouts are also the one part of the pot that may suggest masculinity: some are penile or scrotal. Lids are another element exclusive to functional pottery. Inset or overlapping? Diminutive or generous? Knobs on lids are yet another ingredient in the mix. Related or contrasting? Hidden or decisively terminating the pot?

"Surfaces are one of the great resources of the ceramist."[7] Every pot engages surface qualities of texture and color, which have their own sensibilities and associations. Ceramic glazes, which may be colored or transparent, typically add a glassy reflectivity to the surface, and when the reflection is sharpest it may involve viewers themselves in the surface, or the environment that surrounds the pot, making the view anything from optically playful to chaotic. Matte glazes and sandblasted surfaces eliminate reflection and look softer.

There are texture variations of many sorts: for example, a salt glaze (sodium chloride is thrown into the kiln during the late stages of firing) may have a pebbled surface whose character is aptly described as orange peel, or a gentle sheen sensuously suggestive of damp skin. Firing a kiln with wood can provide a sharply distinctive surface. In the kiln, wood ash may melt on the hot pot, creating a greenish, often runny glaze. If there is less ash, the portions of the pot facing the fire may be "flashed" with a blush or a streak of orange that is a permanent effect of being struck by the flames roaring through the kiln from the firebox at the front to the chimney at the back. Pots are placed in the wood-burning kiln unglazed to capitalize on these effects, and some wood-firers seek the crustiest surfaces possible. But pots may also be positioned to mostly avoid the direct effects, or protected by cylinders called saggars. On the other hand, saggars may be packed with combustible materials to create individualistic smoked effects on the surfaces of the pots within.

Before anything else, the clay substance itself may have a visual interest. There are three basic clays: earthenware, stoneware, and porcelain, which are most often red, gray, and white, respectively (although stoneware may have the other two colors and porcelain may be altered by added pigments). Only porcelain can be thrown thin enough to be translucent.

For most of history, potteries were established where there was good clay, so every pot had a regional character. A few materials were mined and shipped, desired broadly for their particular qualities, such as dark Albany slip from the Hudson valley. In the 20th century, clay was increasingly a commercial product, refined for consistency and dependability. If that product is equated with chain hotels—you know what to expect when you make a reservation—local clays are like boutique hotels, each different. Even nonexperts may perceive particular qualities of less refined clay, such as how grainy it is and whether there are bits of stone and other inclusions. A number of younger potters are digging their own clay, so their material is unique.

Identifying it isn't necessary, but noticing differences is interesting and sometimes is part of a specific primal or other message. One of the recent contemporary-art explorations of ceramics, the exhibition "Dirt on Delight: Impulses That Form Clay," organized by the Institute of Contemporary Art in Philadelphia, chose to focus on this essence. Catalog essayists reveled in its association with "base impulses" and called it "the antithesis of the virtual and synthetic."[8]

Interest in the material itself is one explanation for the practice of clay cognoscenti turning over every pot they handle to examine the foot: it's unglazed, so that it won't stick to the kiln shelf, and thus it reveals the visual and tactile character of the clay, undisguised.

The importance of material—an emphasis that defines all the crafts—sometimes seems to be a partnership of maker and medium. "I think that materials suggest ideas about form," Warren Seelig has written. Expression is recorded in process, he added.[9]

While some glazes with distinctive coloration, such as uranium and lead, are no longer used for health reasons, pottery has become more colorful in recent decades. Stoneware, the dominant material in the '50s and '60s explosion of interest in clay, is fired at high temperatures that burn out bright color. But since then, the growing popularity of lower-temperature earthenware has offered more color opportunities, and also new glaze materials and stains have expanded the range. There's the old option of underglazes (a flatter color usually protected by a final layer of clear glaze). And there are new and unorthodox options such as actual paint—although that restricts the utility of the ceramic object and is not found in functional pottery.

Color, in any art medium, can seem to advance or recede and can give an impression of weight. Since most clays are, of course, earth colored, lots of pottery is brown. For some observers this is a problem. Brown is dirt-y (not dirty) and the opposite of white, which has been associated with purity. Yet, brown might instead be regarded as embodying chocolate- or coffee-richness, or honeyed warmth. The historic brown-black Albany slip and the dark Japanese glaze called *tenmoku* have a soothing depth. Of stoneware, potter Randy Johnston says, *It's not Fiesta ware.* [Laughter] *It's not uranium glaze. But there is, in fact, I think a tremendous range of hue and value in all the surfaces that you see on the pots. We wood-fire. We use slip that tends to flash into the red spectrum, so there's a lot of contrast between black, yellow, and red,* although not, he concedes, in the sense of light, bright primary colors. To that degree, color has always been a contributor to pottery's aesthetic effect.

A balance of emphasis on surface along with form tends to distinguish ceramics from classical or modern sculpture, in which form has been primary. Sculpture has become more colorful in recent decades. Perhaps ceramics was the inspiration.

An underglaze, which is low-fired, usually stays where it's put. But many of the young potters drawing on their pots today take pleasure in allowing the glaze to move, so that it sometimes resembles a wash on an ink drawing. Wood-fired pottery offers an entirely different range. There have always been potters who regard the kiln as a collaborator in the process and enjoy the risk of changes that cannot be entirely controlled. Flashing or drip effects are clues to the pot's position from front to back and side to side within the kiln, as well as its orientation (vertical, horizontal, right-side up or not, etc.). It is not essential that a viewer be able to puzzle out these clues, but even the simple awareness that those conditions affect the surface can make the object more intriguing. It's another dimension, like meeting a person with an interesting history.

In addition to explicitly ceramic qualities, a pot can be read for the formal qualities possible in any artwork, such as a diagonal line conveying dynamism, a horizontal line seen as stable, and a vertical line seen as aspiring. In addition, pots can carry imagery, with its staggering variety of qualities and meanings. They can carry graphic emblems, and they can carry text. These three systems of information may simply appear as if on a piece of paper or a wall, but they may also be integrated into the form, moving around it in three dimensions and perhaps responding to details such as edges, curves, or handles—an opportunity for complex expression.

One may experience the topography of the pot mentally, as if climbing a mountain in thought. The object remains a pot even when its impact includes the image. When a painting captures you, you forget that it is an object of wood and stretched canvas (or the like), but the pot always retains its identity. (One possible exception to that statement is Yixing teapots that convincingly take the form of a log or an animal; the illusion is persuasive.)

The traditional patterning of surfaces is almost always fitted to the pot, following its contours and adapted to the available space. Patterns don't require imagination. Instead they encourage a numeric or spatial sensitivity and can be read as rhythmic. In some cultures, the rhythm of pattern is like an incantation and makes magic.[10] Here and today they are more likely to offer the optical pleasure of ornament.

The visual capabilities of pots are too many to fully catalog. The important thing is to realize that all carry expressive meanings. They are more likely to be small scale and subtle. No matter what their meaning, pots remain in essence containers, with an interior volume that can be revealed or concealed but is always suggested by the contours of the overall form.

One difficulty of reading a pot, however, is that function can't be evaluated by vision alone. A critic studying a pot in an art gallery would not have the opportunity to use it and so cannot judge how a handle feels, how a teapot pours, etc. To discuss a functional object without mentioning its utility is lamentable but often happens, especially when it is presented and considered in an art-supporting context. The buyer of a pot does not share that limitation.

Another dilemma is that since the move of crafts into academia in the middle of the last century, goals more intrinsic to painting or sculpture have infiltrated. Functional potters, facing the expectation that their art, like any other art, should display experimentation and individuation, have responded "with work romantic in its impulse toward exaggeration, asymmetry, expressiveness, and dominance of the parts over the whole. Classical ideals of harmony, symmetry, restraint, and dominance of the whole over the parts fell out of favor," writes Clary Illian.[11] It's a matter of degree. One could argue that potters have always experimented and created their own signature looks; even for the most utilitarian objects, a distinctive style, like a brand, would encourage sales. And traditional forms naturally provide a starting point for form exploration. The changes may be nuances rather than bombshells. Writing for the "Dirt on Delight" show, Glenn Adamson asserted, "What is at stake is not the status of clay, but the viability of human-scaled artworks in general. Perhaps it is only under the present circumstances, with their unprecedented profusion of the larger-than-life, that a total commitment to object-making could seem radical again."[12]

At the same time, it's impossible to deny that wishing to be defined as art has had a pernicious effect on pottery, perhaps undercutting its purity of purpose by making "use" seem irrelevant, outdated, or even mindless, which it certainly is not. The artists profiled in this book have worked it out for themselves that straightforward function is inherently beautiful. And only rarely does the political appear in functional work. Meanings are more usually suggested than stated.

Painting exercises the eye; sculpture echoes the body, but pots express and are addressed to the hand. "They acquire their full meaning within arm's reach, in the confiding zone—the ambit of embraces—where the sovereignty of sight blurs into that of touch," Peter Schjeldahl has poetically observed.[13] The experience may be individual—just you and your mug—or it may be designed for sharing, as a bowl that's passed at the table.

The pot is not something to be studied from afar for a powerful impact. It's more nearly an experience, or an exchange in which the viewer turns into a participant. But within that more intimate compass, its interests can include form, contour, line, color, rhythm, directionality, apparent weight, image, text and other visual forces, and most notable of all, the information and the delights of touch. ∎

1. Clary Illian, *A Potter's Workbook* (Iowa City: University of Iowa Press, 1999), 13.
2. Garth Clark, *American Potters: The Work of Twenty Modern Masters* (New York: Watson-Guptill, 1981), 27.
3. Richard Zakin, *Ceramics: Ways of Creation* (Iola, WI: Krause, 1999), 271.
4. Philip Rawson, *Ceramics* (Oxford: Oxford University Press, 1971), 110.
5. Illian, *A Potter's Workbook*, 14.
6. Ibid., 36.
7. Zakin, *Ceramics: Ways of Creation*, 271.
8. Ingrid Schaffner and Jenelle Porter, *Dirt on Delight: Impulses That Form Clay* (Philadelphia: Institute of Contemporary Art, University of Pennsylvania, 2009), 8, 31. The exhibition traveled to the Walker Art Center, Minneapolis.
9. Warren Seelig, "Craft and the Impulse to Abstract," in *The Haystack Reader: Collected Essays on Craft, 1991–2009*, ed. Stuart Kestenbaum (Orono, ME: University of Maine Press, 2010), 46, 47.
10. Rawson, *Ceramics*, 159.
11. Illian, *A Potter's Workbook*, 92.
12. Glenn Adamson, "Sloppy Seconds: The Strange Return of Clay," in *Dirt on Delight: Impulses That Form Clay*, 80.
13. Peter Schjeldahl, "Feats of Clay: Ken Price's Ceramic Art," *New Yorker*, October 6, 2003, 134.

CHAPTER FOUR

ROLE MODELS

The story of today's functional pottery starts in the mid-20th-century postwar period, with the sudden expansion of the whole crafts field. Many people made utilitarian works. Leading figures, whose names are heard often in interviews with today's potters and who served as models and whose work has been influential to younger potters, are briefly profiled here as a starting point. An interview with Clary Illian, a senior figure whose analysis of pottery form contributed to the last chapter, serves as a transition to the interviews that make up the remainder of the book.

During the 1940s and 1950s, **Robert Turner** (1913–2005) was an exemplar of functional potting as a moral choice. A Quaker, Turner studied painting and during World War II was a conscientious objector, working at a forestry conservation camp and at a school for the "mentally deficient." By the end of his service he felt the need for something more practical than painting. Clay was his choice. After earning his MFA from Alfred University in western New York, he was hired to establish a pottery program at Black Mountain College in North Carolina. Although Black Mountain was famous for its experimental arts, Turner identified himself not as an artist but as a potter. After two years he resigned and returned to the Alfred area, where he taught occasionally but concentrated on his pottery production cycle, which he regarded as like a cycle of seasons.

He developed simple forms with some of the quiet clarity of Scandinavian design, which was popular at the time. In his own words, he made "unassuming, practical things."[1] He worked for integration of all aspects into a state of harmony. The glazes are soft and not reflective. Surprisingly

for someone who started as a painter, he concentrated on form rather than elaborating on surface.

Turner gradually moved away from pottery, seeking introspective and spiritual inspirations. His subsequent objects retained a resemblance to vases and covered jars but became strikingly allusive of the physical nature of landscapes and structures in places he traveled to. Probably a certain mystical bent was always in him. M. C. Richards, a poet who also taught at Black Mountain and who took up pottery and later wrote the classic *Centering: In Pottery, Poetry, and the Person*, recalled how he gave a demonstration there: "He was centering the clay, and then he was opening it and pulling up the walls of the cylinder. He was not looking at the clay. He had his ear to it. He was listening. 'It is breathing,' he said; and then he filled it with air."[2] Everyone who has written about him at length has noted how he and the clay engaged in an interchange that altered them both.

After a very informal introduction to the material, **Karen Karnes** (1925–2016) was first involved in industrial ceramics, making lamp bases. Her talent brought her an invitation to design them as well. She and her then husband, David Weinrib, moved to Italy after World War II, where she studied at a school that taught factory workers how to throw. She had a gift for it. She had a wheel built and set it up in their apartment. She also molded "free-form" works in the amoebic style of the time. Back in the US, two pieces that she'd made in Italy won a purchase prize in the Syracuse Ceramic National, the most important exhibition of the day.

She was in residence at Alfred University (although not taking classes) when she and her husband were offered the position of resident potter at Black Mountain College, following Robert Turner. Soon after their arrival they made serving bowls and ashtrays for the dining hall "to demonstrate a possible role for the production potter in a community."[3] Bernard Leach came to Black Mountain that fall with his Japanese friends, philosopher Soetsu Yanagi and masterful potter Shoji Hamada. She said later, "Watching Hamada work was the most important ceramic instruction I, as a young potter, could have."[4]

Karnes and Weinrib remained at the college for two years. In 1954, M. C. Richards invited them to join her at the Gate Hill Community in Stony Point, New York, where another of the neighbors was composer John Cage. Karnes was quickly successful, with the support of the American Crafts[men's] Council and the upscale store Bonniers. She made a great variety of functional forms, including cups, jam pots, plates, and containers of all sorts, and also encompassing garden seats, bird houses, fountains, ovens, planters, molded sinks, and even a urinal. Richards later wrote of Karnes, "Her work is clean, expert, uncluttered, useful, beautiful, restrained but warm, full of a feeling of original plasticity as well as the advantages of stone."[5]

After being introduced to flameproof clay for cooking on top of the stove, Karnes developed a casserole that she made and sold for decades: low and wide mouthed, with two grips at the fullest point, throwing rings that made it look stable, and an inset lid capped by a fluid, somersaulting pulled handle. Karnes was a rare potter who never formally taught. But she both led and benefited from workshops, using them as pivot points for changes in the aesthetic character of her work through changes in process.

Her functional forms continued to be stable, simple, sensible, and fascinatingly tactile. "A nicely thrown pot has a life from the wheel. Fussing with it can destroy that," she said.[6] The low-key confidence of her wares and her long success at functional work made her a hero of the field. She focused on utility until the late '70s. She began to add various sculptural vessel forms when she started showing her work with Hadler/Rodriguez Gallery in New York.

Betty Woodman (1930–2018) found clay early and enrolled in 1948 in the two-year journeyman program at the new School for American Craftsmen, then located at Alfred University in western New York State. Although she was introduced to the ideas of the East when Bernard Leach toured America,

stopping at Alfred, what shaped her future was a trip to Italy in 1951. She returned twice over the next decade or so and then, in 1968, with her husband, George, a painter, bought an old farmhouse near Florence. Thereafter she divided her time between Italy and the US.

The effect upon her was that she worked in earthenware even as, in the '50s and '60s, "serious" (manly) American work was made of stoneware. She also clearly responded to the colors of Italy, although she did not adopt maiolica surfaces (tin-glazed—bright colors on a white background over the red earthenware). Over time, the historicism, cultural mixing, and dense decoration of Italian traditions may have subtly influenced her work, and even more, the Italian approach to food changed her life and work.

In her early years, Woodman was a conventional potter, making serving dishes, mugs, and even some dinnerware sets. For a number of years her husband decorated her forms. When he stopped doing that in 1971, she briefly left them undecorated and then began to work with a palette inspired by Islamic pottery. She began making what she called "Sunday" pottery, such as oversize dishes for very specific and not-very-common purposes, such as a mussel server. In doing so she was exaggerating the ceremony of dining; she might be said to have put this important pottery-centered sharing ritual onto a pedestal.

The couple began living part time in New York City and engaged with the Pattern & Decoration movement of the mid-1970s, which celebrated the visual qualities of the decorative arts. She began using color almost as antiform: her spontaneous applications of vivid hues were discontinuous, rather than underscoring the details or unity of the form. Her decoration has been compared with the painting of Henri Matisse and Pierre Bonnard. Ceramic influences were surely Chinese Tang-dynasty three-color ware, and the mix of solid and pattern in Japanese Oribe ware. She moved into making large-scale and multipart works, wall pieces, and installations. But she continued to make reference to function by placing flowers in her vases rather than treating them purely as abstracted vessel forms. During her Metropolitan Museum show in 2006 the niches in the lobby featured enormous bouquets in her pots.

Her signature work after the '70s might be discussed in relation to architectural ornament and structure, since she emphasized construction and space. But her devotion to clay and the occasional tableware she made (such as porcelain teacups made at the historic manufactory at Sèvres in France) maintained her identity as a role model in the escape from narrow definitions of how clay might look, where it might be found, and how it might be appreciated.

John Glick (1938–2017) achieved renown as a master organizer in the pot shop. He also wrote extensively, sharing his business skills. He made limited-edition and one-of-a-kind functional pots and took commissions for dinnerware, at one point amassing a seven-year backlog of orders![7] His use of an assistant was uncommon in his early days and seemed more like a European production shop practice than the informal and personal habits of American studio potteries of the time. The assistant threw pots or assembled handbuilt parts, so that he could concentrate on decoration and finishing. He gave a good deal of thought to his showroom, since he sold primarily there rather than in shops or galleries. That gave him immediate feedback on users' expectations and needs.

Glick also led an expansion of the use of the extruder, then primarily used for handles, to form parts of his slab-built wares. In the late '60s he introduced mold-made forms, which does not quite fit the overall image of his body of work, which is loose and exuberant. In the late '70s he was commissioned to make table settings for the vice president's house during the Carter-Mondale administration.

He favored large plates and long extruded boxes because they provided a generous field for decoration. His first signature treatment consisted of iron spots bleeding through glaze, and later he used a variety of means (including slips, stains, and oxides) in a combination of dripped and brushed color that could recall J. M. W. Turner's painted fogs or might suggest abstracted flowers. The fluid, transparent color patches and lines through the glaze seemed to richly respond to the notched rims of the plates, and they can also be associated with abstract expressionist painting. Looking at the surfaces often feels like looking through water, with colors floating in uncertain depths. In his later years he worked on panels, giving his motifs a pictorial platform.

Warren MacKenzie (1924–2018) came to clay as many people have done since. Unable to get into a painting class—when he returned to studies at the School of the Art Institute of Chicago after service in World War II—he enrolled in a ceramics class. There he met and married Alixandra Kolesky, who thought ceramics would be useful at the settlement house where she worked. Together they looked at pottery from other cultures and times in Chicago's Field Museum of Natural History. They responded to the vitality and practicality of the work. Their school did not teach throwing, but another student found Bernard Leach's *Potter's Book*, which had been published in England in 1940. It was a revelation, not only introducing aesthetic criteria but giving guidance into how one could live as a potter. They taught themselves to throw.

Soon after moving to Minnesota for a teaching job at the St. Paul Gallery and School of Art, the MacKenzies concluded that they didn't know enough, and they fixed upon the idea of apprenticing with Leach. They traveled to England the next summer, presented their pots, and were rejected. However, Leach allowed them to hang around for a few days, and with the extended conversation that occurred, he changed his mind. They returned the following spring and were trained by Leach's son David in the exacting production of the pottery's standard ware. Over two years, they became quick and skillful throwers. Equally important were the long discussions with Leach of pottery history and the character of various pots in his collection. "My close friendship with Bernard, which lasted until his death, has been the most important influence in my life. My work is more influenced by Shoji Hamada and Korean pottery. But in attitudes and goals, Leach has always guided my thinking," MacKenzie has said.[8]

Back in Minnesota, the MacKenzies established a studio and set on a course of proselytizing, creating an audience for their work through talks, demonstrations, and a studio salesroom. That, combined with his teaching at the University of Minnesota and thus generating more potters who also went on to sell, teach, or both, gradually made Minnesota into one of America's centers for ceramics, much of it utilitarian.

The MacKenzies worked collaboratively, with Warren throwing and Alix decorating in a linear, modernist style. Her death at the age of 39 was a double blow. Feeling unable to match her decoration, MacKenzie took to creating surface interest through form—fluting, faceting, pinched or doubled rims—and direct mark-making such as roller patterns or finger wipes through wet slip. All give a sense of process and touch and create a distinct aesthetic of subtleties, details, nuances—one that MacKenzie himself has compared with the nondramatic character of the midwestern landscape around him. He said that getting to know a pot was like getting to know a person, something that best develops over time.[9]

MacKenzie's forms embody vitality, propulsion, or inflation: the energy comes from within. He has never tired of functional work and has never shown the urge to emphasize expression.

Byron Temple (1933–2002) opened a studio in New Jersey in 1963 and continued to produce utilitarian pottery that blended Scandinavian, Japanese, English, and American character until his death. His preparation for his lifework involved coil building in high school, throwing in college, and working as a technician at an art school, but perhaps most crucial was that before opening his own pottery he apprenticed as a thrower at the Leach pottery in England. Temple followed his own course with his admiration of the minimal and angular qualities of Scandinavian design, which Leach did not share.

Temple practiced efficiencies that he learned at the Leach pottery, such as throwing by weight and working so that trimming was unnecessary. He produced about 10,000 pieces of tableware per year, often half-glazing them so that part of the surface was left bare. He also fired pots inside saggars packed with sawdust, introducing an element of chance into the surfaces of standard forms. Temple argued for the value of repetition. "As a production potter I limit myself to designs which can be easily repeated. I do not find this restrictive or inhibiting; rather I'm able to explore more intensely the very basic qualities of the clay," he said, adding that repetition reduced the likelihood of affectation or preciousness.[10] He marketed his work by producing a poster that cataloged seven standard objects that could be ordered by individuals or shops.

Temple's work was self-effacing but elegant, reserved but entirely open to the "intimacy of use."[11] As such, it was a quintessential example of the philosophy of the functional, which puts the user ahead of the maker and does not strive to make pottery live by the rules of painting or sculpture. Temple adhered to the simple and practical values of the farm life in which he was raised. He taught at Greenwich House Pottery in New York City and the Penland School of Crafts in North Carolina and took apprentices at his pottery.

Cynthia Bringle (b. 1939) is indelibly associated with the Penland School of Crafts. In fact, she has been called the "mayor" of Penland, having long taught there, served on its board, done "missionary" work promoting it, and established her home and studio along the road leading to the school. She was among the first craftspeople to take up residence nearby; there is now a considerable community. Her comfortably creative life has been available as a model for all who pass through the school, and the Southern Highlands Handicraft Guild once honored her with an exhibition including works by 23 potters who acknowledged her influence. She has even served as a matchmaker for students.

Bringle started in art school as a painter but was seduced by clay. She earned an MFA at Alfred University, where she studied with Robert Turner, and she took a two-week workshop with Shoji Hamada. She especially responded to Hamada's brushstrokes, and her own vocabulary of brushwork has been one of the most characteristic identifiers of her work. She thinks of it as painting, just on a three-dimensional surface.

Her first studio was near her hometown of Memphis, but she found living there too solitary. She moved to Penland in 1970, and she and her twin sister, Edwina, a weaver, taught the school's first Concentrations (eight-week programs) in pottery and weaving. She built her studio in 1975; house and studio are on land she leased from the school, which will revert at her death.

In graduate school Bringle experimented with color and clay bodies. However, the majority of her work has been stoneware because of its durability. She continues to prefer functional ware and to make tableware for daily use. She declines to characterize her own work because of its variety. Some visitors to her salesroom assume there are multiple makers.

She laments that many young people working in clay today *don't talk to the general public*, she said in an interview for this book. *They make their work and they think it's just gonna sell. People of my generation have spent all this time educating the public, and if they don't do that, the public is not going to be there.*

I always tell them, "Go talk to the third and the fourth graders," 'cause those are your customers. And it's true. Kids that came to my studio in Tennessee when they were young, some of them are still my customers today. Because they came with their mother and the mother bought pottery.

Michael Simon (b. 1947), a farm boy from southwestern Minnesota, discovered clay as a teenager and attended the University of Minnesota, where he was a student of Warren MacKenzie's in a class that included several other soon-to-be-significant potters, including Sandy (Lindstrom) Simon, Mark Pharis, Wayne Branum, and Randy Johnston. He recalls that MacKenzie was always anxious to get to his own studio to work, and that was impressive to him as a student. He observed MacKenzie's "dedication and how much he saw in the pots. He had ultimate confidence that the pots could carry his total self."[12]

After graduation, Simon moved to Georgia with his wife, Sandy, and first set up a live/work studio in a chicken coop. They produced what he called country crockery. After getting established and then adapting to a divorce, he earned an MFA at the University of Georgia. When he returned to his studio he had simplified glazing and built a salt kiln, which gave him a surface that he felt was more integrated with the pots. He and Ron Meyers, who taught at the university, became close friends and for several years had a joint sale—eventually discontinuing it because great crowds of purchasers had become aggressive and unruly.

Simon is a low-key individual who never became involved with high-visibility galleries, yet his reputation grew steadily, both for his teaching—workshops at Penland and sessions in Italy run by the University of Georgia—and his quiet but influential work. His forms are simple, often a softened, rounded-off geometry and never with splashy glaze effects. He is best known for boxes and covered jars, often embellished with simple drawings of animals that may be brush-painted or incised and filled with stain. He has often told the story of his "Persian jar"—a footed, squarish vessel with an overhanging lid—which he had been making for years when a student stumbled upon a photograph of a little-known 3,000-year-old pot unearthed in Kurdistan that looked as if Simon had made it. He was thrilled with the unexpected continuity across eons.

Simon was diagnosed with leukemia in 2004, and although he has been in remission since 2006 he is no longer able to make pottery. But with the aid of his wife, Susan Roberts, and the Northern Clay Center in Minneapolis, in 2011 he produced an exhibition and an accompanying book of lasting value. He had, since his early days, saved one pot out of each firing. Selections from that panorama of development made up the exhibition, and the book includes his commentary on many of the photographed pots, calling attention to details and effects and explaining changes. It is, in effect, a portable studio visit. ■

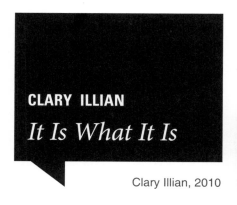

CLARY ILLIAN
It Is What It Is

Clary Illian, 2010

Clary Illian (b. 1940), like Warren MacKenzie and Byron Temple, apprenticed at the Leach pottery in England, and like them she has remained committed to functional pottery, although in recent years she has made a sharp change in her work from stoneware to earthenware and from firing with gas or oil drip to electric firing. She lives in a small town in Iowa and supplies useful things to a familiar local audience to whom she feels a sense of responsibility. She also has a wider audience through leading workshops and through her writing. *A Potter's Workbook* (University of Iowa Press, 2003) consists of a series of exercises for the pottery student, but it is informative reading for anyone who wants to better appreciate the character of pottery forms.

As a student at the University of Iowa, Illian met MacKenzie when he did a workshop. *There was something about Warren and the way he worked that made me feel that I might be a good match to this vocation. There was a rhythm and a philosophy occasioning what he did. I think I was probably pretty oblivious to the visual aspects of the pots, but he talked about his apprenticeship, and I had a very great need for that sort of underpinning. I could never have been a sculptor because I needed the structure and the grounding of a body of knowledge and practice.*

That jibed with the work ethic she was raised with. Also, she was a tomboy and had gone to a camp that *was very achievement oriented. There were all these skills and if you were a long-term camper, like scouts, you would go through various stages of learning and achievement. I don't always remember to talk about that but it's super-influential in my work.*

Since she knew of no apprenticeships in the US, she "dropped in" at the Leach pottery. *I actually went upstairs with Bernard and showed him these funny little black-and-white photos of pots I had made. He said, "No, you're not at the level."* But Leach's wife, Janet, who was running the pottery, told Illian to come back. *Because she would rather take someone and mold them. So I went back, I hung around for a week—it was hard for me to do; I'm not a hanger-arounder—and at the end of it they said, "Yes, you can come." I think they just wanted to know if I was an okay presence in the pottery.*

She was trained to make the pottery's standard ware. *But the apprentices could always stay after work and come in on the weekend and make their own work, and Bernard would critique it for you. So you had a small personal production going at all times, as well as the standard work. But I learned an enormous amount from the standard work.*

Leach had taken women apprentices early on. *He had no notions about women not being able to do this. He saw them as equally able.* During Illian's time at the pottery there were two other female apprentices, from England and France. *To show you that I bought into some of the sexual stereotyping, I remember being a little bit jealous of the other women. I liked to be the only woman!* She recalls that she was assigned simple forms at first, so that what she made would be sellable. The second year, after her skills had improved, was the "payback year." *And then one was ready to go. By that time you were a little bored.*

I called it the Outward Bound of pottery. [Laughter] *Fantastic personal collection of pots, fantastic collection of pottery books, shelves and shelves and shelves of the wonderful Kodansha Press books. People dropping in. Bernard gave us . . . about once a week we would get together of an evening and maybe have a little calligraphy lesson, or talk about some of the pots in his collection. Each of us Americans who apprenticed there had a vastly different experience because we hit Bernard at different times. Another part of that education was a wonderful man named Bill Marshall who was one of the village lads that he trained up* [this was Leach's original conception of apprenticeships, but few of the local boys stayed with the pottery] *and who made wonderful, wonderful pots. He was sort of an unofficial foreman.*

I think that what the Leach training did was show you the rhythm of a production pottery. And because we all made clay and glazed and had duties firing the kiln, I think we felt prepared. Then again, it was a simpler time. Who thought about resumes or income tax, or any of the myriad of things that students are quite aware of now? Or promoting yourself. No one talked about that kind of thing. You were just going to go home, work incredibly hard, and the world would recognize that. It required plunking yourself down in a nonurban situation, where you could make community ties.

She came home to Iowa. That default location turned out to be beneficial *because the Midwest was low overhead. I wouldn't have liked to live on the coast and try to be a potter where the cost of living was so terrific. I was scared shitless. That's something you notice with students; they keep thinking there will be a point when they feel that they have enough behind them in terms of experience and knowledge that they'll feel okay about starting. I always think you never feel okay about starting. You have to start anyway; you have to work through your fear, not wait until it goes away.*

She set up *in a farmhouse. Built a kiln and started. And I had a few part-time jobs but only for about two or three years and then I was on my way. But I mean there was only like $5,000 a year. We're talking middle to late '60s.*

After eight or ten years in her studio, she began to get invitations to do workshops and sabbatical replacements, starting with an invitation to the Kansas City Art Institute, where Ken Ferguson taught. She had met him when she was still in college. *He kept an eye on every person in the whole US, and when he thought I was kind of ready he invited me up. He was a great teacher in that way. He really took care of people.*

The workshops were the genesis of her *Potter's Workbook. I would go to workshops and see that people were always making the same mistakes. Not so much mistakes, but lacking the same realizations, let's put it that way. Just thought I'd write it all down. And once I did, I lost my steam of doing workshops.* [Laughter]

As for her own work, *I think I made for many decades a kind of work that was based on the influences of the Leach pottery; that is, Asian, Japanese, Chinese, Korean work, with an admixture of medieval English, some Continental folk pottery, American stoneware. I just kept sucking it up from there, like a great big straw, and I just sucked and sucked and sucked.* [Laughter] *I think ultimately just through sheer numbers I began to develop a slightly more personal vocabulary. Those are generic forms with a little twist in the dynamic of a curve, or some of the ways of treating edges and beginnings. But probably when the work started to become more personal was*

when I built the soda kiln. Because that pushed me into some surface treatments that were calculated to interact with the atmospheric fumes of the soda kiln. Maybe about '90, '92, I think I built that kiln. I would say my glazes were generic, too, up to that point; they were the tenmokus, the celadons, the oatmeal glazes.

I think most potters develop ways of dealing with the terminal edges of pots, and kind of stick with it through their career. Maybe something that's a little different about me is that I was constantly trying out different things and becoming aware of what is most akin to architectural detail. The trim of crown molding or different layerings that happen when a window is traditionally trimmed out as opposed to with vinyl siding. I grew to be very interested in playing off that kind of improvisation with detail against different curves, different volumes, different angles and planes, and that sort of thing. I noticed it first in pots, then I noticed it in architecture, in clothing structure; you name it. And then it read back into the pots. It always keeps going back and forth.

A few years ago she downsized to a small bungalow with a studio in the garage. With her new electric-fired earthenware, her use of imagery seems to give the work a more distinctive personality, she thinks, *but the formal elements and the formal exploration is really the same. It isn't meaning necessarily; it almost always comes out of doing, dividing up space, noticing the formal elements. Pattern. It is what it is. It isn't something you translate into another language, it's its own language.*

Her intention *always has been that they'll end up in the kitchen, or with plants, or flowers. Even now that I have what I would call collectors, they are the kind of collectors who are putting the things into daily use.* That means she keeps the pots inexpensive. *There's also a little personal piece to that in that I'm a tightwad. I carry along the context of the '50s and '60s.*

In no way did I exhaust the possibilities of the undecorated pot, but I was very happy to slow down and discover the pleasures of the decorated pot. It just happened that when I changed to earthenware I had a little trip to Italy and saw a lot of wonderful, early maiolica pots, the relaxed ones. And for sure I looked at Spanish pots and of course American pots. As I have always done through my career, I was happy to make things that are almost copies. I have no problem about that sort of theft; appropriation, you might say.

In her production, her consistency, and her conscientious self-awareness, as much as in the work itself, Illian has been another role model for present-day potters. ∎

1. Emily Galusha and Mary Ann Nord, eds., *Clay Talks: Reflections by American Master Ceramists* (Minneapolis: Northern Clay Center, 2004), 109.
2. M. C. Richards, *Centering: In Pottery, Poetry, and the Person* (Middletown, CT: Wesleyan University Press, 1962), 13.
3. Mary Emma Harris, *The Arts at Black Mountain College* (Cambridge, MA: MIT Press, 1987), 191.
4. Galusha and Nord, *Clay Talks*, 22.
5. Richards, *Centering*, 28.
6. Dido Smith, "Karen Karnes," *Craft Horizons* 18, no. 3 (May–June 1958): 12.
7. Garth Clark, *American Potters: The Work of Twenty Modern Masters* (New York: Watson-Guptill, 1981), 42.
8. Galusha and Nord, *Clay Talks*, 6.
9. "A Dialogue with David Lewis," in *Warren MacKenzie, Potter: A Retrospective* (Minneapolis: University Art Museum, University of Minnesota, 1989), 37.
10. Lee Nordness, *Objects: USA* (New York: Viking, 1970), 60.
11. Rob Barnard, "Byron Temple: The Gift to Be Simple," *American Craft* 51 (August–September 1991): 35.
12. Interview by Mark Shapiro for the Archives of American Art, September 27–28, 2005.

CHAPTER FIVE

ST. CROIX SUCCESS

The Upper St. Croix Valley Pottery Tour was formulated in 1993 by a group of makers living and working within a few miles of each other about an hour north of St. Paul, Minnesota. They decided to organize a joint weekend open house / sale at their pottery studios. The first concept was a larger group organized on a roadway theme, but they settled on six or seven potteries located in the farmland not far from the St. Croix River.

The lineup has changed over the years, with a few subtractions and additions. Warren MacKenzie, a local icon, participated at first to help draw an audience, and then bowed out. The tour has become one of America's most celebrated grassroots marketing ventures for functional ware, inspiring direct copying in other locations, such as the Art of the Pot tour in Austin, Texas. Two of the successful and reproduced features are holding it on Mother's Day weekend (the weather is usually good, Minnesotans are ready to get out and about, and moms may get a wish) and inviting potters from elsewhere to participate (that adds novelty and also good quality, since no one is going to invite a potter who wouldn't be a credit to the event). While not all the hosts have the same depth of experience or national renown, all are respected figures dedicated to making reasonably priced functional ware. ∎

JEFF OESTREICH

For the Joy of It

Jeff Oestreich in his studio, Taylors Falls, Minnesota, 2016

Jeff Oestreich (b. 1947) started his career in ceramics outside the sphere of Warren MacKenzie's classes at the University of Minnesota but followed in MacKenzie's footsteps by apprenticing at the Leach pottery in England. His early work was classic stoneware, but midcareer he made a sharp change. He has been a stalwart of the St. Croix Valley tour, as well as a mainstay of the national workshop circuit.

In Oestreich's farmhouse living room there are two grand pianos. He sees them as a legacy of love of music that came through his mother, a university graduate with a degree in music, as well as a pianist who gave it up to raise six children (he's the third, the youngest boy). His dad was an intense businessman who sold his company at age 49 and took the kids on a trip around the world, to get to know them. That was 1966. *That trip around the world opened up a floodgate for me of exploring the world. And my parents would go back with us year after year to the various parts of the world that they loved. My parents came to visit me in England when I was at St. Ives, and they fell in love with St. Ives. Their last trip they were 88, and it was their 76th trip to St. Ives. They were on TV when they made their 50th trip.* There might have been an inheritance had his parents not so loved to travel.

The family lived on White Bear Lake, near St. Paul. *We had a big house, and we were a family of makers. We all had our craft projects. My brothers made leather purses and saddles, and my sisters sewed all their own clothes. I loved making crafts. I was taking art classes throughout junior and senior high, and in my senior year we had a segment on ceramics. We each got 15 minutes on the wheel. They had an Amaco tabletop wheel with a switch: high, low, and off. And I remember throwing a ball of clay on there, and wow, this is magic. I wanted to figure this technique out, how to center it and all that.*

But especially he credits his love of arts and crafts to his Aunt Judy. *She was a wild woman. She's not married; she's a lesbian I'm sure, way back when. She had this enormous life. She had a degree in I guess it was commercial art. She would come to visit us, and she'd bring her paints and things. I just adored her. When she was in her mid-50s she wanted to teach high school art, so she went to Bemidji State University to get her certification. And she said to me as I was going there later on, "Take a pottery class from Westy*

James. It will change your life." As an incoming freshman I took a pottery class and I loved it, and within two weeks she [Westy] put me in Ceramics 2 and gave me credit for the first one because I just flew. At the end of his second year she recommended that he transfer schools and work with Warren MacKenzie.

In retrospect, he says, *Our sources were extremely narrow. We were just fed Leach Hamada Leach Hamada. And we were not encouraged to look elsewhere for sources at all. It wasn't until the '70s that I began to look at other sources and think about this.* But it was great at the time. *My first teacher made a dozen pots a year for the faculty show and for demos. She wasn't a working potter, so I had no idea what that life was about other than what I read in Leach's book. So I got to the U, and Warren would invite people up to his place and you'd see his studio just full of pots, because he was a working potter. I loved the lifestyle; I loved it all.* So that was a huge influence on me.

The Leach pottery beckoned. *I remember walking into Warren's office with this idea. He said, "I'll write you a letter of recommendation." So he wrote me a letter on his yellow legal pad [Laughter] that he still uses today, and he sealed it up, and he gave me two porcelain covered jars that he had just made. He said, "Take these to Bernard." So I went with my parents to St. Ives and I met with Janet Leach. She was a dragon. Legendary. Just mean. She said, "We have a spot for you in a year's time; come back in a year." And then she took me down to meet and talk to Bernard.*

So that started my two-year stint, and it was the most exciting, the most difficult couple of years of my life. I was entering into this family, a very tight-knit group of eight people working there. And it was this divided faction. Janet was very difficult, and she had her side. I wanted to be in the middle and like everyone.

Bill Marshall trained all the apprentices. I learned more from Bill than anyone in my entire life in terms of pots. There was one little alcove where just these two wheels were, and I was right across from him. And so he was always leaning over and saying, "This isn't right there, change this, that's not right, the lines too, the lugs," de de de, always criticizing. And also he brought me into his private life. Bill would bring me home for meals; I got to know his family, and I just cared deeply for Bill. He was a remarkable man. And I hated how Janet treated him.

Two months of making the same bowl over and over and over until it reached the standard. And I have that soup bowl, the bowl that humbled me. When I got there, I thought I was a pretty good potter. But I wasn't. I wasn't disciplined. Bill's constant criticizing my work—that was the gift. He was a good teacher. I realized for this one bowl that I made thousands of, that a good pot was a composite of all these nuances that had to be spot on. It was all these subtle things happening. I had no idea you could get so much information in this small little soup bowl that he was criticizing. That line isn't right, the kick isn't right on the bottom there, this line's too low, it's sagging off the pot, bring it up maybe an eighth of an inch. And I was just: Huh? What does this matter? And I finally got the message that all this mattered; these details mattered.

We were on the wheel eight hours a day, and I'd come home and just crash in my bed I was so exhausted. [Laughter] *It was consuming. We just lived pots. We'd meet at night in a pub, and we'd still be talking about pots. I would be working weekends, too, to make some extra money. And then we'd go visit Michael Cardew and help him fire his kiln. And we'd go to museums. And on my vacations—we had vacation time—I'd sometimes go to London and look at pots in museums, or go to Spain and look at pots. It was a total immersion into pots.*

Upon returning to the US, *I fell right into the back-to-the-earth movement, and I'd go, "I want to live in the country like Warren." My Dad had built a building, bought a kiln for me on their property, which I used during summers during my undergraduate years. When I came back from England that was still there, so I just made pots there, saved money for a down payment. I could not find a place to buy. I found a place to rent; it was $35 a month and it didn't have running water, and I thought, "Oh, this is so cool; I can just go pump water from the well." And I fixed up the barn for the pottery. Oh, how romantic, you get to use the outhouse. Until winter hit. And then my* pottery burned down. I left the wax on the burner, and it burned down to the ground and I didn't have insurance because we were anti-insurance. [Laughter] *So I just lost everything. But I got back on my feet. They organized a benefit sale, and I was able to buy a wheel and have materials.*

He finally bought a farm in 1974. He's been there alone except for about 15 years when he and Scott Goldberg spent six months there and six months in Maine, both potting and both playing piano. *It was an old wreck of a farmhouse. It's had a new foundation, and I ripped up all the floors and leveled them and put down new floors; I've gutted it and done all the work myself except for the concrete work. I do electrical, built the studio, did all the plumbing, heating, laying tiles.*

The studio was originally a small granary. You could see the sun through the roof—it was all rotted out. But I was able to shore it up and insulate it, and over the years I added on a kiln room and the showroom. I'd do construction during the day, and at night I'd make pots. When I bought the place I signed on July 4, and I was making pots by September. The house was livable, the studio was insulated with a new roof on it, and I had the kiln built. He has gradually added to his land and now has 45 acres, with the house and studio at the center of it.

The work that I was doing was very much in the Japanese aesthetic. I was using the tenmokus, the kakis, and the celadons and wheel throwing. I was not doing any altering except maybe a few faceted things. And the work was simpler in cross section than the work is now. And then in 1980, I think it was, I taught for the summer in Kansas City, and they had a wood kiln. So I came back and built a wood kiln. There weren't as many wood kilns in 1980 as there are now, so I built a big one and I realized it was so much work. And not being terribly organized, I would be cutting the wood and splitting it and stoking at the same time, like a madman. That lasted for 10 years.

His next phase was altering, especially faceting. *I love the state of the clay when you do it; how you can take a knife and you can take this piece that's got curves and you can square it off, make it sharp and crisp. So you've got the softness of the clay and you've got this hard edge. I'm known for faceting; you can't get the knife out of my hand.* [Laughter] *It's such a simple technique, and if you've got it down, it's an easy way to transform a piece in two minutes.*

Changes in my work mark those decades, like the first decade was gas reduction, the second was wood firing, and then it was soda firing. I was invited in 1990, '91, to teach for a year at Alfred to replace Val Cushing. The students there had a soda kiln—I didn't know what that was—which they were firing in oxidation. I come from the school of reduction, which was so big in the '60s that you were a real potter if you did gas reduction. If you did electric you were a hobbyist. So I get to Alfred and they're doing oxidation. I loved the results. They were just amazing. More-colorful palettes, just wonderful changes.

I was teaching a sophomore class, and I decided to do a big, huge celadon-testing session. All celadons have a little bit of iron in it, but this one didn't have iron; it had copper in it. So I gave that formula to Nick; his name was Nicholas Seidner. We had about 1,000 samples, so we fired them and tested in gas reduction, wood, salt, and soda. And we laid all the tile out on all the tables. The range of them was unbelievable. And Nick's were this beautiful turquoise-gray color. And that just opened up the world for me. So I named the glaze in his honor; it's called Nick's Misfire. [Laughter] I wanted that glaze so bad I ripped out my wood kiln and put in a soda kiln, but Nick's Misfire just didn't work in my kiln. Because my kiln naturally wanted to reduce a bit. So I've never been able to get that glaze. But just that one glaze and that experience at Alfred opened up my thinking to types of glazes other than the Japanese. I began to look at glazes from the Arts and Crafts movement.

Some people have called Oestreich a handbuilder, but he denies it. I can take a cylinder and I can just go off anywhere and have fun. Give me a slab, I don't know what to do with the damn thing. [Laughter] And then he backs off: I use a Leach wheel; it's tough on your body. Because you're kicking with this foot; you're leaning over looking at this. One of my goals is to spend more time doing handbuilding off the wheel, just because it's good to balance out your movements by doing both. My work is about angles now; it's not about curves. When you're dealing with a curve there's this dialogue, back and forth, very elusive. But if you cut and join you can get away with murder. [Laughter]

All his work has been about use—except the period that I worked with [New York gallerist] Garth Clark. I think it was early '80s to the early '90s. He wanted me to focus on a couple of different shapes, so I worked with the teapot shape, the compound base, and the large platters. And so I'd divide my time between making those very complicated forms and then my tableware, things like that. But I really missed just making dinner plates and cups and bowls. So the work is about a domestic setting. It's about use and it's not about high end. It's just going back to my roots.

Oestreich says he is not interested in using assistants or having apprentices because of my odd work hours. I'm on the road a lot, teaching workshops, and when I come home I really like to just have it quiet and work to my own rhythm. I want to mix my own clay; I want complete control. I'm just very particular about it being done in a certain way. And I'm not good at managing people; I'm not good at being bossy. I live in my head. [Laughter]

He tells long shaggy-dog stories of trying to make a production line when he first came back from England, but only one shop bought any and they didn't pay him. And then he was going to start making tiles and did some for a friend's house, and the friend got divorced. And he thought he wanted a full-time teaching job but didn't get it. He now sees all these as providential failures. I was doing it for the wrong reason, so all these flops happened for a reason, to get me where I am now, doing things for the joy of it.

Oestreich has been in the pottery tour from the beginning. We're the second-oldest studio tour in the country now, aside from 16 Hands in Floyd [Virginia], the one with Silvie Granatelli and that group there. That's a year older. You know, what I like about it is it's returning to what potters did a thousand years; they sold right from their studio. And I love that. We need galleries too, though. We need it all, internet, gallery sales, home sales, tours; we need it all to reach the public.

We have such prominence now and validity, but there's still a lot of work to be done. We have to keep reaching more people, because gosh, people our age, their houses are full of our pots. [Laughter]

I have not saved a nickel for retirement. Not a penny. I have nothing in savings. I spend it on this environment or pianos or something. There's no inheritance coming my way. So I'll have to work until I'm 90. [Laughter] I'll have to, just to survive. The Social Security is only $1,100 a month. I can't live on that; I'll need double or triple that. So I'll have to work until I'm dead. It's not a bad sentence, is it? [Laughter] ■

LINDA CHRISTIANSON
The Idea of Daily Practice

Linda Christianson,
Lindstrom, Minnesota,
2015

Linda Christianson, another of the founding members of the pottery tour, lives in a patch of woods, an unfarmable dip in the mostly flat farmland around Lindstrom, Minnesota. She and her husband, Jeff Strother, seasonally kayak and forage and cross-country ski. They have a large studio in which she has her wheels on one side and he has his woodworking equipment on the other. Attached are two kilns in which she and Jil Franke, a St. Paul ceramist, fire together. Some years ago Franke asked Christianson to build a kiln for her; Christianson suggested they try firing together so Franke could be sure that was what she wanted. The trial became a permanent condition.

Christianson was born in Rice Lake, Wisconsin, in 1952. Her father drew and printed maps and was a fur trapper as well. She would accompany him on his twice-daily rounds to check his traps for muskrat, mink, and beaver. From this experience she gained an appreciation of detail, an ability to pay attention, and an attraction to *the idea of the daily practice, doing something over and over with a narrow focus. It's a specific kind of attention that probably most people aren't too terribly interested in, frankly.* She imagines an ideal life as being *dropped somewhere, anywhere in the world and to be told your job is to make something that is visually interesting or compelling and you can only use materials that are within maybe 10 feet.* She thinks she could be happy doing that for her whole life. *I guess my main drive in life is to be outside and to make something.*

Clay was not part of her childhood—except for coming across natural deposits in the woods or along the road in front of their house. She found an Amaco electric wheel and a little block of dried-out clay in the janitor's room at her high school and tried to work with it. The effort was not successful, and that annoyed her. There were other frustrations, such as wanting to take architectural drawing but only boys were allowed to do so. And the high school principal didn't want her to take a regular drawing course because she was an A student. *So that made me want to take it even more. We had an art teacher who basically taught how to draw ducks, how to draw grass. Although we didn't really draw ducks, we drew from pictures of ducks. But I loved it.*

And then I tried clay in college. I was an art major, and I was interested in music as well. I had to take ceramics or printmaking, and I was terrified of the printmaking teacher, so I took ceramics to complete my requirement. The minute I touched the material I remembered as a child that wonderful feeling of the clay and how plastic it was. At Hamline University in St. Paul she was away from home but not too far, she had a scholarship, and she found a community. *I felt like the world sort of opened up to me in the art department.* Her ceramic experience started with Mark Pharis teaching as a hurried faculty replacement. *That was my introduction to clay, and that was just perfect for me because that was his studio as well; he made pots there, and that was really wonderful to observe. I did a lot of observing. I was very shy. I wasn't the natural that picked it up and excelled. But I loved the feel of it and I loved trying.*

The feeling of it, that's the part I latched onto, and the purpose of it, the fact that these objects weren't expensive; you didn't have to go to a museum; you could have them in your homes. Wow, that really appealed to me. I thought of them as useful sculpture—an added bonus that you could use it.

She had a different teacher every semester, which was fine because it exposed her to many different ways of working. And she had the opportunity to build kilns without much supervision, which taught her to do research and be resourceful. *They had a fifth-year program where basically you were the assistant and they paid you, so I did that for a year,* but then she didn't know what to do. *I didn't have very good guidance.* She happened to notice *a poster with a little line drawing of a mountain, and then it said ceramics and it said scholarship. And I thought: oh, that's for me, whatever that is.* It was for the art program at Banff, Alberta, and she got a scholarship for a two-year residency. There she encountered *beautiful landscape, skiing of all sorts, and I discovered mountaineering, and that was just heaven for me, skiing and hiking. Although I was a good student and I spent my time at school, there was a whole group of us that would go off on weekends camping.*

She also learned from visiting artists, especially John Chalke (about historical work) and John Reeve, who had worked at the Leach pottery, but most of all Harry Davis. *He was fascinating, not in an aesthetic way but a "you could make anything you need" kind of way. He showed us all sorts of things, like how to cut steel without a torch, without using heat, how to dig clay, how to make do, and that was right up my alley.* She was there almost three years. *It was just really great. Writers, dancers, opera, jazz, and as a student you could go to anything for free. If you weren't driven to work in the studio, you would be lost to all these wonderful things. I was always disciplined from playing the piano, and I guess also helping my father as well. For some reason, I didn't get lost.*

Back in Minnesota, *I looked for a run-down place in the country to move to. I found, not too far from here, a house to rent. I had a boyfriend who lived in St. Paul. He took one look at this house and went "uh-uh,"* [Laughter] *and I thought: okay, it's over for us. I built a kiln and very quickly ran out of money. Very quickly. I don't know what I was thinking. I just got to work making pots and then decided I had to make a little money so I took a few part-time jobs and treated them as a hobby. I always did outdoor jobs and it was seasonal, my idea of tolerable jobs. I worked at a fire tower, firefighter, skier, making snow, chair lift; you know, that kind of thing. Maintenance. I taught community-education ceramics.*

She was also selling pots, which she had begun to do in student sales at Banff. *I just put out a sign in my driveway that said Pots. Jeff Oestreich was my neighbor, although I didn't know about him, had never heard his name, and I didn't meet him for quite a while. I just kind of stuck to myself. It was really lonely, actually.* But she didn't stay there long because she couldn't afford to fill the LP gas tank.

She house-sat for a while, and then she rented a little farmhouse for $25 a month, and she could work off the rent by cleaning the barn once a month. *It had electricity, which was free, and no water. It had a hand pump outside, it had an outhouse, and I could heat with wood. It was fabulous. I made a lot of pots there. And I had some friends by then, too, so I wasn't so lonesome. I had 1-2-3-4 rooms in the house, a kitchen, and then the living room was the showroom, and a porch, and I kept wood on the porch for the house. And then upstairs was the studio, two rooms, and I slept in one of the rooms, where the pots dried. It was really crowded but great. And then the kiln outside. I'd go to the state park for a shower, and I had a little sort of homemade sauna there and a little garden. I would have sales like four times a year, and, you know, very few people would come. I don't know why—I got invited to be in some exhibits, and I got invited to teach actually. I couldn't believe that.*

I learned how to take slides of my work in Banff, and I always kept a resume. I always made a good poster when I started having sales. I was careful to present it in as beautiful a way as I could. Even though it might be hand-lettered I would try to do a beautiful job of it. Eventually I'd go to a printer and have a nice poster made, and put it up at the grocery store and the gas station, and over time people came. I kept a mailing list. Some people who came all those years ago still come.

About this time she met her husband. She decided she wanted her own house, but *I had no money; I couldn't even afford what they called a handyman's special or a fixer-upper, so I thought: I have to do it a little differently. I found a log house and then moved it, and then my mother lent me about $7,000 and I bought this piece of property. I paid her like 50 bucks a month or something.* The property, to which they have added, was considered waste. *It's a ravine, basically. There's a little creek that runs through here. It was a glacial riverbed, so it's all sand and gravel. Goes down like 300 feet. And then the banks, the hillsides are really rich black soil so there's ginseng and trilliums, and it's a maple-basswood forest, so it's perfect for skiing and making maple syrup, and it's very private. It's really important to me that it's quiet. Anywhere I look I can't see another building or people, really. I like that, and I like in the wintertime that we're sort of down in a bowl. There's hills all around, so it's perfect for observing.*

Relocating the cabin didn't halt her productive work. She lived and made pots in tents. With all the tree cover, the site was so humid that pots wouldn't dry, so she set up a wood stove in the tent. *I think I lost a lot of weight—it was so hot. I didn't wear very much in there. I had to keep working. And the people let me keep my kiln back at that old little farmhouse; they let me keep that kiln for a year, so I was able to keep firing. And then we moved in, and I had my studio right in the kitchen. You just do what you need to do. Actually it wasn't our kitchen then; it was our living room. We had a kitchen / living room, and then upstairs was bedroom, office, everything else, you know. And my husband worked here too.* At first they had no electricity, to avoid the expense of bringing in a power line. *We had some propane lights, propane refrigerator, propane stove, wood stove, white gas, those Coleman lanterns,* and more. But she calculates that it ended up costing more to keep various fuels going.

In the meantime, of course, her professional situation improved. Her goal was always to keep working. *So when things came along, like exhibits and invitations to teach, I was always sort of surprised at that, and pleased. But I wouldn't have let on that*

I was pleased. I mean I wasn't ambitious in a career kind of a way, like I think maybe one should be. But it did please me because it could further my goal of keeping working. But I was always so shy, and kind of embarrassed, I guess, with attention, which is a dilemma. There's another part of that, needing to support yourself and trying to figure out ethically what are you comfortable making or not making, and do you make things just to sell—those kinds of questions. It was important to me to never make things just to sell, because even though people would buy them, it did something to my spirit that I didn't like. I was not a production kind of potter that would make products that didn't interest me or didn't hold my attention.*

I remember the first workshops. I was just terrified. Working in front of people seemed really odd for starters, and you have to keep kind of a banter going, you know, talking. But I found over time that all I had to do was just be myself. That's all that's required in general in life, which makes it kind of easy. You don't have to be smarter; you just have to be who you are, flaws and all. I can't believe the places I've been invited to. Israel, of all the far-flung places, Japan, Scandinavia, France, England, South America—Chile, Venezuela—New Zealand, Australia.

She looks at making pots as *possibility with limitation. Make the best out of the situation, given this limited set of circumstances.* This kind of focus, she speculates, is why she lives in the kind of place she does, because the limits allow attention to subtleties.

Christianson remembers her efforts on the first wheel she bought. *It was like a traditional Korean wheel, the kind where both feet go at the same time and you had a little wooden wheel head and a little upright bench. The only way I could get it to work was if I made the clay really soft, just shy of soupy, just barely hung together. I got really depressed and I thought: oh my god, I'm never going to get this. And one day I just gave in; I said: well, make the best you can with what you've got here. So I relaxed into it and started paying attention to what the clay wanted to do.*

The next step was to get a treadle wheel, the kind she'd learned on, and *it all sort of started coming together for me. Not that they were great pots, but I had some hope. I think over time I became more and more selfish. I mean selfish in the way of: I really paid attention to what am I interested in, how does the clay* react, how does it move when I hold my hand this way, when I use this tool? You're sort of stuck with classical forms in a way. I mean, if you think of musicians, there's standards and then there's theme and variations. I don't think I've really been an inventor or a composer; more of an interpreter, I guess. The choice to fire with wood—you know right away nobody was really too interested in that, so I had to make some decisions around that, too, I remember. Anyway the public didn't necessarily come along with the idea of no glazes really, or just a liner glaze. I remember even my mother would say, "Why can't you make something pretty?" And I'd say, "Well, I think this is pretty. It looks like a garage floor where you spilled oil; I think that's really pretty." But the general public didn't really respond to it. I did try some art fairs and didn't get much of a response, so I didn't grow up with the art fair scenario. I was more the studio sale. Eventually a few galleries did ask for my work.

She regards her early aesthetic as having been this Scandinavian kind of clean and stoically stiff. Well, that's about the last feeling that I ever could cozy up to, feeling stiff, but that seemed to be what would come out. I guess I always was a student; all along I had this hunger to be able to feel like it was me, and I never knew what that was. I mean basically that's everyone's problem with whatever material you work with, whether you're a writer, painter, potter, football player. You want to use your skills and what you pay attention to, and you want to be fully engaged and loving it. And disappear in it; that's what you want to do, I would think. So if you're self-conscious about it and feeling like you're not in that position, how do you go there? I think my guide became the material, paying attention to the material, and I guess looking at things. I didn't really look at pots. I didn't look at magazines. Someone gave me Ceramics Monthly early on, when I set up. I'd get it in the mail, I'd quick look at it, I'd feel bad, and I'd burn it. I just bumbled along, and over time, I don't know, I guess I just kind of pared it down.

Eventually she realized that a cup could just be a cup. It didn't have to have a landscape on it, or a painting; it didn't have to mean anything; it didn't have to have any content other than being a cup. That was a really important realization for me. She had already recognized, during her undergraduate salt-glazing experiences, that she didn't share the popular attraction to orange-peel texture. She liked it better when the other side showed quiet calm. And then at Banff she was exposed to wood firing. I remember looking at the pots that had flashed, that were quiet and had something different on one side, and I thought: wow, there's something, that's interesting. Again she went for the unpredictable and understated, and she has continued that with her own kilns, convinced there is benefit in going along with what you get. Which is kind of the rest of life too, isn't it? [Laughter]

I really liked seeing the clay by itself. I don't want to cover it up with clothing. In Minnesota she found a beautiful clay. You could make anything out of that; it was just fabulous. I just love that color, just by itself, fired in the wood kiln. It's so beautiful. But the beloved clay is now mined out. She came up with a new one but tended to apply colored slip because she wasn't in love with the clay body itself. She's interested in digging her own, but the local clay is earthenware. Which may at some time mean she will switch to earthenware.

Christianson avoids characterizing her work. She concedes that her forms are sturdy. She notes that her husband says they're heavy, and calls them her Gibraltar ware. Sometimes they can really look heavy, but they're surprisingly light. I like to see the seams. What you see is what you get. I usually define things. I don't blend in the handle; I let the viewer see that I added it. I guess my way of working is to set up the situation with a minimal amount of motion, with the minimal amount of tools to get a feeling or a line or a motion that I'm interested in, that I can feel some emotional connection to, and a visual connection. And then call it a day. I don't want to go back and fuss, try to make it better. I'll try to make it better in the next one.

I make what I want to use, and I guess I don't really use a lot of big pots. The biggest pot I've ever used is a canoe, when we've gone wild-ricing. And that's fantastic. Not that we've done it that much, but you end up with a canoe full of rice and it's down your shirt, and the canoe is a basket. And it originally was a basket too, made out of birch bark. It's such a beautiful thing if you think about it in that way. ■

WILL SWANSON
Quiet Pots

Will Swanson and his wife,
Janel Jacobson, 2001,
at the kiln that Janel
built in 1983

If there's a classic Minnesota pottery look (actually, there isn't, but let's pretend), it might be Will Swanson's gracious ware. Warm in color, efficient in form, it is a kind of ceramic minimalism without being in the least ascetic. In a word: serene. Swanson lives and pots in rural Sunrise, Minnesota, with his wife, Janel Jacobson, who is returning to pottery after years of making tiny wood or bone carvings, like Japanese netsuke.

Swanson (b. 1947) grew up in small-town Minnesota. His father had a hardware store (which Swanson loved) and then went to work with the Federal Land Bank, loaning money to farmers. Swanson thrived in high school, active in athletics and music—he's always been a singer, and he played in the band too. *I was the journalist in the class, gathering information and putting it together. Which is funny because for many years I've done the coordinating for the pottery tour. When I work on the poster it reminds me of working on the yearbook in high school.* He was on the college-prep track, but in his senior year he chose to take art instead of physics.

Both his parents had grown up on farms and were handy and hard working. *I was always very connected to the history of the farm. When I decided*

to become a potter, I remember thinking it's a little like being a farmer: you borrow money from the bank, buy seeds, plant them, harvest them. Potter: you buy a bunch of dirt, clay, and you make things and then you try to find a harvest, a place to sell them, at the end of the year. But also the physicality of it, the fact that you're in there moving things around, dealing with really basic materials, the earth. You're making things out of the earth.

Swanson started at a college just 30 miles from home. After two years he decided it was too close and too small. He was about to take an assignment with VISTA—Volunteers in Service to America—when he discovered that if he did so, he would be drafted. The Selective Service System gave postponements only to full-time students. Since that was during the Vietnam War, that was not a happy prospect, so he transferred to the University of Minnesota, where he felt slightly lost. *I vacillated, majoring in philosophy, humanities, and music, and ended up with a degree in social welfare, social work, taking lots of psychology and social-work classes.*

In a long and ultimately successful effort to win conscientious-objector status, *I volunteered to do alternative service. I would serve but not in the military. And I ended up finding myself a job in the Twin Cities as an orderly, and my draft board assigning me to work there for two years. You're working as a civilian, you get the normal pay or whatever, but it had to be a social service job of some kind.* He worked in a hospital psych ward for parts of the next 15 years. *I worked as a psychiatric technician mostly. It means I was seeing a range of human behavior that most people don't get to see. I grew to be very empathetic and a very good listener. My last couple of years there I helped run a program called the Wilderness Treatment Program, where I took kids up to the Boundary Waters* [a wilderness area in northern Minnesota] *on canoe trips, winter camping trips.*

At some point I made a decision that when I go home at night, I don't want to be thinking about so-and-so and if they're going to kill themself, and about how to help this person or that person. I'd like to be doing something creative. I thought there are probably places in the world where people are up and energetic and entrepreneurial and making things happen. I'd like to be in that world a little bit. I went back to the university as an adult taking evening classes and summertime classes. I took drawing and sculpture and ceramics. He also took a design course and became caught up in it. So for two and a half years he worked on a master's degree in three-dimensional design and taught design classes.

Part of the reason why I ended up making kind of universal, simplified, elemental forms—those are the things I love—some of that came from my education in design. I was not in a studio arts program where I was encouraged to be expressive, you know, to say everything about my social, sexual, and political life in my pottery, that kind of thing. I was much more focused on making a functional object that will have universal appeal. He took ceramics classes and spent long hours at night in the studio arts building.

I always knew I liked ceramics. In 1969 I went to Warren [MacKenzie]*'s sale and started buying functional pottery and using it. And that's really my entrée into pottery, buying functional pottery from Warren and Jeff Oestreich. I started coming up to Jeff's quite often to his sales and got to know him a little bit. I started using the pots, especially pots by Warren, and I think I had some of Clary Illian's pots. Wayne Branum and Mark Pharis were actively making pots. Some were by Randy Johnston. I'm the same age as these guys but I started making pots 12 years later than they did.*

I always see myself as the person who used to do something else, who decided to make pottery, who never would be totally accepted as a potter. It might be different if I really launched off into some personal expression that was unique, but I haven't chosen to do that. People say, "You must have studied in Japan," or "These look like old Bernard Leach pots." People see them, I think, as not expressive. For me, the personal expression is in the life I lead to make these pots.

He focuses on *the meditative process of making them, forming them, all the little decisions you make about, you know, is the interior of this pot what you want it to be, imagining what someone's going to use it for, trying to make the pot that becomes someone's favorite not because it knocked them dead when they first saw it but because of how much they enjoy using it every day. When they go to the cupboard, that's the one they pull out because they like it.*

We project so much onto things, and we're so complex and so varied that in a way, the simpler the pot, the more it's open to however we want to see it, whatever we project into it, what meaning we attach to it, whether it's by what we did with the pot, or what it reminds us of. Anyway, that's part of my explanation for making simple pots. Swanson was surprised and pleased when someone recently called him "a potter's potter." He adds, *I do sell a lot of pots to potters, whatever that means.*

In 1985 he joined Jacobson in the house she had bought about ten years earlier. She was a country potter, making her living that way after graduating from art school. He began assisting her, including sales at the Minnesota Renaissance Festival. *It was a little bit of an apprenticeship for me in that I could make coffee mugs and things that were kind of dumb and dumpy, and I could take them to the Renaissance Fair and sell them for $4 or whatever we sold them for. It was a ready marketplace where you could sell simple pottery at low prices, get some reaction from people. That was a good experience for me.*

Jacobson was working in the parlor of her house, with ware racks on the walls of the dining room. That changed after their son was born. *By the time he was around two, we felt it was hard to have a toddler and a pottery studio together.* So they put up a 28-by-52-foot studio building—Swanson's father giving them a bit of money to get started—and they also sold a building Jacobson had at the Renaissance Festival. They moved into the studio in 1995.

I know there are potters who would just as soon not ever have to go to an art fair and have to stand there in front of their pottery and tell people about it, but I like it. He has had an exceptional run at the Philadelphia Craft Show. *I think part of the reason they keep inviting me back is that I have 600 customers who come every year, and they come to see what's new this year, and they tell me stories about the pots that they gave to their kids when they got married and stuff like that. It's a connectedness with the customer that I kind of focus on a little more than some potters, I think.*

The other part of that is that over the years I've done lots of dinnerware sets or groups of plates and bowls, and I'll take orders for things, which I'm telling myself I'm going to do less and less because it kind of bogs me down sometimes. The idea of making groups of things, whether it's cereal bowls or dinner plates, helps the bottom line too. People really appreciate that. I don't buy pots that way, but a lot of people want to buy a group of things.

His commissions usually result from taking 12 or 15 plates to a show, and the person who sees the last few would like more. He asks about sizes, lets them participate in the design process a little bit. *But then at the end I always say, "Okay, now see the way this one looks? The ones you're going to get won't look like this. [Laughter] We're going to make it like this, but it won't come out this way. So if you're willing to give me the order for a bunch of plates knowing that they won't be exactly like what you think they will, then I'll take the order."*

I spend a lot of time trimming, more than other potters do, especially dinner plates; I trim down the bottom because I don't want people to open the cupboard and think: oh, I don't want to use those plates; they're so heavy; they don't fit in the dishwasher. I want ones that are enjoyable to use, so I trim them down a little more. But I still want them to be distinctive pieces that are obviously handmade.

As a student at the U, I right away gravitated to these earthy carbon-trap and shino glazes which a lot of people thought were just kind of dead, not much there. I was always attracted to the sort of aged quality that a plain brown pot can have, the kind of timeless look that it can have.

I admired Warren's pots greatly, the simplicity of them, the undecorated surfaces. My pots are not as spontaneous as his. I don't leave little shards of clay, I don't trim them quickly and leave quite so much of the process on the pot as Warren and some other potters do. My pots are a little more finished.

I have a range of colors in shino, from dark, toasty brown, where the pots look kind of like antique pots, to shiny gray sort of shino with a lot of wood ash on. It's a little livelier. I layer the glazes sometimes so that I have a range of earth tones from dark brown to medium brown to gray. [Laughter] Still just brown and gray. Every firing is a little different; the atmosphere is different. So when I have three firings full of pots, I'll have a range of earth tones for people to choose from, and they kind of work together. It's a family of pots, family of glazes over the years. But I also make white pots and black pots.

Most are small tabletop pots; they're plates and bowls and cups. I also make baking dishes, and I make some bigger bowls. I have not launched into making very complex pots, teapots, coffeepots. I'm threatening to make teapots one of these years. I did it one year and they all sold in about five minutes, so I guess I should do it again.

The decorating I do on my pots really has to do with the way the glaze flows over the pot, whether I dip it in or whether I overlap it, whether I deliberately make it thicker on the edge so that it will be dark and light, some kind of contrast. I don't take a brush or my finger and decorate the pots at all. Thick and thin is a big deal with shino glazes, so dip it in, pull it out quickly, then pull it out slowly, maybe swirl the glaze around a little bit. And that's my decorating.

People say my pots are quiet pots. That's a common descriptive word.

When I was a conscientious objector, when I said, okay, I'm not going to participate in the military, I'm not going to spend a minute of my life carrying a gun and being trained as a killer and being sent off to another part of the world to represent our country, when I said I wasn't going to do that, I think part of my brain started thinking: Well, what can you do that's very humane? What can you do that accentuates positive human values? Well, you sit down and you eat meals with people and you share a community and family, and what's more positive than a family eating together? And then I met Warren MacKenzie, saw him making pots, and was thinking: Isn't this a generous cup and isn't this something you'd love to share with your family? His focus on these intimate objects that are in our everyday life kind of slipped right into my thinking about what's a valuable thing to spend your life doing.

Swanson and Bob Briscoe started the St. Croix Valley Tour. But the precedent was that Jacobson, Oestreich, and Christianson all had moved to the area near the same time and had made a brochure with a map to all three places to announce simultaneous sales.

I met Bob through the Minnesota Crafts Council; we worked together. He decided to move out of the Twin Cities and build a house out here. He and I were looking around and saying, "Well, we should have our sales at the same time; obviously it would make sense." And because Janel and I knew Jeff and Linda, and I knew Richard Abnet, and Warren said, "Sure I'll support you," and he was part of it for the first three years. Warren had had sales for years at his place, and there was a group, mostly his students, who had their pots at his studio. Rick Vincent we knew from the Renaissance Festival, and he was in the area. Jeff had the best history of people coming up for sales.

Bob had the energy and initiative. He's the guy who's managed to make a living making pottery better than anyone else I know. He brought in a spirit of marketing that we didn't have before, a kind of can-do attitude, which not everybody has. [Briscoe has retired, and his place is now owned and hosted by Matt Krousey.]

The most important thing is we're just under an hour away from two and a half million people who live in the Cities. We're in a location that's somewhat interesting; people enjoy coming up to the rural area to visit, spend a day driving in the country, that kind of thing. People respect Jeff Oestreich, Linda Christianson, Briscoe, they know these people, their distinctive pottery; they're worth going to visit.

Jacobson adds, *The things that make the tour wonderful for people is that we each make a unique experience for their being at our site.* She and Swanson spend the winter stockpiling homemade cookies in their freezer for their guests; Connee Mayeron's site—now Ani Kasten's—has a fire pit and s'mores as well as a tire swing for children.

We've had lots of people over the years say, "Gee I'd like to be part of it." But we've kept it at seven studios. We think that's enough.

The potter has to be there. The whole idea is to go and meet the potters, see 300 of their pots, so it's really a different experience from going to a gallery and seeing 8 or 10 pots and having some employee of the gallery explain it to you. There are still lots of people who walk in the door and say, "Oh, I'd like to live in the country and make pottery." [Laughter] *There's that vicarious thing of how do these people live, how do they do this?*

So what else makes it successful? Well, we have a great mailing list, we keep track of people, and our poster tends to be sort of distinctive. We want it to be our identity; we send out this big thing every year. Hospitality. It's important to have a good time.

Jacobson notes, *When there are 100 or 200 people, it kind of feeds the enthusiasm because other people are there and they're holding up their pots.* [Laughter] *In the spring sometimes it snows, sometimes it rains, sometimes it's gorgeous. People are ready to get out. Bob put up a map, and people would put pins in the map for where they were from, and people were from Hawaii and England and Canada and Alaska and all around the United States.*

Swanson adds, *Forty states or something last year, or some amazing number. Guillermo [Cuellar] did a survey last year, and 24 percent of the people at the show were from outside Minnesota. That's pretty good.*

It's a group project. We don't hire a marketing expert; we just do it all ourselves, so people have to really chip in and make it work by contributing their mailing lists and beating the bushes out there and letting people know about it. That's the other part. Jeff and Linda go all over the United States teaching workshops, you know, taking our flyers and giving them to people and writing down names and letting people know that there's this great national event here in Minnesota. It's not just your local potters trying to sell you some pots, it's really good potters from all around the nation. ■

GUILLERMO CUELLAR

Country Pots

Guillermo Cuellar
demonstrating at Anoka
Ramsey Community College,
Coon Rapids, Minnesota, 2011.
Photo: Marcia Paul

Guillermo Cuellar is a Venezuelan with long ties to the US, to the Midwest, and to pottery. He went to boarding school and college in the US and married an American. While they were living in Venezuela, he met Warren MacKenzie and connected with several Minnesota potters who came to present workshops. Economic and political difficulties made the family decide to relocate to the US, and they found a house in the St. Croix valley. Since 2009 he has been a host for the pottery tour.

It's been kind of starting over again, you know, setting up a studio and making pots. We moved to the United States in 2005, and I had my first firing here at this studio in 2007. We built an addition, the showroom and the area downstairs where the kiln is, and it took about a year to do that. During that time, I made pots at Warren's and I worked as a guide as sort of a day job. (He started guiding tours for Wilderness Travel in 1984 in Venezuela. After 2005 he went to Patagonia and Peru.)

The first five years were taken up with establishing his pottery: *trying to get it going, trying to make all of the links in the process that allow you to have something that is functional from one end to the other—finding materials, setting up, building, finding galleries, and getting all the clay and glazes and all that part of it structured up. And then to connect, to*

go out and start to connect with the community, locally and around the state and who knows.

Cuellar's father was from Colombia, and his mother was born in Chile to English immigrant parents but raised in Peru; both studied in the US. His father, in animal husbandry at the University of Illinois, became very fond of the Midwest. Cuellar was born in Venezuela (in 1951) but regards himself as being from all over, and a mix of everything, including Indian. He was sent to English-speaking schools as a kid, and there were lots of foreigners in Venezuela—English, Dutch, French, Italian, Spanish, and Portuguese. *I hung out with a lot of kids; we spoke a lot of Spanglish. When I was fourteen I was sent to boarding school in the States.* When he graduated they gave him the choice of going to Cornell College (in Iowa, which his mother had attended) or striking out on his own. He wasn't thrilled with the options but *Cornell turned out to be absolutely wonderful. It was a really a warm small school.*

I discovered pottery in my first year. I could have sort of deleted the following ten years and just gone ahead and become a potter [Laughter]*, but I didn't have the self-confidence; I didn't have the courage.* His father was horrified with the idea. *He worked his whole life to get out of this, to become part of the developed world, part of the future, and his son was going primitive on him, you know. This was 1970, so there was all of that back-to-the-land kind of thinking going on at the time, and I'm sure that had something to do with why I was fascinated with ceramics. But also, I grew up in an apartment, and making things was alien to me.*

I was just absolutely fascinated with pots, and I ran into [Bernard Leach's] A Potter's Book. *I've learned 98 percent of what I do with pots from working with Warren, but in a sense my inspiration was the same as Warren's. And actually that's still where I am today. I have stayed in the same general vocabulary that Warren uses. I don't feel that absolute necessity to go out and invent something new. I'm really happy. I think that exquisite beauty can be found in pots made for use. That doesn't mean that others can't go out and do their expression, that's fine, but the whole Mingei philosophy to me is absolutely still a guiding reference.*

During my first two years at Cornell, I found out that Clary Illian was in the area. She was at the time living in Garrison, which was a town of 200 people, in the most spare and frugal manner you could possibly imagine. She had a fairly big old farmhouse, and she had hung rugs and curtains and blocked everything off except the kitchen, so she had a wood stove and her bed in the kitchen, and she was making pots in an old beehive kiln that belonged to a factory that made drainage tiles. And this factory was just the horriblest thing too; it was like something really medieval. So anyway, I talked to Clary and I said, "Would you take me on as an apprentice?" And she said no, because at the time she was focusing, and for all I know for all her life she has really been a mentor to women; you know, nurturing women potters. I can respect that, but at the time I thought: that's really cool, man, but it didn't help me out! [Laughter]

Cuellar was ignoring his other classes, so his parents stopped paying and he left school. Back in South America, *I drove to Chile with a friend along the West Coast and spent about six months just staying in places in the different countries and seeing things. We were exposed to the culture of Peru and the culture of Bolivia. We were exposed to the music of the Andes, the weaving, ceramics. Any small town in Peru, a little hole in the wall, would have a museum. And it would be floor to ceiling with pots, lots of those things unfortunately not very well presented or taken care of, but the wealth of stuff was just unbelievable. That made a big impression.*

He worked for a while but decided he really needed to finish his education. So he got scholarship help and went back to Cornell. He did a senior thesis in drawing and pots and married Laurie, whom he had met the first year of college. It was a government scholarship that required him to return to Venezuela for two years. There was an economic boom, and it was easy to find work. He got a job with the World Wildlife Fund, and Laurie worked for a bank. *I got to travel all over the country where we had projects. We had a manatee status survey, we had a project on the Orinoco crocodile, of repopulating sea turtles, we had many different projects like that.*

During those three years I worked there, there was a Venezuelan newspaper called The Journal, *in English. It published three articles about the deaths of Michael Cardew, Shoji Hamada, and Bernard Leach. I was depressed and heartbroken every time one of these things would come out because I was thinking: this is the connection; this is the access point that I could have had to that historical body, you know, the continuum. I don't want to get too carried away here, but that's what excited me, to be part of that tradition. And I said, "If I'm going to become a potter I'd better try it now; otherwise I'm going to end up never having done it, never having tried." So I started trying to make pots about 1980, 1981, and I struggled very hard. It was a little bit of a pioneer situation. You couldn't get the same quality or kind of materials; there was no real source for equipment to build a kiln, burners; you had to try to figure out how to import them from the US. I had no money, so I had a very minimal setup and I was making earthenware pots, firing them in an electric kiln, and they were really bad. Fortunately there are not many pictures of those pots left.* [Laughter]

People were secretive about their information. Once, after talking with a not-very-helpful potter, as he was leaving he heard someone else ask "about this MacKenzie visit." *I heard the name and of course I knew who Warren was because he was in our textbooks at Cornell College. And so I turned around and came back and said, "Is Warren MacKenzie coming to Venezuela?" And they said, "Yeah, but the class is already full."* [Laughter]

Just when I was at a point where, you know, it may have been the difference between me becoming a potter or not. Because I couldn't really afford to go to the United States and look for something. I just didn't know how to make it happen. The group that was bringing him was this potters' group, the Venezuelan Association of the Arts of Fire. There was a very lively ceramic buzz going on in Venezuela at the time, too. In fact, Leach had been in Venezuela in the early '60s and had planted a seed. When Warren came, there was great receptivity to all of his ideas, and Warren is a great inspirer.

So I met the woman who's the president of the association, and I convinced her that she couldn't possibly do this without me [Laughter] *because I could do everything. I ended up being the interpreter and general assistant. The first time I saw him throw, my jaw literally dropped. I had never seen anybody who could throw so easily, so effortlessly, so casually. He slapped it down and it was centered, and to me it always seemed that he was taking the pot off the wheel before it was finished. So that experience was like, oh man, this is my window into this kind of pottery that I would like to make. And Warren and I got along. I asked him if he would teach me, and he said, "I can only teach you one kind of pots." And I said, "Warren, those are the pots I want to make."*

I came up to visit in 1981; I invited myself. [Laughter] *John Reeve was working there. Warren was teaching at the university, so John got stuck with me. I sat with him, I followed him around the studio, and we talked about pots for four days. And I still do some things thanks to John, that experience. I was like a sponge. Anything that I saw, I asked what that was, how it was done.*

In 1984 Warren wrote to us in Venezuela and invited Laurie and me to come up and make pots in his studio with two other potters, Clary Illian and Christy Wert, a Twin Cities potter. So we made pots for a month. I think it was in April, and part of the experience of living with Warren at his house, having many potters coming by, dinner discussions, arguments,

living with Warren's pots, you know, his collection of all the pots that he had, and working together, looking at the pieces, all of that, it was so intense. At the end there was a group sale. That was my first experience with the idea that you could make pots and that people would buy them. There was so much wonderful interaction between the potters and the clients.

So I went home with that experience, and eventually Laurie and I moved to a place about an hour's drive outside Caracas, and we set up a studio there and I started making pots, started getting them into some galleries, and of course coming here to the States every so often and making some pots here and having shows here as well. But I had always had that thought about the group sale, so I contacted a group of potters in Venezuela, and we got together and had a group sale. And it became a huge thing. Well, huge to us. [Laughter]

Working for the World Wildlife Fund, I got to travel around the country and see a lot of handmade stuff, I mean real Mingei, that was being made at the time by people who were just using these things for themselves. We traveled a lot with Indians, who have a wonderful body of creative expressions of different kinds. Carved wood, baskets, fiber hammocks, just wonderful stuff. So when we had our pottery sales we had access to some of those people. We had two sales a year, one in May and one in November. I think we had about 25 sales before the whole thing kind of wound down and ended. The effort was recognized with a front-page article in the national newspaper, and a book.

But things were going downhill. *Everyone was disgusted with the political situation in the country. It was getting very difficult to get anything done. Security was getting much more tenuous. You couldn't buy materials; all the companies that were providers of materials were either broke or they had left the country. When Cuellar's car was stolen before their eyes, that was the tipping point, and they began planning to leave.* A friend who was teaching in the Twin Cities was going to China for a year and needed someone to house-sit. That was in 2005.

Cuellar had been potting at MacKenzie's in the summers since 1984. *I was learning the ropes in the studio. I would make pots and I would help with whatever I could, and Warren was there and we would make pots together. That was fascinating. I used Warren's clay and his glazes, because I wasn't going* to make up separate batches of glazes that he couldn't use. It made the pots look more similar. After a few years he and Nancy would leave and I would stay and take care of the studio, make pots, hold the fort, and they would do a workshop or a trip or do something that they had planned.

After Warren came to Venezuela there was a whole list of American potters who came to teach, most of them from around this area. Jeff Oestreich, Mark Pharis, Randy and Jan Johnston, Linda Christianson, Clary Illian. There was such an influence on Venezuela. I became friends with so many potters in this area. So he was prepared for a working life here.

One of the media we've embraced is the internet, and the first thing that we sensed when we got here is that we had to have a web page. Laurie's been the person who's mostly learned about working with the web page, so she takes the pictures and uploads the pots. And we have a certain amount of internet sales. I can't tell you exactly how much now, but I think it may be 10%, 15% of our total sales. You have a market that's national. People are becoming more and more comfortable buying things online.

It doesn't matter what era you're working in; you have to develop an audience. I prepared a little slide show that I can offer people, or if they want to bring kids from schools and stuff, to walk around the studio. Warren when he was beginning did a demo in the window of a department store!

I think that the most exquisite pieces can be functional pots, but at the same time if you price an exquisite teapot at $500 nobody's going to use it. So it's no longer a functional piece. So you just have to come to terms with what your intention is to begin with, and my intention is to make teapots that you can make tea in, and have this wonderful thing that happens around a life of pots. I'm making pots because I think it enriches people's lives to have that kind of stuff hanging around the house. And it's much more so if they're not off-putting, if they're not on a shelf, but if they're part of your song and dance.

There are pieces that I have in galleries, and I like to have them in the galleries because that raises awareness that I exist. I have come to a final decision, and my prices are a little higher than I'd like them to be, but they're still low compared to the general pricing. If I send anything to galleries, they're the selected pieces from the kiln. It's a promotional cost to me, and I don't

really make a whole lot of money from galleries. I thought that you could have a showroom, and over time people would find you and they would come and buy the pots, and that would be a way of making a living. It's not that simple. Most of the time it's three or four cars in a good week. I've decided to make connections locally, because I'd like people to think about pots when they need a Christmas gift, or ideally if they wanted a pot for themselves. There's an option here. They don't have to go the Cities.

The group sales make a big difference. They are what moves things. But it means schlepping, packing pots, packing the car. Sales events are a great way to connect with people, talk about pots. One of the most wonderful places was the Mill City Farmer's Market on Saturday mornings. Chefs are invited to do demos, and they're installed very close to where my pots are, and so they come over and I give them some pots and they show. We have to be there at 6 a.m. But it's so much fun once you're there. I get back here like 3 in the afternoon.

I think my pots are more country pots; I think that's the direction that I'm moving in now. I'm trying to make the pots looser and more textured. One of the things that I see coming up in my pots often is a sense of both the decorations and the feeling of the baskets that I saw in Venezuela. One thing that I have retained from my work with Warren is to do as much of the decoration as possible right away on the wheel. I try to set up a situation with the clay and then tweak it somehow so that the clay does something, and then leave it that way.

I want the pots to be comfortable. I want them to be warm and giving the sense of some kind of age, some timeless quality. So I've really gotten into using this crackle slip, which with different glazes gives the pots a kind of an archeological quality. I've been making square plates of different kinds for a long time, and I think that's a lot of fun. It's very quick and it's a good way of making something that doesn't have much of a wheel-thrown quality to it. I enjoy that.

The attractions of pottery are subtle, but when you attend to a part and notice the variations, there's just incredible richness and variety. And that's why you need to use them; you need to take the time to have them in your hands and see them over time. ∎

CHAPTER SIX

MAKING A LIVING

While it's not uncommon to hear someone say, "you can't make a living as a potter," there are plenty of examples to the contrary. Still, no one goes into pottery to make big money. There are many other motivations for choosing a life's work.

Functional pottery requires moderate prices to allow people to take the risk of using it and potentially breaking it. While Japan has tea bowls worth the equivalent of thousands, even millions, of dollars, Western culture does not present this extreme. American potters must make a living through high production, efficiency, and skillful marketing if they are to be supported by their work alone. Only a small number are such purists. Many potters have an additional source of income, most often the related activity of presenting workshops. Some have regular teaching jobs and cram the pottery production into their off days (see chapter 7). Some have unrelated businesses (see chapter 8). Some have their cash flow evened out—and boosted—by a spouse with a more conventional job.

Marketing methods constantly change. Amid the crafts boom in the middle of the 20th century, craft fairs, often outdoors, were a common sales venue. Soon there came to be wholesale shows to stock craft shops—which turned into galleries and then into gift shops. The internet developed, and things could be sold through the maker's website, through online galleries that might or might not have a brick-and-mortar space, and through marketing sites, most prominently Etsy. Nonprofit clay centers in several cities have become major sales outlets as well as exhibition, education, and studio spaces. Craft museums developed their sales as well. Potters are increasingly selling out of their own studios, to avoid having to split the profits with a dealer, and sometimes collectively organize pottery tour events. ■

SILVIE GRANATELLI

The Next Iteration

Silvie Granatelli in her studio, Meadows of Dan, Virginia, 2018

Virginia potter Silvie Granatelli (b. 1947) is a longtime master of function known for being self-supporting and for mentoring apprentices—13 so far. Maybe this practical form of teaching appealed to her because, like a disproportionate number of artists, she grew up with some degree of dyslexia. *It took me until I was about 12 to learn to read, so it was definitely there.*

Reacting negatively to her parents' professional lives—consumed by their jobs with little time for home—*I instinctively chose to have a more seamless life between what I did every day and what I did in my home. Being in the arts, I thought, you could do that.* She was inspired by her boyfriend's father, who had a graphic-design business and made art at home. The whole family did artistic things together, *and this enchanted me. So I fell in love with the family more than the boy.* [Laughter] She married him. At the Kansas City Art Institute she tried and rejected graphic design, but when someone in ceramics showed her how to throw, *I sat down and it was immediate. I felt at home. It was that thing that you hear about all the time; if you touch it you have an experience and you don't turn back.*

I didn't have a huge talent. I had a minor talent that I just kept pushing. The motivation for going into pottery was how it felt, that you had nothing and then you had something. That was like a miracle.

They moved to Chicago for her husband's work, but there the marriage ended. *I joined the Midwest Potters Guild, which was an in-city group of potters who built a kiln and had industrial space. I rented space there. For a year I made pots in the city, and I started to do shows.* Then she applied to graduate school and chose Montana State because *I got a full ride.* The two people teaching there did sculpture and installation work, as was the fashion. *My graduate work was about site installation. I stopped making pots in class, but I kept making them in my own time. And it was really quite wonderful because it made me develop a different kind of mindset, and it opened me up to the bigger world of art.* She and another woman did body-centered performance pieces involving clay and other natural materials. *It was the time; yes, it was the time.*

She returned to Chicago and became one of the first members of Lill Street Gallery. *We built a kiln and rented space there, and I started doing shows again and stayed for a couple of years.* With her new partner, ceramist Andy Nasisse, she moved to Athens, Georgia, when he took a teaching job, and set up her first in-home studio there, in the utility room of a rented house. She built a catenary-arch kiln in the carport. *I felt so like a hobby housewife. I felt horrible doing it, and I said to him, "I don't feel professional."* He said, *"If you really want to make pots, you'd do it in the bathtub."* And you know that was not a nice thing to say, but it was the right thing to say to me at that moment. So I changed my attitude and I kept making pots.*

A kiln problem gave her a different, oxidized color palette (the kiln would not reduce). *It really propelled me to having a more original look earlier than I might have. I had to make things that had color and brightness and lightness. I was working in porcelain.* They bought a house and she built a better studio and a better kiln, but she continued to oxidize. *Because now I liked it. I had this other palette of glazes, and I always liked to have a lot of glazes. I like color.*

Four or five years later they split up, and she became potter in residence at Berea College in Kentucky. There she met and married Bruce Gholson, who was the studio technician and had come to ceramics through science. Together they bought a place in Floyd, Virginia—19 acres and a house that was *a complete dump,* for $32,000. They built a small studio, about 30 by 15 feet, that they shared for 15 years.

We spent the years doing craft shows, and eventually we got to the point where we were just doing Philadelphia. We did Baltimore a little bit, but I never liked to do wholesale because I didn't like to make the same thing over and over again. There were a couple of galleries that were very supportive. Then we got into Demarest, which was the [Karen] Karnes invitational, and that went on for many years for the two of us. I think that broadened our audience. We taught at Penland a number of times. We did it together. Our work was never collaborative, but we both applied to things, we often both got in.

They learned to manage unpredictable incomes. *We had a mortgage which we ended up paying off. I also taught at Virginia Tech as an adjunct for a while and used that money to build the studio, so I never took out another loan, I just kept pouring all of my Tech money into the studio building.* Then, for a conference at Arrowmont, she and Gholson were asked *to present what it's like financially as potters, the professional aspects of being potters. At that time we'd been in the field about 20 years. We thought: Why would they ask us?; we're poor as dirt.* They decided to interview other potters who had been working longer. *We asked about insurance; we asked about how did you start, at what point did you feel, okay, now I know I can count on money next year; what were the milestones for you? And it was fascinating and it helped us to see that we were doing okay.*

We got to the point where we were saving 30 percent of every dollar. We were able to manage like that. So at the end of the year, once the taxes were paid and the clay was bought or whatever the thing was, we'd say, "Now, what would we really like to do with the studio, or do we want to travel?" She went on similarly after their marriage ended, while fixing up the house, teaching adjunct at Tech, seeing her parents through old age, teaching at Penland, and traveling more because she did a lot more workshops—including in India and Turkey.

I started having apprentices after Bruce left, because I had this tremendously large studio and I felt guilty about having that much space. People would say, "Could I come work for the summer?" It started out kind of loose. But then Jerilyn Virden, with a good background at West Virginia University, came for two years.

I got serious about trying to mentor and give something back in terms of how do you live this life? So I started to analyze it and think more carefully about it. I always insisted that they had to earn money from the work that they made with their hands while they were here, as a way to test that out. It's always easy to make what you want and just stockpile it or have a little show here and there, but to try and figure out how to make your income from that endeavor is always uncomfortable, especially in the beginning. You never feel worthy; you never feel like you're ready. You just have to do it. I tell them there's an audience out there that's just as sophisticated as you are right now. [Laughter] *And you will grow, and you will bring them with you, and when you outgrow them there will be somebody else that will step in and be ready for you in your next iteration. And so I forced that issue.*

Subsequent apprentices had a variety of backgrounds and futures. Among them are Brian Jones (now potting in Oregon), Dandee Pattee (in Wyoming), and Ian Anderson (dean at the Maine College of Art and Design and married to potter Kari Radasch). *It's a two-year commitment, and I make it serious. They do something for me 12 hours a week, and in exchange for that they get my expertise, whatever that might be, and they get the use of the equipment in the studio and have a place to work. They have to pay for their fuel and materials, clay, and their chemical materials, but they have the equipment. The advantage is that they're in a real working studio and see what it takes. And the thing that I hear from them is they never knew when they were in undergraduate school that you had to make that many pots in order to make a living.*

They see me working and they get it. And I insist that they develop a rhythm in the studio. Most of them have to work outside doing something—waitress, bartender, whatever—and they have to balance these things out, which is what you have to do anyway in life. They realize eventually that they can make more money selling their own work than they can being a waitress or a bartender. And it kind of shocks them. I also make them take almost everything that they make out of the studio. They have to put it in their apartment or whatever. And if they sit on a pile of pots, there's more incentive to sell it or get rid of it than there is if it's in somebody else's space. That's one of my strategies. It's very difficult for them to sell. They resist that like crazy. I've tried to get them involved with writing, doing a statement, figuring out how who you are and what do you see in your pots that really reflects that. I try to help them start to become visually aware of themselves.

I do an economic project with them, which has been very successful. I have them fire a kiln by themselves, a kiln that's for them out in the studio. And I say, for a year, calculate how much money it costs you to live here, your rent, student loan, car payment, whatever it is that you do. Keep track of that, and your food and your bills, and keep track of how much money you make from selling your pottery and then how much money you make at your waitress job or whatever it is. Then after a year is up, your second year here, fill that kiln, count the pots, price the pots, what percent are seconds, what percent do you have to throw away? Calculate how much that kiln load is worth. And then how many of those kiln loads do you have to make in one year in order to support the lifestyle you're living right this minute? I was sort of nervous to make them do this, because I thought: it's going to tell them that they can't do it. Not. One girl that just did this, she only had to make three kilns a year to make the kind of lifestyle she was living right now. Three!* Granatelli also helps apprentices figure out how to price work on the basis of time spent making it.

Apprentices also track her contracts, obligations, and deadlines in some format that they choose. *So they have to read all the small print and organize it in some sort of fashion. And then they make a map for me, so they learn to map out this progression of obligations in the studio.*

For about six years she had two apprentices, because Floyd is a very rural place and they could keep each other company. But she cut back because she had to work too hard to stay ahead of everything they did for her in their two days of work.

Of her work, she says, *I came out of the Kansas City Art Institute, so I was looking at the Nelson-Atkins Museum next door that had lots of Japanese pots and English Staffordshire pots. So those were the early sources. My favorite potter in those years was, and still maybe is, Rosanjin, who was this calligrapher; he was all about food, and I've always been all about food. So a lot of the reasons that I make things has to do with how it presents food.*

There was a phase when I made black and white, and I was probably kind of known for that. There was another look where I used stains to do drawings of fruit, clear glaze over these drawings. I only make those because people like them, and I only sell them here—because she regards it as a phase she has moved past.

In a more recent phase I was doing a lot of throwing in parts and assembling parts to make a range of forms that were off round. That was a trend in the ceramic world with making "altered pots," and I got right on that and liked it. I still do that a lot.

As I've gotten older and worked in the studio for all of these years, it's taken a toll on my body, and I've had cervical spine injuries from throwing and had to have a plate, a fusion in my neck. So making pots not on the wheel has been something that I've tried to do.

I don't enjoy it particularly, but I like the finishing part of it. It helps my body and it helps me to fill the kiln without throwing. Left to my own devices I would just throw all the time because I love to throw.

I was always using porcelain. [Ken] Ferguson wouldn't allow us to use porcelain until we were seniors, but when we got to porcelain I could see that it had a capacity for light and color, and it was clean, and what you did to it was [final], whereas with stoneware, you get the iron coming through the clay body into the glazes, so it's never pure. I wanted to control the colors.

I really liked the Japanese. I liked the culture and the food, and the purposefulness of those pots in terms of food. The things that were used for day-to-day food presentation were the ones that I loved the most. Once I started making porcelain pots, they had a very Japanese look to them; the teapots and the surfaces. And then Victor Babu [KCAI professor] was a slip trailer, so I learned that, which took me to a phase of slip trail work that looked kind of like cake decorating.

One of the things that people would probably say about me is that I've done a lot of different things. The consistency is the porcelain, high-fire oxidation atmosphere with gas. It's always about the table and domestic use. Little forays toward sculpture.

My phases last for a long time. I might be doing two things for ten years. Sometimes I'll go back formwise to things I stopped making because I felt like they were somewhat resolved. But it will have the newer palette, so it's different. It's what drives me, the change. And it's what's kept me interested.

I do tight carving. And I love pattern, so lots of pattern. For years she did swan or crane finials on her pots. *And then the bird image became so popular that I could hardly stand to do it anymore. [Laughter] So I started doing frogs. I thought: take something ugly and make it beautiful.*

I make a lot of dinnerware, and I don't like eating off my own dinnerware because I become too self-critical, so I have other people's dinnerware. Lots of Michael Simon. I use a lot of different people's work. I've always gotten cooking magazines and I've followed food trends, which has been a source of inspiration in terms of objects to make. When there's a food trend, if you look at catalogs like Pottery Barn or whatever that show you what people are thinking about serving food in, as a potter, you could make it. Of course you can't make it as cheap as Pottery Barn can, but the ideas are out there.

I think that potters should look at what we're eating, and go up and down the aisle in the grocery store and rehouse every condiment that's au courant; you know, the salsas and the hot sauces, whatever it is, make something for it. That's what I always say in workshops; try to get people to think about their real environment, their real table. Unfortunately, most of the people that I run into don't cook so much anymore, and they're not so interested in entertaining. So what are we doing?

My father died and left me some money, so I said, "Okay, I love to cook and I'm going to build the kitchen I want and I'm going to make the dining room big enough to have 12 people and go from there." And then I met Jim. He was building a house on the Blue Ridge Parkway, and he was a widower about six years and a very nice guy. After marrying Jim, she sold her house and moved to the house he had built, where she has a smaller studio—but still has an apprentice. ∎

MATT METZ

Perceptions of Labor

Matt Metz in his studio in Alfred Station, New York, 2018

The distinctive carved surfaces of Matt Metz's functional pottery show his touch everywhere and give both tactile and visual appeal. The pots also engage the viewer because they seem to be labor intensive and because they appear to have some not-quite-identifiable message. They are modestly priced, and that's entirely intentional.

Metz grew up in northeastern Indiana. His father was a high school teacher, but probably more significant were the things he did at home. Metz's parents *collected antiques and valued physical objects quite a bit. We'd go to auctions every Saturday, and my dad had a nice collection of furniture and old pots.* That included crocks. His parents *made all their own pickles and sauerkraut and often used those crocks. They had a truck garden and grew most of their vegetables and canned everything. My mom was a stay-at-home mom, but*

canning and putting up stuff and all.

The other thing about my family and about my childhood that I think is important is, my dad probably started us off, but my brother and I were both fascinated with hunting for Indian artifacts and would spend hours and hours doing it. We would go out in the cornfield after it was plowed and it rained, and we'd walk up and down the rows. As a seven-year-old or whatever, I would ride my bicycle out into the country and hunt for arrowheads and walk this 200-acre field back and forth, maybe picking up two or three arrowheads. It has something to do with the romance of the objects and with the history of them and the meanings they carried for me. And also the obsessive labor thing that is in my work, that kind of willingness to lose myself in what others see as boring labor.

Metz had a great art teacher in high school and attended Ball State University thinking he'd major in art education. He gave up that idea but he took ceramics classes, learned to throw, and really liked it. Ball State is Byron Temple's alma mater, and Temple came back to do some demonstrations for the teacher he and Metz both studied with, Marvin Reichle. Reichle, a Japanophile, introduced Metz to the local Bethel Pike Pottery, where he began *a basic, very traditional 20-hour-a-week job apprenticeship, while going to college at the same time. So it paid for college while I was making pots for this fella very much in the Leach sort of model, making what he made and trying to make it in a perfect way and having him knock off boards of pots into the bucket if they weren't exactly what he wanted.*

Metz went to graduate school at Edinboro University of Pennsylvania, which at the time had four ceramics faculty and excellent facilities. Looking back, he feels that even at this stage he was clueless about the field at large. In fact, he feels that graduate school was just the completion of his undergraduate education. But it gave him both literal and figurative space to work, and it was pretty much a free ride. *As an undergraduate I had been really focused on doing fairly traditional pottery things, probably moderately influenced by the Leach tradition and Japanese pots and all of that. In graduate school, there was enough space in the program that I started doing woodcuts and taking drawing classes and a lot of other stuff that ended up coming back at the work, and being in relative proximity to New York, more than I had been before, and more exposed to general art. My final graduate work was large nonfunctional carved platters that were Gauguin-like, I guess, hacked and carved away but painted with terra sig color.*

From there he got a job as a technician at the University of Michigan at Ann Arbor. *To this day I'm not a technical person. And I don't necessarily buy the model of the all-around, everything potter guy. I think the Japanese had it figured out in the sense there was a guy who was making pots and somebody in the village to cut the wood. Everybody could concentrate on what he did best, rather than to try to do everything.*

I was at Ann Arbor for three years, and during that time I had use of a studio and materials and a space to work, but I went through a period of almost quitting ceramics. I felt I had lost my way. I wasn't sure what I was making or wanted to make. Aimlessly, he started making gifts for people, cups with faces. *I was just throwing some cups and pushing out the eyes and the nose and painting them with maiolica, and they are kind of bright colored. I call them hangover cups. They are of not-so-very-happy people, so like expressionist paintings. They weren't great pots, but I actually started having fun again and I remembered what it was like to be productive.*

I started to make pots again out of porcelain; mix up terra sig and put it on the pot and started scratching into it. I got this more intense figure/ ground thing than I'd ever had before. I stuck it in the salt kiln, and the surface was sort of luscious, silky. It was very attractive to me. I started making more of those pots, and they started coming together. He began to do art fairs, including the Ann Arbor fair, one of the biggest. He thought that he might be able to put together a living making pots.

I also started reconnecting with the fact that what I liked about making pots was being productive, and people really liking and wanting them. And wanting to have them domestically. And the way they sat in the culture as opposed to this art thing, which has always made me uncomfortable. He disliked *the jockeying and the hierarchy and the people you deal with in order to sell them and place them. Everything, the whole culture of the capital-A Art.*

The next step was a residency at the Archie Bray Foundation. *The Archie Bray and Michigan were really graduate school for me. At the Bray I was totally autonomous. But Chris Staley was there between jobs, and he had a lot of good advice, careerwise and about my pots. I had a couple of years sort of consolidating, turning it into a business. I got an NEA grant during that time period, which helped a little bit to defer having to make too much of a living. It really let me play around with the pots and push things and build things and develop a vocabulary. I'm glad I had that space to do it in.* And, he notes, with scholarships and fee waivers he had no education debt; his time at Michigan was free and the Bray was inexpensive. Nor did he own a house or have a family at that time, although the Bray was where he met Linda Sikora, and they soon married.

Sikora had been at the University of Minnesota, and her teacher there, Mark Pharis, owned a house and studio in southeastern Minnesota that he was no longer using, which he rented to them and they later bought. Metz worked there for 13 or 14 years as Sikora began teaching here and there, took a job in Colorado, and ultimately moved to Alfred University. They divided their time for a few years before he joined her there. He taught at Winona State in Minnesota and a few other small schools but did not see teaching as his path. *I was always the kind of unstructured teacher who was either looking at the clock or looking over the student's shoulder—like, I really want to be working on my pot over there. I love doing workshops in a limited period of time where I am teaching my process, what I know best. I'm more of a studio person. I like being in the studio by myself, working.*

All his pots are salt glazed, but some would be wood fired and some fired in a gas kiln *if they have flat surfaces and I want them to have clean drawing. Plates tend to get too much wood ash in our kiln, so they are better fired gas.* He likes the results of wood firing. As he sees it, the stiff drawings are warmed up and the figure/ground contrast is softened. *When we were in Minnesota, [Pharis's] wood/oil kiln was available, and it was very cheap to fire because fuel oil wasn't very expensive at the time, and the wood that we were using to fire with they'd throw away from manufacturing lumber and stuff. We could get eight or ten kilns of wood for $50. That's not true anymore. We start off with wood and do that for the first quarter of the firing, and then the rest of the firing is the oil burners.*

He at first did lots of fairs and over time winnowed it down to the Philadelphia Craft Show and other indoor fairs. No more street fairs. *I would if they felt worthwhile, but . . .* He says he is not good at promoting himself, getting into the magazines, etc. *I'm very lazy about pursuing stuff like that. Philosophically I tend to be one who thinks that the work ought to be there, and I don't have that much to say about it.*

Metz's work shows the direct, individual time invested in it, yet he keeps his prices modest. *Well, part of that is Linda and I can be workaholics. For terms of our life, it was like the studio was 90 percent of what we did. I was in there; we were in there all the time. When we were in Minnesota or doing the long-distance thing, that gave me a lot of time to do a lot of work. But having Isabella [their adopted daughter] has sort of shifted that.*

I'm looking at the sales price in terms of the time and what I'm getting, and all that stuff is a difficulty. On the other hand, the work looks slower than it is, because I'm fast and I've done it for a good number of years. Some people think it must be like carving a piece of granite. A cup is about 30 minutes of drawing. A big pot can take an hour and a half. It's like looking at a quilt —you're awe-struck by how much time it takes, but maybe somebody who is very adept at it could do it faster than you would think. My mother quilts and I've always liked quilts, been attracted to that.

The white porcelain pot gets covered completely with a slip, and while that slip still has just the slightest dampness in it, I start carving it. I use a fine-line-drawing tool and sketch out a band and do the initial images. And then it's just about removing the background, and the negative space from it. He does not apply a predetermined pattern. He makes a series of objects—maybe jars, pitchers, or cups—and when he sits down to carve he intentionally makes each one different, within a vocabulary of motifs. *What is so powerful to me about my pots is less the actual image [than] the relationship to the pot; how the volume is broken up and how those things relate to the pattern.* He modestly asserts that *the drawings on their own on a flat surface wouldn't be very compelling.*

The carving is intuitive. *The only time I sketch out anything is if I've been doing some large pots with vines that are sort of intermingling and crossing over each other. If I do that, I'll cover the whole pot with slip and take food coloring and a brush and just pattern out the vines. Just so I don't over-cross or make a mark where I don't want one. And then I'll start sketching the leaves and stuff loosely in between them and filling up the space.*

He has not costed it out. *I don't think about it in terms like that. On the one hand, I'd say that I have no embarrassment and I'm very much involved* and care about making a living from this. And I like the small business part of it and I like the mercantile part of it and I like the idea of making this commodity and having somebody exchange their labors through money for it. I try to make the most ideal things I can, and then figure where I have to price them. I look at the market around me and try to figure out what's fair.

He decided against selling the bigger pots through a gallery for thousands of dollars, and letting the gallery take its slice. *The thing I found with that is there's a very small market, so you saturate that market pretty quickly. And in terms of making a living, you need to keep moving things out the door and selling them. I haven't seen that market stay stable enough that I thought I could make a living doing that as well as I can by going to retail things myself and carting the work. It's a difficult process but it gives me more freedom.* And it also gives him more contact with the customers, which he likes. *In terms of what a drawing would sell for versus the pot, and the amount of labor involved in it, the risk taking, and all that goes into that—I'd like to see the general field be paid better, myself included.*

I think I do better than many potters because I can sell work quickly when I put it out there, in part because of the images and the perception of labor involved and other things that are right out there on the surface of the pot. The young guys are complaining about making a living, but they're doing work that you have to know about pots and the history of pots and something about the making the process and stuff; you have to be educated to those pots to know what's brilliant about them.

Yet, he admits *the things I look to for inspiration are always old pots. I'm a traditionalist in that sense. Most of my input comes from going to the Met and looking in the Persian room or the German pots or the American pots and all those things. Within the last few years I've been trying to meld that with an interest I have in evolutionary science and biology, and I would say environmentalism, and I would say the sense of our interconnectedness. Sort of like DNA, microbes, and things.*

I don't think about it as representation or direct narrative. I've always avoided pinning it down that way. Just the mishmash and eclectic throwing together of a lot of traditions of decorative patterning: Roman, Japanese, German, English, early American. *There's a lot of trees and things that look like they come out of early American embroidery and such. Very much early American decorative tradition: furniture and painted stuff, old pots. I like the democratic part of that. But I don't like to think of them as narratives. I think that they function ultimately at the service of the pot. It's important to me that the pots have a recognition value like a tune that people get, that draws them in. It's the difference between, let me think of a good example, the difference between Gershwin and Schoenberg or something.*

Everything I make has a shape that's recognizable as doing something. I want it to do what it looks like it should do. But on the other hand, I know they get treated as decorative objects, and so they move in and out from the shelf space to the use thing. I don't feel a need to put out a philosophy that says, "I wish you as the person buying this to do this with it, and if you don't it will be a failed object." I like function as a positive limitation that frames the work. Not having rules is just floating. It doesn't feel very productive. I also love pots. I'm drawn to them, and there's that grounding about class and a lot of other things where they feel more substantial to me, and they have another layer of reason to be there besides just my aesthetic interest.

It's all one package to me. Images are decorative and wouldn't function on their own without going into a place that would be more self-conscious. There's a way in which making pots frees me. I think there's a lot of depth to the imagery, there's a lot of things that go on, but that comes through workmanship. Starting in graduate school, *pots were a place where I could lose myself in the making to the point where I'm making decisions without second-guessing myself. That voice goes away when I'm in the middle of making a lot of pots and working hard. I'm lost in the process.* ∎

—Annie Markovich, transcriber

AYUMI HORIE

Grounded in Reality

Ayumi Horie regards her work online as a second studio practice. Obamaware, Handmade for Japan, the Democratic Cup, and Pots in Action all have relied on the internet. 2018.

Ayumi Horie (pronounced *ho-ree-eh*) is admired for her distinctive pottery featuring loosely drawn animals that are engaging but not Winnie the Pooh cute—a real peril of the subject matter. And she has achieved exceptional stature for her professional and very successful outreach and marketing via her website (including videos for particular products), and for fundraising with pottery, for the 2008 Obama campaign, following the 2011 earthquake and tsunami in Japan, and recently with the Democratic Cup. She is one of many potters whose path was not direct, but whose life experiences have shaped her ceramic work.

Horie's parents are doctors. Her mother is from Maine, daughter of a college professor who was a socialist and had a deep interest in other cultures. Her father is from Japan and was preceded in the US by his elder sister, also a doctor. Eventually his brother, sister-in-law, mother, niece, and nephews also came to this country thanks to a 1965 loosening of immigration laws that had restricted non-Europeans. Thus, although Horie (b. 1969) grew up with very few other Asians in her white, French Canadian, and Roman Catholic hometown, at the same time she had a lively three-generation extended family around her. They fished and they had a garden to produce Japanese vegetables that weren't available in the stores.

It was interesting having all these female role models growing up. My mother didn't do any cooking or cleaning or any of that, and my aunt really took on that role, and my grandmother did as well. I feel like I had multiple mothers. Likewise, although she's an only child, because of the constant presence of her cousins, *I grew up being the youngest of four, in a way.*

She did not inherit her artistic inclinations from her parents. *We had CorningWare, which is still in the cupboard. It's really chipped but they don't care. But I was lucky to grow up in Maine; it felt like craft was valued in Maine.* She remembers craft fairs and the craft scene when she was a teenager in the '80s. *Nancy Margolis had her gallery in Portland at that time.*

I think I was just innately drawn to making stuff and craft. I came from a culture of thrift. It wasn't Depression era, but it was very much influenced by my Japanese family losing everything in World War II. So that idea of scrimping and saving was part of the M.O. of the family.

Growing up, I didn't necessarily find it detrimental to be half Japanese, because of the kind of economic privilege I had. I'm sure it would have been totally different if my family didn't have standing in the community. I was very aware of the fact that I looked different, and I often felt like I was an extra-polite ambassador for all Asians, even though I was born here. Looking back now, it feels problematic, but not as much of a burden as being gay was, because there was so much homophobia. There's no question these experiences have shaped my interest in politics.

After I graduated from Mount Holyoke College, I went to Seattle and worked for a couple of those weekly papers as a photographer. At that point I was taking a clay class and I decided to become a potter. I was interested in that kind of lifestyle, of being independent and not having a boss and having more control over my material. It was always slightly problematic for me as a photographer, having an editor that would dictate the angle of the story. There were situations that felt uncomfortable to me ethically, because they had a certain slant on the story, and then I had to kind of play dumb and photograph the subject without them necessarily knowing that the story was going to pan them. When I moved into pottery—and I mean, this is something I absolutely question now—it felt more honest.

I decided, after looking at the resumes of people who were successful in ceramics, that Alfred was probably the best place to go. So I went there for two years as a BFA and just concentrated on ceramics. I considered an apprenticeship, but I had a hard time finding somebody. I grew up with strong female role models, but at the same time it was a Japanese culture, kind of patriarchal, and the idea of getting into an apprentice situation felt uncomfortable to me because I'd already identified myself as a feminist. I do well in academia, and it was a good way to get an education and be exposed to lots of different ways of doing things. I couldn't have asked for a better two years.

I had, I think, a pretty good material sense coming out of there. I was working with porcelain and using it in this very chunky, fat, generous way, not exploring the qualities that you'd traditionally want porcelain for. At Alfred I got a really bad case of tendonitis, so I thought: omigod, my career's over before I started. [Laughter] But Anne Currier [Alfred professor] encouraged me to find a different way to work, so I started dry throwing. It's a form of trimming but it's a way to make work as well. I start with a cylinder of clay, a solid blank, and then take a loop tool and scoop the inside out and push the walls out.

There's a different skill to predict what kind of curve you want, especially in something like a bowl. There's a different sensibility to moist clay rather than wet, slippy clay. It lends itself to low forms, so if I'm doing something more vertical like a cup or a jar or teapot, then I will throw the traditional way but I'll work dry throwing in there somehow, by making a lid, or whatever. I combine them a lot.

Because the clay is moist rather than wet, it shows a different evidence of tearing and stretching and cracking and flaking. That kind of surface feels a bit more primitive than something that's thrown wetly. I've honed the technique, but there's a certain wobbliness to it that stays there, which I love. Another thing is that I can get a certain kind of edge to the lip. It might feel a bit more faceted as opposed to a smooth, finished termination. It feels a little bit architectural.

Today Horie is increasingly moving in the direction of ram pressing forms such as ramen bowls, and she anticipates that technique accounting for more than half of her work in the future. The decals she uses extensively are drawn first in clay by using sgraffito, so that the mark-making is reductive and responds to the material. She cleans up the drawings in Photoshop and silkscreens them to make water-slide decals.

After I got out of Alfred I went to the Bray for two years, and then I went to the University of Washington in Seattle for grad school. Craft fairs were on the decline when I was getting out of grad school, and also it just felt like a lot of work for a potter to schlep all that work around. First I sold through galleries and then set up a website [in 2002], and pretty shortly after that I set up a store online [in 2005]. There were very few potters that had their own websites, and no others who had online shops. Financially it didn't make sense for me to keep selling wholesale or keep pushing those accounts. I sell everything online or through studio sales. And that's worked out in all kinds of ways because, thinking of educating people, a lot of that connection happens online or through reading whatever I've written about my own work. It kind of weeds out people that may not be predisposed to something that's a little bit more imperfect. Since the reach is so great, it feels like the people who want to find me do find me.

She finds that three-quarters of her audience are female, *and the bulk of those people are in sort* of my age group, so between 35 and 44. And it's also interesting that the fundraiser that I did, the Handmade for Japan fundraiser, the bulk of them were women too; 81 percent of our audience. I don't know if we can draw any big conclusions from that, but I think it's interesting. Making functional pots is my main work, but I don't feel like it's my sole work.

Dealing in images seems second nature to her because of her previous work in photography. Her use of the internet is not a generational factor, because other younger artists don't necessarily do it. Anyway, the rise of the internet happened when she was about 30, although she was using computers in college. *A lot of it has to do with control and wanting to have this kind of vertically integrated business where I make the thing, I market the thing, and then I interact with the customers—they send pictures back to me—so it feels like a closed loop in that sense, whereas the old model of selling to a gallery or wholesale, that relationship often ended there. I never got feedback, or at least the kind of feedback I wanted, about my pots, who's buying my pots. I never formed a relationship with a customer through a gallery. It was always mediated through a gallery.*

Another activity—and a significant one on which she spends 10 to 15 hours a week—is editing Pots in Action on Instagram, which she established in 2015 after more than 10 years as a solo project. Guest hosts cover chosen aspects of pottery culture for two-week stints. It has more than 100,000 followers around the world and is a primary source of education for students.

I feel like the best thing about selling online is creating relationships with people, customers. I've invested a lot in defining my aesthetic online and putting a lot of information, content heavy, and branching out and doing things like these videos, which are just fun. They're not really geared toward a ceramic crowd per se because they're not straight how-to videos. They're really about making this fun and bringing in a new audience, which is what I think we need to do as a field as well. We can't keep tapping into the same people over and over again. Especially since the population that was really supporting craft in the '80s is deaccessioning or they're not buying work anymore. So to create a new audience, that needs to happen online first.

I've been giving lectures on this and really

encouraging people to take more control of their own media, and think of their art as more inclusive and think of it in broader terms instead of being defined just by material. Because it's so easy these days to create a website by plugging into a template. To me it doesn't make sense if you're an artist to not think about what your broader aesthetic is, whether it's the clothes you wear, the things you buy for your house, the car you drive. It's an impossible thing to shut off, so why not approach your website in the same way, where you're actually learning some coding, working with a designer to come up with a site that reflects your aesthetic?*

When Horie set up, there were no templates, so she took a class in Dreamweaver, an HTML program, and worked from there. Now she has a web designer who does the more complicated things—*Because on a practical level, I can't keep up with everything* [Laughter]—but she does the updating herself. This reflects a certain intellectual curiosity and openness on her part; others seem afraid it requires expertise.

I'm all about delegating and bartering. The dry-throwing video—a friend shot the video, and then for the music, I basically put it out there as a sort of crowdsourcing project. Somebody recommended a Japanese American group in Japan, and so I traded pots with them for doing the music. We worked on the lyrics together, which was a really interesting process for me. And it felt like it reflected me as well. It's fun collaborating with people, I think. And then the second video, that match-striker video, the director loves my work and she's a photographer and she also had lived in L.A. so she knew people in the film industry. There were probably a dozen people that worked on that video, and I traded pots with all of them. And the music was done by a friend of hers. But all of this stuff couldn't have happened if I wasn't online. I come from an approach of believing something is possible and then just figuring out who can help me make that reality, and then trading pots and a little bit of money for it to happen.

Her first studio, in New York's Hudson valley, where she moved a year after finishing graduate school, was a small, deconsecrated church and attached living quarters that she bought with help from her family and remodeled. *The house was such a mess, and I lived in this mess for three years and* worked as the clay coordinator at the Women's Studio Workshop and had my studio there. *This was really a full-time job and that was a part-time job, and then I was trying to make pots on top of that.* She served as the general contractor and of course made all the aesthetic decisions and was constantly on the hunt for objects and materials. *Renovating gave me a much better sense of what my own aesthetic is, and how important my own geographical history and my own roots are in my aesthetic.*

In the '80s, she remembers, everyone was either doing craft fairs or had a studio with a showroom that people could come to. *It's like you needed some kind of a public space. And I had this beautiful church which I didn't use half as much as I probably could have. I think it was helpful in terms of rounding out somebody's romantic idea of what a life of craft is like, but you don't need that kind of space. You could actually create it all virtually. You could work in a basement and send your pots all over the world.*

In 2012 she made the decision to move back to Maine. *My parents were getting older and I can see them needing help, and I want to enjoy them while they're around. It just felt like the right time. I always thought I'd move back to Maine at some point. It seems like an incredibly fertile place for a small business, maybe not taxwise but in terms of being self-sufficient and finding a community of like-minded people. And I've always been inspired by history, and Maine is such a rich place for history. Until I was seven or eight, I grew up in the house that my mother grew up in, which we actually still have. It's an old Victorian which was filled with antiques and old things. There was a toy closet with toys from the '40s, and the knee walls in the attic are still filled with* Life *magazines from the '30s and '40s, and there's trunks in the old stable, trunks where there are newspapers from like 1880 and dresses. It was kind of a touchstone for me growing up. It's family history.* Having the bulk of her business online made it easier to move back.

I'm lucky because normally what I post I sell about half of it in the first hour or so. And then probably three-quarters of it within the next day. And I spend the next couple of days just packing and shipping. Orders may sort of trickle in here and there after that, but for the most part I can get my studio back to normal and start working again.

On the store I would show usually two or three sides and then a detail. I've only had a couple of people return things, and that has been because it hasn't matched something that they already have, not because it didn't feel right or something. Before I started selling online, I thought: well, who would ever buy something so tactile when they couldn't actually test it out? But people do. Which means that maybe the drawing carries much more weight, and the other stuff is discovered later.

I think I was committed to function because I'm a Mainer. A practical life seems like a meaningful life to me. I struggled a lot to let go of function. For my thesis work I was sewing flannel molds and then pouring plaster into them, so they were these very sort of puffy, white, soft-looking objects. And after grad school I did a series of lanterns that were really a bridge between sculpture and function. Then I started making pots again because it felt really clear to me that my heart was in function. I don't think I was ever really seduced by the art world.

Akio [Takamori, a figurative sculptor who taught at the University of Washington] *took me under his wing. There's a kind of sympathy in his work that I related to, a kind of softness in his subject matter where he wasn't afraid to portray tenderness, and I admired that. I think what I tried to do with my own work is engender a kind of softness in people by using cuteness as a strategy instead of using it ironically. I'm not interested in sarcasm.*

Growing up as a half-Japanese girl and a tomboy and a lesbian, that idea of kawaii [cuteness] *was something I rebelled against, and I didn't see the benefits of it necessarily for myself. It's not something I'd pass off so easily any more. I don't think all kinds of cuteness are the same. I think I'm interested in cuteness as a kind of spiritual pursuit* [Laughter], *if that's possible. A way of connecting. Because often my pots are given as gifts, and that is a very flattering thing to me. As a token of love.*

Also important to her is social activism, most obviously through Obamaware, Handmade for Japan, and the Democratic Cup. *I did those because I could do them, because I was in a position to do them. I had the infrastructure in place, and the interest, and it just seemed like a great project. And Handmade for Japan just felt like I really had no other choice than to try to raise as much money as possible as quickly as possible.*

I was always clear that I didn't want to teach full time. I enjoy and do a lot of workshops, going in for a few days, but I think it takes a toll on the rhythm of the studio, and I feel protective of that. Because I really am happiest when I have a full day in the studio with no interruptions, and I can do what I want by myself. There is something that's very appealing to me about this kind of solitary studio practice. I do email throughout the day or text or whatever, but I feel like the work really moves forward when there's uninterrupted time.

Cup: *The shape has changed some, but there's almost always a bulge at the bottom. On a practical level, it won't tip over. And then visually I actually want to make something that feels slightly dumpy* [Laughter], *because it's more accessible that way. It's sort of the opposite of a palace pot, which I don't really relate to at all. And then there's the Japanese belief that your soul isn't in your heart—it's in your belly; it's further down. I like that idea of it having a lower center of gravity. It's just sort of a practical thing, like wearing sensible shoes.* [Laughter]

Match striker: *This is a shape that I'm kind of known for. I came up with the shape just because I love pastry and wanted to make something where I could fold the flap over and pinch it like a pinwheel is pinched, or a dumpling or something. Linda Christianson, I gave her one of these way back when, and she used the bottom as a match striker, and so I transferred it into the drawing by not glazing that, and also I tend to give them a little bit more fur or* texture to strike on. Obviously the drawing gets marred when you strike a match, so that just is part of it.

Animals: *I started drawing when I got Poncho* [her dog]. *I grew up with a mother who loves books and loved to read to me as a kid, and so I think I had an active animal fantasy life, literary animal fantasy life. Everything from the Berenstain Bears to Winnie the Pooh to Narnia, all those talking animals.*

It was clear to me that I was drawn to work that had animals on it, and so were other people, so it was a combination of a commercial decision and an attraction to that kind of imagery. And it happens that it's a very rich subject historically. Animal drawings have always been a part of pottery history. Our minds naturally want to create some kind of narrative. So it's a perfect substitute without being explicit, without using human figures. It's this rich playground for me.

I tend to draw animals either three-quarter view or in profile. A big part of what I want to do in my drawing is to not create a sense of illusion but emphasize the flatness of the drawings. I don't want somebody to be lost in a world. I want to say: here's this drawing on a plate, and here we are grounded in reality. Maybe that's where my family background in science comes in.

It's interesting, you sort of stumble onto subject matter. I feel like the illustration is really what's going to carry me through my old age. ■

WINTON AND ROSA EUGENE

Listen to Your Customers

Rosa and Winton Eugene in their Cowpens, South Carolina, studio "having our usual discussion"

The Eugenes backed into pottery. Winton owned a carpet business in Chicago, and Rosa was a nurse when they decided to move to South Carolina to be closer to family. Their new career began when she bought him a potter's wheel as a present. Soon she was involved too. They work both collaboratively and individually, and their success can be measured by the honorary doctorates they received from the University of South Carolina in 2016, and the 30-year retrospective of their work at the McKissick Museum in 2018.

Looking back, their practical wisdom is clear. One piece of it is to have no debt. Another is to listen to your customers. That includes both casual comments at the many fairs they do and in the 24-by-28-foot showroom they built between their home and workshop. One oddity, for example, is a cup with a full handle that jogs to the left at the bottom. It was made for a lady with arthritis who didn't have a strong grip; she needed to get all four fingers in the handle. Winton invented this solution. *The thing about it is, once we started doing that,* Rosa says, *everybody wanted it,* says Winton, finishing her sentence.

They have trusted customers who test out new pieces for ease of handling or cleaning, for example. Rosa: *I don't have time to test all these little things, so I give them to certain people and I say, "Will you test this for me? Tell me what you think." And they like getting maybe a free cup or whatever. People know what they want. And you know what you can make and you can't make. It's like a marriage. Give and take, you know.*

Winton: *Sometime people don't even buy anything, but if you care for a little bit of input sometime they have a good idea because they've bought somebody else's work and they figure they can tell you what the other person did wrong. And if you want to listen to it, it might work for you.*

Rosa: *And you learn.*

Winton: *That's another thing too; when you have all these people advising you, they send you books about certain information so you get educated from the public.*

The imagery on their pots includes rustic scenes—Winton loves tobacco barns—as well as portraits, rows of profiles resembling fabric design, and many birds: hummingbird, bluebird, finch, redbird, wren, brown thrush, bobwhite. Winton is a birdwatcher, and they do only birds he has seen. He's a gardener, too, so they are concerned with the environment. Some decorations allude to wetlands. He made a piece featuring cattails and subtly depicted elements of the human body. They titled it "Endangered Species," meaning humanity. But people didn't get it. So he decided to depict faces as if they were leaves. He asked Rosa rhetorically, *How would they like people throwing trash and all this stuff on them?* And with the faces, their customers began to get it. Rosa: *You heard the comment like, "There's no such thing as global warming," that kind of thing. Then we had the discussion naturally in our booth.* They've depicted dragonflies because of their dependence on wetlands and have used a seahorse motif as a protest against a man-made island in Dubai that was created by dredging the ocean floor and thus disturbing habitat, and because of the fishing nets that capture sea life indiscriminately. The Eugenes take it hard.

Besides their attention to local (and distant) flora and fauna, Winton likes to go to the beach in the winter, when there aren't people there and he can hear the surf and birds, instead of human chatter. They also travel extensively (he has been to every state except Alaska), and they follow nature programming on PBS. And they're also (not that it relates to nature) inveterate museumgoers.

Rosa (b. 1949) is the middle of eight children of a cleaning lady and a plasterer. *I was always the one that was in charge, always the one that was telling people what to do. I was always the one that knew what I wanted and knew how to get it and worked harder than everybody else.*

Winton (b. 1945) had been in the military and came to her house because he knew Rosa's brother. He says, *I didn't like her as a girlfriend when I met her. We just used to fuss about everything from religion to politics. We didn't date; when we was together we was always fussing over the whole world. I was trying to fix it and she was trying to . . . I don't know* what she was trying to do. Our parents was basically similar. They call it dysfunctional family, but everybody at that time had dysfunctional in their family. I was from Louisiana, she was from South Carolina, but our parents had the same behavior. Still, the two became friends of a sort, and she went to see him in Chicago, where he was living. They talked of many things, including what they didn't want to go through as husband and wife. So she proposed (he has a funny story about that!). They argue about whether they still argue. Rosa: *But you know what, we've never been to bed angry at one another.* Winton: *I think that's because she can cook.* [Laughter] *Fix the right food to put you to sleep; that's what it is.* [Laughter] *What it is, catnip tea or something?* [Laughter]

She went to Richard J. Daley College and got an associate degree in nursing, and at the University of South Carolina she got a bachelor's degree, so she is RN BSN. Winton has a high school education and never went to art school. But he was good at art from elementary school, and every day he did an illustration for some teacher. In his family home there were five siblings and two cousins, with another taken in later. His mother also cleaned houses, and his father worked at an oil refinery. He moved to Chicago because there were job opportunities and the pay was better. The cost of living was higher, but he was used to living frugally and he had skills. Rosa: *I think he was a saver, and I was a saver. That's why we kind of liked each other. I didn't appreciate people just going out throwing money away.* Winton: *We both love to work.*

They collaborate well because Rosa has ideas but depends on Winton to execute them. She says she can't conceive in three dimensions, as he can, and she can't draw. He likes details. She likes abstraction. When she thinks he puts on too much, she tells him, "That's enough."

They were married in 1968 and came to South Carolina in '79. They didn't want to have a mortgage, because they realized that the mortgage on their house in Chicago would have been more than four times the cost of the house by the time they paid it off.

Winton: *So we said, the next house, we're going to do it a little at a time so we won't be under the mortgage, and it would be paid for. So we started building the house in '76; we gave a guy $20,000*

to shell a house out. So he put the brand-new roof, electrical stuff. And then we came every summer for three years, and we put up sheetrock and insulation a little bit at a time. Go back, work, work, save enough money to put up something else. So by '79 we had the carpeting, the floor down, and all we needed was the kitchen cabinets.

I didn't think television was a good idea. I thought that was one of the worst inventions man made, because it stops people in their tracks and makes them sit down to watch somebody else do something. So my kids hated me for that. [Laughter]

Rosa: *If he was planting trees or flowers, we had to do it too.*

Winton: *Let's go and do something. That was my belief. That's why they bought me a potter's wheel.*

Rosa: *Yeah, so he can have something to do. It's going to take him at least five or six years* [Laughter]*, and we can watch television. Then all of a sudden, in six months he had a whole garage full, he was putting up shelves, and he had greenware. He started carving to remove some of the clay to lighten up the pottery.* His instruction books described throwing thinly, but in the beginning his were all thick. He trimmed, made a foot, fretted about the waste. A sister-in-law saw them giving things away, and suggested that they go to a festival and try to sell. Winton: *And I had some of the ugliest stuff.* It was not only thick; he hadn't mastered glazing. There they heard about *Sunshine Art* magazine, which listed shows all over the US. People told them they could make a living at this. Winton: *My eyes lit up like Christmas lights. When I was a child they said you couldn't make a living at art. Oh, no, you've got to get a real job. Doing art wasn't a real job.* [Laughter] It was also an appealing idea because Winton loves to travel.

I would turn the pots, I would bisque them, turned nice little pots; you know, do little designs on them and stuff, but when I mixed the glaze I didn't care. [sounds of glaze-mixing gestures] *So I said, "God, what's wrong with me?" One day I said, "Rosa, why don't you mix up some glaze and put it on the pots?" So she did.* He was surprised to see her with a gram scale. *She was measuring a little bit of this, and she had this recipe.* He had been measuring everything with a cup and not writing anything down, so when he got a beautiful glaze he couldn't reproduce it. *And that's how we got the glazing system down, because this girl came and she measured everything precise, put it in the little jars, blended it in the blender, and she brushed it on. And every piece she put her hand on came out perfect. So she came back down the next time and added a little bit of color and everything came out. I told her I would never glaze another piece of pottery.* [Laughter] She says he had to come to her on his hands and knees and beg. And she ruled: *If I'm going to mix a glaze, I'm going to pick the color. Everything my husband made was brown.*

Winton: *That's how we became partners, because when she started doing that, I started putting her name on the bottom. Right away. When she started mixing the glaze and everything started coming out, mixing the glaze seemed like half the process. You can make the pot, but if you glaze it and mess it up, you might as well throw it in the garbage can.*

Pricing, Rosa says, is the most difficult part. Winton remembers where he came from, and he finds it hard to think of $35 or even $20 for a cup. But she says, *If everybody understood what pottery really was and how it was made and the amount of time that was placed on it, and what a person should ideally get, then it would be okay. But you're competing with a jigger. That's a machine that makes a plate a second; you just pop the clay on top and it shoots out a plate a second. And you're competing with turners, people who come in and turn a ton of clay for you and just leave the pots there, and all you have to do is glaze them. And you're competing with the commercial Japanese product. You're competing with all that. They just don't understand. So I've been trying to educate the public and gently raise my prices.* As it is, they cover all the direct expenses but do not really factor in their time.

Winton: *You can only put a price on your time if you're doing something that somebody willing to pay you for.* But they get more than their costs, and Winton works very efficiently. They're making a living.

Rosa: *He's so efficient in making the piece. We don't have a lot of loss. Our overhead is for turning and getting stuff out. And because I mix all the glazes, we don't have to buy commercial glazes. Anything we can make that we don't have to buy reduces our costs and our overhead. And we don't have to buy a lot of stuff, like displays. My husband made all those pedestals, all those cabinets.*

He made a table of oak boards recycled from hog pens and carefully planed. They recycled before it was fashionable, they say. And when they wanted to put up the showroom, Rosa, in a Bobcat, was leveling the site and digging the footings. They got some lumber from demolitions Winton helped with, and they traded pots for some work by a concrete man.

If you're not in debt, they say, almost everything you do is a profit. You're not paying interest. Rosa: *We don't believe in borrowing money. How we built this* showroom *building, we did shows for the whole year and we saved up whatever we had left from the show. We found the contractor and he gave us a price. He did his part, and then we went out to find a bricklayer and then paid him how much ever, then I did another show and the man came in to do all the electric. We had money for that, then we paid him.*

They can fire with wood, gas, or electric but use mostly electric now because it makes the work consistent, which pleases their customers. Rosa coils pots. They have a slab roller because Winton makes masks and platters. They do a lot of commission platters. He used to do miniatures, but one person was buying them all, and no one else got to see them.

Rosa: *Winton is a clean freak.*

Winton: *You could spend more time looking for a tool because it's dirty. The tool could be laying right there, but you don't see it because it's dirty. So if you cleaned it up . . . I've been to so many potter's places you couldn't even tell what kind of wheel he was turning on.* [Laughter] He's also concerned about breathing silica in the dust.

Early on, they numbered the pots. But then when one explodes or is otherwise lost, there's a gap. So they date it with month and year and their names.

Winton: *Those pieces that you see over there, that's about women and women issues. I try not being political. I trying being level and calm; I like peaceful and close to nature so when you're looking at it you can enjoy it all the time. She like to do your political aspect of stuff. This is called* Battered. He points to an irregular vessel that folds over near the top, as if cringing.

Rosa: *We talk about social issues. But political to some other people could mean that you're active in politics. It's not that kind of political. It's to speak of issues. When you're in an art gallery, you might* fold your hands and you're quiet because when you're looking at that art, you don't talk. But when you go to a pottery show [Laughter] *and you've got a piece of pottery, people are talking. They're asking me questions. So they say, "What do the names mean?" So that's when the explanation starts. I usually have lots of people in my booth, so the discussion starts there. But political, that's what I'm talking about; us women, we have to kind of stick together and realize that if it's left up to the devices* of men, and I'm not being prejudiced, but if it's left up to the devices of men then the world is not going to last so long. Because men they love war, and the people who suffer the most are the women and the children.

The Eugenes say—laughing, of course—that potters are the strangest people because they make what they want and expect others to love it just as much. ∎

EMILY FREE WILSON

Front of the Cupboard

Emily Free Wilson in her studio, Helena, Montana, 2018

A potter who has her husband and, for a time, her brother working for her is an unusual story. Emily Free Wilson was born in Anchorage, Alaska, in 1979, spent some young years in Hawaii, where her parents had met, and grew up in Oregon. Her father was a pastor in a nondenominational evangelical church. She's not sure how that plays out in her work, but she speculates that at least when she was attracted to ceramics in college, the community or family aspect of it appealed to her. Her father also had a printing business that operated out of their home. She helped with some of his promotional projects and says, *I was really comfortable selling stuff. I didn't grow up in an art family. It was a very common sense, like "how do we pay the bills" kind of creating.*

When I was a kid, I liked to draw a lot, and then I found out I was really good at running and I stopped drawing. Went to college on a running scholarship. I was on track to be an Olympic athlete. It was a pretty realistic goal at the time. And then I got injured. In the meantime I decided to be an art major. Whether it was knitting with my grandma, or tie-dying with my teammates, or making bracelets for them or reupholstering my couch, I was always *doing crafty projects on the side. I could type superfast; I was really organized; I could get any sort of administrative job if I needed to. So I figured I might as well major in something I enjoy. I thought I would go into graphic design.*

She delighted in a ceramics class, took a second semester, and, before she knew it, was president of the Clay Club and taking a busload of people to SOFA, the Chicago craft fair. She also wanted to go to an NCECA ceramics conference, and that forced a crisis decision in which she gave up running, which would have consumed her life, in favor of ceramics, which she felt allowed a more balanced life. Pottery was not particularly encouraged at the University of Wisconsin–Madison, where she was studying. A graduate student taught her to throw over Christmas break, but her work at the time was large-scale minimal, colorful sculpture.

At NCECA she had met Chip Clawson, who was running the clay business at the Archie Bray Foundation, and he offered her a job. It was a godsend, because at graduation she was still fairly new to the creative field and less confident of her talent than her administrative skills. After arriving in Montana she concluded that the clay business was not what she wanted. The Bray had a small gallery, and she tried to persuade Josh DeWeese, then the resident director, to let her run that. He said the Bray wasn't ready yet. So, in a small studio space, with borrowed equipment, she set about becoming a better potter, inspired by the many great potters in the area.

This community of potters and artists is really supportive. In the meantime I ran a gallery, helped a friend start a gallery, worked at the museum a little bit. In the process of all this, I met my husband [Matt Wilson]. He figured out that he wasn't going to get to spend much time with me unless he hung out with me in the studio. So he started helping me in the studio, loading kilns and building shelves, doing all these things.

Free Wilson continues to wear multiple hats very happily. She did later run the galleries for the Bray and at the same time was trying to produce in the studio and couldn't do enough to meet demand. Her husband and brother stepped in. Bobby Free went to Utah State and has traveled to China and Korea studying pottery. *Bobby would come here because our parents split and then I got together with Matt, and Matt and Bobby really hit it off. Bobby's home base was here; he would come here for the summer and during Christmas break. One Christmas break we hired him to throw pots so we could keep up because I was pregnant, and that was the beginning. A year before Bobby graduated from college, we were like, "Bobby if you want to keep doing this for us, we need to ramp it up so that when you graduate we can afford to pay you so that*

you can pay your bills." So we seriously started to do that.

I see these artists coming through that are trying to make a living, and a lot of them bounce from residency to residency, or they are trying to find a teaching job, and there are fewer teaching jobs out there. I don't want to do it that way. I decided I was going to start a family business. It's called "Free Ceramics."

She describes the system, as they started. *I say, "This bowl, we need this shape, this size, or this height," and Bobby makes them, or Matt; he really got into mold-making because he has a construction background. It clicked for him, which is great because I have no interest in making molds, but I can make forms and Matt would make the mold. I decorate everything, and Matt and I color them in. Bobby will help when we get close to deadlines, but he prefers to not color in the dots. He would rather just make the pots. Bobby and Matt have no interest in communicating with customers, or creating the marketing part of it. I run the business and they make the work. We all help make it. Matt has learned how to glaze. I used to dip all my pots, and then Matt started spraying the glaze, which is better because it is more consistent. In the studio I was more of the artist, and Matt helped me fine tune my process. I didn't have test tiles with colors; my clear glaze was hit or miss. He is really the scientist side of it and is interested in that part of it. I am more interested in chatting with people and going to openings and doing that part of it. It is a great group that we've got.*

Free Wilson is staking out a production process that few studio potters have chosen to engage in. The emphasis in studio pottery has been the individual doing all tasks. She has looked at other models, such as Heath, a California business that was started by an individual potter but evolved into a factory. *In college I was helping one grad student do his show, and that's where I learned to throw, making parts of his master's exhibition. I would help my professor with his tile project. Being part of a group creates something that didn't seem bad to me. When I did my BFA show, I made all these forms and I filled all the tables in the ceramics studio and I got seven of my friends to show up and paint them with me. I've always taken on projects or things larger than I can do on my own. I think it's part of my personality, and I like that.*

Bobby Free is now a ceramics technician for a California college; Free Wilson and her husband have expanded with three to four part-time employees plus volunteers. At one time the business operated out of the garage studio behind their house, and they had another space where they held children's classes to help generate income. They moved to a larger space in an old industrial building in Helena that included other studios and shared kiln space. In 2014 they bought an 8,000-square-foot former funeral home, where all activities are combined and they rent nine multimedia studios in the basement. Her own high-ceilinged studio space is rented out for fundraisers, dances, and live music and is the site for a 100-artist community show called "This Is Helena."

Working with my brother and my husband allowed me to really push the decorating and become more confident and allow myself to make mistakes without feeling like each piece is precious because I have such limited time to make pots. Her motif is generally lines and dots, but it shifts and changes. *I will sit down with a tray of cups, and each one I will decorate differently. There are some designs that are more typical, but I don't sit and do like 12 of that design because that would be really boring.*

In the art world and in the pottery world, people talk about selling out. I've never done that. I actually really like how I decorate. It is really me that I am putting into my pots. In college I realized, looking at a lot of art and being around a lot of art, that I wanted whatever I made to be a positive part of our world. I mean, we all have our histories or our issues or our things that we have to deal with, and I think that there is an important place for people to make art that comments on current affairs or things they go through. But I wanted to make work that made people happy, that enriched their lives in a positive way. My pots are really whimsical and fun, and people say that they smile when they use them and have them in their homes. It makes them feel good.

It's the looseness and the movement and the joyful whimsical qualities that I try to put in them. Sometimes my designs might remind people of fireworks or flowers, Christmas lights, strands of colorful lights.

I really want this cup to feel good in my hand and my fingers, and I want my plate to fit in the dishwasher. I want it to be easy for someone to have in their daily life. If the pot is inconvenient to use, then it falls further back in my cupboard. I want my pots to be so enjoyable to use as well as to look at that they stay in the front of the cupboard. ∎

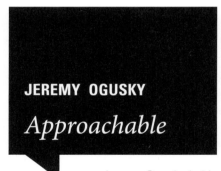

JEREMY OGUSKY

Approachable

Jeremy Ogusky in his studio, Jamaica Plain, Massachusetts, 2018.
Photo: Steve Molter Photography

Despite his health sciences background, Jeremy Ogusky for a time was making himself into the village potter of Jamaica Plain (Boston). His parents are clinical therapists in private practice. He has a master's degree in public health, and it's a measure of his family's professional ambitions that when he told his grandfather he'd completed it, the first question was when would he get his PhD. Ogusky (b. 1976) was not good at hard sciences, but he was good at questioning, he says. He was attracted to the social sciences and was a religion major for a while. He wanted to be in the health field, and medicine was the aspect he was most familiar with. But early on he took art too.

His high school was well equipped for ceramics (wheels, a walk-in gas kiln), but the art teacher didn't know much about it. But a guest, a Korean potter who didn't speak English, sat at the wheel and threw off the hump for the length of the class. *That was it. I didn't want to do anything else. I was mesmerized. So the next day I got on the wheel and I just continued, basically.* While enrolled at Michigan State University he joined a local clay cooperative. *On weekends and late at night I would be there in the studio, from 10 to 2, making pots.* He was the only young person in the group, but *it was fine. I really made some good friendships that continue.*

While a grad student at Boston University, *in all my free time I was making pots. I was just a hobbyist. And when I graduated from my master's program, I went into the Peace Corps and I lived in Mobutu in southern Africa for two years, working on HIV prevention. I did some clay work there. Not a lot, though. There were not that many potters. I met my wife* [Siiri Morley] *there. She was another Peace Corps volunteer. She was working with a weaving cooperative, helping them build their business.* Later the couple spent two years in Ecuador, where he taught public health. *We were in Cuenca, which is actually the clay capital of Ecuador. There's a rich history of ceramics there, and there's a gremio, like a pottery cooperative. I apprenticed with a potter named Ivan Encolada. For generations his family were working clay and it was really great. He just opened his studio; he said, "Come and work with me. We can work with designs together." I helped with some of his firings. I learned a lot, working on a kick wheel, digging clay. It was very interesting.*

We came back to the US and went to Washington, DC. Siiri worked in international development, and I worked with a local community-based organization that does HIV/AIDS prevention. I found a potter in DC who had a studio in his basement. I cleaned his studio for him, and he gave me a key and I could use the studio late at night. I was learning a little bit of technical stuff like loading kilns, mixing glazes, but more I was just cleaning for him. Then we moved to Boston because Siiri got an MBA at Brandeis University. And I got a job with Harvard University doing some global-health academic work, and I worked for them for about six months and then I lost my job. And in retrospect it was wonderful.

His wife suggested that maybe it was an opportunity to give full time to clay. And she suggested that he take a course at Haystack. He took one for production potters, and although most in the group were already working that way, he felt he didn't compare too badly. The session gave him confidence. *It showed me that I could think of this as a business and maybe make money.* He came back to Boston determined to try. He built a website and looked for ways to expand his business.

For a while his dual life continued, but inverted, doing *clay full time and, in the margins, public health. So once a year I got 35 college students from colleges and universities around the US in Washington for two weeks, and I organized a whole global-health course for them. I was doing that every January, which really worked very well because January is a slow month for retail. November and December are at extremely breakneck speed, selling as many pots as possible. I did like a third of my sales for the year in one month. So it was nice to totally switch gears in January and work in public health.*

In 2012 he estimated that one-third of his income was craft show sales, and one-third tableware commissions. *That includes wedding registries. I do about two or three wedding registries per year, and*

I build a unique page on my website for the couple. I try to mimic Bed Bath & Beyond. It has a little photo; it says requested, how many they have, and the price, and then their friends and family can buy it directly on the website. It's not as slick as Bed Bath & Beyond, but it works.

Each registry is like 40 to 70 pieces, so it takes a lot of time, and tableware is a lot of work. It takes a lot of space in the kiln; there's a lot of seconds. But it's hard not to do it, because the margins are quite good. And often registries are great because the couple is not paying for it so they don't care; they're like, "Oh yeah, we'll take one of these, and that one." It's an easy sell to the friends and family because if the couple trusts me, then their friends and family are going to trust me. I don't have to individually market to all those people. The question is finding the couple. And that's a very competitive market, the wedding market. They're being bombarded. I've found my customers mostly word of mouth. If you search for Boston potters, there's not a lot of production potters in Boston, so some people found him that way, online.

Of his work, Ogusky says, It's not anything that you would see in a gallery. I do work with a few galleries, but they're more on the line between craft shops and galleries. I've had a few abrasive and not good run-ins in the art world, and it really turns me off. It's so weird; the code, the norms for the art world are so different than the norms of the world that I operate in. I look for clients, transparently. I have to make a living; I have to market my work; I have to talk about myself; I have to go out and find clients, like advertise.

I was awarded a matching grant from an organization called Assets for Artists. They put me through these art trainings, like artist toolbox types of things where they talk about finance and saving and stuff like that. I was with a bunch of artists, and I was so much ahead of the game. I've got spreadsheets and I know what my margins are. I have to. And so I think I've removed myself from the art world in a way. But that's not to say he's entirely uninterested in it. I think from like an anthropological perspective; [Laughter] it's interesting for me to look at it, not that I would live in that world really.

What's exceptional about me as a potter is not so much my work but how I've used my work. You can only make a mug so many different ways. But the way you use a mug is, I think, limitless. So the application of the mug, that's what I'm very interested in. Getting mugs into people's hands and the idea of sharing the value. I'm really interested in using social media and finding new ways that potters haven't thought of to get mugs, plates, anything out there. He opened an Etsy account because it was low cost. A coffee shop / art gallery planned to offer plates of hot chocolate and asked him to make little cups to sit on a wooden board. He made tableware for a local Italian restaurant. All these young mothers are on a local Jamaica Plain list serve, and someone on the list serve said, "Hey, are you looking for a wedding gift? There's this guy Jeremy."

For a local grocery store called City Feed and Supply, he made mugs with a big emblem that said City Feed, and sold them wholesale to the store. He didn't make much money, but for me it's really good to be associated with the store because they have a lot of social capital, people respect them, and when people see me, they're like, "Oh, you're the guy that makes the City Feed mugs." And that's the kind of stuff I find valuable. I enjoy building relationships. A less successful endeavor was handmade Kiddush cups for bar and bat mitzvah. I was talking with the synagogue, and I convinced them like maybe they could sell my work to these young people who would be interested in something handmade and not just a kiddush cup that's stamped out of metal or something. So they put in their first order for 20. But they didn't sell.

Ogusky also worked with this guy who does usually two or three 5K races per year. He started out during Oktoberfest, so at the end of the 5K race, tons of beer. So I was like, "Oh, why don't we do a trophy that will double as a beer stein?" He always buys like 10 or 20 of these, so at the end of the race there's all these winners filling them with beer and drinking out of this. Always great photos.

He also served on the board of his local arts council. On the other hand, his Etsy sales and some work for Williams-Sonoma were not at all community based.

I did some of the really high-end craft shows in New England and did meet a lot of potters, like my parents' generation of potters, and they're all very negative about the whole industry. They've seen it; the craft show is done. That was the model:

you do some craft shows, some wholesale, and some galleries, and there were potters who made a decent living. But you can't follow that model anymore. You have to be more innovative.

When I first started, I did my local alternative craft festivals. I did the Rock N Roll fair twice—good music, good beer—but I sold nothing. I loved the people I met. I've tried some of the smaller ones, but they haven't been so fruitful for me.

Mostly on Etsy I sell these fermenting crocks for making pickles, kimchee, sauerkraut, which there's a huge resurgence in. It's good money and people are interested. There's this underground movement, not even so underground actually, and if you google "handmade fermenting crock," my Etsy site is one of the first ones that pops up. So people are finding me and they're buying my crocks. That's a niche thing.

This is a fermenting crock. On the front I write "ferment" and on the back I write "foment." [Laughter] *This actually has a lot of my character because I myself am a very big fermenter. I really value microbial diversity. I started making them for myself, and people asked me for them and I started making more. I've seen German-style crocks, but I made this design myself. It holds one gallon.*

I talk about the values in buying local food and preparing your own food and like the Slow Food movement. There's a lot of overlap in the craft movement and the Slow Food movement. So foodies, they get it. But also people that like handmade stuff get it, so it's sort of a niche thing that I'm really proud of, and it's actually selling well.

I'm very interested in the idea of the long tail. So I can reach these people, with Etsy, with the internet. I would much rather do stuff like that than do craft shows, because they're a drag, they're really difficult, a lot of time, and if I don't make money it's a really negative experience. They're pushing the limits of how much they can take advantage of artists, and I'm not that interested in the market really. So I'm trying to change. I think of myself as an entrepreneur as much as an artist.

Sturdy. Functional. User friendly. Approachable, that's the word. I find that the little pieces of myself in my pots come out very slowly and very subtly. After I make 100 pieces, you know it changes each time for sure, and by the 100th one I'm like figuring out sort of the shape of it more, but it's subtle stuff.

I don't look to radically change things. I want it to work well.

Ogusky for some years had studio space at Feet of Clay Pottery in Jamaica Plain. It's a membership organization with about 60 members now, mostly middle-aged women. He liked being around other potters, but with Williams-Sonoma orders, he alone was creating half of the pottery's production, and his work was being picked up on pallets by tractor-trailer trucks. He shifted first to another studio where there was a loading dock, and then set up his own studio in the basement of the house he and his wife bought in Jamaica Plain. Still, Feet of Clay was a good way to begin: the overhead was very low, and his entry costs to being a full-time potter were practically nothing. He got a secondhand wheel for $100 and paid very modest rent because he did some tech stuff in exchange. He had 24-hour access, and lots of kilns. He was the studio recycler because other members were throwing away clay. It was a resource, so he used it.

Gradually he came to a reckoning and gave up craft shows, galleries, and small stores. The Williams-Sonoma orders stopped as suddenly as they had begun. Today about 75 percent of his work is wholesale, and about two-thirds of that is restaurants—as much as 1,000 pieces for a single restaurant. His sturdy, simple, undecorated aesthetic suits many of them. He also sells through wedding registries and open-studio events. He has shifted his public-health interests into the food community, especially fermentation. He does workshops and directs the Boston Fermentation Festival, now one of the biggest in the nation.

I think my work is sustainable. My wife's an entrepreneur also; she started her own business, and we're living in an expensive city. We don't have a lot of money, but I think it's possible to make a living being a potter. It's just a lot of hard work, and you have to be innovative these days. A grant from the Massachusetts Cultural Council enabled him to work with a bookkeeper and professionalize his systems to clarify revenue, expenses, and taxes. It's a new step in his evolution as a potter. ■

ROBBIE LOBELL

Stovetop Sculptures

Robbie Lobell in her studio, Coupeville, Whidbey Island, Washington, 2017

Robbie Lobell (b. 1951) "inherited" a flameproof clay formula from Karen Karnes and has built it into a business, Cook on Clay, which she runs with her partner, Maryon Attwood, on an island in Puget Sound north of Seattle. They regularly take on apprentices and have developed connections with creative foodies in the Pacific Northwest and elsewhere. Lobell's creative journey literally took her from coast to coast.

Lobell was born in Los Angeles *to parents who were socialists and anarchists. I'm a pink-diaper baby. My mother was born in New York, but her father, who was the anarchist, went out to L.A. when my mother was four years old, so they were some of the first wave of the eastern European immigrants moving to California. And my father's family came from eastern Europe to Cleveland, Ohio, and then my father moved with his family out to L.A. My mother went to Berkeley, and she has been a social and political activist all her life. She's more radical than I am, believe it or not.* Lobell's father was a tailor who became a schoolteacher working for educational equality for disturbed or autistic children.

I come from a very strong Jewish background, but it isn't a religious background; it's a cultural background. I hardly knew any non-Jews until later in my life, except people that my mother worked with in the civil rights movement, so I knew people of color but not so much, you know, midwestern Christians.

I didn't really have a formal education. Life was too interesting to me, and I didn't want to be in school. [Laughter] *I got married quite young, and my ex-husband is still an integral and important member of our family. We were married for ten years, and we worked at my father's school together. And when my parents sold the school, they looked at us—Wally was in the rock 'n' roll industry (he was a sound technician), and I was a bartender doing all kinds of crazy things—and they said, "Is there anything you guys want to do?" And we said, "Yeah, let's get a bed and breakfast inn."* [Laughter] *We found the White Gate in Mendocino, California, and we moved there in 1981. We had the inn for about a year and a half and then I came out. Wally and I split; he went back to the Bay Area.*

She now supposes she was doing all these different things looking for herself. *I didn't know what to connect to; I didn't know what I was passionate about. Material was always part of our life. Of course my father was a tailor; both of my grandfathers were tailors, so we had lots of our clothes* made for us, and we got to choose fabric, touch it, and look at it. And my parents traveled to South and Central America, and they brought back lots of fabric. When her parents ran a summer camp for the Jewish Community Center Association in the mountains of Southern California, *that's where I first really got into clay.*

When I first put my hands on, really working in clay—and I think we even had a wheel there—I might have been 9 or 10. I remember that in high school I got serious about it. And 20 years later I went back to it. Around 1985 I took a regional occupation program run by the County of Mendocino. For $30 a month I had full access to a studio and instruction in the mornings. Then I dropped clay for a long time, maybe 10 years. I fell in love with a woman, and we were living on the land in the hills of rural Northern California, living a somewhat separatist life in this very fertile and wonderful lesbian community. That takes us up to the early 1990s. I grew lots of food, I worked in wineries, we grew grapes and made wine, we built houses, we had gardens, and we grew pot. I traveled quite a bit, went to Australia, New Zealand, Mexico, and just kind of lived life the way I wanted to.

Whatever money I had, I used. I wasn't ever thinking about my future. I just wanted to live life as fully as I possibly could. I might have been a little bit too wild. I think if I had been told, "you can't do that," it might have been good for me. [Laughter] Yet, all of that has made me who I am, and I feel good about who I am.

Then in 1992 *the woman I was living with broke up with me. I really thought this was the one I was going to spend my life with. So I moved out and was a puddle on the floor. These friends said to me, "We're going to pick you up, and you're going to this workshop with us." I said okay.* The workshop consisted of a painter and Mikhail Zakin. Zakin was a friend of Karen Karnes, and herself a potter associated with the Old Church Cultural Center in New Jersey, where Karnes had since 1975 been organizing a yearly invitational sale (often referred to as Demarest, for the location) that became a prestigious event. (Lobell remembers being entranced by Karnes when the Mendocino Arts Center brought her out for a workshop about 1985.)

There was an exercise that Mikhail took us through in that workshop, which was to make a solid, any kind of solid, and take one cut out of it and then place that cut in relationship to the hole that it was cut from. She said later that what I did almost took her breath away, and she saw that I had no idea what I was doing. So out of that workshop, she invited me to come east to study with her. It took me about four months to get my affairs in order, but I was done with my relationship and so I thought, what the heck. And I thought I was going for three months. I stayed with Mikhail for a year and a half, including travel to China to do clay work there. I was 41 when I got there. I had been living a fairly undisciplined life up until then. And I went to live with Mikhail, and my education was not as much about clay as it was about life. We went into New York City at least once a week. She lived right on the other side of the Hudson, the New Jersey side.

Mikhail is just the most fascinating person I have ever met in my life. Her dinner table was full of these very interesting people, Koreans and dancers, and painters, and just all kinds of amazing people. My life had to do with social justice, it had to do with exploring the world from the ground up, but it wasn't necessarily about art. What she saw in me was that I had an innate relationship to form and space, to idea and material, but I had no vocabulary, neither a visual vocabulary nor a verbal vocabulary. I didn't know how to talk about how I responded to the world around me in an artistic kind of way. So we talked a lot. We went out in the world together a lot, and I also made clay. Even though I was a functional potter, she wanted me to understand the language of sculpture, object, space, proportion, scale, all those things that we need to think about. She wanted me to explore that outside of the functional object. And so I did.

I made lots and lots and lots of hollow objects and started manipulating them and understanding how the interior pressure affects the exterior experience, and the way that an object might expand itself. I learned that what I care about in objects was—and I may hit it every 50 pots—that moment of inhalation just before exhalation. The absolute fullest something can be. I want to know that there's an interior life to that pot. I want to know that it has everything it can possibly have. The second thing that I learned when I was with Mikhail that continues in my work now is distilling down to what is absolutely essential.

For the time that I was with Mikhail, I didn't explore surface. It was really only about form. After that, I went as an artist in residence to the Wooster Center for Crafts in Wooster, Massachusetts, which is where I met Maryon. She was the executive director there. That was in 1994. When I got there I gave myself the assignment: I wasn't going to allow atmospheric firing to continue to seduce me. I began to explore the idea of interior/exterior and how they relate to each other and if they had to. I was using an electric kiln, working with a light clay body, black slip. I started carving the foot. That became my signature, this foot. And I won some awards at juried shows and such with this foot. And some of my pots got really big with these big carved feet.

I noticed that people were interested in them; they would notice it, start moving towards it, and then move back. And I was like, what's going on here? I thought: you know what it is, it's that reflective surface; people are being reflected back at themselves, and they're not moving forward into that. I decided, okay, I'm going to go back to atmosphere. I had done wood and salt, but I had never done soda. What I noticed in soda pots is that they're soft. I did a couple of different kinds of slips that were going to interact well in soda, but I didn't change any of the ways that I treated the surface in terms of, you know, it was all geometric, it was squares or lines or triangles or circles. And people started paying attention and started wanting to come closer and be more intimate with the pot. And I thought whoo hoo [Laughter], this is fantastic! I worked that way in soda with tableware for—let me see—I'm going to say 10 years. And in the meantime, Maryon and I decided to make a life together.

I moved into her home in northeast Connecticut, in this small historic town about an hour south of Wooster. And I built my first kiln there, my first very own kiln. I built a soda kiln. And then I had my studio there as well, so I was three days a week in Wooster teaching, running workshop programs and the residency program. I had graduated by then from being a student of it to being an instructor and a leader of it. Both Karen Karnes and Mikhail Zakin gave me money to help me build my kiln, because they were really just rooting for me. It was very exciting.

Attwood decided it was time to leave the Wooster Center, but Lobell continued teaching another four or five months while they talked about moving. They had fixed on the idea of the West Coast when Lobell's mother, visiting a friend on the south end of Whidbey Island on a gorgeous July day, called them up and told them it was fantastic and they should check it out. *So Maryon and my mother met up in Seattle. I couldn't come because I was preparing for some shows, but the two of them did, and they found this place. They called me and they said, "We found the place." And I said, "You need to ask these questions, take pictures of these things; I want to know about closets, this, this, and this," and they did and we did, and they bought it that afternoon.* [Laughter] Lobell's mother went in with them on the purchase.

We needed a place for big animals because that's what Maryon wanted, and we wanted a place for a studio and kiln because that's what I needed. This is a 10-acre homestead; it cannot be subdivided. This was the big midlife move, and we can see ourselves staying here until the end.

Earlier, *in the winter of 2000, after the Demarest show, which I'd been doing for years, I arranged a six-week leave of absence from the Craft Center. Karen had invited me to her studio, and she had never invited anybody to work in her studio before. The first time Mikhail brought me up to Karen, maybe '94, '93, Karen and I clicked like that, which is very unusual for Karen. She is not a friendly, come-on-in-have-tea kind of gal. No, no, no. Mikhail is, but Karen isn't. But it was* mishpacha, *you know; we recognized each other.* Mishpacha *is kin in Yiddish. There was a recognition. And I just quietly sat in her house and helped her cook and did the dishes with her and sat and listened to her stories and looked at her books and handled her pots, and it was just lovely. She really adopted me in a way that has been very moving. And so helpful, so generous in opening up the doorways into the field of ceramics and the people, especially through that Demarest show.*

And so she invited me to come work with her, and I just thought: what the heck, I've been invited to do this; this isn't something you say no to. And so I did. And unbeknownst to me she had a plan, and that was to pass the flameware on to me.

The very first week I just made a whole bunch of stoneware cups. And she goes, "Okay, why don't you work with the flameware?" It was so subtle. So I started making some flameware pots and I made

. . . I have pictures of them; I mean they're nothing like they are now, but there's a seed there. I didn't want to make any Karen Karnes pots. Her studio at that time was an L, so she was at one end and then I was around the corner, so we didn't actually see each other while we were working, but we were working in the studio together. She made very few comments unless I asked her, and she wasn't there to critique my work; she was there to introduce me to the material and see what I would do with it. I actually was so excited, but when I went back to my studio in Connecticut and there was white stoneware in there . . . It was a very small studio, and I couldn't figure out how to integrate having flameware in the studio and the kind of firing I was doing. And after about maybe five or six months of rejecting the idea, I finally went, what are you doing, girlfriend; you have just been given this amazing gift, so now it's time to do something with it. And so I was making both.

Lobell had previously helped Karnes recover her flameware formula after a disastrous kiln fire in 1998 that burned down her house and studio. She lost every note she'd ever taken. Every recipe, every photograph. Spodumene, the lithium-bearing material in the flameware clay body, was no longer being mined in the US, so Karnes had stockpiled hundreds and hundreds of pounds of spodumene and it got ruined because of the water being used to put out the fire. So that was gone. I was teaching at that time, and she said, "Okay, Robbie, I need you to give me back my flameware." This was before I had worked with her and before I was internet savvy. I gave a student the assignment to go out on the internet and see if she could find Karen's flameware formula. And it turned out that a couple of people had it.

The student and I did a lot of testing, and I came up with four different bodies. Because the new spodumene didn't have any color to it, there was no iron or anything in it, we had to add certain amounts of iron and use certain kinds of ball clay or fire clay, and we did that. And I sent her four or five—I made up a 10-pound ball of clay; I made pots out of each one of them that were very similar, fired them in the way that she would in a high-fire gas reduction kiln, and sent them to her and said, "You need to choose and we'll go ahead, and this will become your recipe again."

It's formulated to have what we call a low coefficient of expansion. That means that when high heat is applied, it doesn't go through the movement that creates thermal shock. The way I've tested my clay body is I pour boiling-hot water in it, put it in the freezer, freeze it, take it out of the freezer, and turn a burner high under it.

Years ago, other people were using flameware. There was an explosion of one of their pots that injured a child, and that potter was sued for everything they had. And that went around the pottery community; this was before I was in it, and people said don't ever use it.

Every potter can use it. However, it is extremely important that there is nowhere for moisture to get in. If moisture gets in there and then it gets really, really hot, steam happens, and it can blow it off. Karen's pots have been used in ovens and on stovetops for 50 years, and she just never had a problem. But also her pots are extremely simple. So I found a voice in this material, making these kinds of pots, that has allowed me to have a career that can support me. We decided to create Cook on Clay [in 2010] and put the work out in a much broader spectrum. I'm not as interested in being in gallery shows, although I'm still asked to be in gallery shows. I want these pots for people who love food and love to cook. So I'm really interested in gourmet shops. If a gallery now asks for my work, I ask for a culinary event [Laughter] so that people can understand about them.

The exteriors are unglazed. The interior glaze is a common iron saturate glaze, but I've adjusted it to be able to move in the same way that the clay body moves so it doesn't crack. So there's a similar movement with high heat and cold. And then because I love soda firing, I also wanted to bring some of that into these pots. With the naked clay, without having any coating on, it gives that sensation of musculature and taut skin.

Karen said to me, "I think that you are spending way too much time on that pot." I said, "You know, Karen, this work for me is sculpture." Well, this pot would sell for $350. I think that that's not really a sculpture price. Most sculpture prices are going to be a lot more. It's a lot for a pot, a lot for a cooking pot, but yes, people are paying it. I couldn't keep up. And I saw this as a really good problem. It took me over a year to get the idea of the nesting square bakers, and when I did I said, "This is going to be part of solving my problem," and had molds made of these. And now they're ram pressed. For several years, Mudshark Studios in Portland, Oregon, ram pressed the pots, cleaned them up, bisqued them, and sent them to her to glaze and fire in her soda kiln. But since 2014 she has had her own artisan manufacturing facility nearby, with a 130-ton hydraulic press and a 140-cubic-foot soda car kiln; her apprentices and former apprentices press and finish the pieces. *My pots that are ram pressed don't have my individual stamp on them, my RL stamp. They have the Cook on Clay stamp. When I make them by hand, they have both. Thus far, my expense hasn't been reduced, but I'm able to make a whole lot more pots.*

I think the people who meet the maker and use the pots have a special connection to that pot. And that was a big worry when I started selling online. I had up to then probably met 90 percent of the people who were using my pots. And now it's online sales to people who have never met us before. I was reluctant to go there. It probably took me longer than it needed to, because of that reluctance.

When I got to these pots I became even more interested in and able to develop further the vocabulary and ideas of edge, line. Those little tiny details have been really, really important to me. I want it to feel fat. I want it to feel full. Full, full, full. A flat plate, how do you make it full? How do you make it feel like it's a thing of its own rather than just there to receive the food? I really care about that. I think that in my maturing as a maker I've reached for a sense of elegance and grace. There was a lot of bumbling around before I was able to begin to recognize what that looked like.

I wish I were wealthy enough that I didn't have to charge so much. I wish that I was making pots for the people. But right now I can only make pots for people that can afford them.

I'm a really lucky woman to have had these teachers in my life to guide me along and tell me, "You're doing great gal; keep on going." ∎

LISA ORR
Tang Meets Mexican

Lisa Orr in her studio, Austin, Texas, 2018.
Photo: Nick Weddell

Lisa Orr's pots convey her ebullient personality. Her work has an assertive signature look: lots of reds, oranges, greens, and blues on a surface that's also busily textured. The dishes are meant to be used, and if the surfaces somewhat limit the options—how would one get mashed potatoes off that plate?—it makes them highly festive in the places they do find use.

Orr (b. 1960) is a San Antonio native long resident in Austin, the eldest of two girls. Both her parents were schoolteachers. Since she was a small child, her mother has always said *Lisa's so artistic, Lisa's so artistic, so I guess either I am or I fulfilled that prophecy.* [Laughter]

I remember encountering clay—the long story is in third grade we were allowed one ball of clay, and I formed mine over and over. I still have this piece. She remembers taking it home to keep working. *Finally I made this candleholder, very wavy; you'll recognize it as a distinctively Lisa Orr piece, even from third grade. Because it was definitely a more-is-more type aesthetic. I remember being really excited by it, and I badgered my parents for a potter's wheel that I found in the Sears catalog that ran on two D batteries. I got that and used up all the clay, and, you know, I actually could center on that too, pretty good. I'm one of those people that can naturally center. So I used up all my clay. I couldn't fire it or whatever, but again, I remember those pieces. They were short, stubby things, but they kind of had similar curves that I still make.*

After that I badgered my mom to take a pottery wheel course, and so she signed us up for a course we were going to take together. But it turned out to be nativity scene making. [Laughter] *We didn't finish that class. Then in high school I badgered my parents some more, and my dad built a potter's wheel that when you plugged it in it went superfast and flung clay all over the floor.* [Laughter] *To get it to slow down, you had to unplug it. I tried on that a few times but it didn't work. He built it out of—my grandmother had one of those exercise machines that jiggled you; do you remember those? He used that motor. I remember a teacher in high school; she would get out a potter's wheel one day a year. Everybody else had their specialty, and I was just like, "Step aside, that's mine."* (Laughter) *I hogged it. It was the 20-speed Amaco that you put on a table-top. I was really good at drawing and sculpting and stuff; I had always sailed through art and loved it. I identified as an artist all through school.*

When Orr got to college, she thought she'd be a commercial artist (that was precomputer days, she notes). She went to the University of Texas at Austin because it cost only $350 a semester, and she could afford that from savings from a job. *And so I was taking art, not having a direction yet, and somebody said, "Oh darn, I have to throw 12 pitchers for a critique tomorrow." I was like, "Ahhhhhhhhhhh [long intake of breath] is there pottery here?!?" Ceramics was off in another wing; I'd just never found it. So I dropped my tongs; I went over and added myself into a full class. I sweet-talked that teacher; I said, "You know somebody's gonna drop, out of 25 people, you know it's gonna happen," and I would not leave until he signed my course card. And after three days of being in that class, I knew I wanted a career in it. I knew it. That was it.*

Her teachers told her that nobody could make a living in pottery, but someone suggested that she go to local shops and look at the pots, and to write to the makers of the ones she liked, to see if she could work for them. One in Dallas replied, but when she visited, she decided she couldn't live in Dallas.

I started going to craft fairs, and I found a single woman working out of her garage, actually not very far from here. And that was a perfect model for me. She needed an assistant, and so I went to work for her. Her name was Melody Lytle. She's since quit making pots, but at that time she was doing ACC shows, every craft fair, a show every other weekend, supporting herself and some parents. So I learned from her. I worked for $5.35 an hour or something like that, and I basically wedged clay like hell, made glaze, packed, shipped, recycled, just all the stuff. I would work for her five days a week and work for myself two days a week. I caught her up, and together we stuffed all of her shelves for a couple of shows coming up. So then I worked for this other potter named Ishmael Soto. He was doing sort of Mingei; he was the most lawful Mingei guy I could find, really into it. I had read The Unknown Craftsman, *and my teachers at UT did not tell me to do this. I went and read every book on clay in the library, and so I found* A Potter's Book *and I'm like WHOOOOOO, and I found, what's the Cardew one,* Pioneer Pottery, *still my favorite book, and one by Harry Davis. I found that on my own, and because I idealized Mingei—I still do in a lot of ways—I wanted some semblance of*

Mingei experience. Soto lives an hour out of town down a dirt road on the cheapest land possible. So I enjoyed that, but I learned that I did not want to be that isolated. Then I worked for a guy named Dee Buck in Gruene, who is a little bit in the Leach lineage. He makes really good, nice, wood-fired stoneware.

Basically I had three jobs working for other potters, for Melody eight months, Ishmael maybe five or so, and I think six months again for Dee. And for Dee I threw, so that was really good to get up my skill. I would always throw three days a week for him, and I would not leave until I had earned $100. I'd have my boards, and he would toss out the ones he didn't want, and I would remake them the way he wanted. And that way I got my skill.

I worked more and more on my own. I started in my dad's garage and built a gas kiln in the backyard. Part of the reason I needed a functioning kiln . . . at UT at that time you could not turn in earthenware for a grade. You could not. They didn't teach it. Stoneware was a durable material and suitable for art.

I was signing up for shows. I would put my pile of bills here and tried to get that much money from this show to equal the bills. At my first show I made $1 [Laughter], and that was because my sister was there and I had an item for $1 apparently. What I learned from that, I sold the same stuff and the second time I made $700, so yeah. At my next show I think I made $1,200, so I slowly figured out what I needed to make to sell and what type of show to be at. After about three years in the business, I got this little shop that was on a busy street. I could have a store in the front and sit there and work in my studio.

The disadvantage was that she had to drive the wet pots home to finish and fire them. Eventually, I thought, gosh, it would be so nice if I could just fire here, and the only kind of kiln I could have was maybe an electric. That had to be 1985 because finally somebody published in Ceramics Monthly some maiolica recipes. My friends said, "Let's try some low-fire recipes," because if you go to downtown San Antonio, the market was full of colorful Mexican trinket-type pottery, flower pots and stuff, tortilla warmers, and things like that. Everybody was worried about lead glaze, and this maiolica glaze recipe was lead free. It was low fire, colorful.

She saw a future in polychrome 'cause everybody, it doesn't matter if you're Anglo or what, if you have a party there's gonna be chips, there's gonna be guacamole, there's gonna be quesadillas, there's gonna be margaritas, and you're gonna need to have colorful. It suits everybody. So I got an electric kiln and I made this mental shift, which is if everybody defines art by the material, and I don't want to use that material, then I'm not—corollary—an artist. Which is fine. I decided to call myself a craftsman. In my mind. Now I of course know that that's absurd.

I started taking workshops. It was about 20 workshops in six years. I did this three years doing craft fairs and three or more years of having the shop and doing less and less craft fairs, because I got business. She took workshops with Michael Simon, Warren MacKenzie, Ron Meyers, and others to see what was going on, just to know my field better. I was really hungry for teaching and feedback at that time. I worried if I was a workshop junkie [Laughter], and I wasn't, I don't think. I was a starved student.

So then I took one from Chris Staley. I asked him, "If you want to be a better potter, what should you do; should you go to graduate school?" I had always asked this question of all the Mingei people, and they were like, "No, go into your studio and work hard," and I had done that. Chris Staley said, "Look, you need to go to graduate school, but you're not good enough. You need to work and get a portfolio and then apply. Whose work do you like? Who do you want to go study with?" And I said, "Well, I really like this potter named Betty Woodman." Staley endorsed the thought.

After a year of saving money, Orr closed her store and moved to Colorado. I followed Betty around, and whatever class she taught, I went and learned it, because she was great at teaching. She loved teaching beginners, and it was so much fun to watch her. She would pull work out of the trash and put it next to a Richard De Vore. It was hilarious; she was so great, she loved the beauty of their work that they couldn't see.

Ken Ferguson was one of the workshops I took in San Antonio. Ken said, "Quit looking at each other; stop looking through the next Ceramics Monthly for sources. You need to go to the real source, which is historical ceramics." I took him very seriously. That's why I have so many books on ceramics. I really love looking at historical ceramics. Betty was always looking at some 14th-century thing like a muffin tin or something. It was really funny. She would say, "Wouldn't you love to have that in your kitchen?" And yes, I would love to have that in my kitchen; yes, I had permission to make it. My original teacher said you shouldn't make work that is not part of your history; you need to make things of your time and your background. I grew up in a sheetrock, suburban, dull, boring San Antonio neighborhood with gas station glasses—and that was supposed to be my source material?

What Betty opened up was yes, why the heck not? I felt unleashed to sort of freely grab from history anywhere I wanted, like a candy store, and make anything I wanted. So in Minnesota [where she attended the university as a special student], I was a bit too unleashed, I must say, and they would look at decoration on a piece and want me to answer for why it was there, to defend it.

She spent nine months in Minnesota, torturing her teacher, she thinks. It was joie de vivre. I need the freedom to put things there and then figure out later why I wanted to put things there. But with a portfolio of mostly Minnesota works, she got into grad school at Alfred University. Dealing with multiple teachers, including Jeff Oestreich as a sabbatical replacement, she was happy at Alfred. Because I had a potter's work ethic of pretty much just working all the time, they were very supportive. I think I have a weak ego: if somebody's negative to me, I can get crushed easily. But they were kind.

In between her two Alfred years, she went to Europe for a folk dance festival in Bulgaria (folk dance is her hobby). Traveling around Macedonia, Albania, and Greece, she discovered some fascinating unfamiliar pottery. When I got back, I asked, "How can I find a way to go study these pots I found in these villages in eastern Europe?" And they said, "You should get a Fulbright." And I said, "What's that?" And so my faculty helped me find out to how to apply, and wrote letters of recommendation, and so I got to go on a student Fulbright, but in reality it was a travel grant. I spent a year there traveling around—the whole entire 1993, a little of '92, and a little '94. I was in Bulgaria and Macedonia studying village ceramics, and I wrote about it in Studio Potter magazine.

That experience influenced her in an unexpected way. Aesthetically, the only effect was probably a sense of fullness and containment, but exposure to different purposes made me feel freer. I felt like I didn't have to worry so much about Yanagi looking over my shoulder and judging me. They made pots for all kinds of different reasons: for money, it was just plain their job, not necessarily a lot of honorable things. And they made things for fun, whimsy. They would have traded places with me in a heartbeat, a lot of them, for the access to different kinds of images, clays, materials. So it just freed me up to be myself when I got back.

After Alfred she returned to San Antonio and started over. She got a job as a waitress so she could buy equipment and get a studio going. A friend told her about a grant she should apply for—but it had to be postmarked that day. She said, "Get some slides, handwrite it; we'll drive." And literally it was filled out in the car on the way to the post office at midnight. We went up to the airport post office, which was the latest pickup. I said, "I'm never gonna get this." And I got it. It was $5,000, and I bought two kilns and the computers to run them.

So that started me back up again, and I got into like Rosen shows and an American Craft show or two and started wholesaling. So then I started getting bigger and better accounts. When I graduated from Alfred, basically the faculty said, "Send your slides to these galleries." And I got accepted at all but one. They were good galleries, so I started getting some shows. In '95 I got a little storefront and had that for a couple of years in San Antonio on a busy tourist street next to a popular restaurant. I shared it with somebody else.

Orr married and in 1996 moved to Austin. Her studio was the carport, rebuilt all for me—yay! It has a little storage and photo area, a separate kiln room because much of the year it is so hot in Texas and you don't want the kiln heat. So I close the pocket doors, which makes it perfect because the heat stays over there. It's about 600 square feet if you include the breezeway where she stores clay, dry pots, and miscellany.

The candleholder I made when I was a kid is sort of frilly, like the edges of mold-made Mexican pots, probably because I was surrounded by them. When you make things in a mold, you have to deal with the edge, so crimping, like with a pie, is a nice way to finish. But the historical pots that I really love are Tang dynasty pieces; like sprigged Tang is my favorite. And also dripping lead glaze. Another example of that is closer to home: *Oaxacan dripware. It's done in a mold and it's fired so that it gets maximum drip, fired on edge. They just put globs of glaze and let it go. So in me, Tang meets Mexican, basically.*

My favorite glaze in the world is a translucent lead glaze that drips, and Betty was doing that. I spent all my time modifying John Gill's water blue, which is really good alkaline blue glaze; it's a really pretty turquoise. My version is modified, modified, modified. And it's lead free.

John Gill hit it on the head one time; he knew it before me. He said, "These are a garden. You need to go out and look at how land meets mountain." And so I drove around and looked at that and began to see sort of erosion and plain versus mountain. I still think about that when I do my transitions between the flat plate and the edge. I'm also working very hard to get garden, the blooming stuff that comes from nutritious dirt. Mine are the fruits and flowers that are in a relationship with pollinators. The red tomato doesn't exist on its own; it's in relationship with something that's going to eat it and carry the seeds somewhere else. That's what the color on my plates is about, if anything.

I have no interest in sculpting, but like this plate right here, its job is to make colorful food look even more beautiful, and boring-looking food, say mashed potatoes, look gorgeous. [Laughter] *Yes, it's not as easy to eat off this; you can't pick out all the last morsels as easily. I don't care. The trade-off is worth it for me. Everything looks special* [in these dishes].

Warren MacKenzie said, "You must educate the public." One educational effort is that *we copied the Minnesota pottery tour. We started our own central Texas tour called Art of the Pot, named after the iconic film of Bernard Leach. We invite nationally known people to come show with us. We encourage people to visit all the studios. We have little tricks, radio, TV, as much as possible to shine the spotlight on functional ceramics as high art that you want to collect. It's on Mother's Day, the same as Minnesota's. We wanted to copy everything that worked well about the Minnesota tour so we wouldn't*

have to learn from scratch. The only bad thing about it is we can't get academics, say Chris Staley, because usually the time of year isn't good for them; they're having finals.

Another educational effort is films. Orr has made one about Mexican tree-of-life sculptures, one about pineapple pots, and a third *on this great town in Michoacán called Ocumicho—I don't know if you've ever seen the pottery where little devils are riding motorcycles and doing different things. It's kind of kitschy but that has a really good story.* She wanted to know how they were made, and found nothing on them in English or in Spanish, so she took matters into her own hands.

She has been equally enterprising locally. With a friend who had already made a mural at a school, Orr created a 1,200-square-foot mural through community participation that is a tribute to the oldest pool in Texas. Part of the project was a documentary film for local public television. She also teaches workshops, gives pottery lessons at a private prep school, and has a sideline business making house numbers.

She uses molds with textures in them, and she combines different molding techniques, including some she learned from the factories. *I add sprigs sort of like Wedgwood with his little translucent cameo-type designs. It's along those lines, except mine are much cruder. Adhere it to the pot and then you've got texture, which I live for. I do. There's nothing better than a bunch of texture, in my opinion.*

There's trailed slip on some of these, minty green, and then there's underglaze which I make, this red stuff, and then I put translucent glazes over that. Light comes through but there's a color. So I use translucent glazes kind of put on like a calico cat, put on in patches everywhere, and then thicker at the top of the piece and thinner at the bottom because they do run.

I love the blue; the blue is almost like a pool. Water or sky reference but there's so much orange and yellow, which are ripe tomato and mango colors. I've always been interested in food and food issues and was a vegetarian in college and for 13 years because I was protesting eating hamburger. I started doing overt messages on works in grad school, which never got into shows or anything, and then I just began to think about it in another way. Let's emphasize healthy garden systems. The low-relief narratives used to be much more like—oh, I think about a pesticide guy spraying grapes. Now I use grapes as a motif just because they're so beautiful.

I think part of healthiness is having overabundance, having enough for everybody. That way you can waste some; some go to seeds. Some of these can break; they're not so precious, you know. ■

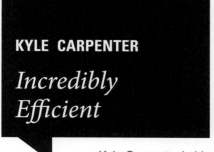

KYLE CARPENTER
Incredibly Efficient

Kyle Carpenter in his Asheville, North Carolina, studio, 2018

Potters try many ways to establish their studios and to market their works. Several in Asheville, North Carolina, combined the tasks by setting up a space called studio + gallery, with each having work and display areas; one of them is always present to transact sales during the hours open to the public, but if things are quiet, the one on duty is also getting work done in the studio. It's a way to contain costs and to share tasks other than making. Kyle Carpenter (b. 1976) was a participant for seven years as he developed his career.

Carpenter grew up in Raleigh in a split family due to a divorce when he was four. He lived with his mother, an elementary special-needs teacher, and her second family, while his father, a landscape architect, lived with his second family in Washington, DC. Weekend visitation activities included museum viewing, which he did not much appreciate. *My dad and my stepmom snicker now that I ended up going to college and getting a BFA degree. They just think it's the funniest thing.*

He had not taken art classes in high school, but in his second attempt at a community college

he took foundation courses and began to focus. His high school girlfriend (now his wife) had started school immediately and was two years ahead of him. He enrolled in the University of North Carolina–Asheville (UNCA) and soon became an art major. He took all the 2-D courses and finally had to take ceramics. *And this is a common story I hear from everybody, I don't know if it's intimidating or undervalued or what it was, why you wait to do that last.*

He already had bought handmade pots, mostly at antique or secondhand stores, and he remembers lots of art in his dad and stepmom's house. But he ascribes his epiphany to a new teacher at UNCA, Megan Wolfe, who had gone to the Kansas City Art Institute and Alfred. *She just brought so much energy to this department and just totally hooked us all.* [Laughter] From then on, even though he took other subjects, it was *I'm going to the ceramics studio, you know. And it parallels life now, when things get neglected because I get caught up in the making cycle.* [Laughter] *It's a labor of love. It's very selfish, but not in a bad way.*

I learned how to make pots, but my perception was pressure to go more towards a fine art. And so I made sculpture, and it was very organic. But I've never been a real conceptual artist. And I think that's why I fell in love with pots.

He finished college and married Carrie; money from sales at his senior show went toward the ring. He worked at Highwater, a clay manufacturer in Asheville, and his wife was a teacher. *I made pots, because that's what I could do in the corner of my kitchen. I bought a wheel. I fired where I could, at Odyssey School or at the UNC Asheville wood kiln. Working at Highwater, I made so many pottery connections that I was establishing this Rolodex of friends and this community. It was really gratifying, but I ended up quitting that job a year and a half into it because I couldn't stand the retail anymore.*

I was looking at city jobs, trying to stay in the arts if possible. He went for an interview at Asheville High School. *The teacher was there and the principal was there, and it just so happened to be my high school principal from Raleigh. We talked and I told him my experience, about art school and all these kilns I could fire. They wanted somebody who could teach ceramics and art. There were a lot of applicants, but I got the job. High school students are incredibly mean* [Laughter], *and I was incredibly young looking. I immediately grew a goatee, facial hair, to separate myself. This was a way for me to find out if I liked teaching without having to go to school for it. I didn't like it.* [Laughter]

He decided to go into business for himself. *My dad gave me $5,000 towards my new business. And that paid for the kiln. Now I had a wheel and I had a kiln, and that's really the two tools that you need. I built a hard-brick salt kiln. I bought two burners and I ordered all the brick from Georgia,* paid $1 a brick, which is very cheap. *It was a gas kiln that he could throw wood into if he wanted to. I started marketing myself. Well, I call it marketing. It was more like saying yes or applying to outdoor craft shows and looking online for opportunities.*

One of the first opportunities I came upon was the MudFire Gallery in Atlanta. It was 2002, and they had put out a call for entries on artdeadlines. com or some site like that. And they were basically asking for new work. It was a little vague, and so I called and left them a message and I said, "So, are you looking for new potters for consignment, or wholesale, or exhibitions?" I knew I wanted to do exhibitions, this kind of white-pedestal track, art pottery, or studio pottery. He called me back and he said, "We're kind of looking for all that but we're new; we've had one exhibition. Send me some photos and we'll go from there."

The second firing I did out of this new kiln, I took some photographs in the backyard in the grass [Laughter] *on some bricks. They were not pretty, and I had to get them developed and scanned and emailed—this was before digital cameras really took off. And he said, "That looks great; let's do a show."* [Laughter] *And I thought: you're giving me a show?* [Laughter] *I did not relay that sentiment to him. I've always been very confident on the surface, and so I said, "How many pots can you take?" And he said, "Oh, 100 pots."* [Laughter] *And I said, "Okay."*

So there was an opening, great response. After the show I was talking to the owner, and I said, "I know a ton of potters"—going back to that Rolodex, that community—and I said, "I could get together a show of people from up there." And he said, "I love that; we'll call it Asheville in Atlanta." And it just stuck. It was the beginning of annual solo shows there, and annual invitational shows that he curated until the owners sold the business in 2010.

It helped his career. The owners had been in marketing, *so they knew how to market their artists and their business. And so I think the second or third year, they sent out a press release for my show,* and Clay Times *magazine picked it up and did a feature article on me. I was in my 20s. I was only two years into my business. I didn't really know how to use that to my advantage, this kind of feature article. Now with the internet, I think you could use it as a springboard to do other things.*

In 2006 we had my son. Carrie had to go back to work because we need the income, right? Well, I turned into a stay-at-home dad. I watched my son during the day while she was at work, and then I worked at home in my full basement. Very convenient although distracting in many ways. So a year goes by.

Carpenter took a studio in the River Arts District in 2007 at *Clay Space Co-op. Some friends were there, and they were all professionals or aspiring to be. The main reasons I moved were for the community and the retail. When I moved in we had a huge meeting. We wanted to make a gallery in the space, and we did, collectively. We split everything five ways or whatever.*

I was there for a couple of years, but I was working out of this very small space, 4 feet by 12 feet. [Laughter] *I was working at night at this point. The place was open if somebody was there, and I could sell my work and get 100 percent of the price. There was no gallery cut. This new schedule of mine, where I'd watch my child and then go to work, I didn't see my wife as much, but I made more money. We needed the money, and it made me incredibly efficient. So I would come in, put on my apron, wedge clay, make work.*

In 2009 their daughter was born, so the daytime child-watching continued. He could say, *I work as much as a full-time potter, just at odd hours, and I do it because we rely on my income as much as we rely on my wife's income. We have a mortgage, Roth IRAs, dental insurance. It's a lot. It's really expensive.*

Although he had to pay rent on the studio, the increased sales covered it. In 2010 he moved to *studio + gallery, where I would have more space, parking right in front, beautiful light; just an incredible studio.*

In addition to the studio retail, Carpenter showed at a half-dozen galleries, rejecting those that photograph the works on crushed velvet. *A buddy of mine asked me, "Why do you use the pregraded background from black to white, for your Etsy shot?" And I said, "That's what museums generally do, and I want to have my work equated with museum-quality work." When I started paying the local professional photographer, it was a confidence builder right there.*

Carpenter says that he is attracted to decor-

ation, although it slows him down. *This mug here with this illustrated bird on it; this takes a lot longer. It is definitely a direction I would like to go. But I still make simplified pots, too, that I can decorate in 30 seconds and charge a lower price for. I have to be compensated for the higher-labor pots. My problem is that I have shows, deadlines that I've created, and so I have to fire. I have to turn around a kiln.*

A couple of years ago he made a connection with AKAR Gallery. *I follow them on Facebook, and so they show up on my news feed and they said, "We're going to try something different; post some images of your work on our wall and maybe you'll be in a show one day." And I thought: what a great opportunity, and so I posted two or three pictures. And then I got an email about 10 minutes later from the owner, saying, "We just looked at these and we love these; can you send us eight more photos?" And I sent 16. This is my chance, you know. Why not? They ended up inviting me to their 30 × 5 show. It's 30 potters with five pieces each, and that's kind of their holiday seasonal show. And then they asked me to send new work.*

Carpenter made a decision not to expand his presence in shops, but to focus on gallery exhibitions, which generate more visibility. He can sell through his website and Etsy. Getting both children in school allows him to branch out. He reflects, *A few years ago, I did 13 obligations in the fall, exhibitions, sales, whatnot, and it killed me.* So he slowly pulled back, and *said no to more things that I've ever said no to,* in order to build up an inventory at studio + gallery, *because this area is becoming a tourist hotbed. It's 100 percent of the sales, and I don't have to ship anything. I don't have to be here. It's direct sales, and you get to meet your customers.*

In 2018, however, he moved to a private community studio as he shifted his focus to pottery tours and shows, and teaching workshops. Since 2014 he has been showing at Minnesota's celebrated St. Croix Valley Pottery Tour.

As for the work, *I started out doing more graphic kinds of dots and stripes and patterns. Everything's individually applied; each leaf is hand painted. I think of them as kind of embellishments, little jewels. And I started doing more botanicals. It started with drawing this pussy willow tree in my front yard. It was abstract. And then I started doing abstract grasses. And then it had a slow evolution into certain things. And Michael Kline was obviously an influence.*

Early on I stuck with a very limited palette, and that allowed me to experiment with form. Putting the same surface color or pattern on it made it mine. And so I can have one-off pieces coming out of the kiln, something I've never made before, but somebody will go, "Oh, that looks like yours." I wanted it to be very organic, no primary colors; I didn't want any kind of commercial feel to it. My evolution in decoration has come very slowly.

He speaks of offering his decoration to the salt kiln, which destroys a lot of the line, but it also embellishes it in beautiful ways. It's kind of a relationship. Basically, salt gives a kind of flashing effect, putting a patina on it in an unpredictable way.

I see more and more young people buying pots, which is very encouraging. And I think there's more and more potters, which can be good and bad, you know? It seems like this area pumps them out like a factory. So many potters around; does it hurt you? No, it creates a destination. So more and more people are coming. ■

CHAPTER SEVEN

THE TEACHERS

With ceramics education today more often involving an MFA than an apprenticeship, academia has altered the pottery context. Those who teach in the university environment are inclined to identify with "vessels" or sculptures, exhibited in galleries and sold at far higher prices than functional pottery. The privileging of sculpture has put pressure on potters to create important and showy works rather than streamlined or simple ones. And the same force has led to a reduction in the number of college programs that support the making of functional pots as every school strives to be up to date rather than traditional.

Despite these pressures, there is still a substantial population of teachers committed to making pots, even if their production is modest or their prices are on the high edge of the functional pottery range.

Many of them are motivated by the sociological and psychological values of pottery, as well as the particular aesthetic qualities that handmade pots can carry.

A great many potters supplement their incomes by adjunct teaching on an occasional basis, and even more with teaching in short-term workshops. This chapter looks at a few full-time teachers in large or important schools. Warren MacKenzie argued that his full-time teaching was not a crutch that allowed him to keep his pots inexpensive; on the contrary, he said, teaching kept him out of the studio and required him to be fast and efficient in his available studio time. Low prices were his choice, because he wanted the work to be used. This is a decision each potter makes. ■

LINDA ARBUCKLE

It's Yours for Life

Linda Arbuckle demonstrating, Southern Utah University, 2017.
Photo: Glen Blakley

Linda Arbuckle, who retired emeritus from the University of Florida at Gainesville in 2016, is an enthusiastic leader in the maiolica decoration of utilitarian ware. Arbuckle (b. 1950) grew up in a Cleveland suburb where many residents, including her father, commuted to work in the Ford and Chevrolet plants.

It was a housing development where most of the houses on the street were identical. As a result, I grew up with a very strong urge to customize my domestic environment. [Laughter] *Another thing I got from that environment: a lot of my friends were first-generation Americans, and the way that the people manifested their pride in what they'd done was by saving it for someday that never came. So they had the living room with the beige carpet and the white couch, and maybe the couch even had plastic on it, but the family was never allowed to use it. I wanted to have more enrichment in daily life. Those are some of the concerns that made me a functional potter, wanting to have something that spoke to me that I used every day instead of the special experience that you get when you go to the museum once a year.*

When I was a kid, all of these people surrounding me had jobs that if someone stopped paying them they would stop doing. My dad thought I should work for the post office because I could work for 30 years and retire at 55 with a good government pension. That was this magical goal: after I'd squandered 30 years of my life I'd have this great retirement to do something with. And I thought, you know, it's kind of putting the cart before the horse. I wanted to find work that was meaningful. My mother told me that I should take typing in high school because it was a good job skill for a woman.

She declined. She went to college with a work/study grant at Miami University in Oxford, Ohio, but without a goal. *I was interested in animals and nature, greatly. I liked science and math. I thought maybe I'd become a lab researcher; that would be interesting. But I found out there's a great deal of animal cruelty involved in lab work.*

So in the meantime, the '60s had happened. I was making tie-dye T-shirts and candles, I was sewing patches on my blue jeans. I'd taken home ec in high school and I made a lot of my own clothing, and I loved the idea that I could pick the style, I could pick the form, but I could also pick the pattern, the fabric, and color. I found all that really rewarding because it was a chance for me to personalize something that I used in everyday life.

So I didn't know how to type, and all the work/study jobs at college at that time involved typing. The city recreation department sent me out for an interview with the woman who ran the recreational greenware-casting program. She taught me how to pour plaster molds with slip and help people in the recreational classes make those big ceramic Christmas trees with the plastic light at the end and the lightbulb underneath. This was my first real encounter with ceramics.

I was blown away! Here was this material that you could customize and fire it and it became a real thing. They let me make some things so that I'd understand how the process worked, and I was just so jazzed. With sewing, the more you like something and the more you wear it, the faster it wears out. With ceramics, unless you drop it, it's yours for life. If you make it and you like it, you can take it with you in the kitchen every day. And it really works well. So once I found ceramics, I thought: this is what I want to do.

There were a few detours first. She dropped out, went back to college, got married at age 19, and divorced at 24. *I decided I was going to move back to Cleveland to go to art school and be a potter. I got a job at Case Western Reserve's library and took night classes next door at Cleveland Institute of Art. I took design, drawing, and copper enameling and put a portfolio together. It was the only school I applied to.*

The first year at the Cleveland Institute I was really aware of the ceramics department. There were two men teaching there, and it was kind of boy's day in ceramics. I wasn't real thrilled about that. By the time I got to my second year, those people had moved on. Judith Salomon started teaching there, and she was really wonderful. The second year, Rob Forbes was faculty with Judith. And in my last year, Bill Brouillard was there teaching. And I think that they were all highly inspirational.

At CIA we learned to throw in stoneware, which is really typical, and high-fire gas reduction. And I was interested in that, but I wasn't all that thrilled about having to make a huge amount of work before I could fire if I was going to be personally responsible for the kiln, or having to coordinate with several other people to make enough work to fire the kiln. When they introduced me to maiolica, they said, "Well, we've seen your printed fabric work up in textiles, and we think maybe you'd like this stuff. It's this white glaze, and you mix some colorants with flux and paint it on the surface." And I could fire it in the little kiln, the test kiln. I could fire every day. And I could make these works that had pink and turquoise and yellow and green, and I could paint on the work and it didn't run all over the surface; it stayed where I put it. So I thought that was a pretty good vehicle for the things I was interested in.

At that time Arbuckle was suffering from carpal tunnel syndrome, so it was best not to wedge or throw. Salomon was then pouring slabs of whiteware onto plaster and cutting and building with them. So I came up with a terra-cotta slip instead of whiteware. I liked the friendliness of terra-cotta. Porcelain always seemed kind of stuck up, it seemed a very prestigious material, a "palace pots" kind of material, and I liked things that were more blue collar. I wanted something that was more down to earth, metaphorically and maybe literally. I wanted to make the everyday glamorous. I didn't want to make something out of a glamorous material.

When I came to the end of that five years, I felt like I had some questions but not very good answers. So I thought I really needed grad school. Judith suggested Rhode Island School of Design. I think my life and my work would be really different if I'd gone someplace that was a pottery club, where they were worshipping at the shrine of functional pottery. People were supportive and interested in pottery, but it wasn't like they thought it was the navel of the universe. [Laughter] During the time I was in grad school, installation art became a buzz word, and there was an awful lot going on that was not about functional pottery.

My first year I had work/study and worked in the library. My second year I had the opportunity to have not one but two teaching assistantships, and my assistantship for ceramics was to teach clay and glaze materials to the juniors. It wasn't because I displayed any particular skill in clay and glaze, but they knew I was a detail person; they knew that I would suffer enough to get the job done. The other job combined literature and art history. The students would be looking at the art history of a specific time period and reading literature either about or written in that time period. The class was taught by an art historian and an English professor and then broke down into discussion groups run by the TAs. I had to read all the literature assignments the students had to read, and the art history. I met with them for a discussion group weekly. And then I had to grade all their papers for mechanics and content. So my second year, when I was doing my show, was just crazy. But it was a great experience. I think I learned a lot more than the students did.

I didn't go to school thinking being a teacher would be a great thing, but those TAs really changed my mind. When I left grad school I thought: I need to have a destination, a five-year plan, because it's hard to get someplace if you don't know where you want to go. So my plan was that at the end of five years I'd be teaching somewhere. I didn't have the cheek to think that I'd have a university job, but I thought, you know, I could teach at an art center.

I figured I needed a big city because I was going to need a day job at the same time. I wanted to live someplace with an art community. I answered an ad in the paper in Philadelphia from Works Gallery and was hired by Ruth and Rick Snyderman to be their shipping and receiving person. Ruth and Rick were very gracious. After I was there a little while, they asked me about my work and let me show and sell it at the gallery. And they asked me if I would like to curate a ceramics show since I'd just come out of school and had all these contacts and ideas about ceramics. And that was really nice. I also did their bookkeeping for a while, which for an artist was a great thing, to understand that money came in and where it went. Everyone has a perception that somehow gallery owners are just siphoning off this 50 percent and spending their holidays in the Bahamas [Laughter], but there's insurance and all these expenses, payroll to be met.

It was great to handle all the craft work in the

course of receiving it and display. When it was really busy I did sales work, and that was really interesting for me too, because I had to wax poetic about things that I might not be that committed about. I had to realize that people came from different places, and this offered something that might work for them.

While I was in Philadelphia I was entering juried shows, going to NCECA, trying to become involved in the field, trying to make the best work that I could. I set up a studio in my basement. I had a row house. The basement had a dirt floor, but it had electricity and running water. The landlord said he would be OK if I had 220 put in for my kiln.

Before I went to grad school I had my hands operated on, and it was successful. It took a little while to recover, but it worked and I could go back to throwing. During graduate school I'd stopped doing maiolica. I felt like I was so in love with the painting part of it that I couldn't see the forms. In Philadelphia, though, I went back to maiolica and surface decoration because I just loved it. The color, the pattern, the way that you could transform the form with what you did on the surface. There were just so many answers.

I was making a lot of things with florals on them, fruit, and then it occurred to me I was a woman making flower art, and I had kind of a revelation about that. I realized that subject matter was just a vehicle to talk to someone about your enthusiasms. And I wasn't trying to duplicate the thing I was enthusiastic about. I was trying to show someone how that made me feel.

After two years at Works I applied for teaching jobs, and I remember being down in the packing room under the stairs with my boxes and my bubble wrap when I got a call from Joe Bova at Louisiana State University. He said, "We don't have any money; we're not flying anyone in to interview. We've looked at all the applications, and we wonder if you'd be interested in this job teaching with us." It was like winning the lotto. It was just amazing. I was very excited. He said, "Well, you know, you can have some time to think about it." And I said, "No, I don't need any time to think about it; I'll come, I'll come."

I went down to sign paperwork and find a place to live, and there were bananas blooming in front of the library. It was all of those exotic things I'd ever wanted. There was Spanish moss in the trees; there were palm trees. I moved into this little house that was up on piers. The ground in Louisiana has a lot of clay in it, and the water pools, so a lot of the old houses are built up on pilings. It wasn't until it was fall and getting cold that I realized that the only heat it had was little vented gas heaters.

Joe was a particularly generous mentor to a young teacher. He was great to work with. So I learned about teaching and I taught at LSU for about five years. I loved the South. Cajun culture was just heating up then and becoming popular—Cajun music, Cajun food—and there I was in Baton Rouge enjoying all this. Nature was really interesting; there were things that you would never find—not that Ohio is a bad place, but there are no alligators in Ohio, no armadillos in Ohio. [Laughter] And the idea that you could see all these things there, not in a zoo, was really just the best.

At LSU, a professor of architecture came from Florida to teach for a year, and since he was also a potter the dean wanted him to be able to use the ceramics studio. And it turned out that this person and I took a fancy to each other and had a really great year together, and after two more years doing long distance between Gainesville and Baton Rouge I stepped aside from my job at LSU—because he'd been at UF much longer than I'd been at LSU—and I moved to Micanopy and got married. And he had a house in the woods and a clay studio.

The first two years that I lived there, I just worked in the studio and did workshops. I think one year I did 12 workshops. It was really good for my work to have that kind of time and focus. And at the end of that time, UF had an opening and hired me as a visiting professor for a year and then did a search, and I won lotto a second time and UF hired me full time in 1992.

I never thought I would become a potter and move to the woods, but I do live in the woods, at the edge of wetlands. My love of nature, while I never made a career out of it, is really important to me, and I live in a very lovely environment with a lot of wildlife.

I served a term as director at large for NCECA. I've done residencies in China and Wales. I've done a lot of workshops, I think in part because the methods that I use are available to the casual hobby potter. Not everybody can have a wood kiln, but most people can have an electric kiln if they want one. So it's a method available to the general public, and people are interested in color and surface design, so I can teach those things.

NCECA has made me an honoree with lifetime membership for my service to the field. I think the combination of having that TA to teach clay and glaze materials in grad school, my library work that I did as a work/study student, and the fact that I am mildly computer geeky all coalesced so that I taught myself how to put up a website, and I put up a lot of my handouts on my website as a public service. I learned how to type a long time ago. I learned how to type on the job, basically. [Laughter] And I've had many, many office jobs.

While I was in Philly my studio ware had to support the cost of my supplies, and now that I was teaching I could think about work that was more speculative. I was wondering where that physical-ness from grad school went. So I had a period when I made a series of really elevated, really extended teapots that were all about being in the South. There was Gone with the Wind, and the antebellum South is still there; there are plantations in Louisiana, they still have pictures of those ladies in big hoop skirts around, and I was thinking if my friends were here, we'd sit on the front porch and have a tea party. So I made these teapots that were kind of like wearing your mom's clothes and playing dress-up.

Once I got to lovely Florida and started teaching at UF, I brought the teapots down off the pedestal. The spouts were still extended, but they were a lot more grounded. And I was making big biscuit jars. And a lot of the work had floral imagery. It was always spring or summer. Flowers are the sexual parts of plants, and buying yourself cut flowers is really indulgent because they don't last long. And as a symbol of beauty, a lot of them peak in a very short window of time. I'm interested in the flower being a symbol of this kind of ephemeral beauty and lusciousness and desirability. And then different kinds of flowers give you a chance to use different sorts of shapes and brushstrokes, and to make dif-ferent kinds of design things happen.

Later on I wanted to talk about being at a dif-ferent point in life, and I was making things like this biscuit jar, where the widest point is at the bottom, the stripe at the bottom is black—we know how this ends—the leaves are falling. But I wanted it to be really beautiful, and I wanted it to look like I was having a really good time even so.

I love Islamic ceramics, and there's some really beautiful calligraphed bowls; there are a number of them in museums and in art history books that are a white bowl with black calligraphy around the edge, and the lines from the letters pull down into the center of the bowl. And those make my heart beat fast. So I was thinking about fall, thinking about leaves falling down, and thinking, oh, I just love that long pulled line. I started at some point making things that were square. In design class they always said three is more about movement, but four is so staid. But I started thinking that four is about cycles, having four seasons in a year, and about going around and coming back again. It was something I would never have done in my early career, I think. I embraced the square.

Most of my work is not narrative. I think when you put an animal or a person on work, people are interested in seeing what the narrative is, and to me that disrupts reading form and surface. But I do occasionally allow myself to fool around. One of my first pottery teachers told me that you're doomed to make pots like your body shape, and I thought: I will not! [Laughter] I wanted to make things that were very uplifted, things that have rising volumes, things that were tall and voluptuous. I've always made forms that went in that direction.

I'm interested in thinking about change and transition. I've had two knee replacements; I think I've had 10 operations on my hands. I'm heavily restored. So I think about my age; I think about my body; I think about going from work to retire-ment. ■

MARK PHARIS

The Arena of the Tabletop

Mark Pharis in his studio, Roberts, Wisconsin, 2016

Maybe the biggest surprise about Mark Pharis, now retired as head of ceramics at the University of Minnesota and former art department chair, is that he is not a college graduate. In this era of credentials, it is exceptional to find that talent is sometimes enough. Pharis (b. 1947) is best known for useful objects made by creating diagrams/patterns on the computer and piecing the work together from slabs. As a student at the University of Minnesota in the '60s, he was part of one of those extraordinary conjunctions of classmates: he, Michael Simon, Sandy Simon (then Lindstrom), Randy Johnston, and Wayne Branum were all there together. Another interesting sidelight is that the studio that Pharis established in Houston, Minnesota, two and a half hours south of the Twin Cities, subsequently was a temporary home to other well-known potters, including Linda Sikora and Matt Metz, Andy Brayman, Sanam Emami, and Karen Newgard.

Pharis looks back on a childhood that was largely dysfunctional. His father was a traveling salesman who was often gone and a disciplinarian when he was home; his mom concealed family secrets of emotional abuse until her old age. Neither was a nurturer, so Pharis became to some degree the caretaker for his three younger sisters and even his mother. Fortunately, he had a very close friend whose family was crucially important to him. *From the time I was 12 or 13 the friend's mother would give me art books on my birthday and at Christmas and at Easter and pretty much any time of the year. I don't know where she got the idea to do that, or how, but it took. I was fascinated with them. And later on, past junior high, she began to coach me to be a college student and to think about taking art*

courses. I avoided art like the plague in high school because I thought it was for dummies; it was for the sidetracked people, the place where they put kids who weren't so bright, and I wasn't doing all that well anyhow. [Laughter] *I didn't need that kind of reinforcement. When I was a senior, she said, "When you go the university, you should take a class from Warren MacKenzie. I've heard he's a good teacher." She maybe had one handmade pot around the place, but she just* [Laughter]; *who knows what she was up to.*

But Pharis wasn't admitted to the university, because he'd been a bad student. He started at a junior college and later began preveterinary medicine studies at the university. *But kind of following her advice, I took a photography course. My friend and*

I built a darkroom in his grandfather's home. So the beginning of the arts for me was photography. It was miraculous to come to know the world visually. I mean, I'd always had a sense of visual stuff, liked making things and putzing and so forth, but I really didn't understand seeing, knowing the world through sight.

He left the pre-vet courses behind and ended up in the art department, where he took a ceramics class with Curtis Hoard. *It was his first quarter teaching, and my first quarter in clay. Being in that studio was like having arrived at home. It was that sense of "this feels okay; I could be here for a long time."* After a second quarter with Hoard, he had his first class with MacKenzie. *I think he became very important for a lot of us. He was so different from other males that age that I had known. He was pretty close to my father's age, the fathers of my friends, but he was totally immersed in his work as opposed to not being immersed in work, which was sort of the case for my dad—I think he really hated his work. So that was a small epiphany, to actually know that people could enjoy work. And it seemed like work that would never be done. I haven't found anyone yet who has said, "I've made the perfect whatever; I don't have to do that anymore; I have arrived."* [Laughter] *You can seek perfection or some personal notion of perfection for decades and never actually get there, or continue to find out that you know more and more and more and also less and less and less.*

Those were difficult days in America, and the clay studio had a front-row seat for campus upheaval, being located across the street from the police station. *It was just a lot of Vietnam-related crap that was going on, and we were all about to be drafted or whatever, so there was a lot of turmoil around that. But it was a great group of young people, and everyone was really jacked about making pots. It seemed like it was an important thing to do. The making of pots was a political statement all by itself. It never occurred to me that making art was political in any way; it seemed that it was an activity more than a viewpoint. Now I think it's just the other way around. I was in and out of school a bit. I would register for a full load of classes and drop everything but ceramics and art history, and eventually I would drop art history.* [Laughter]

I went to Yugoslavia as a photographer, Ford Foundation Grant. They were digging up Diocletian's palace in Split, Yugoslavia, and so I got to Europe. I got to travel a bit and see that there was something outside the Midwest and the United States. I stayed in Europe for about six months. Came back and decided that I was going to finish my degree, and enrolled in school for what turned out to be the last time. I got a call from Hamline University, and they needed somebody in a hurry to teach a set of classes in the fall, part-time work. Both Curt and Warren had recommended me, which was really strange, because they had a graduate program. Maybe they recommended other people too. But anyway, I began teaching at Hamline. I think I probably finished out the quarter at the U and decided, well, jeez, if I'm doing this, why do I need school? [Laughter]

So I did that for a year and a half, and during that period I also had gone to the Archie Bray Foundation and spent a summer there with Wayne Higby and Victor Babu and Bunny McBride. They were the residents. When I was teaching at Hamline, Victor called and said, "Ken Ferguson is going on sabbatical, and we'd like you to come down here and teach for a semester." So clearly, Pharis was launched, although he was 26 and a dropout. I never did finish, just for the record [Laughter], *even though different versions of Wikipedia have me with a degree.* [Laughter]

So I went to Kansas City in January of '73 for a semester. And I walked into the clay studio maybe a week before class began. I'd met Ken Ferguson before. I was unloading my stuff into the studio, which was empty because it was Christmas break, and Ken was like, "Pharis, is that you?," in kind of a grandfather voice. I said, "Yeah, it's me." Well, you know, Ferguson was weird; he was one of these people that either hated you or loved you, and you found out what he really thought. He said, "Well, you know I would never have hired you." This was before day one of class, and I feel pretty insecure about this already, and so I was feeling a lot insecure by the time class actually arrived. The seniors in that class were John Gill, Andrea Gray at the time (later Gill), Chris Gustin, and others. It was a very, very talented group of kids, and I was essentially a peer, but not.

Summer session I went to the University of Colorado for five or six weeks. I had met Betty Woodman at an NCECA conference in '71, and we sort of hit it off in a curious way, and I really liked her energy a lot. She was eager to critique and wanted to be critiqued, and so we had a little bit of an exchange that turned into a much-longer-term friendship. And then I was unemployed after that.

Returning to Minnesota, Pharis looked for property that would be suitable for a studio. He ended up in Houston, Minnesota. *We bought a little place, a farm, a tile milk barn, and house and chicken coop and pig building, like six little buildings and 40 acres, for not very much money. It's gorgeous country. The physical beauty of the place was important. It was a good place for me for a while. I began to build a kiln and turn the barn into a working studio space.*

It was a two-chambered oil and wood kiln, so I'd fire partway with wood and then switch to fuel oil and then salt it. I did that for 16 years, from '73 to '89. While I was in Houston I got two NEA grants, which were godsends. It's just amazing how much the National Endowment money helped. Money always helps. [Laughter] *But it was also a validation, a way of saying to yourself, well, maybe this will work out.* [Laughter] *Often it didn't seem like it was going to work out. I would go to art fairs time after time after time and almost always come home with the number of pots I had left with. There was something about what I was doing that wasn't working in the market, or I was in the wrong spot, or I was dumb about it. I actually still don't know what the deal was, but it was very, very hard to sell pots.*

I was trying to figure out what was interesting to me. Warren's package was so attractive, the package being essentially his variation on Leach's ideas, which had to do with accessibility and usability and the notion that pots should be sold at prices that allowed people to use them and use them up and to reinvest in them once something broke or chipped or they needed more. I liked that idea a lot; I still like the idea a lot, but there are some structural problems with it. The financial part of Warren's model was broken from pretty much the very beginning, except for Warren.

I had, like a lot of us, developed an identity around being a thrower, being good at wheel work. It began to change before I realized it. I was making things that needed modification or additional parts or things that were somehow re-formed when they were on and off the wheel. And there begins to be a kind of interest in geometry, although I never ever would have said that at the time.

Pharis taught part-time in Rochester, Minnesota, and helped facilitate an exhibition of Betty Woodman's pots at the Rochester Art Center. Someone drove the pots from Colorado to Rochester, and Woodman asked Pharis and his wife to drive them on to New York City. *So after the exhibit of Betty's work was done, Marcia and I drove that show to New York City. First time I'd ever driven in New York, and I've got a station wagon full of Betty's pots on 57th Street.* [Laughter] *It was actually very exciting to go there and do this. She was showing at that time, and George [Woodman] was as well, with the gallery called Hadler/Rodriguez.*

That's where those pots went, and eventually that connection led to an invitation to exhibit with them in New York. That was pretty special, to be asked to be in that gallery. I exhibited with them for a few years. That's where my whole sense of price structure got screwed around. Because what they wanted to do with prices was totally outside my ken.

It was more than double, more than quadruple. They were going to sell things that I had sold for $35 and $40 for $300 and $400 at that time. That was a lot of money; it was a different game. So it was like, yeah, I'd love to do that, but what does that do to the rest of my sales life, and maybe more importantly, what does it do to a teapot? Because the functionality, the usability of an object is in part determined by its cost. Pharis's work did sell, including to esteemed collectors such as gallerist Irving Blum. And through Hadler/Rodriguez he made a connection with Garth Clark, who had opened his New York gallery. *So when Hadler/Rodriguez closed, Garth asked if I would be part of his gallery, which I was for ten years.*

I had begun working with paper patterns in 1978, '79, '80, in a tentative way. I'd begun to handbuild and it didn't feel comfortable. Giving up the wheel felt like a betrayal. I wouldn't feel that way today, but it felt bad at the time, like I was doing something wrong. But it was just too compelling, too fascinating, and I was learning all kinds of stuff about how form was constructed and how things went together and how 2-D related to 3-D, and how a plane related to volume and how all of this related to function, and how most everything I was doing was related to throwing even though it was handbuilt and not necessarily "on center" anymore.

A peer introduced him to the paintings of Giorgio Morandi. *There's just something about the line, reductive use of space, and a sense of minimal gesture that could be transitioned into pots. I think it helped me think about and see pots as drawing. I've always worked from sketches, but that's different.*

So I had gotten fairly far into handbuilding, working with slabs and [cutting] patterns. I was trying to create something that was three-dimensional in my head and to make it two-dimensional as a pattern so that I could make it three-dimensional in clay. That going back and forth, I think it must be kind of like reading music. You look at this set of symbols or this kind of cartography of a teapot body, the math of the teapot body, and you know that from its flatness that it makes a certain kind of volume. This was a world that was brand new to me, but obviously there were all kinds of people doing it in other places.

Pharis had found himself wanting to *make things six sided or four sided, or triangular or something, on the wheel. And the wheel, for all of its beauty and simplicity of process, has a lot of rules that come with it, or conditions. The central axis is a condition of throwing, so making a rectangle on the wheel is not impossible, but it's not essentially intuitive. I was curious about other ways of making things. And having that something else still be a pot in the sense that the size was right, the proportions were utilitarian, that it fit within domestic space, that it wasn't clever beyond belief [Laughter], so what you came to notice was its cleverness. They still were pots; they still played in the arena of the tabletop or the cupboard or the dish drainer.*

This kind of space is really important to me. The interiors of homes matter a lot. Like everyone else, I think cooking food and display and conversation and all these things are part of what pots are about. It's part of civility. It's part of a sophisticated society, part of our humanity. Pots make us better at all those things, in a nongrand way. They help to make social connections and raise questions about life and how it should be lived.

There have been a couple of big changes. I think one of them has been moving from stoneware to earthenware in roughly 1989, 1988. I began teaching at the university in '85, when Warren went on leave for three years, then I reapplied for that

job at the end of three years, the job that I had, so I've been at the U since '85, and during the transition, not knowing whether this would be a full-time job or a part-time job or a term position, I had a studio at the university and I had a studio down in southern Minnesota. So I did stoneware down there and I did earthenware up here.

On color and glazes: *I had always been fascinated by earthenware, especially lead glazes. The transition from stoneware to earthenware had to do with wanting to define a palette more clearly. I wanted to be able to have a pink and put it somewhere and it was going to be pink when it came out. And I also wanted the clay body, the sense of clay, the materiality of clay, that earth, to be available. I began to try to figure out ways of making low-temperature clay look interesting or claylike or have some heart. I fire everything in an electric kiln, and electric kilns just don't have much soul. They aren't around for thousands of years and they don't get named and they're really kind of uninteresting things and they're not much fun to fire, meaning it's not a community adventure. But I like the results a lot, and so I keep picking away at that.*

I started to do this sort of color-field application—I don't know what else to call it—a long time ago. This was in response to a Morandi watercolor, a black-and-white watercolor. In that work, Pharis misread a sequence of forms, which provoked thought.

There's the clay body and then there's a white slip and then there's the yellow lead glaze. One of the things that I really like about lead is its luminosity and its transparency, so you can see the body underneath, you can see the slip, and you can see the clay. I go to a great deal of effort to get the clay right, so putting an opaque glaze over it—I'm going to contradict myself several times, so this is just one of them [Laughter]—having the clay body not being available was problematic for me.

There's a large palette of glazes that have come to us through history, and just to choose some from Asia, there's celadon and tenmoku and nuka and a variety of other glazes, kaki, that have a resonance for anyone who makes pots, that are tied to a time and place. So glazes are semiotic in the sense that they are referential to cultures, and historical moments, and maybe artists in some instances. To choose from that palette or to choose from that inventory of glazes means you're bringing that history with it.

On allusion: *Some of this piecing to me is trying to mix things together in a way that references more than one pot at a time. I associate lead with some parts and times of England. And other times I associate it with Turkey. I think potters tend to see these things more rapidly, the same way that a musician might understand the variation on a theme of . . . I think to some degree there is a kind of interpretive effort to this art, which is making a variation on a teapot which is known and unknown at the same time to other teapot makers. The unknown is the part we tend to be most attracted to, I think.*

On interpretation: *A potter working within a format or with familiar materials is like a musician performing a well-known piece. It's an effort to communicate "this is the way I see that piece," and it's probably no different than contemporary versions of* Hamlet. *You've experienced a cup for 15 years before you even know to say that you've experienced one. You know about it all your life; it's sort of embedded in who we are and the way we work and the way we play in the world. To bring freshness to that is difficult. I think it's especially a problem for contemporary potters, who tend to work in isolation most of the time. Our individual reputations tend to come from having claim to what my son would call white space, some space that no one else had occupied before. It's kind of curious. It comes out of academics, I think.*

On other endeavors: *Food Tools was—Wayne* [Branum] *will give you different years than I would give you—but I think it started in '78 and I think we were done in '82 or maybe '83. It was an idea that I had about trying to create an environment that people could walk into and see pots in use and see other things that were utilitarian in use that were analogous to pots, like wooden spoons or certain kinds of fiber or glassware or, you know, things that had an aesthetic appeal that belonged in domestic space, and to create a shop that would not have the intimidation factor associated with a gallery.*

And then we did the food connection so there was all kinds of kitchen stuff, and we did a bunch of demonstrations and we served coffee and did tea tastings and I forget all the things we did, but it was a fabulous idea [Laughter] *that didn't really pan out financially. We had some structural problems. No*

one wanted to be a storekeeper. Everyone liked the idea. So I got a former student who was a farmer, and we got Wayne involved and Warren involved—it was the four of us; we were partners and equals. People still come up and say, "There was this store in Stillwater a bunch of years ago; it was really great . . ." And it's gratifying to have people say that because I think it was really great. We served coffee, and we got the coffee from this little place in Seattle that was roasting their own, Starbucks, that did mail order to begin with. We hired people. The winters were awful because people wouldn't go to Stillwater. The summers were touristy. I think we were in the wrong spot, and I also think it was the wrong time. I think if I had an interest in a store again I could conjure something that would work better, but I'm not going to do that. [Laughter]

On food: *I think there's something about presentation that enriches the whole experience, and I've kind of been playing around with tableware more lately than I have maybe ever. So I've been ram pressing some forms, almost exclusively plates, and that's something that I'm going to keep doing. I'm trying to think about the relationship between those pots that need to be foreground, whose preference is to be extroverted, and those that are more introverted. My sense is that plates can be more introverted. They can be out of the way. And the food then becomes the visual thing. That's what civility is about, it's about deciding that culture is something about order and presentation and aesthetics all woven together to create an experience that's bigger and more interesting. Most of us are trying to make pots that are good for people in some way, as opposed to pots that are bad for people.* [Laughter] *It's an effort to have the world enriched.* ■

CLARY
ILLIAN

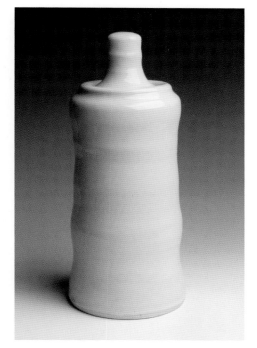

RIGHT Covered jar, 2002.
Porcelain, high-fire reduction, H: 13".

BELOW Teabowl, 2011.
Earthenware, electric fired, 3.5" × 3".

JEFF
OESTREICH

RIGHT Yunomi, 2005. Porcelain, thrown and wire cut, soda fired, 4" × 4" × 4".

BELOW Beaked pitcher, 2000. Stoneware, thrown and altered, soda fired, 10" × 10" × 3".

LINDA
CHRISTIANSON

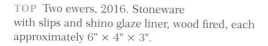

TOP Two ewers, 2016. Stoneware
with slips and shino glaze liner, wood fired, each
approximately 6" × 4" × 3".

LOWER LEFT Sushi plates, 2014. Stoneware
with slips, wood fired, 1" × 6" × 6".

LOWER RIGHT Basket, 1995. Stoneware with slip and
shino liner, wood fired, 9" × 6" × 3".

WILL
SWANSON

TOP LEFT Dinnerware, squared plate and bowl, 2016. Stoneware, carbon trap and shino glazes, plate 11" dia., bowl 7" dia. *Photo: Janel Jacobson*

TOP RIGHT Will Swanson's stoneware and Janel Jacobson's porcelain share the showroom space at their pottery studio in Sunrise, Minnesota, 2018. *Photo: Janel Jacobson*

BOTTOM Three tea bowls, 2008. Stoneware, carbon trap, shino and Albany slip glaze, tallest approximately 4".

GUILLERMO
CUELLAR

RIGHT Serving platter, 2014.
Stoneware, cone 10 reduction,
shino with black trailing, 17.75"
dia. *Photo: Laurie MacGregor*

BELOW Teapot, 2013. Stoneware,
cone 10 reduction, *tenmoku* with
white glaze, 8" × 7.5" × 6".
Photo: Laurie MacGregor

SILVIE
GRANATELLI

LEFT Crane bottle, 2017. Porcelain, matte crystalline glaze, thrown and re-formed square bottle with stopper, 9.5" × 4".

ABOVE Peach platter, 2011. Porcelain, stain decorations under clear glaze, 17.5" dia.

MATT
METZ

RIGHT Pitcher, stained (black)
porcelain, wheel thrown, slipped,
sgraffito, salt glazed, 12" × 6".

BELOW Box, 2018. Stained (black)
porcelain, wheel thrown and altered,
slipped, sgraffito, salt glazed, 9" × 9".

AYUMI
HORIE

RIGHT Jar, 2016. Earthenware, H: 14". From the beginning of her career in 2000, Horie has promoted the idea of photographing work in context, rather than on a blank background.

BELOW Otter and bird cup, 2014. Porcelain, H: 3.5". Pottery shot from underwater in the sink. Photographing handmade pots in new and different contexts is crucial to Horie's aesthetic and branding.

BOTTOM Ramen bowls "in action" by a collector who also loves to cook. Dragon ramen bowl, 2017. Porcelain and luster, 9" dia. *Photo: Steven Sharafian*

ROSA AND WINTON
EUGENE

RIGHT "Elegant Country," 1995. Hand-painted stoneware clay, plate dia.: 10", cups H: 4" and 4.5".

BOTTOM LEFT "Generations" jug, 2002. Low-relief stoneware with brown stain and clear overglaze, 9" × 7" × 9".

BOTTOM RIGHT "Endangered Species" covered jar, 2013. Stoneware clay, etched, Riche's brown glaze, 8" × 4.5" × 6.5".

EMILY FREE
WILSON

TOP Five candy jars, 2015. Cone 6 porcelain, underglaze, glaze, each 4.75" × 4.5".

BOTTOM Plate, 2014. Cone 6 porcelain, underglaze, glaze, 1.25" × 10.5".

JEREMY
OGUSKY

ABOVE Table, 2016.
Stoneware, pitcher H: 10".
Photo: Tina Picz,
https://tinapicz.com

RIGHT Fermentation crock
as it appeared in the blog *Le jus*
d'orange, 2015. Stoneware,
H: 8". *Photo: Betty Liu*

ROBBIE
LOBELL

TOP Covered bowl, 1996. Light stoneware body with slip decoration, carved tripod feet, fired to cone 9 in propane-fueled soda-vapor kiln, 8" × 11" × 11".

RIGHT Nesting square bakers, 2007. Flameware clay body fired to cone 11 in propane-fueled soda-vapor kiln, smallest 1" × 6" × 6", largest 3.5" × 12" × 12".

BELOW Casserole/stovetop pot, 2008. Flameware clay body fired to cone 11 in propane-fueled soda-vapor kiln, 3" × 14" × 11.5".

LISA
ORR

RIGHT Plate, 2013. Earthenware with slips, sprigs, and polychrome glazes, 1" × 7.5".

BELOW Teapot, 2018. Earthenware with slips, sprigs, and polychrome glazes, 8.5" × 7.5" × 5".

KYLE
CARPENTER

RIGHT Teapot, 2010. Stoneware with slip, glaze, and underglaze, fired in propane-fueled salt kiln, 7.5" × 6". *Photo: Tim Barnwell*

BELOW Cups, 2017. Stoneware with slip, glaze, and underglaze, fired in propane-fueled salt kiln, each 4" × 3". *Photo: Tim Barnwell*

LINDA
ARBUCKLE

RIGHT Teapot: Winter Leaf
Chronology Distillation, 2011.
Maiolica glaze on terra-cotta clay,
6.5" × 8" × 3.5".

BELOW Large server, 2016.
Maiolica glaze on terra-cotta clay,
2.5" × 14" × 10.5".

PHARIS

TOP Vase set, 2011. Handbuilt earthenware, 9.5" × 10" × 7".

BOTTOM Teapot, 2014. Handbuilt stoneware,
11" × 6.25" × 5.75".

LINDA SIKORA

The Performative Pot

Linda Sikora in her studio,
Alfred Station,
New York, 2016

Canada-born Linda Sikora was for a time the sole potter—and an exemplary one—on the faculty of historic Alfred University, which has been teaching the art side of ceramics for more than 100 years (she was joined recently by potter Matt Kelleher). Sikora has a reputation as a gifted teacher and in 2017 was awarded the Robert C. Turner Professorship in Ceramic Art at Alfred. Her husband, Matt Metz, is a full-time potter with renown of his own.

Sikora grew up *all over Canada because my father was a Mounty, RCMP. So we were transferred every three years.* Her father, who was born in Czechoslovakia and immigrated with his parents, was also her model of a creative person, since he was a hobby carpenter and *a very meticulous crafts-person. The other thing, he was very physically dexterous*, with exceptional hand-eye coordination. She has three brothers, and all four are close in age.

Sikora discovered clay in high school, where the art teacher was a ceramist. She went to a small art college in British Columbia, where her teacher in the ceramic program was himself a potter. However, there was no BFA in ceramics, so, after meeting Walter Ostrom of the Nova Scotia College of Art & Design when he was a visiting artist, she transferred to NSCAD and in one and a half years earned that degree.

But that's jumping ahead. Between high school and college, Sikora did some traveling, including some time in Europe, and in addition *I took various breaks along the way and I got involved in a porcelain and enamel company. I was a silkscreener and color mixer for this company that was working with porcelain and enamels. We were firing enamel onto steel and working with signage. I ended up being involved in starting a company, and then I sold out of it to go back to art school. It was a great experience as a startup entrepreneur. I got to exercise that entrepreneurial spirit.* She thinks *one thing students need these days is to have entrepreneurial energy of some sort to invent how they are going to put a ceramics life together.*

At first, her work was *very influenced by Hans Coper, Lucie Rie, modernist ceramics. By the time I got to Nova Scotia I was working with earthenware because I got a studio downtown—low fire, electric, just like the students today are doing. So I went that route. The work became a bit more muddy, more "touched" in Nova Scotia. I think those two* sensibilities merged, and I ended up working with more constructed form and color by the time I finished graduate school [at the University of Minnesota, Minneapolis]. *This is a little bit blurred together. I embraced, as a lot of people did then, English porcelain, because so many of us grew up with it.*

My third year of graduate school I moved out to Houston, Minnesota, and was working in the studio out there and using the wood kiln. The forms started to simplify a lot. I became interested in the round, wheel-thrown form. I came through school when everyone was cutting and pasting. We use to call it cut and paste, nip and tuck, slice and dice. It was great fun, but I wanted to throw well, throw a good round pot.

Of course we all have temperaments, and I think I had a certain need for engagement, which meant that the energy that was going into the constructing previously now started to show up in the surface. That's when [decorative] pattern came in. The form became more simplified and the surface became more articulated. It just shifted.

Sometimes when you make something and it's done and you separate yourself from it, and then you come back and look at it and you say, "Did I make that? How did I do that?" It's like all of your resources come together and something happens. And for whatever reason, I think when I hit that combination of that amount of attention to glazing and that amount of attention to form, I seemed to be able to make work that I had to reach for. That hadn't happened in those other arrangements, other types of processes.

In recent years, Sikora's work—in porcelain or either of two stonewares—has been complexly decorated. Unlike paint on a canvas, the glaze colors she uses may move in certain ways, and they are subject to the effects of atmospheric firing—the particular type of first wood, then oil, plus salt firing that she began to do with the Minnesota kiln and has re-created in a kiln built by Donovan Palmquist at her studio in rural Alfred Station, New York.

The complexity of the process is multiplied because raw glaze colors differ from the fired color. *You're translating, sort of imagining what's going to happen*, she says. *When I am actually building the color on the surface with the glazes, I am projecting what the glaze will be, but I'm also really dealing with proportion and form of the pattern*

that's there, and I'm seeing certain colors. When I go to glaze the work, I draw on it. I map out a pattern, and once I get that in place I begin to paint.

I'm not idealistic about them getting used. I mean, I know that they do and they don't. And that's fine. There's a lot of satisfaction in the process, and I think that the process fits my idiosyncratic nature. The other thing that is really more conceptually and philosophically important to me is that I know the work moves into the culture. I know it moves and that the subject matter, the subject of function, is the vehicle for that movement. As a maker you have ambitions about how you want your work to interface with the culture. That might mean utility, or it might mean display, or it might mean performance or something else yet unimagined.

Once someone takes a pot and it's in their house, it's tangled up in the sort of doings of daily life, which aren't terrifically organized or ritualistic all the time. You know, there's times when it's really not seen. It's buried in the dish drainer or it doesn't come out of the cupboard or it's on the sideboard because something else is going on. And there are other moments when it is very visible. It might come to the center of the table or it might be the object that serves tea, so it moves back and forth between. And of course in the gallery it's very visible. And I really do like it going to the gallery on its way to that other place, I like that white box. I like that moment when people prepare themselves just to look. I make pots with both things in mind. I make them to be completely tangled up in domestic activity. And also make them to be really seen—for us to stand back and look at them.

When someone acquires an object like a teapot and they take it home, they are really taking home their own sensibility. They are taking home my pot, but they are taking home a part of themselves. They might not name it or necessarily think about it that way, but that object in that space, if they intend to live with it, it reflects part of their own sensibility back to themselves. So it's sort of written again by a user. Anything that moves into the domestic space is like that. And then the pot has this performative place where it gets tangled up in a certain way—it moves around a lot; it gets dirty; it gets washed.

We may speak of the intimacy and physicality of the interaction of object and person. But *you can use it so often that it's mindless, and I think there's a value in that as well. I think that one could aspire to make the cup that you reach for when you are half asleep. There could be an object that's so integrated into an activity that it's operating almost on the subliminal level.*

Sikora was once described in an exhibition catalog as fourth-generation Mingei, because she was a student of Pharis who was a student of MacKenzie who apprenticed to Leach with his connections to Japan. She finds the idea strange, because, as noted, her early work was influenced by Rie and Coper, immigrants to England from Austria and Germany, respectively, and midcentury modernists. *Mark really showed us the lay of the land; he showed us a lot, so our eyes were opened. But he really did put it out there like choices. I see that I'm of a time, but I don't really think in lineages. I think that where I am now reflects something about color and ornament and ritual, you know, sort of the Sunday dressing up for church, all of those things.* Which are not very Mingei.

An artist once told her that his interest in ornament came from having been raised Catholic. That's also in Sikora's background. *And I thought: oh my God, I've never really thought about it. I was always aware of the ritual. And my mother was just an exquisite dresser. When Walter was teaching us the history of ceramics, I connected it to my* *grandmother's china cabinet. And I have a French Canadian, sort of Scottish side, and that's where all the porcelains came from. But I think there's something that was more broadly embedded in my life, and not just the china cabinet. If I look at the sense of my work right now, it feels more connected to textiles or something like that. And in fact one of the questions I have right now in my practice is: What is the difference between a pattern that is ceramic and a pattern that is textile?*

Part of that came out of unloading the first wood kiln and looking at the color of the bowls with these glazes I started using, and I thought: oh, that's just fabric. I look at ceramic and I look at patterns, and certainly looking at Tang dynasty pots has influenced the way I use glazes and things like that, but this was something else. I was using glazes that are more sort of set. They weren't flowing so much. And it was the quality of the color.

Today I think of function more broadly. In my practice right now, the teapots are the most usable. They're really nice to use. I mean, they're servers, which are just a bit more formal, and the larger jars are more objects where I'm just looking at pattern and color and form. I have both of those things going on. ∎

—Annie Markovich, transcriber

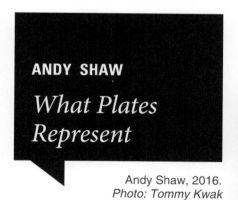

ANDY SHAW

What Plates Represent

Andy Shaw, 2016.
Photo: Tommy Kwak

Andy Shaw (b. 1969) is a devoted maker of functional pottery who has also been recognized as an extraordinary teacher. Originally from a small town in central Pennsylvania, he has been teaching at Louisiana State University since 2008 and has widely exhibited his porcelain tableware.

Shaw's dad ran the family business as director of a funeral home on the main street of the town, so the family knew and was known to practically every local citizen. They lived above the business, *so for me there was no separation between work and personal life; the spaces were totally connected.* The family was church going (Presbyterian), and his father went back to school in his mid-50s to become a minister. Shaw's parents were active in civic organizations, and the family had a strong work ethic.

He was in no way an arty child. A trip to Colonial Williamsburg when he was about 14 reinforced an interest in history that had begun in grade school. Tracing the family roots and studying medieval history in high school led him to apply to the University of St. Andrews in Scotland for his freshman year, to study medieval history, Scottish history, and Latin.

Thinking about pivotal moments, I remember when I was in high school, Scotland sounded really dreamy, but it was also terrifying. I wasn't the kind of kid who would go to summer camps; that was a little too adventurous [Laughter], *but here I am dreaming about going overseas as my first big thing, right? So I remember I got the acceptance letter and I panicked. My first thought was "I can't do this." And then I just said to myself: if you don't do this, if you say no to this thing that you've always wanted now that you have it, you'll refuse these options for the rest of your life. I was 18 years old, and that was probably one of the biggest things I ever said to myself. So I went. And it was a great year.*

I had no idea what I was going to do with those studies; they were just topics that were interesting to me. So while I was there I decided that I would reapply to Kenyon College in Ohio, where I had also applied that first year. I kept studying history. Studied French, too, and eventually put together an independent study on medieval Iceland, which was all about the founding of law and writing it down through literature. That's how I ended college. A great experience of thinking of ideas in a liberal-arts way, where you take one subject and you come at it from economics, politics, sociology, philosophy, who knows what. That's probably the foundation of how I teach everything. So much comes out of Kenyon liberal arts.

But snuck in there, and this is where it gets to the pots, was that through middle school and high school I was a swimmer: on swim teams, I coached swim teams, I was a lifeguard, I was a manager of a pool. When I got to college I started a swimming school. I loved it, but there was a point where I totally burned out and I just couldn't do it anymore. Then I had a huge amount of time on my hands.

So I had the three things. One is the lack of physical outlet. Another was that I needed to figure out a way that my time could be spent doing something useful. He was also struck by an interest in self-sufficiency when his friend Diane, who grew up on a small farm in Vermont, talked about having sheep and goats *that will mow the lawn, and we'll shear the sheep and make our sweaters and milk the goats and have our milk.* [Laughter]

So this is where it really gets good. [Laughter] *My friend Katy wanted to go see her sister in Cleveland, and I went along. And while we were in the house in Cleveland, I saw these canisters in the kitchen, and then we moved into the living room and there were some big serving bowls and a few other things. I don't think I was noticing them because they were beautiful; they were just totally different from everything else there. So I said to Katy, "Where do these come from?" And she said, "Oh, my brother-in-law Jim made them." On the way up to Cleveland she had told me her brother-in-law was an oil executive. I said, "Katy, if he's an oil executive, why does he make these? He could just buy them." And as soon as I asked that question—it sounds kind of hokey, but this is totally what happened—it was like a road-to-Damascus kind of thing, but those three intersections of physical labor, self-sufficiency, and needing to spend my time in a way that produced something—there's like this flash of light.* [Laughter] *I truly don't remember what she said. I just remember asking the question and just going bam! And it was so, I don't know, it was scary, but I knew that it was significant.*

Kenyon had a craft center where students could drop in at any time. Shaw went with a friend who had "done clay stuff," and without instruction they figured it out. *That's where it started. It was an instant love. I hadn't taken an art class since the eighth grade, although I liked art, I liked going to museums.*

These things that I needed in my life for one reason or another landed in this conversation. And I just thought I had to honor this.

Shaw had no postgraduation plans, although he expected to eventually go to graduate school in history. He came across an issue of *Ceramics Monthly* and saw advertisements for clay businesses. *This was long before email and internet, so I just sent them these pathetic letters and I said, "If you have community bulletin boards, could you just post this letter? I'm looking for an apprenticeship, I just want to work with somebody, and I want to work in the Rocky Mountains or in the Pacific Northwest. I don't know what I'm doing. This is kind of a message in a bottle."* [Laughter] *And not too long after that, I got either a call or a letter back from a guy named Patrick Eckman from Basin, Montana. He saw my letter at the Archie Bray, and he lived 40 miles south of there.*

I thought: I'm going to take two years out of school to learn pottery. I'm going to go live some place for an extended period of time so I can feel like I'm invested in the place, not just a traveler. And so I went to Basin for what turned out to be a 19-month apprenticeship.

Pat would tell me what I needed to work on, and then he would just say, "But I don't care if you work on it or not; you have to care about that." He described the job this way: he said, "When you come, you'll cut the grass, you'll chop wood, you'll grind raw materials, you'll clean the gallery"; he just gave me this long list and said, "Once that's done, maybe you'll be able to make something." He said, "Your job is to do everything that keeps me from making the work." And that seemed like a fair trade to me.

I think it was 25, 20 hours a week, in exchange for a place to live. There were weeks that I juggled about six different part-time jobs. They were all on call. When the on-call jobs needed me for two or three weeks consistently, Pat didn't get upset. He knew that when I was at the shop, I worked more than my time. I worked at a pizza shop; I taught swimming lessons; I was a custodian for the elementary school, middle school, and high school; I was a substitute teacher; and I worked at a development center as a food service director, a food service driver, and a custodian again. I really got my custodian skills down there. I think that's all. Oh no, I got to work at the county solid-waste-disposal site. *I was learning so much, but in terms of life, it was brutal. I was living so far below the poverty line. I think on my taxes I claimed $3,500 two years in a row. I was making nothing.*

This was a short-term thing, and the payoff, I thought, was really good. I learned what the Archie Bray was. And I learned aesthetics there. McKenzie Smith was there. He was so kind to me. But I remember seeing his handles and people talk about his handles as being so great, and I'd only seen handles that were smoothed on. And I remember McKenzie's looked like somebody pulled a handle, licked it, and stuck it onto the side of the cup. [Laughter] *At that time I thought it looked junky; I thought it looked sloppy. I didn't understand that craftsmanship is not a look, it's a way of using material to suggest your intentions.*

Eckman urged Shaw to take a workshop with Les Manning on Vancouver Island, British Columbia. Shaw resisted because that was something a potter would do, and he was a medieval historian. Besides, he couldn't afford it. The school offered a scholarship. He realized he had two potential lives in front of him, but he thought it was 95 to 5 against pottery being his future. It was a two-week program, and he had never spent two straight weeks on his own work, because of juggling all the jobs. *I was interested in teapots, and all of my teapots looked like clowns, or like Mr. Potato Head things* [Laughter] *where parts don't fit together. I was frustrated because I was trying to make what I called serious teapots. I spent the first week at the workshop in Canada working on teapots, and I just had a band of clowns. And I remember panicking and I left the studio for about a day and a half. I had a bike and I'd bike around the island. I was avoiding it. What I didn't know at the time was you have to get out of the studio sometimes and let your mind process information. So I went in Sunday morning, and I decided I'm going to make five teapots but I'm not going to make five different teapots; I'm going to make five of the exact same teapot if I can. And I'm going to throw body one, and body two, then body three, then four, then five. And I'm going to throw lid one, then two, then three, then four, then five.* And so on.

And so Les came in Monday morning, and I had these five teapots that were done, and they were the best things I'd ever made. They weren't great, right, but it was a huge thing for me, and I could tell by the way that he stepped up to them that morning that he saw something really profound had happened over the weekend. The rest of the week I just kept making work with a kind of confidence or satisfaction or grasp of methods that just made better sense to me. On the last day, I stepped out of the studio and there's this beautiful bay down there, and I sat on this rock and I just started bawling. I thought: my god, I basically came here with the worst odds that I would ever pursue clay, and now I don't want to do anything else.

After that, knocking around the Bray, he asked various people what he should do now. They advised him to go to Kansas City Art Institute. But he had no money, so he could only return to Pennsylvania and go for in-state tuition at Penn State. *I had heard about this professor at Penn State, Chris Staley.* Shaw called Penn State to inquire about a special student program. Two days later, *my boss Pat and I went up to the Holter Museum in Helena for a David Shaner retrospective, and Pat says, "Hey, I think that's Chris Staley over there."* Shaw met Staley; they talked and made an appointment to talk again. Shaw took a box of work. *So I remember asking Chris, "When I look at this work I don't know how to see it, and you know how to see it. So my question is this: Is there any reason I should keep doing this?"*

And in a very Chris Staley way, he said, "Well, do you think, for you, is there something worth going forward for?" And I came to like that about Chris; he'd usually turn a question you asked him back to you. It worked out. I went to study with him the next year as a special student. It was just an incredible year.

Shaw's next step was a residency at Arrowmont, in Tennessee, a move toward making up for his lack of a BFA. While there, he met a teacher who was going to be on sabbatical for three months and suggested that Shaw fill in for him, and assured him that he'd be fine. In the meantime, he rented Nick Joerling's place in North Carolina while Joerling was teaching at Penn State. *Because I had no job, I forced myself: in this three months I've got to survive only through the studio thing. And I sent out applications. By that spring I had work in about eight exhibitions. Never had that before. I had a*

postcard for myself. That was the fall of '97. Then January 1998 I went to southwest Michigan to teach at Andrews. I'd taken workshops at Arrowmont, but I'd never actually taken a class, and now I get to teach. The route is bizarre. It was an intense and joyous three months. And surprisingly, that class, in a small religious college, included Linda Sormin and Anthony Schaller, both of whom have gone on to recognition in the field, one as a maker and teacher and the other as a gallerist.

From there, he went to Alfred as a graduate student. He became a teaching assistant for the foundations class, which was a revelation to him. When he finished his MFA, he taught introductory ceramics, as an adjunct, at Gettysburg College and then returned to Alfred to teach foundations for a year, full time. He was still acutely conscious of things he didn't know, but he thrilled to realize that *your interest and curiosity, if shaped well, and if shaped into methods, are enough to become a good teacher.*

Then it was back to Gettysburg because the position was open again and it looked like ceramics had potential in the school. There was also a chance to teach a creative first-year class something like foundations, and he was only 100 miles from his family. He spent a year at Louisiana State University as a sabbatical replacement, then two years at the Clay Studio in Philadelphia with a Shapiro Foundation Fellowship, and he stayed another year. And then he was hired for a permanent position at LSU. *Ceramics gets half of all MFA applications for the entire school of art at LSU. So the students that we are get are great. And we have postbac students, too, that also come from all over the country just to spend a year there.*

As a maker, pots make total sense to me. But as a teacher, pots aren't enough, so I do all the rest of it. I feel like there's an obligation for myself to transcend whatever limitations people think are on pots. And that's why I teach some of the courses that I do. He takes on classes without knowing what the forms or the outcome will be, in the same way that artists address the unknown in the studio. But in his studio work he can happily address minutiae.

My work actually has a lot to do with design, but not through industry. When I started the Tableware series, I wanted to turn it into a slip-casting thing. But I never made a plate that I felt like I wanted to see 100 times, because the next one was better. I still like the wheel throwing, and I still like the kind of shimmering and what happens when all those plates are together. That's where the idea is completed.

His first four years at LSU were simultaneously *the best professional record of my career for exhibitions, quality of exhibitions, visiting artist, workshops, publications, all those things.* How can he be so productive when he's teaching full time? *I've got a salary and I teach because I love it; that's why I'm involved in it. And the salary, you know, no one teaches to make a million dollars; you don't do it at a state school in the South. Louisiana is the second-poorest state in the union or something like that. But the teaching environment is great. So I don't have to worry every day about paying; I don't have those stresses like I used to.*

We've got a great studio at school. I have an open-door policy; students can come in and talk as I pull handles or something. I get a lot of work done in the summers. In a normal summer I might fire like four or five glaze kilns worth and then each semester another one or two, depending on what's going on. But I make a point to get in there.

On photographing: *I didn't want to just shoot my work against a backdrop. There's nothing wrong with it, I've done it, but pottery often doesn't look right in a gallery. Ayumi [Horie] started doing her Pots in Action thing—Ayumi is just a genius—so she's taken that whole idea and branded it.* [Laughter] *I don't think I could take a picture of dishes in a dish rack without someone saying that I'm doing Pots in Action. At the Clay Studio, I went to a photographer and I said, "I don't want to shoot my work against a backdrop. I actually want to see it in use or in context." I was thinking of pictures from West Elm catalogs and IKEA, where you could see dishes on the table and just see them involved with things.*

On form: *Even when I first got my wheel in 1993 after college, I was bored with round. I started changing the shapes of the work. Especially during the special year at Penn State. I think I had seven completely distinct bodies of work. So much so that Chris Staley said, "Will the real Andy Shaw please stand up."* [Laughter]

Shaw reflects that when he was making thrown and altered bowls of normal scale, people would ask what they could be used for. *I didn't even* understand their question because it seemed really clear to me. I think the ceramics world at that time talked about educating people. I just stopped one day and said: But visual work is about communication, and if I keep communicating something that people aren't understanding, it's not the listener, it's the speaker, and I'm the speaker. He remembered a conversation long before in which his father had said he wouldn't buy one of those bowls and had pulled down a dish from the kitchen cupboard and said, "That's a bowl."

I thought back to that conversation, and I realized when he brought down the bowl, he understood that this was a bowl because in my mom's cabinet we've probably got 12 of this same bowl, same shape; all the other bowls that we have of different pottery lines or commercial lines, they're still round. Everything that he's used in his life was a round, commercial bowl. So when he sees this bowl he's seeing the cereal, the soup, the ice cream. What was missing in my bowls was the communication about function. I called it the formal vernacular language of function. In functional pots, the round carried a huge association to use. So if I adopted the round, it was already implied that it is meant to be functional. I don't then have to write a little note card next to it [Laughter] *or I don't have to reassure people. So in a really strange way I made the most determined* forming *decision of my life, which was to make something round.*

I started showing things in stacks, like plates. I didn't want to take a picture of one plate, because it wasn't about that object, it was about what plates represent. So this stack makes this plate maybe less important, but it also includes that plate as being important because it's part of this group. I'm not making work for museums; I'm making things for people's homes. Now people buy them in sets. I didn't make the change for sales, but that's always a bonus. When someone sees a set of cups, they see them maybe set around a table, and they see the people who would be with them. The four cups become about the activity.

I needed to change how I made the pots to make that happen. I needed to do something out of clarity, unification of the ideas in the work—patterns that could sort of work off each other, a glaze that feels unifying, in forms that were pared down in such a way that they're simplified, but there's also what I call vacancy. There's a vacancy that forces the people using them to somehow insert something about themselves into them. And by doing that, then they're complete.

Cooks who see the work often say that the color of the glaze allows you to put different colors of foods on it, and that the color is not fixed. It's nice when a cook starts talking about that before I've explained it, because then I know the communication is reaching from me through the work to the person and back again.

Porcelain is connected with thin and translucent. Those are great things, but they just aren't things that interest me necessarily as a maker. I like weight because when I'm holding a bowl or a plate, there's something about the physicality. I like the way it announces itself.

People have different colors in their home, so I want the work to be able to slide into that. And for the patterns, I call it incidental domestic patterns.

So the grids and lines, these are things that are just in people's homes. When a piece of pottery goes to someone's house, people use it and interact with it in ways that I could never imagine.

Tableware started around 2003 or 2004. It's the longest body of work he's done. When he had a residency at Northern Clay Center in 2016, he began experimenting with new shapes for plates, not in the conventional round or the not-uncommon square, but ones that, for example, might reflect the user's reach. He has developed a new line of black stoneware trays. That residency, he says, caused a midcareer shift based on *taking action in the moment of decision.*

I've got a kitchen full of a lot of people's things, but I do use my own things because I have to understand how it works. I know there are a lot of people who say that to use your own work is a conversation with yourself. I actually don't believe that, but I talk to myself all the time. [Laughter] ∎

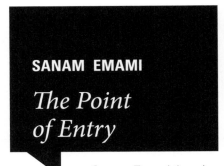

SANAM EMAMI

The Point of Entry

Sanam Emami throwing at the Ox-Bow School of Art, Saugatuck, Michigan, where she team-taught a workshop with her husband, Del Harrow, in 2017

Being an immigrant can be a liability or a benefit, or both. Sanam Emami (b. 1971) came to the US at the age of 10 from England, where her family had spent three years after fleeing the Iranian Revolution. *I have some memories of my childhood in Iran, but they're sort of fleeting. I don't remember things outside the immediate domestic realm. But I did learn to speak the language, and that was a really great thing because I went back to Iran as an adult and traveled and saw many things.*

Both her English-fluent, nonreligious parents had been educated in Europe, and her father trained as an engineer but never practiced it again after leaving Iran. He eventually became involved in an American real-estate venture, and in 1981 the family moved from London to Las Vegas *of all places*, she says with a laugh. *I was a little bit older, but I think it felt more like a culture shock to move to Las Vegas than to London. Las Vegas when we moved there was not the bustling city that it is today. It was a fairly small town. And there wasn't a lot of ethnic diversity at the time.*

It still was the hostage crisis, and I think Americans were dealing with that. I saw how people reacted when I would tell them where I was from, and I think that made me more careful about talking about it when I was a child. In Las Vegas at that time we were just different. We had these thick English accents [Laughter]*, and people were like, "Where are you coming from; are you English?" And they would get really confused. I think we all managed to become Americanized pretty quickly. I wanted so much to be like everybody else, I lost my British accent like that.*

Six years later, when she was in high school, the family (including an older and younger sister) moved to Washington, DC, where they remained until 1991, when her mother died. Then her father, to everyone's surprise, returned to Iran. The three girls chose to remain in the US. All three are involved in the arts in some way, although the parents didn't take them to museums or talk about art. But Emami remembers that in a typical Iranian household, *most people had a Persian rug; most people had a miniature* [a traditional painting] *of some kind. China was very popular, the sort of blue-and-white Chinese ceramics, and then even the more recent ceramics from China with the polychrome palettes of enamels. So I grew up seeing that stuff and always kind of admiring it.*

She had no thought of studying art, although she remembers having made a plate in school in England, and having had a knack for centering and throwing when she had a brief exposure to clay in Las Vegas. She ended up at a state school in Virginia, studying history, with a focus on women and on the Middle East. In her freshman year she took ceramics,

printmaking, and drawing, and art became her minor. In addition, *the art practice and the history practice eventually led to art history, so I started looking at a lot of buildings and historical form from Iran, and from all over.*

Her studies were with Masako Miyata and, in her senior year, Brook Levan. He was a young artist who had gone to Alfred and had artist residencies at Kohler and Bemis, and who *was probably the first person I ever met who made the concept of being an artist a real possibility.* When she graduated, *Brook had just gotten a three-year position at Pomona, in Southern California, and he said, "When you decide that this is what you want to do, give me a call and I'll see if I can help you." And of course I thanked him, but I still didn't see myself as an artist. I saw myself as someone who took art classes and loved it. I took a cross-country trip with some friends and ended up in San Francisco and spent about two and a half years there getting a different kind of education. I sampled different careers for a while.*

A potter friend from her undergraduate days came to town, and together they explored the Bay Area ceramics scene, to which she had been oblivious. She met Sandy Simon, saw a Peter Voulkos exhibition at the Oakland Museum, visited Mary Law's studio. *She said that she was looking for an assistant, and I said, "Well, I . . . I . . . ."* [Laughter] *She told me what she wanted, and I decided to take her up on the offer. And so I worked for Mary Law for about three months. It was an exchange. For however many hours I worked in her studio making these serving dishes, in exchange, on the days she wasn't there, I could use the studio to make my own work. I sat down at the wheel, and I think something must have clicked. I got really excited about working with clay again.*

So about three months in, I called Brook Levan, who was still at Pomona, and I said, "OK, I'm ready." And of course, he said, "You waited until my three-year position is almost finished!" And I said, "It took me this long; I needed this much time." I moved down to Southern California. I helped Brook and his wife at home, and in exchange I had a studio space. And Brook helped me develop and start thinking about being a potter. It wasn't a structured thing. I was working at school but I was sort of more of his studio assistant, I guess.

He said, "Of all my good students, the ones that continued all wanted to keep making pots." Although his own work was sculpture, *there was something about the way he spoke about pots and how much he loved them and how important they were, I think it did affect his students.* Emami decided to do a postbac year, and she chose to go to the University of Colorado at Boulder, where Linda Sikora would then be teaching. But in the fall, Sikora was not yet there, and Emami by default worked with Scott Chamberlin.

I always tell students this: you think you're going to school for someone you want to work with, which is a great reason to go somewhere, but Scott ended up being such an important teacher for me. The thing I remember most is that the students' perception was that he didn't like pots, and he didn't want you to make pots, but my take on it was he wanted to push you till you knew what you wanted to do, and then if that's what you wanted to do, he was going to work with you. He had the postbac students participate in graduate seminars. *I was so green and had such a limited background as an artist or with clay, but Scott just sort of pulled us all together and had me present with the grad students. It was a really important time for me. And then I had a wonderful semester with Linda in the spring. I was thinking that I would go to grad school, and so I applied and I didn't get in anywhere.* [Laughter] *Which is another thing I always tell my students: you have to persevere.*

Sikora was going on to teach at Alfred, and she offered Emami the opportunity to stay at the farm in southern Minnesota that she and her husband, Matt Metz, owned. Since she began teaching they were there only summers, *but Matt would stay in the fall, and he would go and join Linda after he had gotten a few more firings out. I did it one year; Andy Brayman did it one year; Rob Sutherland. In the mornings Matt would get up, have breakfast, and he would go and work. And he would work 12 hours a day. I had never seen that or experienced it, and I think that was really important for me.*

Also he was so generous with his ideas. I think the perception is that he's this amazing maker, but when you talk to him he's so sharp, so smart. We'd sit around for hours and talk about pots. The eye-opening aspect was that this discussion was not an academic situation, but just part of living the life of a potter. *It felt like a window into an artist's studio practice that was very different than I knew. He also wanted to know my thoughts, so it was this great exchange. He became a mentor for me in a different way than I'd had up until that point.*

And then she was on her own at the farm. *School or most situations I had been working at had been very public, and you're always very concerned about making work that might fail. I felt like I didn't really learn how to take risks or make work that was not resolved. At the farm I made a lot of work that I didn't want anyone to see. That was really great. I could spend hours working on a question.*

With the help of Metz and Sikora, she put together an application for a residency at the Archie Bray Foundation and was accepted as a summer resident. When the summer ended, she didn't want to leave. When another resident left for a teaching job, Josh DeWeese called and asked her if she wanted to come back, so in January she returned and was able to stay for a full two years. The best part, she says, was the opportunity for dialogue and exchange among a population diverse in background, age, stature, and style. *I felt like I was always on a steep learning curve because I didn't have the art school background, hadn't done an undergraduate degree. In one of my many conversations with Josh, he said, "You need to just get over it. People come to this from all different backgrounds. It's not that you're lacking anything, you're bringing something else to the table."*

The next step was graduate school. She was admitted to Alfred and was there from 2000 to 2002, a period that she regards as thinking time more than producing time. She was also a teaching assistant, assisting faculty in the classroom. *That was an important part of my education, not actually teaching but being in the classroom with someone who had been teaching for so many years, watching and observing.*

After graduating she moved to New York City. *I was just so ready for city life, urban life that I'd been missing so much, because I grew up as a city person and had spent all these years in very rural places. I cobbled together a few classes at Greenwich House Pottery and a few classes at 92nd Street Y, and I assisted Arlene Shechet; I was her studio assistant. It was a great year, but it was challenging.*

I rented a studio space in Williamsburg. I thought I was going to make a go of it. But she got a call asking if she wanted to teach a few adjunct classes at Alfred. It sounded like a good experience. *I went for one semester and I ended up teaching there for four years.*

Then in 2007 she was hired to teach at Colorado State University, where she is now tenured. Her husband, Del Harrow, whom she met at Alfred, is the other half of the ceramics program there.

Emami considers her real work to have started with the development of *tulipieres*, more correctly called vases with spouts because other flowers were placed in them as well as tulips. For her graduate thesis, she researched the tulip (which originated in the Middle East), and the way the Delft tulip vase in Holland was influenced by Chinese and Middle Eastern pottery, and the dependence both of European and Asian blue-and-white pottery on cobalt from the Middle East. *What I decided to do was take the Dutch tulip vase and remake it with an emphasis on Islamic patterning and Islamic architecture. Islamic art for me was sort of foundation, groundbreaking in dealing with abstraction. Because of the limits of religion and notions of not being able to compete with God, they actually abstracted the world around them into patterns and geometries. The thing about pattern, both representational and nonrepresentational imagery, is that it really is about communicating something. It's both universal and specific.*

In work that she did in '98, at the Bray, *I wanted to find a building block or a motif and try to build the form from that—not wanting to create a hierarchy of first form, then surface. I wanted to make a piece that celebrated the pattern. So I gave myself this assignment to have one tile that was a repeated unit. I found the star cross pattern when I was reading about Sufism, which is the mystical side of Islam. It's not just an Islamic pattern, but the Sufis talk about this pattern in terms of breathing in and breathing out. The star is one act and the cross is another. And I thought that was compelling because it is such a hard-edge geometric shape. I decided that every single star would have a different pattern, but the shapes would be the same. The tiles are about 14 inches.*

The first time she saw a Delft tulip vase was in a museum in San Francisco. *It pretty much stopped me in my tracks, because it was about 4 feet tall,* with hundreds of spouts. For all of the history and the complexity of the form, I felt like the tulip vase was a really great opportunity to create an object that has a specific functional intent but is very sculptural.*

She *started to think about silkscreening and silkscreen transfers. I would start with a found image that I would play around with on the computer and then make a silkscreen out of. The patterns may have come from the Middle East or Japan or China or Europe, and I would cut them and collage them. The work that I was doing before grad school I would try to figure out how one pattern could move around the form. After grad school it was more about layering patterns, so a pattern would wrap around one part of the object, a stamped pattern, and there might be the addition of transfers or sprigs. Like a collage of shapes.*

I worked with darker glazes. I used a red clay body, and later I actually modeled a clay body around the dark-brown Meissen, the chocolate clay from the Meissen factory. I can put a slip over it. In my mind it's a warmer palette. It's very white, but it's not the same white as a porcelain white. It doesn't have those grays and blues that porcelain has.

For a 2011 show in Kansas City, *I made my first and only tulip vases in more traditional Delft shape, that historical pyramid shape. It helped me push the scale. I used silkscreen transfers, but this time I tried to wrap them around the entire form in a meandering way.*

Around the same time, she made a row of slip-cast dimensional tiles, using digital fabrication tools, which *allow me to think a little bit more like an architect, in the way that I can change scale, and numbers. It's very different from sitting down to the wheel and throwing. I think that the more we know about a computer, or any other tool, the more we can use them in a way that is interesting.*

She likes that the tool allows something unexpected to happen, something creative. *I will make a 3-D model, but immediately I want to bring it into the physical world and I want to interact with it. So I think it's bridging the digital and hand, just the way someone would use a plaster mold and then model it by hand.*

Modeling on the computer is *actually a very similar process to throwing on the potter's wheel. You have to think in four dimensions. You can't just* draw. Pottery is so fascinating because you're dealing with the inside, the outside, the top, the bottom; the wheel is spinning.

Cups that she draws on the computer and then prints are subsequently slip cast. Molds help make the work less laborious. *It takes me many weeks to make a small set of cups. A lot of that has to do with all the time of the cutting the silkscreens and applying them.* She also design stamps on the computer that can be applied to the wheel-thrown pieces.

The surfaces are an overlay of geometric and arabesque or curved patterns on top of more-rectilinear patterns. And then sometimes it's also a combination of playing with the Chinese and Japanese—the notion of the Silk Road. I think about all these things, and then I just have all these patterns in my studio. The source material is very considered and is more conscious, but then in the moment in the studio it's probably a little bit more spontaneous and less intellectual.

I make a lot of tableware. Bowls and plates and cups. And pitchers. Tableware is really important. I only make a handful of tulip vases a year, whereas the tableware is an ongoing activity.

I want the object to fulfill its intended use. I'm not saying someone has to use it, but if they're going to use it, I want it to really work. I want them to be able to have that interaction with the work. Without that grounding, I think it would be a very different body of work. That to me is what studio pottery is about. That's the structure. That's like the point of entry into all the work. ■

CHAPTER EIGHT

OTHER DAY JOBS

Besides the innumerable unrelated part-time jobs such as waitressing or construction work that provide a steady supplementary income without sucking up the time and creativity that potters want to put into the studio, some people have jobs that are professional level and demanding enough that they could be primary employment, were it not for the call of the studio. Like teaching, these jobs offer challenges, information, and stimulation that can return to pottery, the work of the heart. ■

DOUG CASEBEER

What Else Is Out There?

Doug Casebeer, 2015

Doug Casebeer is not only associate director of Anderson Ranch Art Center in Colorado and its artistic director of ceramics, but throughout his career he has been involved in international development projects involving pottery. Casebeer (b. 1956) grew up in central Kansas, the oldest of five boys, *in a family of makers. My dad's a welder and a fabricator and my grandfather ran a salvage yard, and everybody had some kind of skill that they developed at a young age. Tools and equipment were not foreign to me as a child, and it's been a way to entertain myself as well as develop skills. My dad and my grandfather realized that you needed practical skills to survive in life, especially on the prairie.*

From an early age I had an affinity for material. I grew up understanding metal and steel in a way that I understand clay today. I remember asking my dad one day, "What is it that attracts you to metal?" And he said, "It's very simple; I can do anything I want." That concept has been with me from the beginning. When ceramics came into my life, the notion that I could make anything that I wanted out of this fluid, plastic material resonated very clearly with me.

I spent 12 years as a competitive swimmer. I think that taught me about discipline and practice, that you honed your eye or you honed your physical capacities by practice. I'm a real believer in that.

I was not a particularly good student. [Laughter] *I graduated from high school and thought that I wanted to be an architect. Architecture was a way to train my eye around issues of structure, form, shape, profile, composition. I went off to school, University of Oklahoma. The technical side kicked my ass. I just couldn't get through college algebra, and calculus was just a mystery.* [Laughter] *The same time I was passing geometry with A's, complex geometry. So I began to realize that my skills were in conceptualizing form and shape, to draw it or articulate it three-dimensionally.*

Casebeer left school, bounced around for a while, and then decided he should pursue industrial design and consumer appliances. He enrolled in a small college near Kansas City, where a demonstration by a visiting ceramist changed his path yet again. Casebeer's thoughts about consumer appliances easily shifted to objects for the table, specifically pottery. *Pottery really got ahold of me because of this sense of utility, that you can make things that people want to use and take into their daily lives.* He went on for an MFA from Alfred, concentrating on pottery, studying with Val Cushing.

I graduated from Alfred with no idea of what I was going to do. I wasn't prepared to be a studio potter. I think art school is about making art and the dialogue around the art, and graduate students don't learn the mechanics of running a business. Then he saw a posting for a job: the United Nations Industrial Development Organization was looking for a young potter. The project, in Jamaica, was administered by an Alfred graduate who was a friend of Cushing's. *And so I got Val out of bed on a Sunday morning and said, "Can you make a phone call for me?" And he called this gentleman and said, "This is the person you need. Not only is he a good potter, but he has a background in architecture and building, and he can weld, he can put things together."*

Casebeer moved to Kingston, Jamaica, with his wife, an art educator. *I got there a year after they had kind of internal civil war for about four years, so they were trying to mend social issues and get back on track as a country. I was assigned to this pottery project that had been sort of in place, but when I walked in, there was one broken wheel, no working kilns, 10,000 square feet, and 48 people standing around wondering what to do. At 25, I was put in charge of these people. I was the only Caucasian in a very black, very macho culture.*

The government was trying to develop industries that would support a developing middle-class market as well as an indirect tourist market. So we were making bud vases for hotels and resorts as well as casseroles for department stores and things like that. I spent three years there, working in this factory. I didn't know what my sense of purpose was as an artist until I was put into this environment that challenged everything I knew about right and wrong, values and norms, race. We see things that disturb us, enlighten us, and we use those opportunities to fuel our artistic practice.

There were times when our personal safety was at risk, and we would bond over those issues. I had people that worked with me that carried guns and knives. You would never think that this would be an issue in a pottery. My wife got involved doing some outreach with orphanages. So she could help. Working in that environment made me realize that if artists have any responsibility in their lives, the major one is to speak to their time and culture.

I grew up in a landscape that was vast, and that vastness now is a very important part of my work. When you're in a small town on the prairie, you're an island, and the sea around you is the prairie. And when I was on that island of Jamaica with the water around me, I really began to get the isolation that growing up on the plains was all about. Even though I've lived in the Rocky Mountains for many years now, the vastness of the prairie landscape punctuated by buildings and barns affects the way I think about cups and saucers on a table. So those years spent watching huge skies and sunsets and the way weather moved across the landscape is really what my work is all about. The wood and soda firing that Casebeer does now is "atmospheric" not just in the technical sense, but as a metaphor.

The first year in Jamaica he concentrated on *designing objects for a domestic market—pitchers, casseroles. Because of their being an English colony for so many years, it took on this English sort of refinement in look. It wasn't my work.*

He also had to adapt his behavior. The shop steward clued him in on one aspect, telling him, *"You know, until you go around and say good morning to everyone around here and show some respect, they're not going to do anything for you."* At that point, two things happened. I understood that she was schooling me in what it was to honor these people. I began to understand that what I was given as a gift in life was this ability to make stuff with my hands and share it with other people. And they were doing the same thing, just in a different context. Right from that point on, I went around saying good morning, good morning, good morning, I'm so glad you're here, thank you for coming to work today, and everything was better.*

I began to take photographs and make drawings of my environment. It was through that observation that I got my artistic voice back. I made a body of work that honored the place in which they lived and worked, and it had to do with the buildings and the homes and the shops. He first did drawings and took photographs. He picked 36 buildings that he drove by on his way to work each day, and made plates that featured those buildings. They were exhibited in a small gallery. *I picked three for myself, and the remainder were sold. And I felt—my wife and I had a long conversation about this—that monetary remuneration was not what I was looking for. We find joy and excitement in what we do, and we share it with others. There is an obligation.*

Casebeer and his wife donated the proceeds of the sale to an orphanage for babies under two that was located behind one of the worst buildings on the block. *We bought blankets and bottles and cribs and things like that and delivered them to the orphanage. That lesson still lives with me today. It's a very Christian value; maybe it's just a universal*

value: to give is to receive.

I got the sense of community, the connectedness of how potters need to work within their community, and then their community will support them and sustain their livelihood. Which is what I'm involved in to this day. At the Anderson Ranch we're all about developing networks among students and workshop participants, so when they go home and when they travel they have this connectivity.

I have three projects, four projects in the world that I'm still involved in, one being the Anderson Ranch. I still travel to Jamaica every year, and I do outreach, I go into rural school districts, and I do in-service work with art teachers and school children. But along the way I also got involved with a pottery in Kathmandu [Nepal]. So I have this ongoing project and they call. And in the last seven or eight years, several of us, Randy and Jan Johnston and Suze Lindsay and Kent McLaughlin, we're involved with an art center outside Santiago, Chile. It's all about bringing people together to support each other in this ceramic activity, and people being able to go back to their communities to share that wealth of knowledge. The Nepali project is just incredible. After I left Nepal, Ani Kasten picked up the load and was there for several years helping to further develop glazes. Same people, same project. It's amazing how we're all kind of connected in some way. Clay is the material that keeps me sane, but it's also the field that's allowed me to effect positive social change.

I really believe to do good is to do the right thing. Through what I've been given as a gift in my life, there's this opportunity to share and develop a community around functional pots. I don't take it for granted. I often think that clay saved me. [Laughter] *I'm going to celebrate the value of the handmade object at all levels and in all capacities. I will look at everything, listen to everything. It's not that I always like or agree with what somebody's doing, but the fact that they put themselves out there to say something about who they are or their culture, more power to them. I think that's fantastic.*

Early on, when I told my dad I wanted to go to art school, he said, "I don't understand that. How are you going to support your family? What's the future in that? Even if you want to teach, how are you going to make a living at that?" Long before I'd ever listened to or read anything Joseph Campbell wrote, I realized if I'm not following any sense of bliss in my life, I'm not a whole person. My mom understood it. It took my dad a while to see that me being passionate about what I wanted to do with my life was me being happy and healthy and whole, and all the other stuff would fall into place.

Ceramics has shown me the world.

I had this insatiable curiosity about what else is out there. That took me to Nepal in '85, to help set up a pottery pilot project that now is exporting work all over Asia and Europe, into the States. It's called Thimi Ceramics. And the Ranch has been really wonderful because it's allowed me to maintain these relationships and develop connections.

The Ranch was somewhat of a parochial, regional little summer art center. I was hired in '84 to come in and build facilities, build program. They were hiring my interest in the bigger world.

The very first kiln I ever built was a wood kiln. I built it in '76 and the thing never fired right, never got hot. Wood or soda firing, atmospheric firing is a huge part of my work. Wood firing also offered this sort of athletic participation which was really important for me because I could be present with the process of finishing the pot.

Architecture plays a huge part in the way I think and organize space. Profiles, eaves, roofs, chimneys, stacks; not that it's a literal translation but it's a conceptual translation in terms of organizing and composing objects in space. The relationship of cubes and squares and cylinders to a plane has always interested me. I look towards temples and mandirs and stupas and grain elevators and barns and things like that as a way to conceptualize form and shape. I try different clay bodies or work on different glazes or adapt my firing process in different ways, but I think I fundamentally go back to this architectural vernacular in the rural landscape. Barns are the cathedrals on the landscape.

While this orientation lends itself best to jars, Casebeer has made a range of objects in more production-oriented work. *One of my best clients was a local hotel. When the hotel changed hands, the new owners changed its style. I sat down with the person I'd been working with, and we figured out that over the course of the 15 years I had made 18,000 pieces for that hotel.* Those include soap dishes for handmade bars of soap and ashtrays for the hotel's cigar bar. *When you get out of our insular pottery scene in North America and you travel, you'll see that potters are making things for needs in their community. Hand-thrown roof tiles. Hand-thrown troughs for chickens to feed from.*

There's a younger generation of makers coming through our field that is enthusiastic about placing the handmade object. I don't think there's a better time to be making pots than right now. I think our culture needs it. I mean it's the day and age of computers and digital information and rapid prototyping and 3-D printers. But the fact that you can leave a fingerprint on a cup and that's a record of your presence with that material, it's pretty phenomenal, that record of history and time. ■

SANDY SIMON

A Lifetime Commitment

Sandy Simon outside
Trax Gallery, 2013

Sandy Simon (née Lindstrom) was part of an extraordinary class studying ceramics with Warren MacKenzie at the University of Minnesota. Mark Pharis, Wayne Branum, Randy Johnston, and Michael Simon (soon to be her husband) all were students at the same time. Simon has long been associated with the Bay Area of California, where she established Trax Ceramics Gallery in 1994 and, through that showcase and her own work, has advanced the pottery community in Northern California and the market nationally.

Simon (b. 1949) spent most of her early life in St. Cloud, an hour north of Minneapolis. She had two younger brothers, both of whom lived troubled lives. Her father was an orphaned farm boy who grew up to be a banker. *He was a harsh father figure; he wasn't ever really loving. I don't think he ever supported me financially or spiritually, because of gender. He favored my brothers. My mother was a nurse, and she was wonderful and really supportive. She always let us make our own decisions. I grew up quickly as a result of that because I had to be responsible for my decisions. And I was a swimmer. I was really disciplined that way. I think that the biggest obstacle that people come up against when they're their own boss and when they're artists is the discipline, getting to the studio and making that the first choice of the day.* Athletic demands shaped her, she believes.

Needing to pay her own way through college, Simon chose the University of Minnesota. It was only $350 a quarter at the time, and she made $1,500 over the summer as a lifeguard. She also got scholarships and loans. But she didn't actually finish *because you could not get a degree in ceramics back then. I was really, really enjoying it. Mark Pharis didn't finish either. We were in that studio all the time! And Michael Simon, he was my first love, and he and I married in 1970. I was 20. He was 23. At the university, I was taking watercolor classes and drawing and painting, and Michael was in ceramics.* And that's what drew her there. *It was in a separate building from the rest of the art department. Next door was sculpture and the foundry, and that was raging at that time, lots of energy. Lots of fun and there were no rules whatsoever. You could work all night long, all weekend long. If you wanted to tear down a wall you could. Rebuild a kiln. There were no safety features on the kilns.*

Curt Hoard was teaching alongside Warren. I remember being so frustrated with the wheel. I thought I would never get it. That whole studio was full of Leach treadle wheels. That is another way of working, where your whole body is in motion. But anyway, I was smitten.

There was a lot of drinking, and everybody partied together. Warren had lost his wife, Alix, about two years prior, so he was available as a partier, that was for sure. And Curt too. We did a lot of things with Curt. He would have shows. He was a big promoter that way, just the opposite of Warren. He would tell us how to build a slide library, how to take photos of our work. And one semester he found that they were tearing down boilers in downtown Minneapolis, and he relegated all of us in his class to go get that brick. We spent the entire quarter picking fire brick up and cleaning it. My hands were bloody; there were calluses. It ended up being one of the most valuable lessons of my life because it taught me that free things are available and you have to work to get them. It was a powerful lesson, and I used it several years later, living in Georgia.

That was at Jerry Chappelle's Happy Valley Farm. He had been a graduate student at the University of Minnesota and bought a farm outside Athens, Georgia, when he got a job at the University of Georgia. Pharis and Branum were building fireplaces for income and went down briefly to help Chappelle raise his.

Michael and I had ordered Leach wheels from London, and when they finally came in a box, we put them in our pitiful old van that barely ran, and we drove down to Georgia. It was during the time of Easy Rider, *and I remember seeing people with rifles in their pickup truck windows. I was terrified. We did get stopped by the police a lot. They wanted to see our driver's licenses, and they would go through our van and finally the question, "What are you, hippies? We don't like hippies down here!"*

Anyway, they were kind of hostile.

Just the opposite happened when we finally got there and settled. People were just wonderful and so friendly. You would go to this big old hardware store and tell them what you were trying to do, and they would just get everything you needed, tell you how to do it. We learned a lot those early years. We arrived in Georgia and we stayed in the Chappelles' house. They had three children, and we helped them by babysitting, but I look back on that time now and I don't know how they tolerated us. I mean we had no money and they fed us, really looked out for us, you know, and in exchange we babysat. Not a really fair deal.

We decided we could live in this chicken coop on their property if we cleaned it out. It was full of chicken litter, old chicken manure, and a dead horse and a Coke machine. We just worked our butts off and we cleaned out one end of it, the most beautiful end that had the view overlooking the woods and the pond. And it had a hard clay floor underneath, so you actually could sweep it and it would be clean. We used that Coke machine for a refrigerator because it still ran. We cooked on a campfire outside our chicken coop.

We were there two years. We eventually built an outhouse. For a long time we had a hole in the ground out in the woods, with a stick you could sit on. And then we built a little bit of furniture. We had a nice stereo (Laughter)—that's where we put our money. Jerry had these big birthday parties—they were called Scorpio Risings—every November. People came from all over, van loads of people. They would pour bronze, and they would have glass blowing and they had raku. It culminated in a pig roast. It was a five-day event. Lot of drugs and alcohol, of course. It was a lot of wonderful energy.

The Simons heard about a sugar refinery that had closed. We asked all the other tenants, who were all involved in clay in some way except for Gary [Nofke, a metalsmith], if they wanted to come down help us get the brick, rent a big truck. And no one wanted to. So Michael and I went; we did all the work and we brought these big burners back too. They were for firing oil in the big beehive kilns. And then we decided we didn't want to stay at Happy Valley Farm anymore. I always felt that I was carrying the load for everybody. If we had a pottery sale where everyone would participate, I was the

one who made the cards, I was the one who did the mailing list. There's always people like that, and I've always been that person.

They found a nearby house to rent for $30 a month, which was two dollars cheaper than what we were paying for the chicken coop. The whole community opened up once we moved away. People came by and everybody was helpful. They helped us plant a garden; they plowed our field. It was wonderful. Southern hospitality—it really exists.

We used to sneak in to the University of Georgia and fire their kilns at night. We never took their materials; we always bought our own materials. But when the head of the department, Earl McCutcheon, found out we were doing it he fired Jerry Chappelle [Laughter], I guess as a result. I really didn't see the wrong in what we were doing. I see it now, of course, but there's a lot of things I didn't see when I was 20 years old. Anyway, when we couldn't fire at the University of Georgia anymore or use their clay mixer, we mixed our clay with our feet, in a big tub that we made that was like a cement tub, because we couldn't afford a clay mixer. It was wetter than you would normally do in a dough mixer, which is all we knew to have. Eventually we had enough money to buy a pug mill, and we started mixing clay for other people too, to make a little extra money. We did art fairs; that's how we made our living. If we made $600 in a weekend we felt rich; then we would go to the beach and stay for a week, then we would drive back to Georgia and start the cycle all over again.

We moved there probably in 1972 or '3. I was asked to come teach at the Chicago Art Institute in 1978. I had never really liked country living. I mean I appreciate it, I respect it, but it's just not for me. I need more going on. When the opportunity came, I went, and I just knew I wasn't going to come back. Michael and I divorced eventually.

The Art Institute was at a point of doing everything conceptually, and they had gotten rid of all their tools because they wanted students to just think. And the classes were one whole day, once a week, so it was quite a different program. Which was nice for me because I brought my wheel and I made work in the basement.

My pots really shifted then. I fired them in a salt kiln, I used stoneware instead of porcelain because it just seemed warmer. It was a cold climate, and you kind of want to feel that warmth of brown clay. I had some really nice pots come out of that one firing. Basically I was very social, so I didn't do a lot of work, but I think I was a good teacher. I was terrified of doing it because I never had taught before. There was a big push, at that time, to get women onto the faculty. It was not just that school; it was lots of schools. I went to Purdue next, then I went to Tennessee, the Appalachian Center for Crafts, which is where I met Bob [Brady] in 1980.

Susan Peterson was the director. She called me when I was teaching at Purdue and said, "I have this job opportunity for you. We will pay your way. Will you come for an interview?" And I said, "Yeah, I'm interested," because I didn't have a permanent job there, even though they did want me to stay. I went down to interview, and she told me I had the job, but there was one more person they were going to interview. That was Bob Brady. She asked me what color I wanted the walls painted, what kind of kilns did I want to buy. It was a pretty sure thing I was going to be hired. Well, she fell in love with Bob when he got there. He was kind of like that. She calls me and she says, "I am really, really embarrassed to tell you this, but they hired Bob Brady. But I want you to come, too, so we are going to create a position for you." It was a studio manager. They had them in every department, studio manager, but I think I got a little more money than the other people. We got a free place to live, room and board, and I think $12,000 a year. But there was nowhere to go and nothing to do, so that was money.

I called Bob on the phone to introduce myself, and I thought he was the biggest asshole. He said, "I'm expecting an important call. I can't talk right now." [Laughter] I just went, "Hey, I'm an important call. Tell me when you are going to call me back." He was the last to arrive, and my impression of him was "Wow, I never ever saw a clay person who looked like this." He got out of his white El Camino pickup—do you know what those look like? They're really sleek; they're like sedans but only a pickup. They're kind of a collector's item now. He had on Björn Borg tennis clothes, very fancy tennis clothes, and Adidas tennis shoes, and he had all these Mexican silver amulets; he had one necklace and he had a bracelet, and he had a green bandana on his head. We were having a faculty meeting already when he got there, and he came in and he lay on the floor

under the table and he put his legs up on a chair. I'm just going, "Who is this guy?" Well, he realized what happened in the job situation. He treated me equally. We critiqued; we were both faculty in terms of . . . in the eyes of the Lord. [Laughter]

In the Appalachian Center's second year, they became a couple. Brady had taken a two-year leave from teaching at Sacramento State and decided he wanted to return. It was decided that I would go with him, and we moved to Crockett. We bought a house there, and it already had a studio, so that was great. We went to teach for the University of Georgia in Cortona, Italy, in 1983, when I was pregnant with Morgan, and that was a very wide-eyed experience. When we came back to California after that summer, we lived in Benicia for three years. And then in '86 we were asked to teach at Indiana University. They wanted both of us because one teacher had died and one was on sabbatical.

Simon and Brady sold their house, boat, and cars because the plan was that when they returned to California they would move into Peter Voulkos's building in Berkeley, which he had agreed to sell to them. But when they returned, Voulkos had done nothing about leaving the building. He gradually vacated over several months. When they finally had access, Bob said it is the only time he has seen me cry. Because it's this huge building, it is so big, it's 65,000 square feet, and it was empty and it was in such bad shape. The sheet metal had big holes in it, there was no inner wall, and we had to sleep in the front, which was less than 30 feet from the railroad tracks. When a train would go by—and they always blare their horn right at the intersection there—the whole building would shake, and I would feel like I was tied to the railroad track.

By the time we finally got the furniture moved in, we hired a contractor; we did some remodeling; we actually made it a really nice space. That building was wonderful to own, really was. All kinds of just really good energy in it.

That's where she started Trax Gallery, named for its proximity to the railroad. I wanted to have a gallery because I was so tired of potters not having a really nice place to show their work, where it wasn't compromised in some way. I have always believed that it was equal to any piece of art and that it should have the same status as far as display goes. I wanted to honor the people I knew who had committed their *life to making pots.*

We built another floor in the front. So you would enter from the railroad track on the north side and go up some stairs. It was about 500 square feet. And we did it really economically. They colored the plywood floor with bright-green aniline dye. *Everybody commented on the beauty of it. And then I had some display shelving made that was bright yellow, aniline dye, too. It sounds shocking, but the pots were really beautiful on them.*

After a few years they sold the building and moved to their current location, a few blocks away, where they built on vacant land. They live over the gallery and Simon's studio, which are in front, with Brady's studio and a guest suite in back.

Well anyway, other than adjunct teaching and raising children, I've had the gallery since 1994. When I first started it, the city would only let me be open by appointment. I look back on that and I wish I had that again. Because now I'm open regular store hours, and it's a very demanding schedule to have to be here noon to 5:30 every day except for Monday and Tuesday. I have had lots of help over the years, but just part time. And I finally realized why people don't sell functional pots in galleries. You just can't make enough money. If I had to pay rent I would never be here, never. And frankly, Warren MacKenzie's sales is what is holding this whole operation up. It has for the last few years. My goal originally was to be able to actually support a few potters. That has never happened, and it won't happen in my lifetime.

When I'm having a show at Trax I have to unpack work, label it, photograph it, upload it to the web, you know. Gallery business has changed tremendously since the internet, and it is three times the amount of work that it used to be. I sell about 80 percent online.

California has never been the best for supporting potters, primarily because Arneson was here, Voulkos was here, and they are not potters. All of the galleries that I knew that sold pots didn't keep on.

I would love to have enough success with the gallery that I could afford to hire someone permanently, afford to pay health insurance for them or whatever it takes so I could have more freedom. It takes a really good person, and you want to pay them enough to make it worth their while. At the most I have had two days a week, maybe three

sometimes, and I have somebody on call if I need it. It takes overseeing by me almost all the time. I guess maybe I am a control freak, but I want to know what's going on, and I want to know that the buyers have been tended to in a respectful way and that they get an email with their UPS document that thanks them for their purchase, and they can see exactly what it cost them.

When I had a mailing list (before the mailing list went to email), my expenses for a show were $2,200. I did six shows a year probably. You have to sell a lot of pots to make up $2,200 just for expenses. So I get it, why people don't want to show pots. But now the dilemma for me is that there's all these online galleries. Many of them, she notes, don't have brick-and-mortar spaces and don't even have possession of the pieces they're offering for sale, which minimizes their expenses.

Simon's early pots were porcelain, thrown on a Leach treadle wheel—both a consequence of MacKenzie's influence. *Also I was highly influenced by Japanese pots and Japanese culture. I hadn't ever been to Japan at that time.*

At one point I was really excited about brushwork. The reason, I think, the Japanese like to do birds is because with thick slip rather than paint on a brush, real simple bold lines come more naturally than other shapes. I made deer on a lot of things; I made shrimp; I made cranes. I never thought of it as Japanese brushwork. We get this input now from all cultures, and everybody is getting influenced by one thing or another. I think that success is when you are influenced and move beyond it in your completion of the work.

Among the Minnesota influences was the limited palette of reduction firing. *But when I got to Tennessee in 1980 and met Bob, he came there with a whole palette of colors that I had never seen before. Never heard of a stain. I started using his colors, his stains, and I didn't fire the pots very high. Then people said that they were growing mold because they weren't vitrified. So then I started using white earthenware— because I definitely wanted them to hold water and be useful—so I could still use the color. So that was a big shift to my work in 1980.*

When we moved to Indiana, I used this image of a tulip that I had drawn, and then I would sandblast the whole pot except for the tulip. I really like those pots. I started sandblasting because I couldn't get the same clay that I had before. I had this porcelain clay body, and when I fired the pots they had like a sugar coating on the outside because the silica didn't melt. So I took them up to the sandblasting machine, and I tried to beat them down. But sandblasting is not fun.

And then I had a show in Japan in 1988 or '89 I think, and I was using red clay and some white clay. That group of pots was really strong; I really liked them. And that's when I started using nichrome wire too, using it for handles and just visually. My idea initially was to put a big lump of clay in the palm of my hand that I would use as a teapot handle so that I could grab it, but I didn't want a big, heavy lump attaching to the body of the pot, so I used this thick nichrome wire and that held it up. It looked like it was levitating above the pot. I really enjoyed that look. I got a lot of feedback from people who didn't like it. I remember Mark Pharis said, "Can sure tell you ran off to California."

She put color on the inside. *I feel these are very sculptural. If you squint and look at that contour of this pot, I want every little curve and detail to matter. There is nothing in conflict; it's in harmony. Then there is surprise inside.* When it's on the outside, all you see is the color; you don't see the contour, you don't see the volume, and you don't see the shape of the pot.

My choice is to fire it in an electric kiln with a clear glaze because there is not a lot of action on the surface then, and I think it shows the form better.

And I am really concerned about the form. That's what I 'm working on.

A few years ago Simon made a striking change to green. She had a supply of a red clay on which a porcelain slip fit perfectly, and she began to apply Lisa Orr's green glaze. *There is no problem with it lifting off or anything. And that is a real fortunate thing, you know. I didn't have to do a lot of testing. I've had a lot more success selling this green, at least right now. I really liked it just because the warmth of the green. It's like a mineral pool. Green is also known as a healing color, and people are responding to it for that reason.*

I love making cups, and there is so much that goes into them in terms of getting them to feel good, to be the right weight, have the right depth. And you could never make the right cup for everybody because it has a lot to do with how you drink. When I was young and living in Georgia and Minnesota, I never took milk in my coffee, always black. And so Michael and I always made really small cups, and they were kind of thick so they really kept the heat. But then after I went to Italy and started making cappuccinos, cups got bigger and wider because they have to be low to fit under the cappuccino spigot. I could make cups for the rest of my life and be content.

This is why potters make things over and over. It's not because they want to repeat themselves. It is because they are looking for the best form, how to better it. ■

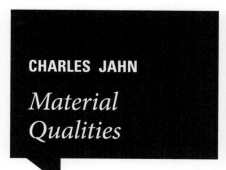

CHARLES JAHN

Material Qualities

Charles Jahn and Moko with burry box kiln at his new studio, LaPorte, Indiana, 2018. *Photo: Mie Kongo*

Charles Jahn's family owned a Chicago-based international manufacturing business, and after art school he started his own business, manufacturing dinnerware. Eventually he gave up both in favor of his personal work, which is obsessed with the characteristics of raw materials. His reserved, reductive pots convey that focus even to the viewer who knows nothing about the chemistry or physics of pottery.

Process is almost as important as form. Utility drives the work, but process is a real passion for me. How do you find the best-quality material and then how do you understand the nature of that material and unlock it or elevate it so that it can illuminate its own inherent beauties? That's a lot like how some cultures cook. They think about the beauty of a particular vegetable or a specific fish, and they find ways to make that fish become the most delicious thing you could ever eat. [Laughter]

I look at the pots that I'm interested in. The Sackler-Freer Gallery is an incredible resource for these pots. I can go to the stacks and they bring the pots out to me, and I get a feeling of what glazes looked like 300 years ago. We've become so used to pharmaceutically refined materials, we've adapted our aesthetic sensibilities to what can be achieved with those modern materials. And it's changed our perception of what beauty is, in a way. The historic pots are a result of attention to detail.

I limit my choice to the rice husk ash, mixed ashes, hardwood ashes, a pine ash, and a crushed stone, and my stone is coming from the Custer people but I get it differently. It looks like cat litter. It's really quite coarse. It's a combination of many of their veins of feldspar. The reason I've done that is because I wanted to get in a step above their processing. There's a lot impurities in the stage I get the material in, and I didn't want those things taken out. From reading things, especially Wilson [Richard L. Wilson, *Inside Japanese Ceramics*], *it was clear that light refracts differently on larger particles. With a feldspar that looks like sand, about 60 mesh, it makes this beautiful opalescence. So I'm fascinated with how you process, or how you treat, or how you understand a material in its raw state. And how it has such an effect on the end result of the glaze.*

Jahn's interests are not shallow. Ask him about rice husk ash, for instance, and he describes a realm. *It's a process where you strip the outside of the husk*

of the rice to make white rice, and the shell is then a waste product or a byproduct and they're currently using it as a fuel. In southern Louisiana they're taking that husk off and they're fueling electrical power plants with it. They burn it and they spin a generator with the steam off that. And it goes on golf courses as an absorbent material. It goes into foundries to cool big castings. They use it as an oil-absorbent material when there's an oil spill. For a potter, it's a really interesting source of silica because it's 90 percent silica and it's about 10 percent carbon, so it's jet black, ink black, until you reach red heat, and then it turns white when the carbon burns off. So it's a fascinating material because it's very different from flint. I could use silica in a bag, you know, flint. Yet, the quality of glaze if I use silica is entirely different.*

He pays the same intense regard to the character of the clay. *I avoid using feldspar in my clay because I want the clay to remain very open. It has a softness to it when you don't add feldspar to the clay, and I think that's again where in commercial bodies we're very accustomed to; it's almost like this is a must. But it's not necessary to add feldspar to your clay unless it's not fitting to the glaze. When you do that you really change the quality of the clay. It gets very tight and it shrinks more, it fluxes, it starts to melt. We think that it needs this, but when you look at Japanese pots, they're soft, they're open, they [don't have] a high-tone ring. And that makes a softer feel in the end. The clay isn't reaching maturity in terms of vitrification. I think that in that openness there's more of a connection between the underneath body and the slip and the glaze.*

Jahn can name the source of this attitude. Although he was born in Chicago (in 1957), the youngest of four children, *my family lived and still does in northern Michigan in the Straits of Mackinaw. All summer I was there in northern Michigan. I lived on an island with my mother while my father stayed* in Chicago and worked. *My mother lived with us kids on a very remote wilderness where there's no electricity, no running water for many years; we drank from the lake. We were restoring a 100-year-old lighthouse. My father was a builder, too, and he would give us projects and we'd be building and he'd go off and he'd come back two weeks later.*

Jahn thinks that the sense of freedom he experienced there *allowed me to hold on to that creativity, and I think that it's a really important part of being a potter, who I am. I know that the surfaces that I'm interested in come from walking the beach, where there's stones—it's a limestone beach—and then the forest is right there, and it's a wall of cedar. So these material qualities were very pure, and they're very influential to me. To this day, I return to that place.*

There's one point in my earliest memory: my mother's reading me a book on Egyptian potters. I'm probably about six years old. It was fascinating. I identified with the hierarchy within the village and what the pottery meant. I felt myself there and then. That stuck with me. I made objects in school from first grade on. Then in high school I met a very important teacher who saw that I was fascinated with clay, and she kept exposing me to more things. I was hooked after that. I went to Northern Michigan University in Marquette, Michigan, for two years, and then I went to the School of the Art Institute of Chicago for four years after that. I could feel the stigma in that school, where painting was first, sculpture was second, and who knows what ceramics was. And ceramics was sort of pushing back and trying to be something of its own, and I could see a community beginning in that way.

I think that from early on I wanted material qualities, and it was always a love of pots that I was seeing in the museums. Those were sustaining my interest far more than contemporary work. He appreciated that instructors saw beauty in historical work or were strong on the technical side of things. At the SAIC he also worked with the painting department, where the influence of Chicago's Hairy Who artists meant that some people were open to historical and primitive qualities. He earned a BFA, but *I didn't think I needed an MFA. I had studied six years. I wanted to make my own work and make pots.*

I worked with a potter, Robert Rosenbaum. And then I began to make pots with industrialized processes after that because I wanted to run a pottery where I could be self-supporting. I spent ten years, actually a little more than that, making lines of work that were designed and made as a hybridization of mechanical forming processes and hands-on work. Under the name Charles Jahn Pottery he was spin-pressing (also called jiggering) and ram-pressing with a hydraulic press. *I would go to trade shows, and I developed a clientele of small shops that were selling tablewares and gift wares.*

I made a group of work that was porcelain with a blue slip on top and then a chatter pattern, chattering with an iron tool. At the height of that we were supplying 80 stores in the country. I had two other people working with me. And we'd be making more than 300 pieces a week, a lot. There were two big car kilns. And it was a production. That was interesting, yet it was very limiting because I was providing the public with what they wanted, not so much what I wanted. I got to a point where I said, "I want to move away from this." I started teaching more, part time, and then I taught half of the week (part time) at the Art Institute for ten more years.

About 2005 Jahn stopped teaching and stopped making his production work. He built a wood-fire kiln. He jokes that if this was a midlife crisis, it was a good one. And he notes that he wasn't going so far afield from what he had been doing, because *the beauty of making that production was utility. Those forms were really functional and people responded to them. I sold many, many sets of dinnerware. And people are still on eBay trying to find it and sell it and asking me if I will ever make it again. But I don't want to do it. I want to make this work that I'm doing now with these simple materials.*

When he made the change, he was too far along in life to think about apprenticeship in Japan. *I wish I could have had the experience because I think I could have used it really well.* He cites the example of Richard Milgrim: *he has access to very, very highly guarded secrets and glaze technology from that country. When you look at his glazes, right before your eyes are the best shino glazes and the best Amé and the Yellow Setos. They're exquisite.*

Wilson says so eloquently that it's about the source of materials, it's about understanding process. That's what makes a Japanese pot a Japanese pot. And we can adapt that, using our own materials here. I think that it gets us to the core, for me, of what pot making is. It's utility, it's process, and material. Three things really.

I look at Japanese forms, and I travel with my partner to Tokyo—her family's from there—so I understand those forms. I want to make pots that have a place here for the American public, yet I also want to hold on to what's important to me.

At the time he made the change, his family asked him to take over responsibility for the business that his father had developed, which produced ceiling suspension systems. They said: "*You understand some about this business, and we really need you." So I did it and it's been a good experience. We stabilized that business.* He then took a communications role, running the board and managing a group of 35 shareholders and coordinating both with the company's management. *It took five years to get to [that] place of organization.* The firm has just under a thousand employees; manufactures in the US, Europe, and Asia; and sells all over the world.

It's a bit about stewardship. There's a desire to just take care of this thing because there's many people who work there and it's a good livelihood for a lot of people, and how can you maintain this? And there's an interest in me in terms of manufacturing things, and I think that came very early from my father, from the experience as a child of being in the factory.

It allowed me to have the financial grounding to be in my studio, to let that thing run and be separate enough from it so that I can focus on my work again. Jahn was able to spend at least 50 percent of his time in the studio. But in 2012 they decided to ensure the company's longevity by selling it to a larger business. And at that point Jahn's sense of stewardship shifted to the natural world, and he bought an 80-acre farm in northern Indiana and is returning it to indigenous hardwoods and native prairies. He has planted more than 14,000 trees!

Jahn fires in a new wood kiln built in 2018 by Donovan Palmquist. He shows his work at Trax Gallery, having known Sandy Simon since her teaching stint at the Art Institute of Chicago. *I sell a lot to Chicago artists, and that's very rewarding. I like that painters and sculptors have my work in their kitchen. That's a beautiful thing. And [Trax is] a place where I can sell work, and they understand what goes into it and they can communicate that to people who are purchasing the work. I think,*

beyond that, I can't ask for more. I want the pieces to be used.

Yet, if I look at what it costs in terms of time, material, and space—that's a very logical way to look at it; you need to understand your cost structure and where you live—clearly I'm supporting what I do now by this other [income]. Richard Milgrim's pots are $4,000, $5,000 dollars here, and they're much more in Japan, and he can make a very comfortable living. But I think there's just very few people in this country that can sell enough and charge enough to be at a very comfortable level with income.

I stopped using the jigger or the ram press because you always have the quality of the plaster when you're pushing clay against a wall instead of stretching clay in different ways. Stretching is direct communication with the individual. I mean, everyone who's stretching clay is going to stretch it differently. And that's what brings vitality to a handmade pot.

The present time to me is about listening and engaging, taking in as much as I'm giving out to the work. You could relate that to many things; our breath, everything. I'm listening to what that clay will do and how aged it is, what I can throw with it. I'm engaged with this group of pots that I'm making at this time, and it's never going to be able to be made again. Even though I could go back and make the same pots over again, they're going to be different. I've made cups for friends in weddings. I made 400 cups, and you look at the cups' middle, beginning, end, and they're different. It was a challenge to me: How am I going to stay alive in this, and how am I going to make this interesting?

Things that are core here are engagement with nature, and the unpredictability of nature, and how do you embrace and work with that? I love the fact that I'm overpowered by this process and there's things I cannot control. I'm a sailor, and I love to be on the water because it's the only experience I get in this world of being up against nature and knowing just how small I am and just how powerful this world is. I want that in the work. ■

MARY BARRINGER

Drawn to Limitations

Mary Barringer in her studio
in western Massachusetts,
2013. *Photo: J. Doster*

Mary Barringer (pronounced with a hard *g*) was for ten years the editor of *Studio Potter* magazine, after the long reign of its founding editor, Gerry Williams. Following a founder is not easy, and a magazine that consists of volunteered articles from nonprofessional writers can't be easy to edit. Barringer, who lives and works in western Massachusetts, was well established as a potter and intimately acquainted with the issues that the magazine might wish to consider, and she skillfully held it together as a social and intellectual center for the field.

Barringer was born in 1950 in the Pennsylvania outskirts of Wilmington, Delaware, where her father was a chemist for DuPont and a history buff. *My parents were very much hands-on people. They bought an old house, which they worked on through my entire childhood. We had a huge garden. My mother sewed all our clothes. There was an orchard. So there was a lot of handwork going on in our house, although it was not creative in the professional sense. Neither one of them would define themselves as artists. My parents didn't know any real artists, but Andrew Wyeth was our local guy. It wasn't as though I had any direct contact with him, or any real clear idea of what his life was like, but I would say that he exemplified a level of identity and seriousness about an art practice being not just what you did but who you were.*

Barringer took art classes in school and in a summer program for high schoolers at Pratt Institute in Brooklyn. She went to Bennington College in Vermont, which *was as close as I probably could have gotten at that point in my life to a serious study*

of art in college. I was there at the sort of last gasp of high modernism. Isaac Witkin taught sculpture, and when she told him she planned to do figurative sculpture, *he said everything that could be done with the figure had already been done.* [Laughter] *And I should learn how to weld. Isaac made it clear that there was only one kind of thing that could be sculpture, and that was welded David Smith, Tony Caro, Isaac Witkin kind of sculpture.*

While I was in college, so many things got their lids blown off. Not just art, not just the discussion of what art was, but also the discussion of many hierarchies in society, and many systems of value and thought, including what our foreign policy was, which was the first place that I started questioning things, and the women's movement. The hierarchy of the art world was very much a part of that in my college experience. Choosing ceramics was part of the repudiation of that hierarchy. Ceramics at the time seemed to me an anti-art. [Laughter] *And also an art form that was democratic, that was accessible, that had at least the potential—not that I had this* very well thought through—of being integrated into the larger culture.

I can still remember the first thing we did in my first ceramics class, which involved feeling the clay. It involved mixing a clay body, like having piles of the dry clay, the different kinds of clay, all out on a big table so that we could actually feel the difference between fire clay and ball clay. And then kind of mixing them all up and adding water, doing this communal mixing thing on the table. I was pretty much hooked at this point. No, we didn't taste it. [Laughter] But there was certainly a smell. I think those of us who are in clay studio all the time forget about that smell, that kind of earthy smell that clay has and that the clay studio has. That was it for me! [Laughter] I said goodbye to sculpture.

The ceramics teacher, Stanley Rosen, had a sort of tortured relationship with throwing as a process, which he passed on to all of us. He made it seem like it was really, really hard. [Laughter] If I'd learned to throw from somebody who was good at it and loved it and thought it was easy, that might have changed how long it took me to learn how to throw. [Laughter]

We all went on the obligatory field trip to Bennington Potters, which we weren't as interested in as we should have been, because it's a factory. Let's just say Bernard Leach would not have enjoyed a visit to Bennington Potters. Leach was our god, and the idea of the shop where the potter is doing everything, including writing influential books [Laughter], that was really swallowed completely undigested and unexamined [Laughter], there not being any other real models.

Bennington had a nonresident term, still does, so in the winter, January and February, you weren't in school; you were supposed to be doing something related to your studies. I went on a cross-country trip with a friend and went to all the potters I could find. The way I found them was I went to the ACC offices when they were next to the Modern [in New York City]. Down in the basement they had a file drawer with 3-by-5 cards in it organized by medium. So knowing more or less where I was going to go, I just wrote down a bunch of names and addresses and phone numbers. Everybody was in there. It wasn't that big of a world then. So I took this address book and headed out across the country with my friend, driving, and we just would call people up and go visit them. [Laughter] Sometimes we'd stay on their floor. [Laughter]

The first place we went was Karen [Karnes]'s, in Stony Point [New York]. I can remember the impact that seeing her in her studio had on me. I'm thinking I'm going to be a studio potter, but I hadn't seen many women doing this; there weren't a ton of examples. Seeing her whole studio full of work, and the way she organized her life around her studio practice, and there she was. I think that's the difference between theoretical role models and physical role models. She was never a teacher of mine, but she was so important to me as an idea. And that came because of actually meeting her. I met other women when I was on this trip, although not nearly as many women as I met men, but I would have to say that nobody stuck with me as an image of what I wanted to be the way that Karen did. I think one of the really important changes in our field is the number of departments headed by women, and the number of teaching positions.

When I started out, despite my having gone to see all these potters and sculptors, what was running through my veins was Leach, and Daniel Rhodes. Rhodes was the how-to, and Leach was the why-to. And my idea of pots was very narrow. They're all about form, they had to be reduction fired [Laughter], there are only like four legitimate glazes that a potter would use [Laughter], and electric kilns and decoration and those sort of things were so far outside the pale [Laughter]—they were like housewife things. You could see it as masculine. You could also see it as a kind of formalist ideal about pottery. As amazed as I am by the kind of surface decoration that is going on now, I have to say I still in my heart of hearts believe that good decoration will not save a bad form. [Laughter]

I had a friend in college who was an economics major, and her boyfriend was a potter. He had a day job, something on Wall Street. Our plan was that the three of us would go someplace, and Rhoda would get a job and Richard and I would set up a studio and be potters. We ended up in Hartford because Rhoda got a job there. I lived there for almost 20 years, actually. And that was another important step in changing my worldview, in that what you're supposed to do with your Bennington education is to move to New York and become an artist. Moving to a place that is not really on anybody's map; I mean Hartford is more like a joke than a place. [Laughter] It's close to New York and Boston; that's the best you could say of it.

But actually Hartford had a very lively art scene in the '70s. It was a right-sized city for me. I could find my way into the local art scene. Moving to a place that isn't on the radar and discovering that there are serious artists there forces you to question the whole center/margin ideology, in which if anything is worth knowing about it will be in New York, and if it's not in New York it's not worth knowing about. So that sort of paralleled having chosen a marginal medium to work in. It all added up to an embracive marginality, of the potential that being marginal gives you to find your own voice.

The real-estate situation enabled Richard and me to find a place. We took out a $5,000 small-business loan. You can imagine what the neighborhood looked like for the bank to look at Richard and me and think that we were good candidates for a $5,000 loan. Richard was older than us; they would not have given me the loan by myself. Apartments were really cheap. So we could just get to work, which is what I wanted to do.

We had a storefront and then a place behind the storefront where we made our pots. And then we had an area in back where we taught classes, which was pretty laughable considering that . . . I mean, I did know more than my students, but only a little more. [Laughter] We were in that space for three years, and I would say that was where my education as a potter really began. I hadn't really given much thought to what pots are in modern life. I mean, I was in school. I was in an art department. So the discussion within an art department is about how these pots are art-like.

I thought my job was to make good pots, and that they would somehow sell. But I didn't understand my part in making a case for them, connecting with people around them, until I was forced to do that. And I was forced to do that by having a storefront. With $15 or $20 for a plate or a cup or a cooking pot, you could see people walking by. There are other stores around; you know that they're spending their money on something—you'd think if you put good pots out there they'd want to spend their money on this, and that would improve their lives [Laughter], and the world would get better. I think when you hang around with artists, a lot of times there's a kind of instinctive aggrievedness that artists have about the fact that people don't appreciate us and people don't understand what we do, and they don't value what we do.

My experience is that there are so many things in the world to look at and maybe buy that very often what connects people to objects or gets them from looking at it to deciding they want to have it actually has to do with the human encounter, not the power of the object. It might be the encounter with the maker, or a gallery person who you trust or who seems to speak your language, or it might be through a gift. There are a lot of ways that can happen, but the objects themselves don't necessarily carry that kind of mandate with them out into the world. It's all context. [Laughter] It's human context as well as sort of societal, spatial, conceptual context.

In Barringer's early work, there was a stony white glaze and a celadon and an Albany slip glaze. There might be a little decoration. And I made the whole range of different kinds of things. Thinking seriously about function had not been part of my training. In that sense I'm self-taught. Although I think I've had a strong training in visual language, the functional language came about in dialogue with a very vague buying public. And with images. You know there were images of pots in Craft Horizons and stuff like that. When you have a storefront, people are just wandering in, and they say idiotic things as well as useful things. You get the range. You find out what these pots look like to people.

To take somebody who had never used a hand-made cup and try to win them over, like why would this be better, is an ideological argument, but it's also a seduction, in a way. You're trying to introduce your own beliefs about what attention to a very mundane activity could give. Introduce that to somebody who maybe doesn't pay that kind of attention to those mundane activities. They just think of a cup as a kind of caffeine delivery system. [Laughter]

I could support myself. I think it's important to acknowledge that I got out of college without any debt. When I talk to young people now, I'm staggered by the amount of debt they take for granted as part of their future prospects, before they do anything. I know that influenced what I saw as possible and what I saw for myself in economic terms.

I don't know if I would have had the nerve to

do this on my own, quite apart from whether I could have gotten a small-business loan. Eventually we not only taught classes but rented space. So we had a little community there. I was a local potter for at least the first eight or nine years that I lived there. Central Connecticut was pretty much my turf. It suited me to be a local potter. We moved out to a place called the Farmington Valley Art Center. It's an old factory building that had been turned into studios. Our neighbors were artists. You could come and see artists at work. There was a gallery at one end. And so it was like an extra validation. During that time, Richard decided he really didn't want to be a potter. So I continued on my own.

I wasn't doing strictly functional work anymore. I started handbuilding in 1979 or '80. So I tapped into other parts of ceramic history, in a way. Because when you're not working at a wheel, you're in a whole different realm of history of the medium. I was feeling frustrated by the limitations of function as a driving force. I think I have a sort of oscillating relationship to limitations in general, where they serve as a kind of focusing mechanism and as a way to keep me from being just all over the map. I think potters are in some ways drawn to limitations. The form language of our medium pretty much sets out from the very beginning that you're not going to attempt to make something that's never been made before. If that's what you're interested in, don't become a potter. So you're already embracing the possibilities of permutations within a formal structure. I started making big handbuilt pots. They're not huge, but they're definitely bigger than the functional pots I was making. They were about an abstract idea of a vessel as opposed to the pot.

In '83, while I was making those kinds of pots, I moved back to Hartford to the Colt Building. It's a huge complex, and they had huge spaces, like 1,000 square feet. Lots of artists were moving in; a lot of them lived there. It was a great time to be there. And 1,000 square feet with utilities for $200 a month was pretty great. My friends from New York would come to visit and be blown away because they all worked like three jobs just to pay the rent. And I felt a little bit vindicated, I must say, having chosen to be in a place where I could keep working. My first show in a real art gallery as opposed to a craft gallery was probably in '83. I showed pots and drawings. It was the '80s. The line between art and craft was really going to just disappear for once and for all, right? [Laughter] There was a lot of crossover.

I participated a little bit in the scene outside my region. I used to go to Rhinebeck [ACC show], I did craft fairs, and I would occasionally enter juried shows. But my base was in Connecticut. And I was supported by that, in a way that I didn't fully appreciate until I left it and came up here. Art schools, galleries, that kind of concentration of places that people can rub up against each other; those don't exist in the same way in rural places. And I thought, wow, this is lonely up here.

I had lived in Hartford my entire adult life. And as I got into my 40s, that seemed a little scary to me. I was aware that I had landed in Hartford without making a really considered decision about it. It felt like time to shake things up. It suits me to figure out how to be an artist in places where there are people who do other things, some of which are by hand and some of which are serious practices which are outside the creative realm. I like living in a town that still has some farmers in it and has a range of people, and to have that as the backdrop to my life as an artist.

Another thing about moving to a small town; there's not as much real estate. You don't have as many options. I've always had a studio away from my house, since the very beginning. I rented the bottom of a barn on Route 2, and I was there for 11 years. I'd always kind of had my eye on this building, actually. It's been a bunch of things, but it struck me as being an ideal studio. A freestanding small building that is not on the main commercial street and also doesn't go with a house. There are very few of those in town.

I owned my house. Actually, my one and only smart decision in the real-estate market was to buy a two-family house in Hartford, discover that I was not cut out to be a landlady, but we lived in it for five years, and we sold it for more than twice what we had paid for it. Then we moved to a place where the money that we had from selling that house went a lot further.

In the early '90s I had a spell of teaching. That's when I started to be out in the national ceramics field more. I had started going to NCECA; I did a little bit of workshop teaching. In like '92, somebody approached me because they were looking for a *sabbatical replacement at Ohio State. They wanted a woman; they wanted somebody who had been in the studio; they wanted somebody to bring that studio experience into their teaching. They offered me the job, and I was really sort of terrified to go.*

Going someplace for six months was a big deal. I felt a little like a tourist in academia. [Laughter] *And for the next three years I did another visiting artist at Ohio University in Athens. Actually I got started teaching ceramic history at Ohio State because that's part of their curriculum. They usually try to fob that off on somebody coming in* [Laughter] *because it is a ton of work. It was sort of like a late-firing chromosome* [Laughter], *after all those years of living with my father, who loves history and has an extremely catholic interest in pretty much the history of anything. So our dinner table conversations often involved some boring droning* [Laughter] *of some sort of history, and I was like, "Why can't I have a normal father?" What interested me about it was that the history of ceramics has the potential to be the history of everything.*

Starting to teach kind of unleashed the part of me that's interested in things outside of what goes into my own work. There's a fairly clear link between that, in my mind, and Studio Potter. *That also used the parts of me that don't go directly into my work. The kind of outward looking.*

Barringer was already on the magazine's board. Williams *would have people guest edit a topical section of the magazine, and I think he was trying people out. I suspect that what he saw in me was somebody who had the same kind of polymath interest in the field as a whole and was also not institutionally aligned; someone who didn't come out of an academic background and yet saw that potters as a group are curious people.*

To be a potter at this point in history is very much a choice. We didn't take this up because it's what our families do or because we're indentured into it. So to choose to be a potter already involves some thinking and some active drawing of connections between what we do and both the world around us and the history of people who have done what we do. I think potters tend to be curious about a lot of the different ways that what we do intersects with the world, whether it's the natural world, the political world, the design world, the style world, or the art world. And Studio Potter *is really about that. It's*

really not about the object; it's about the mind of the maker.

Changing from working on the wheel to hand-building was a major shift for me, because the ways that my ideas are informed by process really changed. I think I'm very dependent on process. I love words and I love thinking about things, but it's really hard for me to imagine articulating my intentions and then making work that expresses those intentions. And when I go into schools, and kids are always having to talk about what their work is about, I'm so glad that we didn't do much of that when I was in school. We did some, but it's really ramped up since then.

For me the process opens up ideas, and suggests possibilities, in a way that thinking really doesn't get at. There are times when my dependence on that process is expansive. It allows me to go someplace surprising. And then sort of cyclically, the negative side of it is that the process is a kind of groove that's worn too deep.

When I was making pots on the wheel, I was in love with the wheel, with the flow of it and with the discipline of it. And also in love with function, with the challenge of making things that worked, that were the right weight, whose lids fit, whose handles were comfortable to hold. There wasn't any literature about that. I really love making covered pots. One of the things with covered pots that went really deep had to do with the fact that it's a compound form. And you have to resolve all the parts of it so that they go together, but knowing that at some times you're going to experience the parts separately. I find an almost emotional charge in the fact that there's an interior that you can only discover by interacting with the piece. You can't take in all of a covered piece except by touching it. And there's something really primal about the way that the pieces go together in a pot like that. When I used to do craft fairs, I noticed that even in our very touch-averse culture, where becoming socialized means, among other things, learning not to touch, people come into my booth and they are drawn to pick up the lids. [Laughter] *There's something about that relationship, almost a kind of force field around the parts of a pot like that that compels exploration in a kinesthetic way.*

I began firing in an electric kiln in like '90, because I moved up here. I imagined that I was going to build a gas kiln, but there's no question that electric kilns are more portable. So I thought I should really figure out this electric-firing thing. That was when I had to think about the surface of the pots, because the kiln is not going to help you out at all. In my first handbuilt pots, I didn't really work that much on the surface. The coils would show a little bit, but mostly it was very plain. It wasn't until the kiln forced me to take responsibility for it and resolve the surface that I started doing more what I do now, putting layers of slip on and really trying to make something there, which was a great challenge. ■

ALLEGHANY MEADOWS

Luck and Timing

Alleghany Meadows at the Archie Bray Foundation, Helena, Montana, 2017.
Photo: Jake Brodsky

Alleghany Meadows had a peripatetic childhood, got into a good college, learned to speak Japanese and Nepali to dig deep into those cultures during extended stays, organized a mobile gallery, co-owned a brick-and-mortar one in Aspen, Colorado, and still managed to have a family and to make utilitarian pottery with an emphasis on serving forms.

My name has to do with the time I was born, in 1972. The name Alleghany comes from a little town up in the Sierra Foothills, where my parents met. It was a gold-mining town in the 1850s, so people must have come from the Appalachians or the Allegheny range. In California the town is literally six houses. I was conceived in a meadow outside a valley. Our last name was Meadows. My mom had adopted that name a few years before. It was very much a part of the alternative culture. She lived in a commune at various points and traveled around helping to put together light shows. My mom was a hippie. I was raised just by her. She was also a painter, an artist. She was trained at the Corcoran.

I did not have a father figure. I did have two older brothers. But even then, you learn. I think some of it is genetic, and some of it is, you know, it takes a village, which may not be the best way to raise a kid. [Laughter] But that's what humans do: we adapt, we find what we need. Or what we think we need. Now in my 40s, I've figured out all that. [Laughter] *I have children now, so I get to figure out what I needed and what I can give, and it's a very important process.*

We had a lack of financial security, and of stability. And so I want roots. I want a home. So those things I have in my adult life. But there are huge things about my childhood that affect how I work in my studio, or how I approach a project. I'm very excited about the newness of a project. I don't shy away from crazy ideas, because I think that some of those push me into a new territory. So I don't have inhibitions in that way, and I think that comes from a childhood of inventing play and dealing with your surroundings.

When I was four, we moved from California to a commune in southern Colorado, very rural and isolated. After a year, I think, we moved to a house in a very small town and lived in that rural area until after I finished eighth grade. My mom had watched my two older brothers struggle with the lack of academics in the school system there, so she moved me to California. She said, "With my last child, I'm going to give him a good education." We ended up in Santa Cruz for a year, and in high school I took a ceramics class.

The next summer we moved to Mendocino, and I enrolled in ceramics again because there were art electives and it looked like fun. By the end of the year I was there at night. There was something in it that really had meaning for me. The head of the Mendocino Art Center hired me to help him in the summer, so I was wedging clay, chopping wood, firing kilns, that sort of thing. And then I switched to an alternative high school for my third year, where I could independently study a lot of different things. In the Art Center at that time, there was an artist-in-residence program and there were people like Josh DeWeese; there was this group of young people just out of Kansas City Art Institute. So I was an impressionable high school student who was seeing these guys making amazing work and having so much fun doing it, and that community and that sort of hard-work ethic and making something with your hands really drew me in.

My junior year of high school, I got a National Foundation for Advancement of the Arts award for high school students, and I was able to be a California Art Scholar. They sent me to a summer-school program at CalArts in Valencia with about 100 other similar-age art students, from dance and poetry to sculpture and ceramics. It was an awesome, eye-opening experience.

I also assisted workshops at the Mendocino Art Center. Paul Soldner came to teach a workshop, and I helped. And I asked him at the end of his workshop, "Where should I go to college?" And he said go to Scripps. I was applying for college, and I was also very interested in geology and the science field. With the name of Alleghany, I was sent an application and I was reading it and I was like, "Mom, what? I can't go to school there; it's a women's college." I called Paul and said, "I can't go there, I'm a man." And Paul said, "Oh, go to Pitzer." So I went to Pitzer College. [Laughter] [Pitzer and Scripps are two of the five schools collectively known as the Claremont Colleges.]

There was an amazing education there. Small liberal-arts college, incredible faculty and mentors. At the end of it, my major was art and Asian studies. I took Japanese classes and studied Japanese culture and religion and was very interested in going to Japan. But my time with Paul was amazing. At that point he wasn't critiquing anybody's work; he never spoke with you about the aesthetics of your work—it was the technical advice, if you needed help with technology, firing the kiln, mixing glaze. Otherwise it was "Oh, you figure it out." That was very empowering. He was asking his questions of his own work, and he was working in the classroom setting.

It was his way of sifting out who had motivation and would be serious about making work. Everything was there. A small gallery space, funding to put on exhibitions, materials. And there were graduate students working constantly at the same time. All of these really amazing figures in sort of post-abstract-expressionist clay would come and work. There was a class they had me take called graduate seminar, and I was a freshman. [Laughter] *It was a potluck dinner once a week at Paul's house, and Paul's house was full of an incredible collection. There would always be a visiting person. It was very important because of that camaraderie and community, and discussions that would happen about artwork. They don't have to happen in a rigid classroom. It was a very California way of educating.*

At the same time, for an environmental-art

class, the students met James Turrell and visited his Roden Crater project, and they visited Paolo Soleri's Arcosanti, and Sedona, Arizona. *I didn't just live and breathe in the ceramics studio. I was involved in many different things.*

I feel like luck has played a huge role in so much of my life. [Laughter] *Or timing. I wanted to go to Japan, and the head of study-abroad programs had lived in Japan and had married a Japanese woman, and he was very interested in Japanese culture. His name was Tom Manley. Tom gave me various books and things to read, and once a week I'd meet with him. It was like an extra class because we'd sit down and talk, and we would read poetry together, he would take me to dinners, or we would cook dinner; there was just this great friendship that evolved. And he didn't want me, and I didn't want, to go to a standard study-abroad program, so we formed an independent study where I could go to Japan for a year.* The first four months were the introduction to Japanese culture.

That was the time of the letter. I would write letters home, and these letters were 10 to 20 pages of answering questions and really going in depth about what I was trying to learn about Japanese culture. I would live with a home-stay family, I would study Japanese language, and Tom set it up so I could practice Zen meditation at this place called Tōfukuji monastery, a 14th-century monastery in Kyoto. So twice a week I would go and I was the only white guy there.

My roommate my sophomore year of college and good friend is Shingo Francis. He's a painter and the son of painter Sam Francis. Shingo said, "Oh maybe my mom can find somebody for you to work with." So when I first arrived in Japan, I went to Mako Idemitsu's house, Shingo's mom, and stayed there for about five days. And she said "We're going to meet somebody at the museum." I was this 20-year-old; I had a portfolio with pictures of my work, didn't know what I was getting into, didn't know who she was. We had a meeting at the Idemitsu Art Museum, which her father had founded. [Laughter] *In Japan those introductions are very important. So I said I wanted to study pottery, and they said what if you were to go work with Takashi Nakazato? I didn't know who he was. Luckily they were patient with me. So Takashi had a phone call or letter from them asking if I could come and work, and being the*

museum with the biggest collection of his whole family's heritage [Laughter]*, he was really "Wow, come on down then."*

Meadows wasn't entirely sure he wanted to get into that, because he had read Leila Philip's account of her own apprenticeship, *The Road through Miyama.* *That was a very influential book. And that was part of the inspiration of wanting to go work in Japan. But also in that book were a lot of things that I didn't necessarily feel like I just wanted to dive into and become a part of, so that's why I was skeptical about going to be an apprentice.* Nakazato invited him to come for the party after a firing. *His cycle was to fire the huge kiln, it cooled for a week, and during that week they would set up for a massive party.*

He put me to work to see how I would do, and I wanted to see what was going on. There were probably 300 people coming to the party, and that included museum curators from all over the world. There were three musicians from England who performed in his living room, the viola di gamba, you know, 17th-century instruments. It was just this unbelievable experience of celebration of food, and he was also very relaxed and casual about it, and everybody was working furiously to have it all done. Everything was served on his pots. I obviously wanted to work there. [Laughter] *At that point I really got it, like what an opportunity was in front of me.*

I was trying to understand Japanese culture and why these pots were Japanese, and I knew that I had to immerse myself in something like this, all of these connections into the aesthetic. There's obviously the individual artist's voice, but I needed to understand what tradition was, I guess. So I moved there shortly after the New Year. I was more a student of his. Even though I did all the work of an apprentice, an apprentice would be there for three to five years, and I was there for six months. I learned how to use the wooden kick wheel. I tried to do everything possible to fit in with the other four apprentices.

I was the newest one, so they were all showing me what type of work I would be doing with them each day, from mixing clay to mixing glazes and loading kilns, all those levels of work that sustain a pottery. Early morning before 8, or after 5, we were able to use the wheels to practice. I would sit and practice centering at this wooden kick wheel, and at some point Takashi would see me working, and if I was doing it well, he would show me the next step, and if I wasn't, he would show me that step again. It was mastering each little bit as you go. So in six months I learned how to center, cut off, flip over a little disk, and trim it, all of this off the hump on this wooden kick wheel. I never completed a piece. We did two more firing cycles, and then Takashi left for the summer. He was doing this tour with Malcolm Wright. It was great. I was there seeing Malcolm's work and helping load that into the kiln, and they had these exhibitions around the States.

The whole year away I got credit for, it was like going to classes. When I came home, Soldner had retired; there were different people teaching at different places; everything had sort of shifted. Brook Levan was the new teacher at Pomona. He was a very influential and motivating teacher like Soldner was, energizing everybody. It was like: You have an idea? Go for it, do it, let's go. Slightly competitive with each other in terms of who can stay up the latest, make the most work, and that kind of thing. He had an apartment in his backyard that I rented. He and I would stay up really late looking at pots. He was trying to get me to loosen up, in a way. I like control, and so I had a teacher who was wanting me to work more quickly and a little more vigorously.

There's a great program to study abroad in Nepal. My friend Gail came back from Nepal, and I admired her very much, and she said, "Alleghany, you have to go to Nepal." I took that to heart, so I applied for a Watson Fellowship and luckily I got it, and I was able to go to Nepal for a year.

In Japan I used to go and sit in Kanjiro Kawai's house and read and write and work on these letters, because it was a museum and it was open. So the "unknown craftsman" thing steeped into me, and that's a big reason why I chose Nepal. There are potters working there within the culture, and they don't do it for reasons other than cultural. I mean they make pots the same way somebody builds roads, and they're making them for their culture, their religion. Religion hadn't been separated. They weren't doing it in a self-conscious way. It was very real and very important to them. I lived with a family in an immersion program five days a week and learned how to speak. I was pretty fluent in conversational Nepali, learned about religion, all these different facets of the culture. I looked at how things were used in homes. But I wasn't working with potters at all in that first four months.

I went as an anthropologist, on my own idea of a cultural anthropologist. After becoming confident in the language, where I felt I could go anywhere in the country and do anything I wanted to, learning how to stay healthy and things like that, I went off to a village that Doug Casebeer has been to many times, in far eastern Nepal.

I met Casebeer in this village. I knew Anderson Ranch was bringing a group of American artists to work in this village, so I set up to help logistics on the ground for them. Doug and I really connected. He told me more about Anderson Ranch. I had left some portfolios with my professor, so if I needed to apply he could send an application from the States. So I was able to apply to the Ranch residency program. I didn't know that I had gotten it for a long time, but those seeds were sort of set for a return.

I realized at one point that I had gone with a one-way ticket and I could have stayed. I had been looking at what a pilgrimage is—where you go away to remove yourself from your comfort and from your things that you're familiar with—and to complete the pilgrimage you need to return home. I realized that I was on was a type of pilgrimage, and I needed to come back to the States to understand why I felt like I could live in Nepal forever. There were a lot of expatriates there, and they were not coming back to the States, or back to Sweden, or wherever. They would never be Nepalis. They were always expatriates.

His next plan was a further benefit of the Watson Fellowship, which *was more than enough money to travel the world and do these things, and it was also wide open and flexible.* He thought he would go to Spain, learn Spanish, and investigate the beautiful local Spanish pots. But he arrived there and concluded it was not the right thing, that he needed to digest the Nepal experience. He traveled a bit, and then stayed with friends in Italy while he wrote his fellowship report. *And at that point in Italy I found out that I had the residency at the Ranch, so I had a place to land.* [Laughter]

So Anderson Ranch. I was there for about a year working. I realized I had never actually made pots, which was an important realization. The other residents were Michael Connelly and Julia Galloway, who had just finished graduate school, and Jill

Oberman. It was an amazing group of people. I really, really needed to make pots. I didn't want to go study cultural anthropology and write about making pots; I wanted to learn how to really make. Now I was around some folks who were very critical and were intensely trying to make the best work they could. I wanted to think about that. So I sort of set myself on this path of working all the time, trying to figure out how to make good work. Hands in the material, getting critiques from people. I assisted the summer program at the Ranch, just being bombarded with all kinds of different perspectives and ideas, not much time to work. I assisted John Gill.

Meadows's request to stay for a second year was accepted. In the fall he did a college tour and went to the Utilitarian Clay conference at Arrowmont School of Crafts and was able to watch Chris Staley, Linda Sikora, and Michael Simon work. He sent off a bunch of applications and then went back to Nepal as Doug Casebeer's assistant on a group tour, since he spoke the language and knew his way around. He returned to the US to learn that he'd been accepted every place he applied. With some trepidation, he chose the two-year program at Alfred, knowing its one-time reputation of "ruining" potters, although he was disappointed that he would not be able to study with Linda Sikora, who was teaching at the University of Colorado, Boulder. But his good luck continued, because that's just when she was hired at Alfred.

I feel like I started at Alfred at an amazing time, where making pots was not questioned. What you did with it was thoroughly examined, and how you expressed yourself in that art form was clearly questioned. His first summer at Anderson Ranch, he had begun a relationship with the woman who became his wife. She came with him to Alfred, and their daughter was born in March before his April grad show. He was reluctant to start with a teaching job because he felt that if he did that, he'd never learn how to be a potter and make a living from it. They chose to return to Colorado, where she could return to her massage therapy practice and he became studio manager for the Carbondale Clay Center. After eight months, he knew it wasn't for him. I found a studio at a high school there, and I only had to talk to the advanced students for an hour and they watched me work.

My friend Sam Clarkson put together a tour where his dad gave us this old white van, and we drove around the country and did home sales, sort of like Tupperware parties. We went to Dallas and did a visiting artist thing with Peter Beasecker and drove on to Arrowmont, the Utilitarian Clay again. We set up pots and tried to sell them there, out of the back of the van. A friend's parents had a brownstone on 72nd and Central Park West [New York City]. They hosted us for a big party, and we had a home sale out of their home and sold a ton of work. I think Syracuse and a couple of other places we did workshops.

I had a different studio at this point in Carbondale. Somebody had given me a big barn and said if I put the effort in, they would provide the materials, so I could remodel it for my studio. It was beautiful. And Sam and I taught at Penland for the eight-week Concentration. My mom was still relatively itinerant, and I thought, wow, if there's an Airstream for sale I could fix it up and park it somewhere that she could live. So I had enough money from some recent sales that I bought this Airstream from the classified ads, and then September 11th happened. We were supposed to leave two weeks later to go to Penland, and we weren't interested in going with a young child. Cynthia Bringle said, "If there's anywhere you need to be, it's Penland in this time of panic in the country." So we went. Sam and I were trying to figure out how are we going to make a living as potters, and this idea popped up to make the Airstream into a gallery and take it to NCECA.

So we came back from Penland and had already set up six of us who were going to be in the first show, and we were going to do it in Kansas City at NCECA, and that was in four months. Andy Brayman was from Kansas City and was going to be there over the holidays. We knew it had to be legal and legit and safe, and so he got us the parking permits, and the police set up where it would park, and they blocked it off. And I did the remodel work and polished it, and we rolled out of Colorado with a trailer of pots, this silver shiny thing, on our way to Kansas City. Our first customer was Betty Woodman.

It was great for young people to feel like the whole field wasn't just watching; they were supporting it. We sold a bunch of work directly to the people. We had folks saying, you've got to bring this to New York, to Minneapolis, or wherever. It started to snowball. But it was a huge team effort. If I had to *do this on my own, I couldn't have done it physically, and if I had done it with just my work, it would have been more egotistical or self-serving. Whereas a group of us doing it, we brought in all of our connections and friends from all over, and it became exponentially more highly regarded. It was more like we were doing something for the field rather than our individual careers.*

My side of it was to always do the bookkeeping and paperwork. Elizabeth Robinson always does the publicity side of it: posters, things like that. And we always try to do something fun with it. One time I was demonstrating with Mark Pharis at Utilitarian Clay again, and I was watching Mark's computer program, how he could design a pot that was flat and then build it, and I said, "Mark, can you help figure out how we can do a poster that people could cut out and they'd build their own Airstream?" [Laughter]

During graduate school, Meadows had met his father for the first time and learned that he had a half brother five years younger than he was, *who is in digital animation and uses the computer the way I use clay, where it's just at his fingertips. So Brian took this idea and made it real, so that we could actually fold this thing up and make an Airstream. And that was for a tour where we were hosted by the Museum of Arts and Design at their old location, right when MoMA had opened after the remodel. There were five or six stops on that tour. We'd gotten to where if we wanted to go to the Northeast, we could make some calls to people we knew, and between all of us we knew somebody who ran something or at a college or something where we could go park and be hosted. It was great when you were in a venue for more than one night, so you didn't have to set up again.*

The logistics included taking as much work as possible in the Artstream and in a towed vehicle, and strategically picking up the work of others to replenish as they crossed the country. *The biggest tour that I've been on was the first time we went through the East Coast. It was three weeks, 12 or 13 venues, and that included driving from Colorado across the country, stopping in Kansas City and doing various things for shows. When I got home I had zero energy left, and the amount of money I made was the dollars on my own work.* [Laughter] *Which was not very much* [Laughter], *in the $3,000*

range. After that amount of effort and work. So yes, the project continues; no, it doesn't make money. There were other years that we figured out how to do a lot better than that, but that's kind of the bottom line. A lot of the tours are visiting-artist gigs where a college will pay us to come, we'll sell work, but the expenses are huge compared to the amount of income. And so what I've done is make sure that all of the artists on the tour and myself are getting paid honorariums from the colleges.

Sales were not good for NCECA in Tampa, but they were very good in Seattle, where they hired an espresso caterer so buyers got a free drink with a purchased cup. They went to Minnesota in March. *I think it got to 6 degrees that day. The sun was out, though, and Minnesotans are incredible. We had a hugely successful day* [Laughter] *even if we couldn't feel our fingers. It was because the sun was out, and everyone was so happy and thought it was great we were doing this.* [Laughter]

I'm not going to be going on the road very much. I have three children. To be with my family is a much more important priority for me. So Artstream in the summer is used every Saturday at the Aspen Farmer's Market. We have the same parking place; we're there from 6 in the morning to 3 in the afternoon. That venue is more for my own work and some others who live locally there. It's a very important venue for me. And it goes to NCECA.

A developer came to myself and Sam Harvey a few years ago. They had buildings just outside Aspen that weren't leasing very well, and they made us an offer we couldn't refuse, to start a land-based gallery. Sam and I, realizing Aspen would be an amazing venue, and the work we loved wasn't being represented, we went for it, borrowed a couple of thousand dollars from a friend to start a business. We did all the work, made pedestals, stripped off carpeting in the place, put in lighting, and made the Harvey/Meadows Gallery. We signed our lease in July 2005 and opened in early August.

We had a buzz; a lot of people were interested in what we were up to. And Sam had been one of Betty [Woodman]*'s students, so he called and asked if she had any work we could show in the gallery. She was like, of course. There were three huge, wonderful pieces in a show at the Boulder Library that we drove down and got. We were able to have an opening of work that we were really excited about,* from pots to large woodblock prints from John Buck, to Betty Woodman, to Voulkos's work. We had some people who said, wow, we have this collection; we'd like to sell a few. Sam had worked in Kansas City at the Morgan Gallery, so he understood some things about the art world and collecting which were really important. How resale work, secondary market work, could lend a huge stature to our gallery from the start. We didn't have a relationship with artists of that stature, but we could still have their work.

We moved from that location, where we were a destination gallery, to downtown Aspen, where there's a lot more walk-by traffic. We kind of reached that seven-year point where we weren't successful enough to hire staff and to have financial security to pay ourselves all year, but we were successful enough that it was hard to walk away and close the gallery. It's a struggle, expenses and income.

In all this, I make my own work. The work is dishes, porcelain for many years, and for the last couple I've been splitting it with earthenware and porcelain. Just trying to keep my own process fresh and to figure out new materials and new technologies. I felt like my work and my risk taking was really conservative. And I wanted to be challenged.

My dishes were in these phenomenal homes with art collections around Aspen, but always in the cupboards. And I thought, man, I want my work to sit out on something. In the Airstream that was primary, and it wasn't a lot of space in there, so I started to figure out how things stacked together and fit together. That's where this spiraling-set, connecting-set idea came from. And that's been really fun to play with, where small elements can become something much larger.

I'm interested in the way glazes feel on my skin. I very much pay attention to the insides of the work. The form on the inside and the detail on the inside of a cup is as important as what's happening on the outside visually. Storage forms are something I don't work with much; it's more about eating and presentation of food.

I'm looking at Chinese ceramics, as far as glaze. So with fluid glazes, I'm building up a form and structure that will catch the glaze and create areas where the glazes are thicker. In porcelain it was clay and glaze, and with earthenware it's clay, slip, and glaze. So having thin slips that let the clay body sort of burn back through, and the way that that happens

differently on one side of the piece to the other because of my direct touch as I'm applying the slip and trying not to be even.

I assemble a lot of things, but it's always thrown. I've worked a little bit in some other ways. I made a series from molds made off garden tools, like a shovel trowel that turned into a dish. It's pressing it on a mold. So there's a sense of touch and hand on the outside of the work, and then the inside is more narrative, the way a coffee cup can be narrative about what it's going to be used for.

I have worked for restaurants quite a bit. One chef in particular I traded for years for credit in the restaurant. It was a place I could never have afforded to eat. He'd say, "I have this beet salad that I'm trying to figure out how to serve. Come in and let's talk about it." I would figure out a shape, sometimes geometric, sometimes round, for these specific dishes.

In the summer where we are, the gallery and the farmer's market are very, very busy. When my family goes away to see the in-laws, I'm in the studio from 5 in the morning until 10, and then I'm in the gallery from 11 till 5, and then I'm back in the studio at night. I work on deadlines, and so when I have a show somewhere I can be in the studio 10 hours a day and still be in the house with the family and still be functioning on these other levels somehow. I can continue that pace for three or four or five weeks, and then something's got to snap. [Laughter] *I'm more of a binge potter.* That may change, since in January 2019 he left the gallery to devote more time to his own work. ■

CHAPTER NINE

JOURNEYMEN

David Stuempfle (see chapter 11) was a journeyman in the traditional sense of the word, a skilled jobber who for many years worked for various employers rather than for himself. But the American ceramics world today seems to have journeymen in another sense: art-school grads who spend ten years or so after earning a BFA moving from one temporary situation to another—special student, postbac, grad school, and residencies—before they are able to get the money, skills, and well-developed work that enable them to set up a studio on their own. The good thing about this journey is that it takes potters to far-flung places, provides them with varied experiences, and encourages networks of acquaintances they might miss if they held to the long hours and isolation of studio work from the beginning. ∎

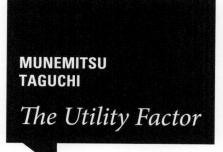

MUNEMITSU TAGUCHI

The Utility Factor

Munemitsu Taguchi
in his former studio in
Philadelphia, 2012

Mune (pronounced *mooney*) Taguchi is a Vermont-based regular American guy with an unusual background. He's the third child, first son, of a Japanese man and an American woman. Just before his birth, his father was traumatically injured in a car accident, and his family took him back to Japan for rehabilitation. The wife and daughters ended up staying with her parents in Washington State, where Taguchi was born in 1978. Not long thereafter the marriage was dissolved, and a few years later the American grandparents died in quick succession, leaving Taguchi's mother financially well off. So she chose to move with her children to England. He was there for second, third, and fourth grades and rapidly picked up an English accent despite summer visits to the States. *We had long winter breaks, and I remember going to Paris for two weeks, or to visit friends in Greece, so I had a very lucky childhood, a great mom, always around, very nice.*

When they moved back to the US, he had to adjust to American schools—first a Jesuit school, then the local public high school. This one, in Tacoma, Washington, drew both from affluent and poor neighborhoods and so had its tensions. He took his first ceramics class as a junior. *I really didn't get it until I went to Thanksgiving dinner my senior year at my girlfriend's uncle's house, and he was a potter. His name was Reid Ozaki. All of a sudden it was like, "You can do this with clay? Really?" Around his house there were a bunch of really wonderful pots, a lot of them he'd made.*

Because of being a bad student in high school, I didn't have a particularly high GPA and didn't know what I wanted to do, so I went to Tacoma Community College. They had an amazing ceramics program for a community college. Among the features was a faculty relationship with a teacher at Tokyo National University of Fine Arts and Music (now Tokyo University of the Arts, commonly called Tokyo Geidai).

In 1998 there were a number of people from TCC going to spend a month or so at Geidai and make work, and I decided to spend some time reconnecting with my father as well. I lived in Japan for nine months and made pots and sort of started to get an understanding of Japanese ceramics, a better understanding of the history and tradition. Returning essentially broke, he took some time off school. His mother had moved to Bethel, in western Alaska, an isolated and mostly Native Alaskan community. He joined her and worked unloading planes for an air cargo company, driving forklifts, and in the summer working for a contractor. With the money saved, he

returned to Tacoma *because for the fall term there was another trip in conjunction with the faculty and students from Tokyo, to the Central Academy of Art and Design in Beijing.* So he went to China for two months. *What am I going to do, say no?*

It was also through the community college that he experienced wood firing at the kiln of Hiroshi Ogawa in Elkton, Oregon. *There were a bunch of Pacific Northwest potters who would gather and fire this amazing, beautiful kiln that he built. That was the best experience in the world. The effects, and the community, and the whole thing. Like the typical thing that gets kids hooked on ceramics: you're spending 12 hours at a time with a couple of people, removed from everybody else. You're gonna talk about the things that are closer to your soul than you normally would.*

I decided that I would transfer to the University of Alaska, Anchorage. My mother was teaching at their satellite campus in Bethel, and she informed me that dependents and spouses get free tuition. So in January of 2000 I moved to Anchorage. Didn't know anybody. I spent the semester getting my prereqs so I could take ceramics. It was a really great class, me and Deborah Schwartzkopf and Jen Allen all in undergraduate school together. I feel really lucky to have both of them; we just had great conversations.

But what next? The special-student program was still fairly new. Taguchi wanted a place without distractions, and someone recommended Wichita State. He called, and they were surprised because they had never had a special student before. He moved to Kansas sight unseen and plunged into working. He calls it the *first really focused time of my life. And finally at the end of the fall semester, six weeks of really concentrated effort on a body of work that was good enough to get me into graduate school.*

He went to Indiana University. *Four faculty, 12 grad students, fully funded private studio. And during my first year, NCECA was in Indianapolis, so it was awesome. I was still maybe a little more interested in spending equal amounts of time in the studio as in the bar, so I was a little less productive. But it was a three-year program, so it was okay. My first year I was trying a lot of things.* Akio Takamori, the University of Washington professor born in Japan, was in town for NCECA and gave Taguchi succinct and valuable advice: he should focus on form. *The second year was a little bit stronger, and then deciding that I was going to make pots.*

By the time of my orals, fall of my third year, I made this beautiful mahogany coffee table and did this whole setup with white pots, and they were fine. Then everything sort of changed for me. I had a really good critique and started thinking about generosity of material and our preconceptions about porcelain—it must be light; it must be all of these things. No, it could be a doorstop and it's beautiful and it has all these other qualities that you can start to embrace. By the time I put up my thesis show, I had gone through the whole gamut, being stripped down to nothing to being in a place where I felt like I was onto something.

The work got him a residency at the Clay Studio in Philadelphia, a city that attracted him because it had something for him and for his then girlfriend, now wife, who was in apparel merchandising. He flew out the day before the jury and had a conversation with a guy he thought was amazing because he was *so ready to embrace the place of utilitarian ceramics.* That was Jeff Guido, then director of the Clay Studio. Taguchi until that time had felt that he was *butting heads constantly, being challenged all the time* because he wanted to do pots. During his five years of residency in Philadelphia, he added to his income by spending six to ten weeks working in Alaska, where the money is good and he can see his mother and others important to him. He returns ready to work.

Looking back, Taguchi says he can see that he spent too much time *just fighting a lot of things about who I am and how I want to make things. I make really tight work, you know? There's nothing natural about gesture in throwing. It's a controlled action, and I fought that for years and was never satisfied with the result. I finally started to get crisp when I put together this pseudo body of work to get into graduate school with. My pieces now deal with some of the same ideas, from the most abstract idea that we have two faces—your public face and your private face—and that dichotomy of the human spirit and how it's represented in the form. So having the interior space and the exterior doing different things.*

I let the interior feel like pure utility; just keep it simple, a really clean parabolic shape, which is ideal for a utilitarian object both in how it functions and cleaning and all that. Porcelain, celadon. I was making these 1½-inch-thick forms and trimming them. I started trimming the whole outside. That was like a big breakthrough for me because, you know, you're only supposed to trim the foot. The rest should have been taken care of when you were throwing. I was screwing around one night in my studio and cut off a piece and said, "Oh, I made this giant facet." So then it was about creating forms that were thick, asymmetric facets. Then it expanded into this idea that you can create two different profiles in the same object.

Taguchi loves porcelain because even when it's not thin enough to be translucent, it has a luminosity that *gives a finish that is unlike anything else in the ceramics world.* Besides that, *somewhere in my mind I wanted the glaze to be a part of the object as opposed to being so separate. With porcelain, the clay starts to turn into glaze, starts to become more glasslike, so there was less of a distinction between the two materials.*

At the time of his thesis show he was making jars that ranged from 18 to 24 inches tall. *At the time I thought they were very successful because they're super sculptural and they're massive and they had this dynamism that existed in a faceted wing. But in hindsight I don't find them so attractive. I don't think of them as being resolved.*

When I moved to Philadelphia, my first year at the Clay Studio was horrendous. I had catastrophic clay and glaze failures. I brought my clay from graduate school to the Clay Studio, but I mixed my glazes here, and the water was so different. The tolerances for a crazeless, transparent glaze are really slim. So I unloaded six kilns into the trash, literally nothing salvageable out of it. It was so disheartening. It was the closest I'd ever come to quitting. But by the end of my first year, I was starting to move forward.

I had decided that I really wanted to make dinnerware. I wanted to focus on utilitarian objects, but with more interest than something you'd buy at IKEA, which is my biggest competitor, I think. [Laughter] Still thinking of the dichotomy of exterior and interior, with two different profiles in one form.

I realized that part of success now is financial, because if this is what I'm going to be doing 40 hours a week, it needs to earn a profit. So I came to this conclusion that you make what you want and figure out how to market it, as opposed to letting the market dictate. It's super idealistic, and who knows if you can always hold on to that, but what happens now is, let's say I have 15 objects in my arsenal, it might be that there's three that are really popular and sell better, so I might make more of them. But they're still part of the objects that I decided to make. That's the way I rationalize that to myself.

In his carved series, one of the first forms he calls a whiskey cup because that's what it was first used for. The specifics of the contour changed periodically, but the idea was always that the sculptural protrusion would not impede utility—the user could drink from any side. *The ergonomics, how that object interacts with your hand, can be specific. These have definitely gotten tweaked. When I was in grad school, I had a dishwasher in my apartment. I didn't have to think about washing the stuff that I made. We moved to Philadelphia, didn't have a dishwasher, so the proportions of these objects started to shift. Little things that visually don't affect the overall statement of the object much, but they enhance the utility greatly. So this flare at the bottom of the foot used to be so narrow that it would get filled in with glaze, on purpose. I had put that in there as like a stop for the glaze. But then having to handwash all my dishes, it's really nice to have something to hold with two or three fingers when you're washing a dish like this, to shake it. So the utility of the objects started to influence subtleties in the form. The aesthetics had a greater importance when I was in grad school, and my time in the Clay Studio let the utility catch up. Little things like having parabolic interior*

shapes. If you're using a spoon and you have a square corner in the bottom of the pot, how are you supposed to get the last little bit of ice cream?

And how did the shapes develop? *To me it just made sense both ergonomically and visually. The wing is about one-third of the cup, but it's not exactly one-third. Its visual weight is greater than the plain side.* The forms are thrown and then the whole thing is trimmed in the round—*inside, outside, top, bottom, everything.*

One of the formal influences for these is ceramic insulators. I used to play with them when I was a little kid. My grandmother had some of those blue soda glass ones, and she had my grandfather turn wooden bases for them to sit in, and used them as candleholders at their beach house. Because we were on an island, power would go out all the time, so you had to have a lot of candles around.

But even good things come to an end. A few years ago he concluded that the idea was finished. *In 2011 I started designing, thinking about a new body of work. In the carved works, the trimming process really allowed me to compress, to really define those indentations, sort of an external force working on the object, so it's pushing in, squeezing, cinching.* The new body of work was a reaction to that.

He began to deal with volume. He throws them a little thinner, but he continues to contrast interior and exterior. *The exterior form is just a standard bowl, and instead of having expression on the outside it's shifted to the inside, so it's even more minimal and more reduced.* Each piece is monochrome, but they come in three compatible colors building on the same base glaze: pale lavender, pale blue, and pale green. Thus they can harmoniously interact because the undertones are the same, and they continue his policy of making work that doesn't interfere with the food that's presented on it.

The new series has a range of dinnerware forms, but the plate was the last one added. *I feel like the handmade plate is the one place where potters get in trouble, because most handmade plates are doorstops, and they don't fit in the dishwasher. They're so heavy that if you have a stack of eight, how are you ever going to pick that up? So I felt like, as a maker of a handmade object who's going to compete with other commercially available tableware, I want my plates to go with the rest of my body of work but* not be so massive that it's going to impede someone using it.

Taguchi has no interest in casting, because he loves to throw. *Every day that I get to come to my studio and throw is a happy, happy day. For me there's a joy in manipulating clay. The other reason why I don't cast is because I enjoy difference. It keeps me interested. I can change anything anytime I want to.*

I polish the feet of my pots. So if you feel the bottom of that, it's not glazed; it's polished. And that's another thing in the utility factor. It started as a tactile deal, so that you have that extra experience. And this is a Jen Allen: "Consider all surfaces." She used to put these little surprises on the feet of her pots, so it would give the viewer or user a reward for paying attention to the whole thing. I wanted it to be a surprise, but also if you're handling a cup you're going to have your hand on the bottom. The polishing, which he does after the piece is fired, also means that it will not scratch a table surface. He regards the polished bottom as a signature, because he does not sign his work. The new series pushes this a little further: it is distinctive because it's so elegantly reductive, and he doesn't want that to be interrupted by a signature or stamp.

I try to work at a sustainable pace; I sort of pride myself on that. My wife works from 8 till 5:30, and I go to work from 8:30 until 5, Monday through Friday, and I don't work on the weekends. I think that lifelong thing of leaving summertime to work has given me a healthier separation from my studio than many people have, the ability to walk away from it and not feel that the world's gonna end. Sometimes, like maybe one Saturday or Sunday a month, I'll have something I have to get done, so I'll go to the studio for a couple of hours or whatever. But I'm pretty good about keeping that distance. I'm trying to because making pots is what I do, but it's not the entirety of who I am. ◼

DEB SCHWARTZKOPF

Working Hard

Deb Schwartzkopf in her Seattle studio, 2018.
Photo: Jayme Verfaillie

Deb Schwartzkopf (b. 1978) could be described as Ms. Initiative. She has always been interested in multiple things, and her home at the southern edge of Seattle includes a large studio and kiln yard constructed with Kickstarter help. She calls it Rat City Studios (after the neighborhood's World War II association with a Reserve Army Training Center made it a Restricted Alcohol Territory, she explains). She offers classes and has three studio assistants and a studio manager plus resident studios. She was president of the Washington Clay Arts Association, and *Ceramics Monthly* named her Ceramic Artist of the Year in 2018. She gardens and keeps bees and chickens. And she has developed a distinctive body of work that focuses on table functions and is innovative in form.

Schwartzkopf grew up in Seattle in a creative and active family. Her father makes casework (cabinets) and taught her to use tools, such as the scroll saw from which she and her sister made jigsaw puzzles. He mother taught her to sew; her grandmother taught her to crochet. They did not watch television. In her family, *that was just what people did, was making things.* She took continuing education classes in painting, flower arranging, herbal medicine, and more. In her small private high school she was able to test into college and take writing, photography, mechanical drawing, and clay classes. Clay was just one among many things she enjoyed. At Seattle Pacific University, she took a lot of religion classes.

Is this a problem of focus? *I think I'm really focused, actually. I just focus on a lot of things. I don't sit still very well. After I went there for about a year, I transferred to the University of Alaska in Anchorage. Mostly I just wanted to have some space and kind of reevaluate. I am really lucky to have crossed paths with the people that I did when I did, because I was at this really big changing point in my life. I just fell into an amazing crowd and an amazing ceramics program, and I also worked with some production potters. My family is really practical, and the idea of an art degree is a little abstract. So working with potters—Kris Bliss and Peter Brondz—was a really practical way to use art.*

Brondz has a timber-framed studio *in this really picturesque valley, and he has this lovely family. I just sort of bought the whole thing, hook, line, and sinker. I really wanted to have that as a goal. I'm very goal oriented, and having something so clear and concise and wonderful was the motivator for me to work super, super hard. So I was in school, and I overloaded almost every semester on classes, and I worked for the potters when I wasn't in school. I had my hands in clay many, many hours every day. It was great.*

A good friend lived off the grid, three miles off the road. And I learned how to ski to get to her house. We were hauling water and cutting down trees for wood on their land, and that was interesting for me. It's good for me to get out of my head and just be really present in the experience. I also built a cabin up there with the person I was dating at the time, so I had a major building project that was incredibly

challenging and a very good learning experience. My mom always says I learn best the hard way, and that was one of those projects. And just being able to see the vastness of that land. There is something really special about that place for me.

Steve Godfrey, who was one of my main professors, was a great example as far as making his own work and demonstrating a work ethic, and I also worked with Robert Baker. I made wheel-thrown pots with Steve, and Robert's was more of a sculpture/handbuilding class. But I was really stuck on making pottery, so I made handbuilt pottery in that class. (I had two bodies of work that were very dissimilar, and over time those two have merged.) And I was in a—what do they call it now—a cohort, with Jen Allen and Mune Taguchi; we were all in the same undergrad class. And there were a few others too. We were a pretty serious group. And then I also had people like Kris, who was like my clay mom. She's just very generous. I had all these different personalities really pushing me, I guess.

After graduation I kind of wanted some sunshine, so I moved to San Diego. Actually, I felt like glaze chemistry was my weakest point, and Richard Burkett, who teaches at San Diego State University, is kind of a glaze materials guru. I called him up and sent him a packet and said, "Can I please come work at your school and take your glaze chemistry class? Like a special student." I helped reclaim clay, I helped fire kilns, mix glazes, whatever they said, so many hours a week, so I was basically a tech. And I took glaze chemistry and tested glazes like crazy. It was really, really fun. I tested cone 6 electric because that's what the class was, and also because I was going to try to apply for graduate school the next year, and I couldn't fill a gas kiln because they're huge and I don't work that fast. So I started firing electric.

I got into graduate school at Penn State. That's a two-year program. I wanted to work with Chris Staley; I had done a workshop with Chris at Haystack. And when I went for my interview and met Liz Quackenbush, I was just blown away because I didn't know her and she's amazing. So I feel really lucky that I got to go there. And Chris was on sabbatical one year, so I also got to work with Nick Joerling and Margaret Bohls, each for a semester. I feel really fortunate to have had a really large number of influences in my school career. And I think that program was a good fit for me. It was smaller; it was really studio based. We did some teaching, but Liz and Chris both went out of their way to keep us working in the studio.

I finished in 2005. I went to the Archie Bray Foundation for two years with a fellowship. That was the first time I was not in school. So it was a pretty major difference. You know, setting my own goals, keeping myself going without a critique deadline or something like that. It's hard getting started.

I'd never really sold pottery. And so that Christmas, I made packets and sent them to 20 galleries to introduce myself. I got a really amazing response, and I had five or six solo shows that year. So then I really made a lot of pottery.

After that I applied for one job and a whole bunch of residencies but I got the one job. It was a one-year teaching job at Ohio University, which was scary and fantastic. I'd just been in my own brain, working in my studio, and then all of a sudden not only do I have to teach ceramics but I have to teach 3-D design and lead critiques and help students grow.

After that, I went to Boston for a year and I worked at Mudflat Studios. It's just a little residency program. I had a studio there, and I taught at Massachusetts College of Art and Design and at Mudflat and at Harvard for the Arts. I did all these part-time jobs. I wanted to live on the East Coast for a year. I never really set out to teach. I wanted to be a studio artist. But I keep being offered teaching positions. I really love teaching, so I do them. I also did a short stint in China for a month and Berlin for seven weeks and a one-month residency at the Philadelphia Clay Studio, or maybe it was a two-month residency. I can't remember anymore. Then I finally moved back to Seattle. Since I left Seattle and came back, it was ten years.

When I couldn't earn a living, I had a little extra support. I mean from my school because I had an assistantship, from my mom and from my dad some, a little less there. [Laughter] And then I also always had the support of a residency. It's a huge expense to have a studio, to have a kiln, and I have all that stuff now. Over the years I stockpiled away the things that I needed. Kiln shelves and posts, I bought those when I was in China and had them shipped back.

Before RAT City, Schwartzkopf supported herself from sale of her work and from doing workshops, which ranges from a third to half her income. *I have a lot of theories about teaching that I've formed because of teaching workshops, and at some point I would love to go back to school for psychology because I'm so interested in how people learn. I've read quite a few books about how people's minds form pathways because of practice and because of repetition, and so I'm constantly trying to see that in my work and also bring that into workshops, to make learning this playful, kind of blind process.*

I don't really believe people are innately skilled at pottery, but I do believe people have skills with problem-solving or having a connection between their hands and their brain. I really think that a lot of it has to do with practice. I feel like if you want to succeed at something, you just have to find a way to breathe it constantly.

Schwartzkopf has dealt with various ideas and approaches as she has developed professionally, but she has managed to make a coherent body of work. For example, she has been interested textures inside her pieces, to make them more interesting to look into. She looks to the model of potter-designers such as Eva Zeisel for the sensuousness of curving lines, the dynamism of diagonals, the confusion of zigzag lines. *I really wanted to make something that had this feeling of curiosity to it and also had a sense of momentum. I wanted this sense of direction, and I wanted a sense of expectancy.*

I wanted colors that made my work feel more buoyant and light. I also wanted there to be these kind of more neutral, broad colors and then little bits of color to accentuate different areas, maybe where your hand would rest, or the underside of something. Speckles sort of came out of this idea of how animals have speckling, like trouts' backs are speckled and it helps them hide from birds, and their bellies are white, which helps them hide from whatever's looking up trying to eat them. And trying to bring in that sort of natural coloration with a really intentful breaking up of the surface.

I have a pretty big repertoire of forms, because I really like figuring out new things—to me new. What happens inevitably is that a new shape teaches me something which I can bring back to the rest of my body of work. They just feed each other that way. ∎

Life Lessons

Sunshine Cobb at the
Penland School of Crafts,
Penland, North Carolina, 2018.
Photo: Matt Sloan

Sunshine Cobb is known for her good nature; her name seems appropriate. But it was bestowed upon her when she was born in 1972, because her draft-dodger father had taken the family from California to cloudy and rainy Canada. Other interesting aspects of her childhood include living on a boat, as well as her parents wholesaling hamsters for Southern California, which turned into a business in exotic birds. They had a retail pet store for years. Her father is also an abstract painter and a musician, so creative arts were always around. And in Canada they ran a small antiques business. *So we had a lot of handmade bottles and vases and things like that.*

A lot of this is relevant to my ceramic life. I have certain opinions about painters, and they stem from my father being a painter, in that my father is a highly egotistical person, and artists get free license to behave any way they want. As a young person I objected to that a little bit. Being creative doesn't give you the right to treat people poorly. So, although she feels lucky to have had a lot of art in her life, *I refused to refer to myself as an artist for a very long time just because I didn't associate it with positive thoughts.*

I liked functional ceramics because it contributed positively to people's life. It was an outlet for me to be creative and not have it be about me particularly. No offense, painters, but painting is not a community-oriented art. It's a solo, ego-driven art.

I wanted to have a potter's wheel when I was maybe in my teens. And I wanted to learn how to throw. But it was one of those unfulfilled dreams.

As I've gone on in school, you know, finishing

high school and undergrad and grad school, it blows my mind that I did that because I was a terrible student. I mean, I hate sitting in class. I had social issues too, but I made it through. I think grad school is great because you get to choose all the things you do. You know, it's so self-driven.

When I first started in junior college and college, I wanted to be an anthropologist or a social worker. I just loved groups of people and the dynamics between them. I felt like I found such connection with far-away communities that I lack in my own life as far as structure goes. I did religious studies and things like that, the beauty of ritual I was attracted to.

Cobb worked for a few years in random jobs, from customer service to Jack in the Box to doing production coordination and costume work in the entertainment business. She tried video and sound engineering, and massage school. *God, I have done so many weird things.* When she moved in with her sister, who was studying at the University of California, Davis, she started working in daycare and then became a sort of nanny for two families.

Taking care of the kids was a huge growth period for me, overcoming a lot of childhood stuff and just growing up and meeting people that I tremendously respected and who respected me and trusted me with their children. It was my first introduction to some really well-educated, ambitious people. I was looking for new role models, and I am of the school of "fake it till you make it," so finding people that you admire and striving to adopt what you admire about them.

I took my first ceramics class at the UC Davis craft center. You could exchange volunteer hours for a class, so I worked the front desk two days or a day a week or something and took a beginning ceramics class, throwing. I missed the first class because I had some other commitment, and I showed up for the second class and she was demonstrating plates. She had everybody go along with her, and so I started throwing and went along step by step with her. And she was like, "Oh, good, you know how to throw already." I was like, "No." She is just like, "Oh, but you didn't have any trouble centering," and I was like, "Oh, are you supposed to?" [Laughter] *I just had a real affinity for it; it just came quickly. I really loved how much focus and energy it took. I couldn't think about anything else, and that sort of focus was new in my life.*

After a brief period at Chico State, where her teacher was encouraging, she went back to Davis and then transferred to Sacramento State, where Scott Parady was just joining Robert Brady in the ceramics department. *I just hit the ground running with making pots* as a studio major. Initially she was hostile to Brady, with whom she never actually had a class, and she didn't respond well even when he said she made nice pots. *Bob is one of those guys who gets fans, right? He is a wonderful artist and a tremendous guy, and people want him to mentor them. I witnessed that a lot, and that just turned me off. One of my goals when I left there was to be more open to advice and criticism from people. I need to work on that!*

She had begun to wood fire with Parady at his kiln in Pope Valley, a couple of hours from Sacramento. It showed her the impact that wood fire can have on the work. During her three years in the program, she participated in a couple of firings each year. *The roughly 10 or 15 people that came and worked have all become family, basically. We just spend lots of time together.*

After graduation she moved in with her grandparents to assist in the care of her grandfather, who had developed Alzheimer's, and was there for a year and a half. *It was a 24-hour-a-day job. I did have a small studio set up out in the garage, but it just became impossible for me to do that. So I put a lot of my creative energy into cooking and baking. It was something I could do in the house and keep an eye on my grandpa, and feed them well. And to me, another part of being a potter is cooking. Funnily enough, it's what we make stuff for.*

For grad school I chose Utah State because I went to the Portland NCECA and they had a wonderful, like a 21-year sort of alumni show, and it was the most diverse bunch of beautiful pots that I had seen. I was like, "This is a place that promotes the individual, and everyone has the freedom to do what they want to do." When she arrived, John Neely, half the undergrads, and three or four grad students were in China for an extended stay. So she and the other new grad students had to teach classes, starting immediately.

I made some crazy stuff, came up with a new body of work every three or four weeks for crits. I am tremendously productive compared to some people. I work through ideas by working. A lot of the times by the time the crit hit, I already knew what my next step would be.

After wood firing with Scott and then going to Utah State, which is known as a wood-fire school, I came out making electric-fired functional ware. Part of the reason may be that *in my opinion, Scott has one of the best wood-fire kilns in the country. The surface that he gets out of his kiln is beautiful, and it has all of the things that you could want really, and it is not flashing and it is not dry and it has got some real depth to it. When I went to Utah, the train kiln atmosphere didn't speak to me because I was so accustomed to Scott's kiln.*

My thesis exhibition was all about traveling. I lived three miles from school, and in my three years there I still put 10,000 miles on my car 'cause I drove back and forth to California. The basis for a lot of the work is what the world looks like at 70 miles per hour, sort of the blur of lines and machines and traffic. And then what interests me enough for me to pull over and take pictures, 'cause I am a big picture taker. I am a collector of ceramics too, I love pots, and I love pots that I can't make. I sort of hip-hopped. My very first self-assigned project was making salt and pepper cellars, and then for my thesis project I made these large vessel containers that were for fruit or . . . I called them buckets and pails and troughs.

I think, you know, in the world that we live in now, it's important to be able to talk about your work and sell yourself and understand where other people are coming from. My function is to make work. That is what I am supposed to do. As much as I dissed Bob in the beginning, what I learned from him is a tremendous work ethic and how much just working contributes to what you do. If you are making, then you are growing. I always think of Bob and Sandy [Simon] as my ceramic mom and dad. Sandy's voice is always in my brain, like, "Go experience life outside the studio, because that will feed your studio life."

After a brief stay in Portland, *I came back to California in January of 2011 and did a residency out at Sonoma Community Center with Forrest Lesch Middleton. He was director of the ceramics department and started a small residency, like a six-month gig. You are there and teach some community classes and do a show. I started with the garlic boxes. I did flowers and architecture with large vessels. And I started doing a lot of this candy-colored sandblasted stuff. Which was present in my thesis exhibition but not to the extent.*

She next did a summer at the Archie Bray Foundation, and then a two-year funded residency at the Bray. *That is just a tremendous place to be, and really such great positive energy in the amount and sort of people that you meet and the passion that everyone has for ceramics. It just feeds my soul. It is home for me.*

In between she was essentially artist in residence at Sacramento State, *not teaching but just using it as a studio base, which was good because Scott is only on campus a couple of days a week. Scott also offered me a show. Being one of the few students going on in art, with the department struggling and stuff, good press for me was good press for them.*

I do love teaching. Utah was a great learning experience for that. I learned in Utah that I am not necessarily just teaching ceramics skills, I am teaching a lot of life lessons.

When you are so passionate about what you're doing it's all you think about, and all you do, and all you dream about. But you think that it's like that for people all the time and that there are students like that all the time. I know that Bob, over his career, has had maybe five or six students like that. I have been really blessed because I've moved from situation to situation that I find pretty magical and pretty compelling and full of passion, and everybody is on the same page with their love of ceramics. I have not been in one place where I have 150 students that couldn't give a shit.

I keep moving forward with the idea that what I need will show up. It took me a long time to find my bliss, as people say. I love ceramics; there is nothing I want to do more than make pots. I force myself to be more of a business person. Growing up in retail, I have a lot of business experience and understanding of how to sell stuff. I live a very cost-efficient life. In my world, I can fit everything in a Subaru and a U-Haul. I love my life. I get to choose what I do every day. I have contributed greatly to a lot of people's lives who reciprocate that. I am workshopping, and I am doing the circuit of getting pots in shows. The Ceramics Monthly *cover thing* [May 2012] *was really pretty tremendous and unexpected and opened a huge number of doors.*

My work has always been what they classify as loose. I don't particularly like that, because people assume that it's unintentional. I think there is a softness to the way I work; I want there to be depth to the forms. My inspiration are these metal objects that have rust bleeding through these layers of paint, and they have been dented. Once metal has been beat up, it's soft. It's structural and soft at the same time. It was perfect but it is now worn. It has a, what do they call that? A veneer of time.

Cobb wants the work to make you think of *your favorite object that you have worn down.* One way to create the effect is sandblasting. *It has worn off the shine of an object, it is worn down with love, and that is what I feel about pots. They have to be used, and if you break them you break them. That is what I always tell my students: ceramics teaches you about loss.*

A lot of it is sort of candy colored. It has to do with my reference materials, metals that have been painted garbage-can green or garbage-can turquoise and then yellow over the top of it to match whatever building it is next to now. I do white slip and then crackle slip over the top of it like peeling paint. When I sandblast, it pulls the depth out a bit.

Cobb says she is not looking to invent new forms. *Everything comes out of making. I am making these forms that look like little houses to me; I want to put windows in them, so I am like, "Oh, it can be a garlic box." I make up whatever use I can find for it after the fact. A lot of this is a weird sculptural leaning. I am adventurous when it comes to form* because I am not attached to it. She likes to have pots *litter a space, because it's like countertop landscape.*

Now I preach ceramics. *You don't have to buy my pots, but you should buy somebody's pots. Don't buy them from the store; buy them from someone that has spirit and interest in design. Sometimes we are not just selling pots; sometimes we are selling our lifestyle. People enjoy that aspect. They find it romantic. People live vicariously through your struggle.* ■

KENYON HANSEN
I Can't Stop

Kenyon Hansen in his former studio in Arkansas, 2017

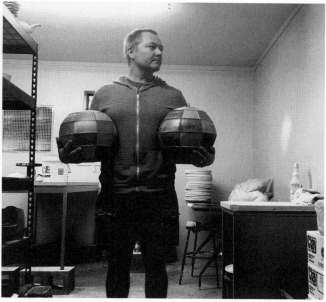

Kenyon Hansen (b. 1980) is the middle of five children of a single mother who was a preschool teacher in the Upper Peninsula of Michigan. *Very lower class, she made maybe $20,000 per year, so we were pretty poor growing up. We had a cooking wood stove in our house for a very long time. Lots of antiques that were still in function. We had one of those old-fashioned wringer washers.*

His life changed unexpectedly. *That's a pretty good story. I was a senior in high school; I really had no intention of going to college. I'd planned on being a construction worker like my brother. An art class was offered, and I took it because I thought it would be a great way to slack off. I didn't know anything about art; I had no interest in it. For the* first half of the year I actually failed this art class. *It's really hard to fail an art class. [Laughter] I didn't do anything, I skipped class, smoking cigarettes, being a mischievous kid. And my mom came in for teacher conferences and asked, "How are you failing art class?" And the teacher said, "He doesn't do anything; he's always fooling around, talking to* girls." My mom said, "He kind of has this interest in photography." The teacher said, "I didn't know that." My mom had recently got this old camera that she'd given me, and I was taking pictures with it.

And the next day I came into school, the teacher said, "You can't sit by your friends anymore. Here's where you're going to sit." It's a small little desk off to the side, sort of a wall barricaded me from the rest of the class. And he gave me this project to build a pinhole camera. I was fascinated by the idea that I could build this camera out of an old oatmeal box. Then we went into the darkroom. It hadn't been touched in ten years; there was a lot of dust. To make a long story short, within a couple of weeks I was showing up to school early [Laughter], I was staying late; I was taking pictures in between my classes. I became really fascinated, truly this love, obsession with it.

So at the end of the year there was this thing called the ASA show, the Association of Student Artists. It's about 13 high schools throughout that area, Wisconsin and northern Michigan. They had a big display. I wouldn't really call it a show. It's something parents came to and saw the work. Universities came to recruit students for their art programs. I ended up getting a scholarship. This person saw the photographs I had taken, and decided I was worth a scholarship. It was a scholarship to any school from a private donor. It wasn't that much money, but it was enough money to make me go, wow. I think it was somebody believing in me is what it came down to. This lady, who didn't know me from Adam, said, "I think this kid could do something."

I think there were several things that were unique about the photos. This huge emphasis on technology was pushing the field forward, but I was using something as ancient as a camera obscura or a pinhole camera, finding ways to bend the film to create fish-eye effects, kind of warping effects. And the subject matter was something you probably don't see a lot of. It was school kids on buses. It was very much hands on. You were loading the camera by hand, you were developing a negative that was printed right on the photography paper, and then you were flipping it over and creating the positive. I was showing a lot of the images connected, two worlds colliding, the negative and positive image sort of folded into one. That was something different.

I went to the school that was close by, Northern Michigan University, and I took a handbuilding class with a guy named Sam Chung while I was a photography student. I was really very shy. I kind of sat in the corner and didn't say anything. But with that class, I felt my interest was moving toward clay.

I was really interested in art, but I wasn't very interested in the other things that I had to do to get that degree. [Laughter] So I took a semester off, and I started making pots in my mom's garage. I had this Amaco wheel that had a slow and slower switch. And a friend of mine gave me a box of clay. So I had 25 pounds of clay, this junky little wheel that worked, and I sat in my mom's garage and threw pots all summer with the same 25 pounds of clay. [Laughter] I would throw a pot and I would squish it and then I would smear it over some plasterboard, and by the end of the summer I think it was more plaster than clay. [Laughter]. It was all chunky; there was paper in it. But I think I have this addictive personality where if I find something that I really respond to, I can't stop. And that was making pots on the potter's wheel.

After that summer, I transferred to a small private Finnish school in Hancock, Michigan. It's called Finlandia University. It's a sister school to Kuopio Academy in Finland. I'm not really sure why I went to this school, but it turned out to be a good thing for me. It had some really great teachers. There were scholarships and grants that I got as soon as the program saw that I was really dedicated. The acting dean asked me if I would be interested in studying abroad, but I didn't speak Finnish so I went to England. I studied at Stoke-on-Trent, which is Staffordshire University. It took me out of my comfort zone of making pots to getting a real taste of history. There was Wedgwood there, there's Spode, there's Royal Doulton, and then there's this wonderful history of smaller potteries that got snubbed out by bigger industry. At that time the school was focused on industrial design, so instead of having a studio and a potter's wheel and a slab roller, it was a classroom and you had a desk, which was a real shift in gears for me. But it opened me up to a whole other avenue and approach to clay.

After graduation Hansen faced the "what to do next" quandary. When he looked at photos in magazines, he tended to respond to wood-fired pots, although he had no experience with that. *I didn't feel like I was ready for graduate school, so I sought out somebody who took apprentices. I contacted, I don't know, 15 or 20 people, and all of them said no except for one, and that was Simon Levin. He was hesitant but ended up taking me. Simon was in a really rural area, and his family was very much intertwined with his studio life. In some ways you just became a member of the family. You'd eat meals with them, watch his girls when they went away, walk the dog. We built a kiln in Illinois together, and we did repair work on the kilns there. Certainly I learned about firing wood kilns. My entire life was built around firing and filling these wood kilns. It was a really great year. It felt like everything was open; there was a million possibilities.*

But I still didn't have a strong set of skills, so from there I went to Penland School of Crafts and worked with Matt Kelleher and Shoko Teruyama. They were Penland residents at the time, and I was a studio assistant for the two-month Concentration, which had nothing to do with wood firing. It had to do with bisque molds and earthenware clay. So again I was taken out of my comfort zone. It was good.

After that, I moved to Illinois and was a resident artist at a place called Center Street Clay. I made pots there for a couple of years and then moved to North Carolina and worked with Matt and Shoko again, in their studio. They were really good at pushing me. I was going to apply for grad school, and I came down to see them and the deadlines had passed, and they said where did you apply and I said I didn't apply and they said they weren't sure they wanted me working in their studio then. They started to doubt my commitment. They insisted that he apply for something. So he applied for residencies at the Bray and Red Lodge and decided to go with the longer two-year residency at the Bray. There he stopped wood firing and began to soda fire, appreciating its much more rapid turnover rate.

Hansen feels that he had his biggest leaps *in terms of thinking about pots, different ways of making pots,* in North Carolina. *I grew up using very heavy things, cast-iron pans. So weight to me speaks of quality. Today so many things are made out of plastic, Styrofoam, cardboard. You pick them up and there's no skeleton to them. And that's a big concern, I think, to many people. I think all of these things are contributing to the loss of rituals.*

He crosshatches the bottom of the forms, most of them thrown. *The crosshatching is something I started doing in North Carolina. I started using it as a way to even out slabs over bisque molds. It's just this technique to take down high areas and level things out. And I became interested in the texture and how slips and glazes could pool and accent that texture. I think it grew out of rope-impressed work I was doing.*

He also ribs or lines the work in relief. *Originally, the exaggerated hips and shoulders of pots were made with the intention of collecting and pooling ash, because I was wood firing. Those are very old ideas. But now that I'm soda firing I see that it's pooling and collecting in a different way, around the entire piece, whereas wood firing is much more directional and it would maybe collect in a small area. Moving things around on the cups gives your hand a place to rest. It's from using a metal rib on the outside and pushing out from the inside with my hand. I want my pots to celebrate the hand.*

Long spouts sort of grew out of those old aluminum percolating coffeepots. My mom probably had 10 or 15 of them throughout the house, and that's how she made coffee. I always thought it was a form that was beautiful.

I started looking at old kerosene lamps, another thing that was sort of littered around our house. When I was in Stoke-on-Trent, there was a really great museum, a wonderful collection of pots on three or four floors. And there was this vase that had been made at Wedgwood, a similar form. I found it really beautiful, and I couldn't explain why, but of all the pots there, and there were tens of thousands of pots, I kept coming back to this one vase. I just couldn't stop looking at it. I think that's a form that shows up in a lot of different places, the variations of it. I've seen variations from Taiwan that were made in a similar way, even these old African pots with all this form down below and then this long tapering neck.

The thermos certainly evolved in North Carolina. Matt and Shoko lived on this big hill, way up. You can't drive up it; it's too steep and windy. So it was a long-enough walk, and I did it too many times in a day. I'd have lunch and this thermos. Each day at lunchtime I'd pour some tea out. I began thinking about the possibility of making one with clay. I hadn't seen it done before. So how would you make such a thing; what does it take to contain a hot liquid and keep it hot? I don't think just having a thick wall does it so well. It helps making a double wall, that's what struck me. Trying to make a double wall form that is tall and slender is really challenging. Making it out of two pieces of clay made it significantly easier. I think it can be done and works really well. It's not that heavy. It's not like carrying around a cast-iron frying pan [Laughter] or a box of clay. [Laughter] But it's also something that requires care. You need to be aware of where it's at; you don't want to knock it over. It's not an idea suitable to somebody who works in a coal mine, but it may be suitable for somebody who works in an office. It's fitting into many different kinds of lives, but not everybody's life. And that probably goes for all my pots. Still, he has discontinued making them because of the loss rate.

Hansen also developed a tea infuser because he likes loose-leaf tea, and it was a nuisance to clean the tea out of one of his own teapots. And a side-handle teapot that he thinks pours much better than the common arch handle. Although Levin and Kelleher and Teruyama were mentors and influences, he doesn't think his pots show any similarity to theirs. It took a lot of time to find my own voice and find forms that weren't theirs. It required me to make a lot of really, really bad pots before I could make a good pot. There's no doubt about that. The pots are stoneware or "dirty porcelain."

Once his grandmother was telling me about growing up in the Depression; how hard it was. When they sat down as a family for dinner, everybody felt really grateful because they were eating okay. On really, really rare occasions they would have dessert. It was this luxury at the time. And she said, "When we would have dessert, our plates had to be so clean that you could flip then over and eat off the foot of the plate." And I thought: That is such a beautiful story, a really great story. I wanted to figure out how I could share it. So I started making these plates that has sort of a dinner plate, and as a foot, sort of a dessert plate. I think in today's society we don't need to talk about not having enough but maybe having too much. And talk about how we consume today, how much we waste. I love ideas, and when ideas can come forward in form, I think it makes pots much, much better, much stronger. And for me it was one of those revelations.

Hansen is now back in the Upper Peninsula, and he and his wife, ceramist Lindsey Heiden, have bought a house with a studio. ■

GWENDOLYN YOPPOLO

The Peril of Structure

Gwendolyn Yoppolo in her Kutztown, Pennsylvania, studio, 2016

It's not at all unusual—it's a standard joke in the arts—that families resist a child's desire to make a life in art. But many of those stories are not entirely funny: the ending might be an unhappy person trapped in the role the family chooses, or a person estranged from the family by insisting on an artistic destiny. More often, families gradually come to accept this unexpected career and see the passion that drives anyone who chooses the arts.

Gwendolyn Yoppolo in some ways embraces her roots, but she does so from an expressive rather than a business perspective. Her father ran a hobby craft store. *He had a pretty large store with all these really fun materials to use. There weren't the big-box hobby stores yet. He had models and just a lot of crafty things. My mother eventually started to work with him. My brother runs an eBay business, which is also craft based or art materials now. So he in a way followed and updated what my father was doing.*

I don't think I showed any special talent for art, but I did show that inclination of always trying to make something or do something. I was pretty academic in school, though. I really loved the reading and writing and studying part of school. [Laughter] I grew up near Philadelphia, and I trace my roots in wanting to make things back to Isaiah Zagar's mosaic murals and the magic garden on South Street. When I was a teenager visiting Philadelphia, just seeing his work had a huge impact on me. And that's how I started working with clay. I started by making mosaics. It was during college.

She was enrolled at Haverford, in sociology, but living at Bryn Mawr. *They had these old coffee tables in one of the buildings where they had coffee hour every morning. They were built to have tile tops, but the tiles were all falling out. So one of my first renegade art projects was to steal one of those tables, put it in my dorm room, and mosaic the top. Then I sneaked it back into the space. During coffee hour I would sit near it and watch people interpret the imagery that was on it. I was working with more narrative imagery at that point. It was fun. I guess from the beginning, my drive to make art had that kind of surprise element.*

I used a lot of found objects, and things I had collected over the years, stuck in with the tiles. It was a lot of how I was feeling about being female. I was struggling a little bit with my parents' *traditional views on gender roles and things. It was imagery that questioned the male/female dynamic. I was using commercial tiles, just breaking them up and using that for the mosaic.*

She took clay classes at Mainline Arts Center and Moore College of Art, at first with the goal of making her own tiles. *And then I moved to Manhattan to go to school for education, but I was also at Parsons taking continuing ed. One was a tile class. And then I took throwing there. Once I started throwing, I decided to go into that direction and stop doing the tile making so much.*

In maybe my second year of graduate school for education, I found this tiny community pottery on the Upper West Side, called Super Mud Pottery. It was like a closet, basically, but the teacher there was Louise Harder. Her energy was really thrilling. The first day she's like, "Oh, we are going to build a wood kiln out in the country." I was like, "Whoa," because I had just had this intense dream about firing with wood a couple nights before. It was mostly women, and we drove four hours out of the city to build this wood kiln up in Walton, New York.

That experience made the decision to work with clay irreversible for me, because the group was so supportive. We collaborated on the kiln and then collaborated on the firings, and I felt like we were sharing so much knowledge, and it was this time of awakening for a lot of us. Many of us are still working in clay today. I went on in wood firing for a long time. That was part of the excitement for me. Louise was all about enjoying meals with people and making the meal a special event through the use of handmade pottery. It changed how I felt about eating and how I felt about people, everything.

Yoppolo completed her education degree, but *I was trying to figure out how I could change tracks again. My friend Kowkie Durst and I were working at Women's Studio Workshop in Rosendale, New York. We were trying to get them equipment and* trying to get a clay program going with classes.

I was basically just really poor and learning how to be an artist. I didn't really have great skills. I went from there to teaching first grade for four years. I would wood fire at Chester Springs Studio in Pennsylvania.

When I decided to quit that job, I moved to Southern Illinois University, Edwardsville, as a special student, and that was partly because Dan Anderson has a big wood-firing component. I began to clarify what I wanted to do. It was the first time I was in the academic ceramic art environment. He slowed me down and got me to really think about what I was doing, and also to give the piece in front of me full attention. That's when I started swearing off clock time in the studio. I had this antagonism toward measuring how long a piece took, until a couple years ago, when I was appalled to time myself in making mugs. It came out to be like two hours and nine minutes a mug. [Laughter]

I went from there to Eastern Kentucky University, where I worked as a studio tech for Joe Molinaro for two years. Another special time in my life was working for him. He really values people and community. His vision for what ceramics means in the world is very broad. He travels a lot. One of his ongoing projects is to study indigenous potters in Ecuador. He took me down there, and we went into this remote jungle village. It's like adventure travel for potters.

The villages are being more and more connected to the city economy and using money. Thinking about that in terms of what I make and how what I make influences the way people live, I made the decision to work with the utensils line, for people to use in the kitchen, so mortar and pestle and citrus strainers and colanders. For me that focus on getting people back to processing their own food is pretty revolutionary. Ecuador made me think about how the way we eat is completely connected to how we feel about our environment, and it made me a lot more aware of the ways that pottery can fit into that relationship between people and environment, and people and other people.

She went to grad school at Penn State but didn't do a lot of work with clay. *I did a lot of sewing and a lot of knitting, and I also started working with the electron microscope. At SIUE, I would hang out in the library, and I was always drawn to the biology*

section and looking at life forms, and I loved the microscope imagery in the books. I have always had this philosophy that small can be just as powerful and intricate and infinite as huge. I've also always been interested in the way that we perceive the world, and the microscope for me is like extending our capabilities into the infinitely small world.

At SIUE I discovered the microbiology books; I discovered diatoms. Their cell wall, which is made out of silica, is incredibly perforated; beautiful forms and infinite variety. I had images photocopied at Penn State, and they were up on my wall. With faculty support she contacted the microbiology department, and armed with some grant money she went to Haystack in the summer, picked up beach rubble, and brought it back to Penn State to examine. *It was so easy to just take a tiny piece of beach rubble and prep it and put it in the microscope, and there were diatoms all over it. So I started taking my own pictures on the microscope, and then I started looking at sugar cereals and then, from there, bugs and plant parts, like pollen grains, are really interesting to look at. The bugs actually got me on a side track of this fascination with how bugs perceive the world. That is one of my writing projects. I am working on expanding our ideas about the senses and to include other senses besides the five or six senses we commonly think of.*

I was drawn to the diatoms' perforated forms and their waterworn edges. It is similar to how bones in our bodies get eroded by flesh so they are rounded edges. At Penn State I was trying to figure out how to make that in clay.

From grad school I got a teaching job right away at Juniata College, where Jack Troy retired from. It is right near Penn State. I got hired by them for a tenure track job right out of school. I felt like my studio life was embryonic still. I knew if I stayed at Juniata, I would give my everything to that because I wanted to be a good professor. So I left that after a year. That was a second time I heard it from my family about leaving a salaried job.

Interestingly, her father's business had been evolving and had become a clay business. But that didn't actually help when he heard from his customers how hard it was to get a teaching job, and she had just thrown one way.

She jokes, *I am lucky I have my midlife crisis so young, you know? Or how many of them have I had so far? I moved to Alfred and did a tech job there for a year. It was a really good job. They had a scanning electron microscope I could use, and they also had every kind of kiln that I could use. During that year I figured out my glaze palette and how to fire these runny crystalline glazes. So I finally got the work to some point there. Something clicked. From there I went out to the Bray for two and a half years.*

The Bray's emphasis on exhibiting helped her get over her qualms about that. *Before I went out there, I felt so exposed and vulnerable when I would have an exhibition. It became more like part of the process for me, part of breathing in and out, like breathing* in *in your studio and breathing* out *to show the work. I started getting enough recognition that my father relaxed a little bit, I think.*

The residency program can be really supportive for someone like me who doesn't have the financial backing to set up a studio. When I left Alfred, I had a goal of five years in studio residencies, because I knew that my artwork needed that. And I was lucky enough to provide that for myself, two and half years at the Archie Bray and then three years at Penland.

When she was at Penland, one night she asked all the core students, *"What is it that made us come out artists, and our siblings are normal people, relatively normal people?"* It was really funny, the answers they had. They were all pretty much negative traits. They were like nonconformist, or stubborn, obsessive.

But are those really negative traits? Maybe the world needs them.

The work goes through these phases. After working with a technique or a process in the studio, I have to ban that process because it doesn't serve the work anymore or I find myself applying it to every piece indiscriminately.

I was making things that hang; I was really interested in that and also my early interest in perforated walls and seeing through into the inside form. So the hanging thing became my tea infusers, the ones that either sit in the mug or else click up into the lid of the teapot. I was making an inner bowl that hung in there. One of my mantras during this period was "the peril of the structure is the cage." Structure gives you something to grow on and grow into, but it also can become a cage; you can become limited by your own kind of scaffolding.

A tea infuser set with a mug is an example of her once-favored process of faceting with wire, which was the first process she had to ban. Another early interest *was this idea of the vessel, the multiple vessel, the compound vessel. I guess my hanging oil jars are a manifestation of that, with the two forms joined together.* A garlic roaster was a double-walled vessel. *I got into doing a lot of forms that were different on the inside from the outside, and that whole metaphor is really compelling to me.*

When she was doing compound vessels, *everything was lobed, and I felt like the functionality of them was getting sacrificed. I had this epiphany that I was working from the outside/in too much. So when I banned lobing, I basically made this commitment to working from the inside/out, and working from the functional space and the emptiness/out.*

If I had to sum my goal up in one word, it's abstraction, but to me that abstraction is not geometric perfection. It is actually born out of imperfection or born out of irregularity.

My first summer at the Bray I was really into this idea of vertigo. All of my cups and everything had this craziness to them and this off-kilterness. And from a pot you want stability. This idea of the object as dynamic is something that I returned to when I started focusing on using the rare-earth oxides that change color under different lights. Our mind has to assume some constancy in our environment, you know. With these color-changing glazes, I wanted people to be able to pick the pot up and walk around through different types of lighting and watch the color changing, which was not often possible in gallery settings where you can't touch the work. I started to think about how to create food events. I want to go beyond the visual and the tactile, which are the two main senses that we use with ceramic art.

That led to *feeding events and creating utensils that are designed to feed someone else with, rather than feeding yourself with. Another idea is pots that are designed to fit in your hand. I have been all along trying to figure out how to incorporate the knitting and sewing that I do into the work. I have tried making wraps and carrying cases for pots, or in terms of presentation to have the pot be wrapped in a nice fabric swatch.* She has carried this on in performance/event objects that involve paired people speaking/listening, sharing tea, and otherwise interacting. It is a form of social action.

She sees such works as *breaking down binaries. It is about recognizing commonalities and recognizing humanity. It is about listening and empathy too. I'm still interested in the idea of the hole, as in the perforation, as a structure that can be permeable. The same thing is coming out in the knitting, and I do a lot of lacework, open work. I think of the* opening *in terms of listening and being open to the other person too.*

I need to teach to be fulfilled, I think. I have enjoyed the years of studio time immensely, but part of that is because I have been in communities where I feel like part of something larger than myself. The studio explorations continue, although she has stopped the feeding events. And she is now an assistant professor at Kutztown University. ∎

NOAH RIEDEL

Product-Designy Pots

Noah Riedel at the Archie
Bray Foundation, 2016

The journeyman's journey may not be so much in miles as in the development of focus and ideas. Noah Riedel's imaginative, problem-solving work has come through despite obstacles. But then, his parents are an architect who for a time had a computer business, and an English professor turned wildlife biologist; his sister was in advertising in New York, then a yoga instructor in Massachusetts, and then pursuing documentary films. So maybe it's not surprising that he, too, has trodden a varied path.

His interest in art is long standing. As a kid, Riedel (b. 1979) wanted to be a painter, but an older cousin to whom he was very close went to RISD, and, without talking to anyone about it, Riedel decided that only one person in a family could do that, so he couldn't be an artist. In high school, living in North Carolina, he took a ceramics class and didn't do well.

The teacher didn't know how to throw, and *I didn't know much about pottery and didn't like what I did know, because most of what I'd been exposed to was those country kitsch things. I grew up in an architect's house, and he had modern conceptions.*

Riedel sort of slid through high school, not sleeping much and getting obsessed with things other than his homework. *My parents had these old beads from when they were younger (and they were hippies), bits of bone and different kinds of beads, and night after night, instead of doing my homework, I'd make a bead necklace. But they weren't for wearing. I would always do them in patterns, like the Fibonacci sequence. For some reason I got addicted to that, and I didn't want to tell anybody because I was embarrassed about making jewelry* [Laughter] *and doing it in the middle of the night.* [Laughter]

He applied to a single college, and that only because his mother insisted. *That was the college that almost everyone in my high school went to, sort of a party school on the coast of North Carolina, UNC Wilmington.* Yet, there he was engaged by a 3-D design class. The teacher gave them sculptor Richard Serra's list of action verbs. *And then he said, "Make boxes that embody one of these words." I had such a good time with that, and it got me so zoned in. It was actually, now that I think of it, a lot like the beads, I would get so absorbed in it. I made these transformer boxes, and the idea is you do one action, pull or twist, and it would change from one shape to another. They were just cardboard and rubber bands and glue. The teacher also taught ceramics, and so I decided to take a ceramics class.*

Despite getting more and more into clay, *I thought I was going to get a sculpture degree and then go into product design or something like that. So I graduated and I moved back home with my parents, because I didn't have any money. I got a job at a design gallery in Chapel Hill. I decided, well, I know how to work in clay, so I need to build a little studio and get a wheel. I can start out doing some dishware. And meanwhile the design gallery went out of business.*

I got a job as a picture framer; I became the head wood framer, someone who cut wood frames. It was fun to come up with interesting framing options for people. In the meantime I built a studio on my parents' property. I got a wheel. I didn't have a kiln, and I thought that's okay because I could just practice and make prototypes. So I did that. Then I saw an ad for a job for managing a studio for a lady in a nearby town who did wholesale garden art, all in ceramics. It was slip casting, press molding, and extruding mostly, both high-fire salt and midrange electric with stains and stuff like that. I worked for

her for a year, managed her studio. I got some experience managing people, which I found I'm not particularly good at and I don't like very much. But I got good at popping molds and working really fast, because that was what we had to do.

Her business failed because of competition from China. In the meantime, Riedel met someone teaching at a community college in Siler City, about an hour from where he lived, who was starting a ceramics program. The guy offered Riedel a scholarship to do glaze chemistry there and use his salt kiln. *So I did that, and I had a great time. That's when I found out a little more about the history, found out who Leach was, read* A Potter's Book. *I sort of got caught up in that,* but being a potter was still not his goal. *I was there for a semester.*

He met Mark Hewitt when he went on a tour of artists' studios. *I didn't know who he was. I went and was blown away.* When Riedel was taking a class on documentary filmmaking (encouraged by his mother), *I decided to do one on Mark Hewitt. I emailed him and he said he was up for it. I went out and interviewed him and went prepared, so I knew things he had said. And just by happenstance,* both of them had recently been to New York to see the van Gogh drawings show at the Metropolitan Museum. *Since college there would be one artist after another that I'd get hooked on, and I'd look at everything they did. I was really into van Gogh at that point, so I went there just to see his drawings. It was really fortuitous; it was just a good connection. I had been going to Mark's openings at that point for a couple of years, and of course I asked to be an apprentice and he blew me off, in a nice way, but he had people always asking. He was talking about this new kiln he was going to build, so I emailed him while I was editing the documentary and asked him if I could help build the kiln.* Hewitt said he could fill in before a new apprentice arrived.

It went well, and Hewitt recommended Riedel for an apprenticeship with a potter in London who had to cancel at the last minute for personal reasons. As consolation, Hewitt agreed to try taking Riedel on as a third apprentice—his first time having three. *And I stayed, and it worked great. I got along with the other guys, I got along with Mark, and I worked hard. I learned a lot. I had worked really hard at throwing, and I thought I'd gotten decent at it. After working for Mark I realized I wasn't* such a good thrower.

That made him think maybe he wasn't meant to be a potter. *Plus I love Mark's work, but somehow the ones I liked were not the ones the other guys liked, and more than that, they tended not to be the ones that Mark liked either.* [Laughter] *I liked some of the underfired stuff, the stuff without as much decoration. I was surprised when I got there that Mark was decorating. He said you've got to have at least three colors; you have to decorate this; you have no option. I was having to do these things I wasn't comfortable with, and I'm glad I did but I'm also glad I don't have to anymore.* [Laughter]

After the stint with Hewitt and attending a wood-firing symposium in Denmark, he thought, *now I'm really going to pursue this product-design thing.* Still he hesitated. *I love looking at product design, but everything started to seem like it was made out of plastic, and not just the things that were made of plastic. If you don't know a medium or a material very well, you sort of think in basic geometry. Then I thought: Why don't I just be a product designer who's independent, essentially a potter, but my angle would be that my pots aren't pots; they're products designed as functional pottery. I wouldn't say it like that because it sounds a little snooty, but that's how I would think about it.*

He had heard many people say, "*Pottery has been around for so long that you can't make a new bowl; you can just make your own bowl.*" *And I really didn't like that, and I still don't. With product design, modern design, you make your mark by making something completely different. The more different you can make it, the more you might get attention. And I thought you could use that type of thinking and then also use material knowledge that I felt like I had a little bit in pottery.*

So his concern was this: *How can I make this so you couldn't slip cast it, or you couldn't make it any other way than throwing it* [to protect it from commercial competition]? *I ended up with a couple of pots where I feel like at least it would be really difficult to, and it would be pointless. I could make things that were just for a few people. With the internet, I could sell it just to those few people because there may be only two in my town, but if there's two in every town I can still do it. Before the internet, you couldn't get your stuff out as easily.*

But I've left Mark's, I'm working two jobs, and then *I'm also making my pots on the side. So I'm killing myself, you know. I'm so exhausted after working the other jobs, and they were boring, tedious jobs. They didn't exhaust me physically, but I would come home and I just didn't care anymore. I was seeing too many faces. So I quit my jobs.*

My parents let me live at home all this time without paying rent. When I left Mark's I was 28, so it was between the ages of 28 and 32, four years. I had a friend help make a website, which we got halfway through. I started out trying to sell pots, mostly making just modernized Mark Hewitt pots that were then electric fired. I started doing fairs and shows, and selling everywhere I could, then I started entering competitions and I got in some, and it was motivating. I got into this artist collective being formed in Chapel Hill. I worried that I'm going to have to deal with a lot of people. I found out that I really loved it. They all called me their son [Laughter] *because it was their joke that I was the only one under 40.*

So I thought: a residency is not a bad idea. I applied to a few, and Wally [Bivins, director of Pottery Northwest in Seattle at the time] *called me up one day.* It was a good experience and led him on to a subsequent residency at Archie Bray Foundation in Montana. He stayed on in Helena.

Riedel's efforts to develop his work involved sequences of dilemmas. As he conceived *these product-designy pots, I thought it was such a good idea that people would copy it. I was overly concerned about that. I didn't want to release it until I felt like I could really produce it. I'd labor and labor on each one. I think it was my mom who said, "You need to just start doing your ideas."*

Among his inventions were *stem-showing vases. The idea was to come up with as many different ways of showing the stems off. It always came down to some way of having the middle part open or exposed.*

He developed squared bowls in sets of five. *Made them to stack: Even though this looks random, there's a pattern to this, and you can go pretty high. It's really stable; you can shake it around and it won't tip over because the corners fit into each other as long as the bowls are the same size. The only problem was if I was going to send the bowls to a show that I wasn't going to set up, I had to tell them left, right, right, left.*

He adapted the faceting he had learned at Hewitt's, so that every pot looked different from every angle. In Denmark he had developed a mug that could be grabbed from the side. *I showed them to Mark, and he pretended to drop it. It was a comment that they were going to fall out of your hands. Which they're not, but I found that a lot of people thought they wouldn't be able to hold it; they were scared of them. So that was a good lesson to me too. Even if something works, if it doesn't look like it will, they won't use it.*

Mark doesn't trim anything except bowls and plates, and I decided I was going to hold on to that too. I liked the thinking and the systems in Mark's practice. It goes along well with a lot of the ideas behind modern product design.

He developed what he called *Heat Shield Lap Bowls. Essentially I'd throw a jar, then turn it on the side and squish the side in. I called them that because you could have a bowl of hot soup in your lap and sit in front of TV, and it wouldn't burn you.* Then he made colanders and what he called *Drunken Whisky Cups, because they wobble around, and I've worked the rims so they're even.*

His originary efforts continue, not always to his satisfaction. He has been trying to create a new kind of glaze *where any color could be achieved with different ratios of a few primary frits. Hubris. I still don't have a reliable clay body or glaze for my standard tableware.* But his creativity comes through in elegant modernist forms, including fruit bowls (unglazed) and a canister with an inventive and graceful grip on the lid. He has been adding metal and wood to his pots, and learning woodworking to that end. ■

CHAPTER TEN

A WAY OF LIFE

Probably every potter who establishes a studio can be said to have worked out a way of life. But there are some makers who seem to have struggled harder to achieve that goal, overcoming exceptional odds or completely shifting gears or demonstrating extraordinary ingenuity to find a satisfying and coherent life. ■

JOSH COPUS

Half Artist, Half Community Organizer

Josh Copus, Marshall,
North Carolina, 2018.
Photo: Jack Sorokin

Surprisingly, a good example of focused life-making is embodied in one of the younger artists in this book, Josh Copus (b. 1979) of Marshall, North Carolina. Copus grew up in Floyd County, Virginia. *We moved there when I was five because my parents wanted to be a part of the back-to-the-land movement and the alternative community. I grew up more or less on a commune, and we lived in a bus and things like that. My mother was very invested in education. The families that we lived around started a school loosely based on Steiner's education philosophies and Waldorf. It is more of a real school now. When I was a kid it was kind of like a big playground experiment thing.*

I feel so fortunate to have been raised as I was. My life is all about creating very holistic, integrated experiences, and there is no way to separate my childhood from who I am now. There are days when I wake up out here and I am like, "Oh my god, what am I doing? I am just re-creating this thing that my parents did." There's a huge number of us that grew up in Floyd that have more or less embraced the teachings and the lifestyle.

Having potters as neighbors was just normal in Floyd. Only when he was a student at Warren Wilson College in Asheville did Copus happen to see the inscription in a book belonging to his ceramics teacher and discovered the Rick Hensley was someone more than his Little League coach. *When you're a kid, you don't realize. I didn't have any notion that Silvie Granatelli was anything more than just one of my mom's friends that happened to make a living making pottery.*

The father of a friend allowed free play in his ceramics studio at night. *We were just playing around, learning about the material in this really kind of cool, unstructured way, which is a lot like the education and principles that my parents were trying to create. Experiential-based learning, and learning where kids are making their choices. One of the most influential experiences as far as my career is concerned was this idea that, wow, this is actually a viable way to be in the world. I had these great models.*

The friend's father encouraged them when they made face jugs, not like the traditional southeastern US ones but based on Narnia, Dungeons and Dragons, *Lord of the Rings*, and the like. He took some to a show, and when they sold, he split the money with them. Copus thought he had discovered the secret of life: *As a 16-year-old kid, I was like, "You can make money doing something that you would just do anyways, 'cause you thought it was cool? Wow, I can get into that."*

Still, he *felt this weird pressure from somewhere that I had to go to college and do something serious. Warren Wilson is a work college, so everyone on campus has a job. I was interested in it 'cause the educational model was work and service and academics.* His first-year job was on the recycling crew, but the second year, because of his ceramics

background, he was on the ceramics crew and had a key to the art building. *The studio was supposed to close at 10, but I was like, "Hey guys, we can stay as late as we want." And I remember being on my way to my biology class, and stopping in my tracks and thinking, "I don't even like biology. I'm going to the pottery studio!"*

Once I figured out that I wanted to do ceramics, I dropped out. He worked in the warehouse of the Highwater Clay Company while he waited to get into Heywood Community College, a professional crafts program that often had a waiting list. *I went there for two years. During that time I started getting involved with Penland and having all of that experience. And then when I finished Heywood, I knew I needed a more complete art education, so I went to finish my bachelors.* He chose the University of North Carolina, Asheville (UNCA), for a broader perspective, including art history and other mediums, *so that I can discover where I fit within that whole wider world. Because my aspirations are not just limited to ceramics. I want to be able to have a debate with somebody about why functional pottery is art, and you can't do that if you don't know the history.*

When he started at UNCA he also began renting a studio in Asheville's arts district that he shared and named Clay Space. *I got my friend's band to rent part of the space, and I convinced two kids I knew who went to UNCA to stop working at school and instead come work at the Clay Space, and it was like a free-for-all.* The rent was $500 a month, and dividing it among several people made it almost free; the only additional cost was electricity. *I lived in there for like three years, and it was great. A lot of people were living in the building at the time. The space was so cheap you could afford to do weird stuff. There wasn't this kind of push to make things and sell them to pay the bills.*

He received a grant from UNCA's research scholarship program, as a team with his friend Matt Jacobs (who was also part of Clay Space), to investigate *local and nonindustrially processed ceramic materials in contemporary ceramics.* That involved digging clay, and wood firing was part of it. *I had a vision for the work that I wanted to make and how I wanted it to look and feel. Honestly, a lot of it has* to do with my history and my background in Floyd, and taking responsibility for your food and your materials and that kind of stuff. I am always drawn to that. And in response to the art-school urging that he "find his own voice" and make an "individual statement," he thought, *well, if I am supposed to make this unique work, what if I start with a material that is unique to me?*

In a lot of ways the physical qualities of the clay had a huge impact. In school I was digging this clay, and my ceramics professor would say, "Let's figure out what the problems are with the clay, and we will add stuff and amend it and fix it." And I was like, "Well, what if I just change what I'm doing to fit what the clay is capable of?" I realized that what is unique, more than the physical properties, is your experience with it.

When I was in school at UNCA, I feel like I had two educations going on. I had my education in school, and then I had my education in Asheville. I think a lot of students didn't take advantage of Asheville. I would hang out with people or fire with them. It was more like friendships, informal, not like workshops. Michael Hunt and Naomi Dalglish are really key in creating my passion for the potential of local materials.

He describes his approach as empirical. *We did some work with the North Carolina Geological Survey group, but mostly we just drove around with shovels and talked to farmers and potters and construction guys. The clay that I use, pipe clay, is pretty bluish, so it is actually kind of recognizable. But we didn't really find the clay.*

At an out-of-state kiln-building project with Hunt and Dalglish and others, Copus proclaimed his need to find his own clay. *When I left that project, I came back and I walked into my studio, and there was a bag of clay on my table with a phone number and a guy's name written on it. Matt Jacobs told me, "This crazy guy just came in here the other day; said he found some clay and wondered if we were interested in it." I had just created this conviction in myself that I was going to find some clay. It found me!*

So we called this guy up. He took us out to this place and showed us where this clay was. But it was not on his property. The first day we went out there, we were like, "Well, there is all this clay; we might as well just get some while we're here." Not knowing whose property it was or anything, we kind of drove down in this field a little bit, and we were loading the clay up, and the next thing I know, this pickup truck pulls up and I thought: We're in trouble. This guy just thought we had run off the road, and he was going to stop to see if we needed a hand. Copus explained, and asked whose land it was. *And he said, "Well, that's Neil Woody's land."*

It's cool talking to people about clay around here because people know it. In some parts of the country, if you tell someone you make pottery, they think of Pottery Barn. I called Neil Woody and when I said, "Hey, I make pottery," he said, "I know pottery; I got some." And sure as shit, I go over to his place, and he has got all of these old folk pots that were his family's; they were his grandmother's pottery. I didn't have to sit down and tell Neil what I did because the image that he had in his mind was close to what I actually do.

It has been interesting for me because we were outsiders in Floyd. It's a lot like here. There are families that go back to settlement, and the local community didn't exactly open their arms to the hippies. When he told Woody where he was from, that made them seem like neighbors. *When I was growing up, there was a sense that "I am different; I am not from here; I will never be fully accepted by the local people." But the truth is that I am from there, and that's what I know. That's who I am.*

The first dig that we did, we put all of the clay on Matt Jones's land (see chapter 11), and I had a percentage. There was a total cost, and then we figured out what it cost per dump truck, and I got so many dump trucks and he got so many dump trucks. And then when I bought this place, I still had this relationship with Neil. So I got eleven dump trucks out here.

When I was in school, I was a little bit older than some of the kids 'cause I had done some other things, so I was super driven and I wanted to make awesome stuff. I did really well in school, and I felt like I accomplished a lot, and I got nominated to apply for a Windgate [Charitable Foundation] *grant. I wrote a proposal and it was accepted and they gave me $15,000. One of the things I am most proud of in this life is what I did with that money. That money was a miracle.*

I was going to build a kiln, and it was all tied to the local materials research, and there was this huge community component. When I wrote that proposal, there were things I didn't mention, like I didn't have anywhere to build the kiln; I didn't own any land. I didn't lie! I said, "I am going to buy some property, and then I am going to build this kiln." I just didn't tell them how any of that was going to happen, honestly because I didn't know. I actually did exactly what I told them I would do, but the way I did it was a little bit different than even I expected.

I'm a pretty good scrounge, and I'm pretty creative with materials. I gave them this budget that was line itemized. I did all the research, I knew what everything cost, I had a kiln, and the materials fit the budget perfectly. The truth is, I knew "I am going to have to figure out how to get a bunch of those materials for not that much money," because I put $3,000 down for this property, which came from the Windgate [grant], and then I bought the Airstream Travel Trailer for $3,000. I was $6,000 in the hole before I even did anything.

I never would have built this kiln if I had not created a certain connection, 'cause all these bricks were free. I went to this conference for wood-fired ceramics in Arizona, and I met this guy there. Maynard Leeman is his name, and he was a character. We were on a firing shift together, and he was asking me all these questions.

Maynard Leeman knows the foreman at this huge brick plant. I feel like he went to that conference with this piece of information to give it to someone, and I gave him the time of day, and he gave me the information. And this guy is my absolute angel; all of these bricks are because of him. They are flawed for various reasons: materials impurities, underthickness, odd lots, overruns. So a lot of times when I build, I am working with stuff that is a little bit weird. You've got to be a little bit creative. Probably like $60,000 of retail material for . . . I've got to drive to Alabama to get it, so it's not fun, but it allowed me to build this kiln for practically nothing. In fact, multiple kilns. And he insists that they are not personal property but a community resource.

I've been given this incredible thing, and the best thing I can do with it is make it available and make it affect more than just me in a positive way. There's probably 50 people who have been out here firing these kilns with me. None of them could afford

to do this for themselves. So it has been really cool to afford that opportunity to other people too.

Copus organized a workshop with a friend. *It was just a simple trade labor for knowledge. And Rob* [Pulleyn, a philanthropist and former publisher] *is such a big supporter. He's got a guesthouse at the top of the hill, and he let everyone live there. We worked for a month; we did it every day. We put the right group together, and that's stuff that I am really interested in.*

I haven't made the strides that I want to make as far as the development of my work is concerned. Because I haven't had the time; because I am doing all of this other stuff and also the pressure of making money. I make work to sell it. Yeah, that's how I live. Sometimes I feel like I don't have enough time to just make, to explore.

For example, there's the Foundation, a collective he established in the face of possible gentrification of Asheville's arts district. *I feel like half artist, half community organizer.* Another distraction is travel. *I kind of got on the circuit, especially for the wood-fire things, so I got to present in Germany. They had the European wood fire conference there, and I had a talk. Then I had another talk at this conference in Denmark and met a bunch of people. And actually the whole Australia thing started with the* Studio Potter *article about local materials.* He has made several trips to Australia for months-long stays. These exposures have led him to bring makers from other countries to Asheville, so he says only half joking that he is also *an international residency organizer.*

My pottery is primarily made with local materials and/or nonindustrially processed materials, and it is wood-fired. Those are the two defining elements more than anything, and the clay is a pretty powerful influence. The clay is pipe clay, which is a local vernacular term 'cause they used to press-mold tobacco pipes. Its major physical characteristic is that it is very high in iron, really nice plasticity, kind of a nice mixture of coarse and fine particles. It is most similar to the clay from Bizen and Imbe, in Japan, or Korean Punch'ong, Choson-dynasty Korean pots that are also made of iron-bearing clay. Dark clay, white slip, finger wipes, or brush decoration and simple clear glaze.

What I am trying to do with my work is make things that have a timeless sense. Not like a reproduction of ancient things. I want it to have the feeling that it could have been made a thousand years ago but still have a contemporary relevancy. I want to make things that feel like rocks. When people tell me that something I made looks like it has been in a shipwreck, that is a huge compliment. Artifacts, things that got dug out of the ground, are big influences to me. A lot of hewn qualities. I'm enjoying a lot of African carving work. I like tool marks, and the mark of the hand is really important.

I don't want to get overly analytical about my work. I don't want to make work that just feels like it's from the mind.

I am so influenced by the fact that most of what we know about ancient peoples is through their ceramic record. When I was at school, I was feeling that division of importance based on medium, where painting is this and ceramics is this, in Western culture. I totally feel the opposite; I feel like clay is the most important material. There are all of these theories about life coming from clay, like the beginning of bacteria comes from clay. I feel like as far as humans go, clay is our original medium. That is why I love it. That is how I want my work to feel, something like that.

I want to make stuff that feels like the earth and gives people a chance to have a moment, even if it is just when you are driving to your office job and you are drinking your morning coffee, but you are doing it out of something that is so handmade and so earth. I want to be independent and create an environment that is sustainable.

Copus continues his life-shaping. He married in 2018, and he and his wife are converting the Old Marshall Jail into a boutique hotel. She also raises flowers, on his pottery land and at her main farm 2 miles away. Their plan is *to have everything center around the land in Marshall. It's our core, and everything we do emanates out from there.* ■

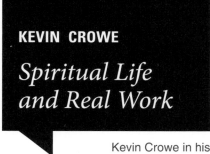

KEVIN CROWE

Spiritual Life and Real Work

Kevin Crowe in his studio in Nelson County, Virginia, 2017

Deep in the woods of central Virginia, Kevin Crowe pots and fires a large wood-burning kiln. From a transient childhood—including some influential years in Japan—to his rooted existence at Tye River Pottery is a long way, and not without some painful interruptions.

Crowe was born in 1949 in Evanston, Illinois, when his father, an Army officer, was stationed at Fort Sheridan. He grew up the second of six surviving children in a devoutly Catholic family—*Catholic school, high school, going to daily mass, spent three months in a seminary actually. Kicked out for fighting.* [Laughter] *First fight I had in my life. And I think it was a way to get removed without quitting.* [Laughter] *My heroes in Catholicism were people like Thomas Merton, the Berrigan brothers, Dorothy Day, and priests that were involved with social-justice issues. The seed of my stopping Catholicism was the contradiction between the liturgy that we were learning and the faithless practice by the institution, especially during the Vietnam War and race issues. It was overwhelming. And all my heroes were getting excommunicated.* [Laughter]

I lived in a world of militarism and Catholicism, which were real bedfellows, you know. So I lived in a world of ritual and discipline. I was an altar boy until I was 18. You never put that stuff down. And there was a beauty in it, especially in ritual. I think that has played a big part of my life and attraction to tea ceremony, and pottery, and craft. The integration of a spiritual life with real work. And I think I drifted in the early '70s, like most of my generation, in political activism. I was a draft counselor, a war resister on Vietnam.

But backing up a little: *I was born in Illinois, we moved to Kalamazoo, Michigan, then we moved to Germany, then we moved to Japan. I lived in Japan for four years. I was seven through eleven. And that was the most remarkable experience. Every day, even now, something about that experience replays.* The first surprise was that their housing came with a maid, a young Japanese woman who didn't speak much English. *That wasn't a relationship that my mother was comfortable with or totally prepared for, so Yoko-san basically became one of the family, you know, more than a maid. And she sensed early on that I had a real interest in things Japanese. If you don't leave the post, it's like living in the United States. Yoko-san started taking me places on weekends, like the Buddha at Kamakura, Shinto shrines and festivals, bunraku puppet shows, my first sumo match, viewing cherry blossoms.* The rest of the family was not interested.

He was already an artistic child. *I was drawing, I won a couple of art contests, and my reward was I think two months of classes in this Japanese art studio. I would go there, I was like eight, and there would be five women and three men drawing pictures of plum blossoms, so I would sketch and draw.*

All of these things Yoko-san took me to, I didn't have any visual vocabulary for, nor did I have language. So I would go to these events with this sort of visual epiphany that I couldn't make any sense out of. After about a year and a half, I was fluent and then I could interact. But up to that point, I mean imagine walking into a small stadium, this enclosure, this arena, and everybody is quiet in seats and there's this circular mat, and then these enormous Japanese men in jock straps come out. [Laughter] *And then watching this whole thing go on, these two whales smashing, and this Shinto priest with the fan watching. I just loved everything about it. The architecture, samurai movies; I was just mesmerized. And I think I was fortunate that in those four years there was no television or anything else, so you could really ratchet it into your attention.*

Being introduced to how Yoko-san's family lived *was a profound experience for me, to see what minimal looked like in relation to materials. I remember the first time I wandered into a large bamboo grove, stopping dead in my tracks because the canopy was high, and the way the light comes through the bamboo and the clicking sound that it makes. I remember being transfixed. And the sound of wooden geta* [shoes]*; you know, in Tokyo even business men and women were still wearing geta then, and clopping. All these beautiful sounds. I wake up in the morning and it's Boys Day and every roof is flying a carp banner. That visual baptism into another way of seeing, another relationship of form and light and ritual, profoundly reshaped the way I saw life and saw images and saw materials. There was always, for four years, that conflict between the life I lived with my family and this other life I was being introduced to, this other way of being.*

Back in the States, in Virginia, the Japan experience and the art stopped cold. *The Catholic school I went to had no art. It was all college track and nothing extraneous. By the seventh grade, I started playing guitar and I started writing. So I was in* bands and playing music constantly, growing up. He continued to write and play during college at William & Mary, where he was an English major. After college, *I actually went to Nashville and got offered a job writing for ABC Dunhill. I remember my wife, Linda, said, "Whatever we're going to do is fine." But she didn't like Nashville. I realized that to do this I would have to have a lot of people with me all the time, and that seemed improbable. So I didn't do it. We stuck around Williamsburg, and I was working as a glassblower on Jamestown Island, the colonial thing, wearing a colonial costume. And coming home in January, my motorcycle got hit by a truck and broke everything.*

An elderly driver pulled out in front of him. *I remember thinking: let go of the handlebars. I hit the top of the truck and went over about 100 feet and landed in the road. I remember my body moving really fast, but I never felt any pain. Even when I hit the road, I didn't feel anything. Everything just stops. Then a state trooper pulled up and they said each other's first names. The guy said, "Yeah, this long-haired hippie drove into the parking lot and hit me and he landed out in the road and he's dead." I could see my body. I couldn't move anything. Everything in my body was wrong, so I thought: maybe this is dead.*

And then I heard this car pull up, and all of a sudden there's this face in front of me that's a young guy in a Corvette who said, "I saw everything; I was just coming over the hill, and this guy's trying to tell the cop"—and he fills me in—"and don't worry, I'm going to tell him." And I remember thinking this would be a good time for an Advil; why doesn't anybody do that? Then I kept thinking, well, because I'm dead. It was so surreal. And then the cop said to the guy, "When did you call the ambulance?" And he said, "I didn't call; I thought you were going to call." Now cars are lining up and kids are looking out windows at me. And then I remember hands moving all over me, and I saw this guy's face, and he said, "I'm a doctor. Your back is OK and your neck is OK and your head is OK. Everything else is probably broken, but you're going to make it."

I was 23 then. You do have this profound excitement that you get another chance; it's not over. I got married when I was 21, and the thought of not seeing Linda again was overwhelming. There

are two Lindas. My first wife Linda died of cancer, and I remarried, and this woman is also named Linda. I knew my first wife in high school, so we'd been together since we were 15 and went to college together. The accident is important because just before then, I had suggested to Linda that she might enjoy throwing pots.*

Everything indeed had been broken, and his left elbow was crushed. The doctor gave him a long list of things he'd no longer be able to do, including swimming and playing the guitar. *I had only about 10 percent use of my left arm. He said, "Here's the good news: when you came in, that arm was going to be amputated."*

There I am in all these casts, back then in plaster, so to take care of me, Linda would put me in the van and take me to college and prop me up and just, you know, face me toward the light and water me like a plant [Laughter] while they were making pots. So I would just watch. And during that time, a Japanese potter came to William & Mary as a resident. So he's making pots and I watched. I thought it was interesting, but I had no wish to make pots. But I started reading books that were around while I was there, Bernard Leach's Potter's Book *and* The Unknown Craftsman *by Soetsu Yanagi, all the books available then. And something clicked for me about that combination of ritual, discipline, commitment, service, spirituality. After getting out of the casts and stuff, I tried throwing a pot one night, and just throwing it I knew that this was what I was supposed to do.*

I think one of the advantages of growing up under my dad's discipline and work ethic and athletics is that I just approached therapy with a mania and got myself back on my feet. And by the time a year went by, Linda said I was using my arm for things that were impossible, that I shouldn't have been able to do. I have limited motion, but I can do a lot with it. And it actually locks, which is great for a potter; I can lock it up and use it as a lever. I lost some dexterity. It took a long time to play guitar again. I'm playing in a geezer band now. [Laughter]

So that's how I came to pots. Maybe 15 years after I began throwing, when I looked back at my relationship to my experience of clay and the community it provided and the discipline and the sense of ritual, that dovetailed with everything in my background without the responsibility to enlist in

LINDA
SIKORA

RIGHT Covered jar, Tortoiseware
series, 2011. Stoneware, 12" × 9" × 9".
Collection: Everson Museum of Art,
Syracuse, New York, 2011.5a–b.

BELOW Yellow Ware Group,
2014. Porcelain, monochrome glaze,
oxidation electric firing,
13" × 28" × 18".

ANDY
SHAW

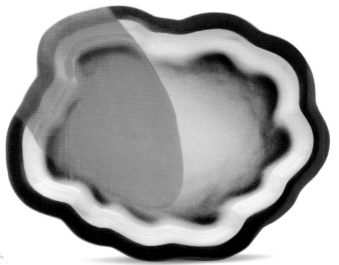

RIGHT Dinner tray, 2017. Black stoneware, cone 6 clear glaze, orange stain, 1" × 12" × 11". *Photo: Jim Osborne*

BELOW Tableware, three-piece setting, 2014. Porcelain, cone 10 celadon, varied sizes. *Photo: Kevin Duffy*

SANAM
EMAMI

RIGHT Dinnerware, 2018. Chocolate brown and buff stoneware, slip, laser-cut stencils, oxidation, sizes varied.

BELOW Garniture of three vases, 2015. Buff stoneware, salt-fired oxidation, each 12". *Photo: E. G. Schempf*

DOUG
CASEBEER

TOP LEFT Silo vases, 2017. Stoneware with slips and glazes, wood fired to cone 11, 14" × 8".

TOP RIGHT Place settings for 14. Installation at Harvey/Meadows Gallery, Aspen, Colorado, 2018. *Photo: Alleghany Meadows*

RIGHT Teapot with yellow handle, 2017. Stoneware with slips and glazes, wood fired to cone 11, 8" × 8".

SANDY
SIMON

RIGHT Pippi (covered jar), 2016. Earthenware, nichrome wire, red seeds, porcelain slip, green glaze cone 03, 4" × 4" × 5.5". Collection of the Weisman Art Museum at the University of Minnesota, gift of Trax Gallery, 2017.31.

BELOW Teapot, 1970. Porcelain, nichrome wire, needle-prick decoration, soda fired to cone 10, 6" × 5" × 9".

CHARLES
JAHN

TOP LEFT Tea cup, 2012.
Brick clay, white slip, wood ash
glaze, iron decoration, wood
fired, 3.25" × 3.25".
Photo: Mie Kongo

TOP RIGHT Tea cup, 2018.
Stoneware, rice husk ash glaze,
wood fired, 3.25" × 3.25".
Photo: Mie Kongo

RIGHT Jiggered bowl, 2006.
Porcelain, cobalt slip, chatter
pattern, 3.75" × 6.5".
Photo: Mie Kongo

MARY
BARRINGER

TOP Three plates, 2011. Stoneware, handbuilt, with multiple slips and glaze, 5" × 5". *Photo: Wayne Fleming*

BOTTOM LEFT Cookie jar, ca. 1980. Stoneware, wheel thrown, with "Korean" celadon glaze, 8.5" × 8.5".

BOTTOM RIGHT Creamers, ca. 1998. Stoneware, handbuilt with multiple slips and glazes, H: 4.5". This is a form she made from 1998 until around 2015.

ALLEGHANY
MEADOWS

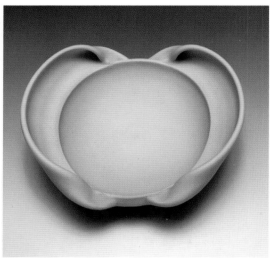

TOP LEFT Pitcher, 2015.
Earthenware with slips and
glazes, salt fired to cone 1,
10" × 8" × 6".

TOP RIGHT Ear bowl,
2017. Porcelain with glaze,
5" × 8" × 9".

LEFT Flora series, nesting
plates, 2016. Porcelain with
glazes, 11" × 23".

MUNEMITSU
TAGUCHI

TOP Table and serve ware, 2011.
Porcelain with celadon, cone 10 reduction fired;
serving bowl, 8" × 15".

BOTTOM Cloud jars, 2012. Porcelain with
celadon, cone 10 reduction fired; jar on right,
8" × 14".

DEB
SCHWARTZKOPF

TOP Plate, 2016.
Wheel-thrown and handbuilt
porcelain, cone 6 electric, 9" dia.
Photo: Vanessa Norris

BOTTOM LEFT "Merry-go-round," 2017. Wheel-thrown and
handbuilt porcelain, cone 6 electric, 6" × 8". *Photo: Jon Johnson*

BOTTOM RIGHT Tiny bowls, 2017. Wheel-thrown and handbuilt
porcelain, cone 6 electric, 3" dia. *Photo: Jon Johnson*

SUNSHINE
COBB

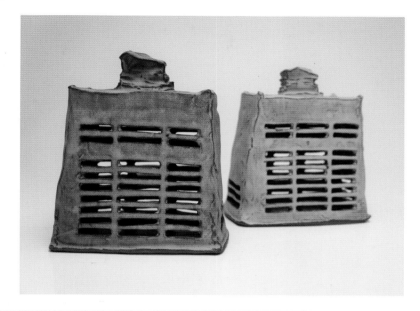

RIGHT Garlic boxes,
2017. Midrange red clay,
glaze, sandblasted,
7" × 6" × 4".

BELOW Ice cream bowls,
2017. Midrange red clay,
glaze, sandblasted,
3" × 3".

KENYON
HANSEN

TOP LEFT Set of plates, 2014. Porcelain with
multiple glazes, 1.5" × 10".

TOP RIGHT Teapot, 2017. Soda-fired stoneware
with slip, 6" × 9" × 5.5".

BOTTOM Thermos, 2013. Porcelain
with multiple glazes, 9" × 4" × 3.5".

GWENDOLYN
YOPPOLO

RIGHT "crossing boundaries," 2016. Handmade table and stools, matte crystalline-glazed dinnerware designed for feeding another person; platter 2" × 9" × 27".

BOTTOM LEFT "regard," 2012. Matte crystalline-glazed porcelain, hand-knit and felted wool, hand-knit linen and silk; cups and saucer 6" × 13" × 5", table runner 108" × 18".

BOTTOM RIGHT Mug and saucer, 2017. Matte crystalline-glazed porcelain, 5.5" × 9" × 7".

NOAH
RIEDEL

TOP Espresso set, 2015. Stoneware with terra sigillata and glaze, cup 3" × 2.5" × 2", saucer 2" × 5" × 3".

RIGHT Banana frame, 2015. Stoneware with terra sigillata, 19" × 11" × 6".

UPPER RIGHT Split basket, 2017. Stoneware with terra sigillata and engobes, 8" × 26.5" × 7.5".

FAR RIGHT Canister, 2015. Stoneware with terra sigillata and glaze, 8" × 8" × 8".

JOSH
COPUS

RIGHT Stone vase, 2016. Wood-fired
wild clay blend, 14" × 7" × 7".
Photo: Tim Barnwell

BELOW Segmented tray, 2015.
Wood-fired wild clay blend, 4" × 16" × 3.5".
Photo: Tim Barnwell

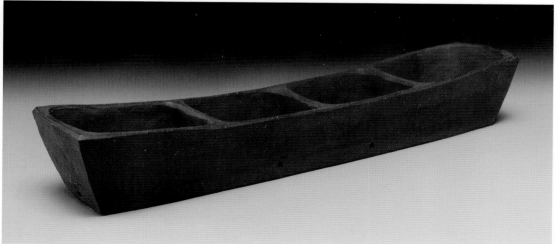

KEVIN
CROWE

ABOVE Tea bowl, 2015. Stoneware, wood-fired eight days in anagama kiln, natural ash glaze, 4.5" × 4.4".

RIGHT Teapot and three vases fired on top of an interior firebox grate, 2015. Stoneware, wood fired in anagama kiln, natural ash glaze, teapot 14" × 11". *Photo: Crimson Laurel Gallery*

the army. Also, I realized that males are always looking for their father's approval even when we think we're not, and I think there are enough bricks and fire and heavy bags to lift that at some level my father would have approved of it.

I was totally overwhelmed with the excitement of being a potter. Read everything I could get, threw pots constantly, and Linda and myself and a couple of other friends found a beautiful old barn in Williamsburg that we rented and turned into a studio. And I did my first carpentry ever, putting steps in and opening the lights. There was no electricity in the barn, and I went to a small electric supply place and told the guy that I wanted to figure out a way to get electricity to a house and run it to a barn, which is completely illegal. He wouldn't cooperate. So I went up the electric pole and spliced into the wires. It was a real epiphany for me, the excitement of creating something. When you look back, you wonder how you're still alive. [Laughter] I was capable of unbelievable stupidity. [Laughter]

Linda had just learned the rudiments, so I watched her and just sort of went at it. I remember getting hold of Susan Peterson's book called Shoji Hamada: A Potters Way & Work, reading and looking at the black-and-white photos with the hands and what you do. It certainly isn't the way to learn, but that turned out to be my path. So we made pots there and built an oil-fired kiln.

To say that we didn't know anything is generous. [Laughter] I just threw cylinders for six months. I was like a human pug mill. And I think I have a telescopic personality. When I'm doing something I'm zeroed in, completely focused on it.

The barn was condemned in two years. We wanted to move to the country and start a pottery. We found Nelson County through an ad in the paper. This place was $430 an acre. We needed a loan to buy it. Neither one of us had jobs; we had $3,000 [from the motorcycle accident]; there wasn't any way in the world anybody was going to give us a loan. Well, they did. They sold it to us, and it was $100 a month for 10 years. So we moved here with two tents: a big tent to put our tools in and a small tent to live in. For the better part of three and a half years we lived in a tent. There was no electricity here at that time. We looked, like everybody, for an old farmhouse and a barn that we could turn into a studio for $15,000, and, surprise, it wasn't out

there. Linda said, "Let's just build a house." I had built a set of stairs more like a ladder than a set of stairs [Laughter], but I said, "I can do that." I got books about alternative methods of construction, and unhampered by either conventional wisdom of construction techniques, or experience of anything, plunged in, drew up plans, got them passed by the local building inspector.

It went on for three years, and then we finally got the thing closed in and then power came, and then I realized, well, there's no way of getting enough money to build a studio. But I saw an ad in the local paper, Amherst, across the county line, wanted a building on Main Street torn down. So I went in and I thought they would pay me and I could get the materials and they laughed. But they got in touch with me later. It turned out the town charter required that it be taken down by hand, because it was three stories tall, right on Main Street . . . with 2 inches between it and the building next to it, so it couldn't be exploded or demo'ed. I was the only one who was smart/dumb enough to do it. [Laughter] So I went in and took it down piece by piece, and they paid me $3,000 to take it down, and I got all the materials. The whole studio, the kiln shed, and the work shed are built out of that. So 1980 it was built.

I worked as a carpenter, finish work, framing, outside framing. A friend of mine formed a small company. I was learning as I was doing it. I turned out to have a good eye for finish work and trim. Then after that, I started working with a good friend. The two of us would build one or two houses a year. That would give us time, he would travel through Nepal, and I would make pots.

Then the kids came along, and I thought, okay, I've really got to tighten up my act and make pots that are accessible and marketable. I just kept working with the wood-fired pots, making the pots I wanted to make. Three mornings a week I'd get up at 3:30 and work in the studio until 7:30 and then have breakfast and go to work. If you look at your life and think, "if I'm going to make pots," either make them or don't make them, but don't whine about not having time.

I continued making pots in between the cracks whenever I could and selling them, going to shows and selling some things at galleries. It started out one-quarter pots and the rest carpentry, and then it was half and half for a number of years, and then by the time the boys were in the sixth grade, I was merging into making pots full time. And it's been full time since then.

There are many full-time potters that are full-time potters because of their personal economies. Parents paying for them, spouses paying for them, or they're an academic. When I was young, I'd look around and get really frustrated with myself that I hadn't been able to create this economy that would allow me to make pots full time, when I saw other people doing it. So you have doubts about your organization skills. And then you realize everybody's money is different; everybody's life is different. So that was a lesson for me: never be cynical about somebody else's advantages. That erodes your responsibility and your relationship to the options that you have.

I'd really been frustrated, early on, listening to all artists and potters saying, "I'm poor." I think it robs the dignity of people experiencing poverty. Poverty for me is: no choice. These are all choices we make. I think it's important to maintain that perspective, because if not, cynicism will eat into your work and you won't be able to make pots. As soon as you see yourself as a victim of anything—a critic, a show, the lack of taste that you think the public has—then I think you just go through the motions.

Crowe's workshop specialties are firing wood kilns and throwing large pots. Throwing large-scale pots is probably the big one. I've gone all over Europe and the US teaching that. It started out when I first got here. I didn't have enough money to do kiln shelves, so I had to make 3-foot pots to fill up the space, and the pots would fire wildly erratically and inefficiently. And of course they'd never sell; they were so big. And I remember Linda asking, "How many of these are we going to have around?" [Laughter] But I was fascinated. The learning curve was so energetic and so exciting, so electric, that I couldn't stop making them. The market that developed was not the pots, the market was other potters hiring me to teach them how to make big pots.

Three hours south of here the market for pots is transformed. The sympathy for clay work of all stripes is typical of North Carolinian clients and absent in Virginia for the most part. Outside of Native American work, that's the only indigenous tradition we have in the US, and North Carolina made the commitment at the turn of the century to have crafts be the bedrock of their tourist industry. And the investment shows. Charlottesville is town for us, University of Virginia. It's a wonderful town, and there's a strong presence and support for 2-D work, for sculpture, for film, for drama, for theater, but not for clay. There's no place in Charlottesville to sell clay work. I sell most of my pots to North Carolinians.

Crowe was drawn to wood firing by the surface effects it produced. And watching the communities that were required to fire those pots excited me. I was drawn to the human relationships built around a common effort. At first, Crowe fired with oil and wood, for economic reasons. The oil was used motor oil that I would pump from gas stations and school bus depots. It's toxic. It's horrible. It's free. That's what you do when you're 25. He stopped using oil in 1982.

He fires in a three-chamber anagama (including one chamber for shino glaze and one for salt) that he built in 2001. Kai was going to college and Bram had a couple more years of high school, so I realized my work force was leaving. When the boys left, working by myself I could just turn into a hermit out here, so I thought: I'm going to build a big kiln and I will have to have other people in my life to fire this. And that's exactly what's happened. And since about 2005 I've had apprentices. That's been great, having young people. I give workshops here too, for four people at a time.

The apprenticeship arrangement is this: I supply work space, unlimited clay, and I fire the pots in the kiln, and instruction. And oversee their development of artist statement, portfolio things, and take them to any events, workshops that I'm teaching, take them to a conference, as much as I can. And in return they help me with the grunt work. They help me cut and stack wood, recycle clay, wad the pots and stack the kiln, and fire. And they help at the shows here and the sales after each firing. And that's it. I make it really clear that I don't need any help with making pots; I need help with the grunt work. I'll get calls from people asking me what the pay scale is and what the benefits are, health package. [Laughter] And I say, "You know, there's really nothing you can help me with." It's been a wonderful experience; it's been great having the energy and the help, and the excitement of young people around me, which I love.

I've always felt that there's no separation between a spiritual path and the activity that you're engaged in. One of my mentors, Thich Nhat Hanh, a Vietnamese Buddhist monk, was nominated for the Nobel Peace Prize. He said, "You know we're all headed for the shore, and you need a boat." There's lots of boats. And for me, pottery is a boat. Whether you're an engineer, a nurse, a janitor, a potter; all those activities invite an integration of your spiritual self to your work. So everything is practice.

I think what's important is to make what you love. There's nothing that goes into the kiln that you haven't committed your heart to. So you don't make things that you think, "Well, I don't like this but they're selling," or "This is not why I make pots, but I know if I glaze it somebody will buy it." You take clay, and if you live long enough you convert acres of it into rock. [Laughter] It's an irreversible process. So that's a sacred responsibility.

I don't do commission work. I don't partner up with people. I'll make 100 teapots, but they're my teapots. I'm convinced that if you make work from the heart that you're committed to, people who are serious about looking will see that and support that work. So I think that's actually the best social security I can come up with. You can't do what I do online. You can't have it reproduced somewhere else. And somebody else isn't going to make it bluer or cheaper than me.

A lot of the functions you would make functional pots for no longer exist. But I think the need for touch, a sense of ritual in our lives, is probably more urgent now than it's ever been. I see it in movements that young kids have come up with, like the Slow Food movement. And insistence on recognizing and embracing more handmade, more local; that's important. A sense of community. All those things I think have become more urgent as they become endangered. So the needs have morphed into something beyond storing food, cooking food, and shipping tea.

Larger-scale work is traditionally part of a potter's vocabulary. Once you experience the vocabulary, you have a different experience of a larger form in the corner of a room in relationship to the space that it's in. When you get to a certain scale, you scrutinize elements that you gloss over a little more quickly with smaller-scale work. So I found that making larger-scale work makes me a better potter than making small-scale work.

There's a lot of alteration and movement in the pots. I have a lot of nuances. Right before I stop throwing, I take my right hand away and I make a quick pass with my left hand on the inside. The left hand, connected to the right side of the brain, is the artist part of you. The right hand holds the rib, and it's the accountant and the engineer; it's always countering, trying to control and get the exterior to be very tight. So when you take that away, it allows for more expression.

They're almost all paddled and cut and moved in some way. And the work is natural ash glazed. And I fast-cool the kiln as opposed to reduction cooling. I move more toward glossy, shiny surface. I'm all about ash buildup.

When we sell our pots we're selling stories. When people come here they have an experience. They tour the kiln and they actually get an insight into the process of making. And they see the site of the life that's built around that process. So from then on, when they use the teapot or the bowl or the incense burner, they're back here. Culturally we need stories.

This is it for me, nothing but. I think it's the interaction with other people. I think it's the challenge of being as engaged and careful in the making and the placing and the setting and the preparation for firing as possible, and then partnering with forces that are beyond your control. Even when I see events on the surface of a pot that I am enthralled with, I will try to set that stage and exploit that experience in the next firing, but there are too many variables. Each piece of wood is a different BTU load. It has a different oxide content. It has a different moisture content. It's split differently. All of those things. There's low pressure; there's wood; the people on that shift are as responsible as you are, but they're making different decisions about what they think is a full fire box. All those things change. That's the challenge, and I find it's been a real teacher for me. ∎

ELLEN SHANKIN

In Love with the Life

Ellen Shankin in her studio, Floyd, Virginia, 2018

See photos in color section following p. 216

Ellen Shankin, with her woodworker husband, Brad Warstler, lives and works in rural Virginia and raised two children there. And that's exactly as she wished: she says that the pottery process and the life were what initially drew her to clay, rather than love of the resulting objects. That came later.

Shankin was born in New York City in 1952 and grew up in suburban Mount Vernon. Her father was a doctor who loved lapidary and collected Chinese ivories and Japanese netsuke, which she also appreciated, although her attraction was more to painting. But an extraordinary experience opened another door for her.

I was 13 and I went to probably what was the best summer camp in the world. It was a place called Buck's Rock, in New Milford, Connecticut. It was run by the Bulova family, and you had to be 13 to go there, 13 to 17. It was a place that completely changed my life. It was an art camp, and it was all camper driven, all about self-motivation and pursuing your own interest.

You woke up when you wanted to. If you woke up late, you missed breakfast. Too bad. There were live models, nudes to draw. I learned to weld; I

learned to carve wood; I learned macramé; I learned all kinds of things. The person that taught pottery was a RISD graduate student. He was really good. He just sort of sat on the wheel with me day in, day out, getting me through all of the difficult things. I ended up centering and making things pretty quickly because I had a lot of help. It was two months, all summer. There's something about mastering a skill, and throwing was way more compelling than carving wood or welding. It's so hard to imagine being able to do it, and then just getting an inkling into it was like candy for me. [Laughter]

Because I had had this Buck's Rock experience, of course it was also 1969–70, so that was a very hippie culture anyway, I chose Goddard College as a place to go to school. It's in northern Vermont, and it is exactly like Buck's Rock. You have maybe six people in your classes; you grade yourself. My first semester I wrote to my parents and said, "I'm taking one class you expected of me, and it's early childhood education (because I thought I would be a teacher), and then I'm taking pottery and revolutionary anarchy." [Laughter] *Those were my three classes.*

The first year that I was there, Gwyn Hanssen Pigott, a potter from Australia—she worked with Cardew and Leach, this amazing woman who had a pottery in the center of France—came to Goddard College to teach. Gwyn had wanted to work with the Bread and Puppet Theater. She had seen them somewhere and fell in love with them, and they lived at Goddard. So the college said you can come and work with the Bread and Puppet Theater if you teach pottery for a year.

She and I became good friends. She is the reason I'm a potter, for sure. And we are like 100 percent different in our things that brought us to where we were. I loved clay, I loved trying to master that skill, and then I fell sort of in love with her and her life. It was seasonal; she was a woman by herself (her husband had died already and she lived alone), and she dug her clay, and she had a wood kiln and fired four times a year. There was something about this that was so much more meaningful than my parents' life.

But I couldn't care less about pottery. It took me years before I was really moved by what exists in the world or even what I could make. I don't find too many other potters that are like that. I was a really dull tool in allowing the language of clay to work its magic on me, for me to be able to have those feelings connected to the thousands of nuances that I have so much feeling about now. Now I'm so bereft when I rent a house at the beach and there are tin bowls to put your beautiful salad out in, how 90 percent of the world lives, and I have this richness of clay everywhere now.

In the beginning, *I loved it as a material, unbelievably loved it. I would dream about moving it. It just completely filled me. You see your mark. You go like this, it goes like that, and it stays there forever. It's a powerful thing, and it got me that it's so ancient; people had been doing this for thousands of years—it came from the ground. It was just so real. That was very compelling to me.*

After Pigott left, Shankin dropped out and apprenticed for a while to a Vermont potter who *had*

two daughters and a husband who also didn't have benefits or a salary, but she made this work. Being a mom was super important to me, I always knew that, and I was really glad to see that she managed all of that.

Then Shankin moved to Peters Valley, New Jersey. *That was in the early days before Peters Valley really had any workshops. It was like an artist community. I knew enough to fire a kiln and make glazes and throw pots. It was the beginning of trying to sell things. It cost nothing to live there, like 60 bucks, so you didn't need to sell a lot. It was mostly to buy more materials. So I stayed there for a while and then I went to Penland.* It was a Concentration session, and she found it rewarding. But more important, *I met Brad, fell in love, had powerful stuff going on there too.*

I think it was because of my time at Penland that I realized forms were starting to feel like they were doing things that I was wanting them to do. But glazes were just like, you know, there were six buckets and you dunk it in this or this or this. I had no idea what was in there, the science of it. It is such a deep field, ceramics. It was wanting more control over that end result that made me want to go to school. She went to RISD and was completely unhappy because it seemed too regimented. After a summer session and fall classes, she wanted to work with Cynthia Bringle over the January intersession (extra motivated by the fact that Warstler was living in North Carolina). But she *butted heads* with Norm Schulman, who insisted that she stay at RISD and take his winter session class. *I just lost it. I said, "I quit; I'm going to North Carolina and not coming back." Now I think: What if my kids just quit college?* [Laughter]

She went back to North Carolina but then transferred to Alfred. *And that place was very much more flexible. Absolutely. They let me take graduate classes even though I was an undergraduate. I took Val [Cushing]'s glaze class, which is one of the most awesome classes ever taught. Alfred opened up my world to seeing pottery and loving pottery, for sure. That library in Alfred was the first place I spent a lot of time looking at books. That was like 1975, and I had started five years before. If I hadn't been opened up to the language of clay—I mean, I can be moved to tears in front of Jomon pots—I don't know that I could have gone on making functional pots, because*

I think it would have gotten boring. Because it became this deeper thing for me, I don't tire of it.

Alfred teachers urged her to go on for an MFA, but she declined. *I wanted to move to the country—this all did happen—live in a rural place, have a rural life with some of the primal feeling that Gwyn imparted to me that she had about her life, and find people to buy this stuff so that I could keep doing it and raise children and have a good and meaningful and productive life. Graduate school was unnecessary for that. Now, the way my life has gone, maybe a graduate degree would have been a beneficial thing. I've had surgery on both hands. This is a hard practice on your body. But let's say the hand surgeries hadn't worked and I was really compromised, then teaching would have been my only option to stay connected to this life. I'm so powerfully a thrower that it would take completely unuseful wrists for me to explore whether handbuilding could take on that same thing for me.* An MFA would have made college teaching an option. But that was never her goal. *I don't want to teach at a university. I just want to be in the studio making pots. But I have really come to like going off different places four times a year and teaching in a workshop kind of way.*

Another change point in her life was receiving a $20,000 grant from the National Endowment for the Arts in 1990. She had been urged to apply by someone convinced that the NEA never gave grants to potters. *I sat down with myself and said this is really a nice honor. It lasts for like 15 minutes, and it's a lot of money, but things will come to you because of this and you have to say yes or that's all it is. I made myself do that, and it was very hard for me. The first was to give a presentation to NCECA. I had never been to an NCECA conference, but I knew what they were, and knew there would be hundreds of people watching me, and I had never demonstrated or spoken or shown slides or done anything, because I was just sitting here making pottery and trying to sell it. I had five slides; that's what I needed to get into a craft fair. And so I said yes, and I was just a nervous wreck. And then because I did that, I got asked to do a lot of workshops. And I had to force myself to say yes because it was so unsettling to me. I was not nervous to throw in front of people, not at all; I just didn't want to talk.*

The money went to several purposes. *We graveled this road and made it passable, because I wanted people to be able to come here and buy pottery. That seemed important to me. I bought an electric kiln. I started saving money for the first time in my life, which we continued to do every year, which was great, because I had two young children and that was not easy. And we took our very first vacation. A friend had a boat in the Bahamas, so they flew down and stayed with him, cheaply. At the end of the year I called the NEA and said, "I have to account for everything. Do you want to know that the electric kiln is $487, or do you just want to me to say electric kiln, road development?" She said, "Honey, we just want to know you didn't go to the Bahamas." [Laughter] I said, "You didn't say that." [Laughter] Needless to say, I did leave that $1,000 off my NEA report.*

Shankin started with direct selling at craft fairs. *It's a big life of rejection when you do that. It was really hard and very discouraging because I had such a desire to make and make and make. If you couldn't sell what you had, what are you doing with this? It was really costly, and if you didn't make money then you couldn't fire the kiln. I started going to the Baltimore Craft Fair, which was a wholesale fair, and not the first year maybe but by the second year I could take orders for the whole year. So for me, that was perfect. I got to stay home with my children. I worked for three weeks, I glazed, I fired the kiln, I took a day off. I worked for three weeks, I glazed, I fired, I took a day off. Every month I sent work off. I felt like I had super control over what I made in the studio. If you go to Baltimore in February, whatever you show is what your next year is going to be about. There were always at least five galleries who I sold to. Their orders were like, "Just send me $1,000 in the spring and $1,000 in the fall; send whatever you want."*

I would try to give them things that worked for them, but I tried to avoid them being horribly specific. I take a long time to work through a form. Maybe it will take me eight firings before I've resolved every part that I'm thinking of. And once I get to where I really like them, I really want to keep making them. So this worked for me in a lot of ways.

I got to control my creative time in the studio by losing money somewhere and making lots of money somewhere else. Salad bowls make a living for me. They're fast, they're easy; I guess I just could say I don't invest as much in those salad bowls as in other things, but it also suits my nature. There are days when I just don't want to have to agonize over every aspect of a pot. Some days I'm in a bad mood; I don't have patience; I just need something that works. And it's great that the somethings that work are the foundations of the income part of this.

I didn't need a lot of money. Our bills are really small. Our land was totally paid off in five years. That was the arrangement with the landlord. It was only $15,000, that's all it cost, but it was hard, really hard, to come up with $3,000 every year for five years to pay this off. But then it was done. And then we did have building costs, but I wasn't pressured the way other potters were to, say, keep making that casserole in a blue glaze because they knew they could sell it and they absolutely had to. What I wanted to do was salable enough that I got to do what I wanted to do and make a living. But I was creative about it.

The fact that Brad was also at home working had a slightly difficult aspect because neither of us had benefits. We always had healthcare. My dad was a doctor, I could never be a person without healthcare. But it allowed him to take care of the kids exactly half the time, so he had them every morning, and I got to be in the studio without a single interruption until noon, and then Brad goes to sleep every day after lunch and the kids would go to sleep with him, so sometimes I could work until 2 or 3, and then I was theirs and Brad was working. It made marriage hard for a bit, or just a little more distant, because when they would go to bed, both of us would be in the studio until midnight. And that was a lot of years, until they went to school.

I pretty much sold everything by wholesale when my children were young. When they got to be 11 or 12 and they would enjoy coming with me to a retail craft fair, I did the Smithsonian. Then she was part of starting 16 Hands. That involves two studio tours each year, and she also does Minnesota's St. Croix Valley Tour in May. The 16 Hands tour draws an audience mostly from North Carolina, plus people who have taken workshops with the 16 Hands participants. Shankin also maintains a gallery space on her property so that anyone can come any time and purchase pots by the honor system.

I did salt firing in Alfred. I'm not 100 percent sure how I got started. I did see Don Reitz's work and was just knocked over. Wow! And without even knowing how much I had absorbed, things started getting bigger. It also owed a little bit to Gwyn. When we moved here, it's hard to have enough room to build a kiln, and it's a huge expense, so Alfred had shown me this way to build a castable kiln. It was actually cheaper than the electric kiln, $400 or something. It was tiny, and I think I fired it 52 times before it caught a roof on fire. [Laughter] It got hauled to the dump, but it allowed me to get out of school and, without having any money, make the kind of pots I really wanted to be making. So for the first five years or something I did salt pots.

Even though I loved salt, everything was of one kind. Everything was noisy to me; the surfaces, they were runny and juicy and almost snotty, which for me was nice. I liked all of that stuff going on, and I liked that it felt kind of like rocks in a way. I would spray blasts of these washes that would make it modulated, but also more natural in a sense, without the hard line of a brush.

I could build a reduction kiln and use either ash glazes or fake ash glazes or something that would give me this but would also allow me to have a lot more quiet surface. So I reinvested in building this. It's like a curse that we're handy. Brad can do anything; I can do a lot. We laid every tile, every stone in this house. So when it came to building the kiln, he can weld; we built this kiln together, and it certainly reduced the money we had to spend. But the curse of the handy is that it takes years. [Laughter]

One thing that I'm involved with when I'm making these pots is fullness. I'm always looking for that, sort of this feeling of breath in the pots. I'm driven by line. How lines develop out of rims. Tautness, pressure, often lift. I was involved in dance when I was young. People have called this to my attention; when I talk about the pots, I start to have better posture. [Laughter]

There's something very organic about it to me that's very chrysalis-like, and seed pod–like, and I think the glazes contribute to a sense of a natural and organic development of a form. But I really feel like the potters who love the process are happier than those who just love the outcome. My glazes need to be sprayed for lots of reasons, and I'm in a bad mood for four days out of every cycle of making pottery because I'm having to wear masks and I have to pay an insane amount of attention to something that's amazingly boring.

I would say there are definitely some pots that are influenced by architecture. I love buildings. I probably would have been an architect if I hadn't been a potter. I learned to build buildings at Goddard College. As a student you had to work for the college, work study, and at the time they were building the art building and my work study was to swing the hammer, and I really liked it. And then I lived with a guy and we built a house in northern Vermont. And then building this.

I like those kinds of basic things. Even the kinds of shoes I wear. I have never worn a pair of high heels or a pointy-toed anything. [Laughter] *Nothing about me is delicate or fragile. I'm big boned. A lot of people have asked me, like at those craft fairs, Where's the guy who made these?* [Laughter] *I look at this work, and I think it's the work of a tomboy.* [Laughter] ∎

MARK SHAPIRO
Commensality

Mark Shapiro in his studio, Worthington, Massachusetts, 2014, drying a section of a pot with a glassblower's torch to prepare it to support additional sections

Mark Shapiro lives and operates his Stonepool Pottery in rural western Massachusetts, participates in a local pottery tour as well as Minnesota's St. Croix Valley Tour, and has studied and collected Early American crocks. All that makes him sound like a placid traditionalist. But he is a child of New York City—with its intellectual and political heat—and he pursued sculpture before committing to clay.

The scene is set when he describes his family, who might have appeared in a Woody Allen movie. *I was born in New York City in 1955. My father was a psychoanalyst, and my mother was a social worker and ended up being a professor of public policy. I have a younger sister who is a veterinarian in Canada, and an older sister who is a professor of Chinese environmental issues or something in Washington. Scattered, yes. My father died a few years ago, and my mother lives in California. Her partner is a Zen Buddhist monk who has her own little zendo.*

I grew up on the Upper West Side. I was 13 in 1968, and we lived about five blocks from Columbia University. I started riding the public transportation in second grade. There was a lot of freedom. I went to a progressive private school in Harlem. A lot of the arts, and a chaotic educational philosophy that seemed to change every couple of years. [Laughter] I met some pretty supportive people there, and I actually remember ceramic objects that I made in art class in second grade. I can't remember anything I painted or wrote about, so somehow that clicked. I think I was probably okay studious but very physical and passionate about whatever I was passionate about. I always was that way.

I was aware of the New York museum world very early on. I'd go to the Met, the Guggenheim. It was a good time to be a kid in New York. By the time I was about 12, I had the sense of this huge change politically happening. My friends and I were on the young edge of this whole hippie, counterculture thing, but we were brought along by our older siblings, especially my friend Ralph. His siblings were very knowledgeable about the music. We would go to the Fillmore East, and we would go to Hunter to see Jimi Hendrix.

My school had a dedicated ceramics room. I had these lovely art teachers who weren't artists. They were like, everything you did was great. Very encouraging, nurturing women, and you never really believed them. [Laughter] By the mid-'60s, there started being real artists who came there as their day job. These people were opening up a big, big world for me, what art could be, an idea of modernism, an idea of art as self-expressive, original, a little transgressive, fun.

I think I was in sixth grade or seventh grade, and this kid came to our school from one of those Quaker schools in Philadelphia. He sat down at the wheel, he centered a ball of clay, and he threw a bowl, maybe 9 inches high. To me it was a complete miracle. When you grow up in New York, you learn how to not get mugged [Laughter], how to negotiate the subway system, but nobody knew how to make anything. It's not a place of makers, so much. I mean there are these tradesmen who come in and do things, but if you're an upper-middle-class kid you don't come into contact with that. Making things is deeply connected to understanding a sequence that has developed over a long period of time. It's very hard to invent that yourself; takes a lot longer. But this kid showed me how to make pots, which was amazing, the sort of peer to peer; it's so convincing.

Shapiro learned of a Greek American potter named Don Mavros. I would go down to his studio two days a week. I think I was supposed to do a little cleaning up in exchange for clay. But I had a very bad attitude. He was doing earthenware, these super-controlled, very Greek, like amphorae, and I thought I knew more than I knew. Japanese, British ceramics was what I was thinking about. So I was kind of using the studio, I would say, which is too bad, the arrogance of youth. I had that Leach book, I had the Herbert Sanders book, the Japanese pottery book, and I had Clay and Glazes for the Potter [by Daniel Rhodes]. I got the books you could get at that time, which was very few. I couldn't really understand the Rhodes book, the technical glazes, but I was trying. That was the beginning of my sort of autodidact trajectory. I remember going to America House when I was only 14 and buying a little Karen Karnes pot. I still have it. I knew who she was; I was starting to know a little bit about what was going on. I was reading Ceramics Monthly; maybe it came to the school.

He found out about a partnership between Haystack and Hinkley School in Maine and convinced his parents to let him go for a summer session of about three weeks when he was 14 or 15. We built a kiln, and we built the burners. The person who was there at the time who was sort of ahead of everybody was this guy named Barry Bartlett. He had been an apprentice to John Glick as a 15-year-old, and he actually knew how to make pots and was very charismatic and technically proficient. It was a real eye-opener. It was my first time to get involved with gas kilns and reduction. I had read about it in Leach and saw those Asian pots. I was thinking: I want to do reduction.

A girl in the program told him about an interesting boarding school in Vermont. He went to visit and said to the admissions people, "Look, I really want to come here, but I want to build a gas kiln. Is that something that could happen?" They were like, "No problem." It's kind of hard to imagine, isn't it? [Laughter] This place was established by someone who'd gone to Black Mountain College. It ran all year round, four terms, and you took one term off, not necessarily summer. It was a great place.

They bought the bricks and I built a kiln, and the plumbers came and hooked up the burners. This 15-year-old kid whose father was an architect and a boat builder was at that school, and he said, "I'll build a kiln shed." He has this tool box with all these old planes and chisels, and he built a post-and-beam *kiln shed over this thing.* [Laughter] *It was beyond my wildest dreams. I was sort of teaching myself and making pots in this art loft, and there was a student a little bit behind me who started making pots along with me, and that person is Bobby Silverman.*

I made pots pretty seriously for a year there, through 11th grade, and then I got so interested in the academics and I let it go. It was very seductive there, the intellectual life. It was a very eccentric and a very good place for me. Of course it folded.

My sister knew about this program that the French government ran for foreigners that was virtually free, and they would teach French language and literature. It confirmed an impulse I had towards independence in some way. I had a great year there and met some wonderful people.

I got into Amherst College. I had submitted my pottery portfolio as part of my package and gotten an amazing response from the admissions director, who wanted to talk to me about my pots. I guess I stood out from the pack. Because I had such a good interview with this guy and connected with him, I wanted to go there, which was probably a terrible mistake because I really didn't fit in there at all. And my expectations were so high, that there would be an even more incredible intellectual experience than I'd had before. It was, at the classroom level, but the students were just so absolutely calculating. They really were not interested in knowledge for its own sake.

I did stick it out. I loved my department, and I really used the Five Colleges [a consortium including Amherst]. *I made it work, but it was a really, really alienating experience for me. There's something about those kind of places; they're so self-satisfied and they're constantly reassuring you and themselves of their virtue. It's hard to describe, and I hope it's changed.*

I majored in anthropology, and I was doing this reading in history, and I finished my degree requirements by the end of my junior year. Thinking about graduate school, I really felt like: I do not want to sit in a chair; I want to make stuff. It came back at me in some really weird way. At Mount Holyoke they have an incredible sculpture facility, this big metal-fabricating scene with casting and welding. It was highly underutilized and had tons and tons and tons of gear. By the end of that year,

I had in my head I wanted to be a sculptor.

I rented this block building for $80 a month, and I paid for bringing electricity in. The roof leaked and I kind of fixed it. I bought a welder and I started raising these aluminum forms. I'd make two halves and then weld them together. I had a show at UMass of that work. They were these kind of curvilinear, maybe biomorphic forms. And I played with light in photographing them. And then I went out in the woods and got these trees, and I took my chainsaw and I squared them off and I did a whole installation at Smith College that was of maybe 20 vertical elements, sort of like these bottles that I make right now, set in this frame maybe 15 feet by 25 feet and with mulch around them. I had a certain ambition.

I guess around that time I met this woman [Laughter]—*ever hear that story before?—I met a woman, she's French, and she was an artist living in New York. I was very smitten with her, and I was trying to put the romance on her, you know. I moved to New York and got a loft in the Garment District. Everybody was so welcoming, and it was such an amazing vision of being an artist in New York. Things were cheap and everybody was having a good time. Within a year Tribeca started to happen; artists started to get evicted.*

I was trying to make sculpture and mostly doing carpentry. [Laughter] *I ended up getting a loft in Staten Island, five blocks from the ferry, and I renovated it. I spent a lot of my years in New York either working for money doing carpentry or renovating the place. And not making so much sculpture. I was also having a hard time getting work shown, and it just takes so long to make sculpture.* The work, in aluminum and concrete, *was all about moving stuff, like clay. At some point I had to be honest with myself and say: you just want to make pots. That immediacy, like drawing in space.*

I had all those experiences about making pots. I mean I had the technical capacity; I didn't have the visual development really. So here's how crazy I was. I was living on Staten Island, and down the road was this place called the Sailor's Snug Harbor. John Perreault was the curator there, and he was very supportive. They had a ceramics studio. I thought maybe instead of doing carpentry I could make some pots and sell them. I didn't realize I was creating more problems.

The more I did it, the more I had to face the fact that to have this freedom and sensuality and immediacy and fluidity, there's nothing like clay. You touch it directly with your hands, and it transforms from water to stone over this incredible continuum, and what you can do with it is so varied along that continuum. It is just the most amazing of all materials. It also has this accessibility; it's not expensive, so it doesn't have this sort of hierarchy implied by precious materials or the fine-art world. It was something I was looking for, this connection to something immediate and tactile, and more relational with a viewer or with a user.

I took a trip to the Springfield ACC show, and I saw Mary Roehm's work. I said, "What is that? How are those surfaces made?" She said, "These are wood firing. I'm teaching a class at Penland. Why don't you come down and take my class?" So I took Mary's two-week summer class. I loved making forms, but I could never answer the question of how glazed surfaces integrated with that. For me it was always unsatisfactory, putting glaze on top of things and covering them up. Salt firing had always appealed to me, that sort of skin that isn't obscuring the piece. I was starting to be aware of the bigger wood-firing world. Mary invited me to come back as her studio assistant for Concentration the next fall. I did that.

I wanted to do wood firing after that summer thing, and I bought my property in Worthington [Massachusetts], *which was like a shipwreck. I knew the area, and my mother was teaching at Smith at the time, and it was close enough to New York. Very pretty and rural, and also quite progressive politically. So I bought that place and started fixing it.*

He bought in 1986 and the kiln was built in '88. His friends Aaron Weissblum and Sam Taylor helped build the kiln and fired with him. *We fired that kiln every six weeks. Aaron said, "You've got to go down to Penland and take this class with Michael Simon." I'm like, "You know, I'm really busy, doing carpentry, trying to renovate, trying to get a little time to work in the studio," and he says, "You've got to go; this guy's unbelievable." He showed me some of his pots. I was really not convinced.* [Laughter]

Michael taught a four-week Fall Concentration. I arrived at Penland, and Michael had put maybe 35 pots on the table. I walked in the room, and everything I ever thought about pots was completely transformed. *They were so expressive and they were small scale. I was trying to get to something being a show-off, and these pots were so modest in scale and yet they eclipsed the frame. They were so powerful. What he was doing was so sophisticated, the kind of alteration, the kind of trimming, and what he was doing with surface, pattern, image and form, and making relationships. It was one of the more powerful experiences of my life, seeing the work. It wasn't the cult of personality or transference. I felt that his pots had something to teach me. Later I found out that he had a lot to teach me as a man also. It was an absolutely unique experience in my life.*

That was probably 1989, so I was 34. To get a teacher experience like that at that age is such a gift. It took me about three years or maybe more to process that experience, you know, find myself.

In that class he met Michael Kline, who eventually moved north to share Shapiro's house and, along with Taylor, be a studio mate. Kline had some training, *but Sam was totally self-taught, and I was pretty much self-taught so the three of us were challenging each other a lot, and competing in a very good way, and supporting each other, and intervening, like, "Hey buddy, that handle's got to go."* [Laughter] *It was a very exciting time. I'm so lucky I had those years with those guys. They're really good artists, and they're smart and really amazing men.*

I started doing ACC shows. I was the first of the three of us going in that direction. Michael was waiting tables; I was still doing carpentry. Michael, I think, lived in my house for about six years and fired with me for about 12. Moved to a smaller place and then to Penland. Sam lives nearby. We used to do a studio sale every year, and there are postcards going back to where we look like much younger men. We showed locally; I tried to do all the craft shows, started teaching a few workshops little by little. And then I was Michael Simon's studio assistant at Haystack; must have been the late '90s or something. I got a lot closer with him then.

I got married when I was 40, so I'm a late bloomer. Well, it's funny; when you're shoestringing it along like that and just wanting to make pots, and renovating a house, and I always worked as an independent carpenter, I was not a good prospect. [Laughter] *I used to work all the time in the studio, really almost all the time. At one point I got quite* anxious because I had to drive someone, and I thought, no, while I'm driving to this place, my pots are drying, so I'm actually still working on them. I had this idea that being a potter was like being an athlete, that if you're not training all the time you're losing. And when I got married and had children, I saw that was a dumb idea. You become quite anti-social when you do that. What's interesting about being an artist is they say, "Do you want to go to the movies?" And you say, "Not really, I'd rather be in the studio."

I'd always known Leslie Ferrin, and I was maybe showing a little at Lucy Lacoste's gallery. That was very appealing after doing craft fairs. In a way I was getting drawn back into that idea of the nonuseful pot that's a gallery object. So I did that for maybe two or three years with Leslie, and I hit a wall with it. It wasn't really right for me. So I returned to making pots that people could use. I'd make a few bigger, more expensive pieces, but I'm not going to try to shoehorn my work into SOFA.

By the time I turned 50, I've always been pretty dissatisfied with the discourse, whatever you want to call it, pottery writing, so I thought I'd better take some responsibility for this if I want something else to happen. I'd always had this love of books and anthropology, history background, and I thought: well, I'll give it a try. For Studio Potter I wrote this piece called "Lyrical Functionalism," about the lyrical in the handmade pot. I used poetics, this idea that lyrical poetry is the unique transmission or portrayal of one consciousness to another, and that pots could do that. Typically, people were saying, "Well what I do is improvise like a jazz musician," as a metaphor. I thought maybe there's another theoretical structure, some other parallel. I read a bunch of books about poetics—there's lyrical poetry; there's epic poetry and narrative poetry—so I was thinking about how pots could parallel that.

That project was very meaningful to me, having to think that through, and I think it was a good piece of writing. Then I think I made a comment to Ann Stannard [Karen Karnes's partner] somewhere, maybe at Demarest, "You know, Karen should really have a book." And Ann said to me, "Well, you're going to do it, aren't you?" [Laughter] So that project got started and it took me about five years to find a venue. Peter Held [then director of the Ceramics Research Center at Arizona State University] ended up agreeing to do it with me, and that was great because he'd done it before and he was supportive. I wanted to make a real book, with different points of views, essays, that would be readable and accessible.

Several institutions just told me, "Well, that may be impossible. We don't do that," or "You can't do that because you've never done that." Nobody took me seriously. I wasted a lot of time with a couple of institutions who basically wanted to plug that into their system and publish a little skinny catalog. It was a very dark time for me. A couple of moments there I would say I was absolutely humiliated. Museums are so hierarchical, and I don't have a title. I could bring the Windgate Foundation money, but still it's like, "Can you just give us the money and get out of the way?" [Laughter] So it was great working with Peter. We worked very well together. The two years that I worked on that book I really stretched myself. I feel proud of that piece of work, and I think I fulfilled some obligation to Karen and to the field, and I don't really care anymore about whether I'm sitting at the right table. I'm done.

I have apprentices. They're incredible young people. Typically they're responsible for making clay, keeping the studio clean, helping me prepare wood, reprocessing clay, bisque firing, liner glazes, and wadding. Pretty much everything else is up to them. They just hang around, and they get influenced by other people, they see the pots I have in my house and the people who I hang around with, and if they spend the time they get good. For me it's probably exploded the talent myth. It's important that they be young and flexible enough, but if they're hungry and they want to do it, they can do it. Typically they have to work two, three days a week, because I also like to have my own space. They do help me, because the wood kiln is a lot of work and this place is absurd for one person.

Why couldn't we set something up to help people get a great education that's free? They help me, I help them, and they start exploring areas that they're interested in. Maybe we could hook up with some of the craft schools. Maybe there could be a university component, some sort of fellowship. But you can't send these kids to Cranbrook and they come out $80,000 in debt and they're like, oh, now I can never be an artist.

Shapiro considers his serious work to have

started after he met Mary Roehm and went to Penland. Of one of those early works, he remarks on the skin-like quality, the thinness, the pushing out, and yet an overall sense of geometry. *It was very stretched, to the point of failure. Which is what I was doing at that time.*

I used kind of a tenmoku glaze as a liner a lot because I like the way the darker glazes draw your eye in. You have a change in gloss and value. I still use this glaze as a liner, especially for boxes and things where you want a sense of deep space. I was starting to understand that when you spray glaze over wax, you could get these incredible little dots of glaze, which I've made use of in a lot of different ways.

I made a lot of pots over the years with different—some square, some six-sided, and more recently with these multifacets—hexagons. No two are exactly alike. It's a repeating pattern but it's not identical. That's where the pleasure is for me. What makes such a pleasure to look at a forest is that you have all these trees and they're not alike but there's a kind of rhythm. There's something magical about the difference, all those slight variations.

I think there are a lot of limitations to throwing, but within those limitations you're invoking tradition, convention, familiarity. And that's really cool. For me, the fact that you hold this pot and you put it to your mouth, that's a pretty powerful position to be in as an artist. To give your viewers, or your customers, or whatever you want to call them, your work in their hand and actually have them interacting with their body in such an intimate way. Pots that are very complex in their construction and in their surface tend to be less user friendly, and they tend to compete with what you put in them. This is about a collaboration between these conventions, and what you could call rituals of the table, and of commensality, which is such a significant form of human interaction, such an affirmation of the bonds among us. It gives me courage to make things that people can use and not to be my own best collector. To make a lot of things and have them go out in the world and live their lives.

I never know how I'm going to sell my pots, but somehow my pots get sold. [Laughter] Sometimes it's through workshops and getting a show during the workshop, and sometimes it's all these pottery tours. If I wasn't doing Minnesota I'd be out of luck. For me the future is not working with galleries, those places that never sell your work and take 50 percent? [Laughter] What's exciting is all this stuff about farm to table, and pottery tours.

I really felt when I was starting out that pots should be a really important part of the culture. And I think that was my ambition. And I'm really feeling now like that is not going to happen. And I think I'm okay with it. Maybe we don't need to move toward the center, because there's some wonderful things about being on the margins. I mean, look at our community. Would it be that way if there were really fame and glory? The quality of people in this field is phenomenal. They're articulate, dedicated, and ethical. This is the best group of people.

The excellence of our community is nurtured by the fact that people are doing it for love. There's some big tent we're involved with, which has disadvantages of including amateurish things, but there's something deeply democratic and inclusive. I would hate to see that go by the way. ■

KARI RADASCH

Stickers

Kari Radasch in her
craft show booth, 2007.
Photo: Chuck Blier

Kari Radasch (b. 1975) is known for her effusive good humor and pottery that conveys the same. She grew up in Wiscasset, which is known as the prettiest village in Maine; it's not far from the Watershed Center for the Ceramic Arts, but she first heard of Watershed when she was living in Berkeley, California.

Radasch (*It's ray-dash. I've been called many things.*) came from a family of makers: her parents, before divorcing, built a log house in the woods, and her father since then has been a builder. Her mother sewed all their clothes. *In hindsight I can see my mom taught me how to sew; I was always beading or crocheting or sewing, whatever the craft thing was at the time. At camp we would macramé, make all these bracelets, but I didn't call myself an artist until my senior year in high school.* That was a big change and improvement, because she had hated school and not done well, probably having an undiagnosed learning disability. But the summer before, working at a camp, she'd been assigned not only to be a lifeguard (which probably made sense) but also to the art barn (which didn't so much).

And we did all these paintings. And I would paint and paint and stay there after hours. With that new interest, school improved. *My senior year I just rallied. I did great in all my courses. I think one term I got all A's. I found out there were art schools, and I felt connected to art making, not that it was capital-A Art at the time, but it wasn't beading or anything. I thought, gosh, I can go to college. And I think my parents were so excited that I was*

going to college that they were very supportive, even of the fact that it was an art school. I applied to Maine College of Art and I got accepted. That was in 1993. I thought I would be a sculpture major, but I didn't know anything about contemporary art. I took a ceramics course that first year, and it was just like you hear about, love at first sight. I loved it first touch.

She started with handbuilding. Throwing was harder. But she assumed that when she got out she would be a production potter. One of her teachers recommended that she try it out and see what it was like. *So that spring, I went down to Georgetown* [Maine] *Pottery and showed them my pots and said, "I'd like to, you know, throw for you this summer." And they hired me. In hindsight I have no idea why* [Laughter], *because I did not have the skills to be working as a production potter. But it was a great job for me, because (A) I realized that's not what I wanted to do, and (B) I came out of there with really good skills.*

So I went through my senior year. I feel like there was a pretty talented group of majors the year I graduated, and I wasn't one of the most talented ones, though I will say I was one of the most hard-working ones. *I feel that's kind of been the story of my life.* [Laughter]

Not feeling ready for graduate school, she applied to two schools as a special student. *But I went to Haystack to be a technical assistant that summer, summer of '97, for Catherine Hiersoux, who's a well-known potter. And she was talking about needing an angel in her studio and her life. I asked her if I could be her angel. And she invited me to Berkeley—I had no idea where that was—to live and work with her in her studio. That would have been the fall of '98. A few weeks later I went to Japan and spent the rest of the summer there on IWCAT program, International Workshop of Ceramic Art in Tokoname. It was about six weeks. There were 20 of us from around the world, four Americans, including Peter Beasecker.*

You attached a picture of yourself to the application, and I later found out that they liked my smile. [Laughter] *They didn't think I'd be a troublemaker, and so I got to go. They took us all over the place. We would go to artists' studios as a group, and Peter would always grab me and say, "Kari, you've got to look at this; this is amazing," and he would say why. He was such a great person to be on that trip with because I was just 21 and hadn't really seen a lot.*

It was excruciatingly hot. [Laughter] *We loaded the wood kiln. I remember there were four of us girls who took our shirts off and were loading the kilns in our bras* [Laughter], *and they thought that was very daring.* Her host family *had these two giant china cabinets full of handmade dishes. And so for this particular fish that we would eat, we would use these particular dishes. When I think about being there, I remember how specific all those dishes were.*

As an undergrad I hadn't seen any colorful ceramics. I mean it was brown town for sure. And to me, at that point in time, good pottery, successful pottery, was brown. Which is really funny in hindsight. I think it's just that canon of pottery that we look to: it's salt fired, it's wood fired, it's soft, still looks wet, loosely thrown, it's Mingei.

She returned from Japan and moved to California. *It felt like my world went from black and white to fully saturated color. There were flower kiosks on every corner; the people were so wild; there were all these art cars all over the place; it just seemed so joyful and so celebratory and so open minded. That was awesome. And just the work that I was exposed to. I worked for Catherine; I worked for Nancy Selvin; I worked for Sandy Simon, I worked for Coille Hooven. I just felt like I was a little ceramic slave or something.* [Laughter] *Not a slave, because I enjoyed it. I worked for Nancy first, and then I went to work for Coille while I was living with Catherine because Catherine was just trade for my studio and for my housing, and I needed money because I had my student loans. So I worked for Coille, but it was only 20 hours a week. I would always find a way to make work. It's always top priority. (Even now with two kids, although it's very difficult for me. I mean I would say that my family is top priority now, but I have to do that to be a whole person or I sort of feel like I'm lost.)*

I worked just enough hours to meet my student loans and my groceries and have a good time on the weekend, but the rest of the time I was always working in the studio. I was there for two years. I applied to grad school, I didn't get in anywhere, and Nancy Selvin told me about Watershed. I applied to do Salad Days, and I got to be a Salad Days artist. I made 400 plates, and I actually probably made 500 because I made more than I needed—made, fired, made all the glazes, in six weeks. That was insane, and the plates were not really good. And then I went back to California.

The next summer she returned to Watershed as a cook, although she knew nothing about cooking, and then spent a year there as a resident so that she could get a body of work together to apply to grad school again. *I got into a bunch of places. One right after the other. One year I didn't get in anywhere, and then I got in everywhere except Alfred. I just had better work.* The next summer she cooked again.

I still feel like those two summers cooking sort of really helped me to be much more organized, a much better planner, a much better sort of a forward thinker, you know. I feel like in some ways that job has really helped me to become a better student, a better potter, a better wife, mom. We had work-study students. We had to plan how to most efficiently use them. We grocery shopped; we made big bulk orders; it was really intense in terms of planning and being efficient because it's very hard to be a cook—it's a lot of work.

She chose to go to the University of Nebraska, Lincoln, where she had a teaching assistantship and a fellowship that added up to about $14,000—more than she'd ever made in a year. *I thought I was loaded.* [Laughter] *And it was really cheap to live in Lincoln. I'm so thankful that I went to school there.*

She felt the work took off during her second semester in the three-year program. It started with a cake stand. *I was making these sort of celebratory multifunctional pieces, like a candelabra, a flower vase / candelabra / toothpick holder.* [Laughter] *So they did many different things. There was a lazy Susan, a tiered server on a Lazy Susan, so it spun around. A deviled egg tray on the top. Another multifunctional piece. And this was about 6 feet tall and sort of riffing on the Delft tulipieres. This had two sets of clocks. And it all stacked; it came apart. And there were these sort of Della Robbia-esque wreaths that I made for my graduate show. So my work in grad school was really rooted in historical ceramics. That was fired about six billion times. And these were all pinched and sort of very loosely put back together.*

Up to then she had worked entirely in porcelain. But ceramics was the first department to move into a new art building, and only electric kilns were available. *We had to take kiln building our first semester because we were building the kilns for the program, and that was so difficult for me. I'm sure that's because so much of it was math based, and ratios, proportions; you know, something that I'm not good at. At the time I sort of felt inadequate because if you're a clay person you're supposed to enjoy building wood kilns and salt kilns. I had no desire to learn anything. I don't even know how to change my own elements in my kiln.* [Laughter] *I'll hire somebody to do that. So I changed to earthenware because I wanted to be able to fire my work. Now there's all these reasons why I work in earthenware, but that's why I switched.*

Another grandiose work was *a cake. It was also 6 feet tall; it was 2,000 pounds of clay* [Laughter]; *it was this tiered cake and it held maybe like 100 vases or something. That was at NCECA at Kansas City. I'd say I spent about two full years making the cake and the Delft piece, these sort of over-the-top multifunctional, celebratory type of pieces.*

I was in grad school; I had a teeny apartment;

I didn't know what to do with all this stuff. And I missed that interaction of knowing that my work was being used. I couldn't find a place for those things to live. Not that I've ever made work that's used on a daily basis. To this day I don't make daily pots, because I think they scream a little bit in your face.

My third year in school I really did just make pots. I made wreaths, but I focused on pots and decided I really wanted to be a potter. Her thesis work included *a big 22-inch platter, handbuilt. Maybe 5 percent of my pots were thrown at the time. With this work I was really influenced by Oribe ware, by Tang dynasty, by folk pottery, by Mexican folk pottery, all that sort of lead-glazed type of maiolica. I was trying to make them very luscious, very drippy. It is a thick application. I still use very thick glazes. Most people look at them and are sort of horrified* [Laughter] *because it's really more like pudding.* [Laughter] *I would also do some things with my fingers. That work was very gravity driven.*

They're kind of shell-like; they're kind of floral, heavily rooted in this sort of European—like this is a jardinière, so a lot of them had these names that reference historical objects. Earthenware was draped over a slump mold, which is how I still work to this day, brushed with a very thick frosting-like slip, and the brushstrokes are really, really apparent, not hidden at all. I would lose pieces because of the glaze. That was the risk I took to get that look that I wanted, this lead-glaze, maiolica type of look.

My last year in grad school was 2002–2003. In 2002 I met Ian [Anderson], who was also a grad student, a year behind me; we got together, I should say—we've been together ever since then, so it was a pretty big event in my life. I got a residency at Anderson Ranch, but that was the year they changed their funding structure to where you had to pay. I didn't have a lot of money, and Ian was in Lincoln, and there was and is an art center in Lincoln. At the time it was called Uniplace Art Center, as in University Place. Now people know it as Lux Center for the Arts. They offered me a residency. I lived really inexpensively; I didn't have to get a job; I worked at this art center where they were really trying to build up their classes. What I was supposed to do in trade was teach classes. But they didn't have anybody taking classes. So I had a big class-room studio all to myself. I didn't have to pay for my studio stuff, my firings, or anything.

That summer after I graduated we went to Silvie Granatelli's studio and worked there for that summer and the next summer. Ian was her apprentice for two years, and they are very, very close.

I wanted to try the craft show thing, and so I applied to the ACC show in Baltimore, got wait-listed, but I got in. That was 2004, so I mean long before the economy crashed. I think I took $7,000 worth of orders. It wasn't huge, but I knew I could live on that for a while. So I came back and I started filling orders, and I still had that residency studio to do them in.

At the ACC show I met some people from the Clay Studio; some residents, Jeff Guido, the artistic director of the Clay Studio, and at the time the gallery director. They encouraged me to apply for their residency for the Evelyn Shapiro Fellowship, because it was going to be the first year that they were going to give it to a potter. I got it. And so we went to Floyd that summer again, worked in Sylvie's studio, and then we moved from Virginia to Philly. They gave me $500 a month, and I taught a class and I had my wholesale orders. We ended up really loving it there. We thought we were going to stay.

But her husband was offered a two-and-a-half-year sequence of sabbatical replacements at the Maine College of Art, in ceramics. How could they refuse? She had done the Baltimore ACC show again and had more orders. They thought their stay would be temporary, but she badly wanted a house and garden, so they took the plunge. Her father rehabbed the house, they moved in, and she went to work. That was in 2005, and they stayed in the house for ten years. Her last year with the ACC show—she had decided that she wanted to be available for workshop gigs at Arrowmont or Penland—she had a "sellout show," which means she stopped taking orders.

That was 2006, the year her work changed for other reasons. For one thing, she realized that at the ACC show she was pricing her work too low. *I think I priced my work for somebody like myself.* Even worse, she began to have problems with her glaze crawling, which required reglazing and refiring. *It's also not my specialty. In glaze chemistry class I could stay alert and pay attention for about 40 minutes, and then after that I was just in la-la land. So my loss rate was like 40 percent.* She asked

the advice of all the more technical people she knew. *I never was able to figure it out. I stopped making that work. I could feel myself losing interest in my work and in my studio practice.*

But that fall I got asked to coteach a Penland Concentration with Meredith Brickell. It allowed this opportunity to play for the first time. Our house in Maine had this little side porch, and it was just a concrete floor and it always bothered me, so I thought: oh, I'll make the tile for that floor. I'd roll out these slabs and I would take my X-Acto and I would just cut out these free-form shapes. They were garden inspired, nature inspired, mostly sort of like leaves and blades of grass and flowers. I just loved those objects. She decided that in addition to forming tiles, where she surrounded them with black grout, they could be applique. *They're sort of like stickers, so I ended up sticking them to my pots.* [Laughter]

One thing that I really ended up loving about this work was the way that the glaze broke on the appliqué. So it would be this really brightly colored glaze, almost like candy, with this really sharp red terra-cotta line around it. You'd sort of have to look for it; it wasn't the first thing that screamed at you about that work. And I always liked to draw, and I was trying to figure out: How can I repeat that element in the work, that line, that linear quality of the glaze breaking on the edge? She wanted to make a Sharpie with black underglaze in it, but then she realized: *ah, I can just do the drawing and make a decal of the drawing. It was actually really easy. So now my work, almost all of it, has these decals, inspired by a lot of the same sorts of things, such as the garden. I do these drawings, I scan them into my computer, I print them off onto decal paper, and I put the decals on like a sticker, which is funny because the appliqué is like a sticker too.*

Since she had her first child, *I tend to make smaller things. I make cups and saucers, mugs, espresso cups, plates. I do make some big platters, some cake stands, but not the sort of over-the-top stuff that I was making in grad school.* She also largely replaced her craft show income with teaching at a local community college. She had some carryover from the ACC shows even after she stopped doing them. *People call me up and say, "Hey, I'd like to have an order of work, and can you email me what you have available?" So I'll take my iPhone* and I'll take a picture of what I have on my shelf, and they'll pick out which pieces they want. So in some ways, if you can make the initial contacts it's a much cheaper way of taking wholesale orders. She also has an Etsy account but maybe is not as diligent about it as she might be.

I do one craft show a year, the Maine College of Art Holiday Show, which is a lot of faculty and students, which is great for me. It's down the street,

it's a local clientele, they call me throughout the year, I don't have to pay for a hotel, [and] I don't have to rent a van. I would really like to do another Smithsonian or another Philly. I like going there, setting my work up in a nice clean space, looking at it for three or four days; you learn so much about it. And then also just listening to people talk about it while you're there or behind your booth. [Laughter]
∎

BRYAN HOPKINS
Buffalo Booster

Bryan Hopkins demonstrating at the Ceramics Program, Office for the Arts at Harvard, 2018.
Photo: Darrah Bowden

Try to imagine that a punk who once sported a 13-inch Mohawk would turn into the maker of inventively architectonic, translucent porcelain vessels. Bryan Hopkins's life story might be profiled as a wobbly start, an almost explosive blooming, and then a comfortable settling back into a constructed stability. He found his way.

Hopkins, born in Philadelphia in 1967, was the elder son of two school teachers, his mom teaching art and his dad teaching mathematics and coaching. But, although he was an obsessive constructor of customized model cars, he was not exposed to art making. He and his brother were into sports, so his mother *never wanted to push us, to sour the possibility of a future relationship with art. And I guess I can appreciate that, but she never took us to* *museums or galleries or anything. And she taught high school art!*

His father *grew up very poor in a household where his father left when he was 12. He ended up putting us through the same thing, because he left when I was 11 and my brother was 8, and we lost our house because one teacher's salary was not anywhere near being a living wage. My mother got into a bad second marriage, and I had a really awful stepfather who did very bad things and was extremely abusive with my brother and me. When I was 13 I was taking care of a 10-year-old brother, and we were both driving cars illegally by the time we were 15. You know, to get around. We were resourceful. We were not getting into trouble only because we were not getting caught.*

I got a near-perfect SAT score in math, but the verbal score was atrocious. But it was enough for me to get into some good colleges for math. Because of the income that my stepfather had but wasn't willing to give us, I couldn't get any grants or anything. I had to get legally emancipated from my parents when I was 18 so I could get money to go to college. Because I did that, the federal government paid for my schooling. And so that helped a lot, getting out of college without any debt. Sometimes people say that's awful that happened, but honestly, it's how I got to where I am today. So I don't see it as being a negative.

I ended up going to West Chester University, which is a state school in Pennsylvania. I loved the math major, but I wasn't a big fan of calculus and I didn't do so well, and if you got below a B, you had to take course over. So I had to retake Calc 3, and that's what broke me.

I realized my limitations at a certain point, and that I should be in college to learn. There's a lot I didn't learn as a kid in dealing with all the family stuff. I started taking classes that would make me (I thought) a better-rounded person, and I became politically active as well. I was a punk rock kid in 1984. And it was just amazing being exposed to different things. It was like: oh my gosh, there's stuff out there.

I took a couple photo courses. I loved black-and-white photography. I thought they were counting for my art credit, so I could graduate, and they weren't. They were part of the communications department. So my advisor said, "You need to take an art class." And I was terrified, because I hadn't taken an art class since elementary school. A girl I was interested in was taking ceramics, so I thought: oh well, I'll hang out with her and get my art class out of the way. So I walked into that classroom not knowing anything about clay. I struggled through the handbuilding. But we got to throw pots at the end of that class, and that's when it clicked. Things just came together in that two-week period. I ended

up taking three ceramics courses over the course of a year and a half before I graduated.

The teacher encouraged him to stay after graduation, mixing glazes and clay and building kilns in exchange for clay and firing. So he did that for three years while at first working in a commercial screen-printing operation. *I was spending all these hours in the studio, and suddenly it got to a tipping point when I was calling into work and saying, "I can't come in today; I'm sick." I started lying about my "pot addiction."* He switched to a half-time job. *I would work in the morning from 8 to 12, and I would go to my apartment, the first apartment that I had a studio setup in, which was just my wheel in the basement. And I couldn't stand upright because the ceiling was too low.*

That lasted for about a year. Then I moved to another apartment, and that was a third-floor walk-up. I had my wheel up there. I was making pots, then I would take them up to the school, where I would finish them and fire them. It's a dicey thing, transporting greenware, and I had started to do bigger pieces that were the size of the kiln I was firing in.

I was still doing photography, professionally. I was working as a stringer for a local newspaper, and I started, through my punk rock connection, to do other photography. So to my line of credits, I have album jackets, and inner sleeves, and magazine stuff too.

The multiple activities were not something new. Hopkins and his brother both had a strong work ethic, he says, and started having full-time summer jobs at age 14. He ascribes this to his grandmother, with whom they spent summers. She made them work as well as do chores around the house. That had a carryover effect when he decided that he needed to go to graduate school to learn more. *I asked people, "Where are graduate schools?" Nobody said, "You should probably go do a BFA first." Everybody just said, "This school is good," and Mary Roehm is who I ended up applying to. That was SUNY New Paltz, and I liked her work and I liked the fact that she was a woman, because my grandmother was my role model, so I was used to being around strong women.*

When I first saw Mary's pots, I thought, "Wow, I have a lot to learn." Because I had been playing with translucent porcelain and doing monochrome work. The three years between undergrad and grad school, I'd been doing about a dozen craft shows a year. All outdoor East Coast shows. None of the big shows. I was building a portfolio; I was getting into a couple juried exhibitions around the Philadelphia area.

I thought I was going to go to grad school to learn process and learn clay mixing and glaze formulation, and of course I had to take the remedial classes. I had to take a drawing class because I had never had drawing before, and what else did they make me take? Oh, art history. I had never taken any art history in my entire life. In hindsight I don't think I was ready, emotionally or even my work. But I got through it. And my second year, there was an undergrad course in glaze chemistry, and they let me take it. That was really valuable, and being exposed to the artists that Mary would bring up. Jim Makins is still my pottery hero.

In a course called Design and Production, Hopkins made a dinnerware set for the first time. *That was really good for me. I made a clunky set, not beautiful. For the critique, Betty Woodman came up. We all knew who Betty Woodman was, and it was terribly intimidating.* A lot of people wanted to work with Roehm because of wood firing. *I still don't really care for wood firing, the process of it. I like the results. But it takes too long, and it's backbreaking work, and being a tall skinny guy it's hard for me to get into an anagama kiln to load it, and place shelves. But I go to visit people when they're firing, and split some wood for them or whatever.* He would cook or bartend for Roehm's parties. *I picked up jobs cooking in college too. I always had jobs because the grants paid for my tuition, but not for my living expenses. Me and my roommate always had jobs in restaurants so we could eat.* [Laughter] *Because you get at least one meal a day.*

Mary started taking me down to New York City with her my second year and introducing me around, but also bartending. I bartended a couple of Garth Clark and Mark del Vecchio's parties after their openings, back at their apartment. This was usually mixed drinks. [Laughter] *Yeah. I'm also a certified espresso machine mechanic.*

There was one last benefit of his study with Roehm, and it was a big one. She had brought the Japanese potter Shiro Otani to New Paltz,

and in turn she was invited to do a residency in Shigaraki and asked Hopkins to assist her. *I said, "Well, it sounds good, but are we going to kill each other over there? Are we going to get along?" Because I had never been her studio assistant. I didn't know how she made her work. She said, "You'll be fine. Bryan, you know me better than anybody; you're gonna be fine. I'll pay your whole way. Will you go?" And I had never been out of the Philadelphia / NYC / New Jersey area my whole life. Because there was no money to travel, and there was no importance placed on the value of traveling, you know, intellectually. So I jumped on the opportunity to do that.*

I think she had been advised to take a male with her because of the chauvinism that exists in Japan, and then also wanting to work in porcelain in Japan and then wood firing it, as a woman, is just bizarre. They don't understand any of that. They wanted to put it all in saggars first, and she said, "No, no, no; I want the ash." Of course, Mary did what Mary wanted. [Laughter] *So when we were there, we got to travel the country for two weeks with Toshiko [Takaezu]. She was having a retrospective at the Kyoto Museum in '95. I learned more of how to be an artist from Mary in that two months than I did the whole two years that I was in grad school with her. It was pivotal in my life, that trip.*

Then I came back. I decided I had never seen anything of my country. I was dating a girl at the time, and I said, "Look, I like you a lot. I like you better than anybody. I want to work for two months, and then I want to get in my car and I want to drive around the country." And she said, "Okay, sounds good." So that's what we did. We worked for two months, saved all the money that we could, sold most of the stuff that we owned, hopped in my 1989 Ford Escort, and then, over the course of two months, we drove around the country looking for a place to live. Her immediate family lives in Buffalo, so we went to Buffalo first, dropped off a bunch of stuff that we didn't want to sell, and we put away enough money to pay two months of rent on an apartment. We put it in a CD, which actually made money back then, because neither of us come from a family with any means who could float us for a while.

After looking from Seattle to San Francisco to Florida, Buffalo looked best. Why? *Well, (1) her family was there; (2) my family wasn't there. A* comfortable eight hours away, and I knew they weren't gonna fly. Also, when I was there—we were only there for a couple of days—I went over to the Burchfield-Penney Art Center, which is on Buffalo State College's campus. It's a museum, and they have a great ceramics collection. The curator there called Hallwalls Contemporary Art Center and arranged for Hopkins to meet the director. And then she *walked me up to this place called the Buffalo Art Studio, which is a 501(c)(3), and I saw the studio space; it was $85 a month for 400 square feet, which included 24-hour access, heat, water, and electric. Electric for my kiln was free.*

So that's in the back of my mind when we were traveling the whole country. I'm thinking: $85 a month including electric, like, really?! I could have a studio separate from my home! And that's a big thing as far as health goes: mental and physical health. It's a separation every day. And I'm still in that studio. I've been there since December of '95. And we've built in it, we've expanded, we've done a lot of grant writing, a lot of fundraising to buy wheels, and get a nice gas kiln on the fifth floor of an old industrial building. And I'm two blocks away from Frank Lloyd Wright's Darwin Martin house, which they've just completely redone, three blocks from the zoo, which is one of the three oldest zoos in the country. There's Olmsted parks there, and we live up in that area too.

There's a lot of good in Buffalo. The city has lost a lot of population since I've moved there. I'd like to think it's not because I moved there. [Laughter] *But they are always losing what they are calling intellectual property, because there's nine colleges in Buffalo. A lot of people come here to study, but then they leave. We bought a house in the northern end of Buffalo, and we're within walking and bike-riding distance of movie theaters and restaurants. There's a Target that's a half a mile away for when you need that. Good grocery stores. So Buffalo has been really good. A place for me to grow. And also to get recognition early on, which is what artists need.*

I teach part time at Niagara County Community College, which is outside Niagara Falls, about 8 or 10 miles. And the way I got that job was, when I moved into the Buffalo Art Studio, they had a gallery, but no director. And they said, "Do you have any experience in this?" And I have always said yes to

anything anyone has offered me, which has led me into a good amount of trouble but has also led me to where I am now.

Let me say that I never lie about my experience or lack of, I just don't give away the full truth initially. It's the truth, not the whole truth (initially), but it is nothing but the truth. So you know, I get two out of three. So the first year I was running that gallery, I wasn't getting paid, but it was good experience and I thought it would lead me somewhere possibly. I put together a show called "Let's Go Bowling." It was just bowls. We had some good people in there. Sold half the show. And no show that they ever had there had sold work before. One of the participants taught ceramics at Niagara, and through that connection Hopkins was invited to teach 3-D design. *And I've been there since the spring of '97. Two classes a semester. One or two students a semester something really clicks and they really get it. But I pretty much think I'm there to teach an appreciation for working with your hands. And for the handmade object and for good design.*

I ended up running the art gallery there because of my experience at the Buffalo Art Studio, and I ended up doing writing as well because people asked me to. So I kind of taught myself how to write, but I still write in what I think of as a down-to-earth blue-collar way. I don't write about my own work, but I like to talk about other people's work.

I'm attracted to craft and utilitarian work because of use. The sense of touch. You can look at a cup that I make, but if it's not properly lit, you don't get that it's translucent, right? So if you can't pick the piece up, you don't get the complete thought. And that leads to my pricing structure as well, why I keep my work more affordable than some other people. That's just an ethical decision that everybody has to make for themselves.

I'll tell people I'm a potter. The conversation grinds to a stop because nobody knows what to do with a potter: "You mean you make pots? What do you do for a living?" [Laughter] *I do call myself a craftsman and want that association because it has a lot more meaning to me. It means that I'm attempting to attain a virtuosity in a given material, and I'm not willing to change from that material to express a given thought. Not like Jeff Koons. I'm going to make it by hand; it's always going to be in porcelain; it's always going to be monochrome.*

Hopkins names his influences: *math in nature, in a nautilus shell, Escher's regular division of the plane, a lot of architecture: I. M. Pei, Louis Kahn, Gordon Matta-Clark. De Chirico and forced perspective. Bachelard talks about intimate immensity and about those intimate spaces we all discovered as children and that are embedded in our minds. I think a lot about architecture because when my parents would fight, I used to go hide underneath the stairs, and I was cramming myself in there. There was also a closet that I would hide in. It's these architectural spaces that are usually so unconsidered.*

I really enjoy translucence. That's my primary reason for using porcelain. I use platinum luster for a cultural reference, but also contemporary too. In the hip-hop world, platinum is it. Platinum has made a comeback with wedding rings and all that too. Sometimes I use it in a way that is traditional, like Mikasa china bands, but sometimes I just do these little reflective dots.

Another reason that I like to use porcelain is the thinness of it. It conducts and transfers heat from your hand, so if you drink red wine, or bourbon, or scotch, they all benefit from a little bit of warmth, right? In opening up smell and flavors. Heat transfer actually does that. I do cups set up on stands. They're just solid pieces of porcelain that I drill out. Kind of like the hem line on a skirt, it draws attention down. People always look at the rims of cups and see the undulation of the rims, but this draws the eye down more.

Cutting windows through the pot walls, you get that access to the interior that you wouldn't have otherwise. I do a lot of drilling out to reveal the interior, to really engage that interior space. The first one led me to all that perforation, and I make thousands of holes now. It's fun. I have a little wooden dowel I push 'em out with.

My ultimate goal is to contribute something to this field that I care so much about. And what I think I bring to it is different textures, which I see as industrial and working class, which I see at odds with the cultural associations of porcelain with upper class. Also, living in a city environment, I'm very sensitive to space. We live in a small home with a small kitchen. It's very nice, we love our house, but you don't have a lot of horizontal space in a small kitchen. So this is a cream and sugar. Cream's the bottom; sugar's the top. It's more of a European sensibility of space, I think. And Scandinavian design. I love midcentury modern furniture, I like some of the American stuff, but mostly I like the Dutch work.

I don't think I'm going to change the world. But I think that just being able to affect somebody's daily existence is a pretty powerful thing. I sell my work at craft shows, where I'm standing there, hawking my wares, and I actually get immediate feedback from people. And I love it.

All these pieces have little imperfections that come from my hand. I don't use an assistant. It's a conscious decision; it's not that I can't afford one, because I can. I use an assistant to help me ship work, or to help me unload a pallet of clay, but never to make. It's important to me because it's my hand making those little mistakes.

The ribbing on these is exoskeletal, especially when you have the glazed and unglazed surfaced next to each other. It also has an ergonomic function. It's easy to pick up. You don't have to squeeze it. You can almost just lazily put your hand on it because there's so much friction in there. And it's really cool to pick those up, and that's an influence from those Good Grips kitchen utensils.

Once you take a circle—because these are all thrown circular pieces—once you take that and make an oval, that's math. A lot of what I do is math. People are so intimidated and unknowledgeable of mathematics that they don't really know that. ∎

NAOMI CLEARY

A Part of Something Larger

Naomi Cleary in her basement studio, Philadelphia, 2016

Naomi Cleary's route to her pottery life in Philadelphia was long in miles and effort. Although it's impossible to tell from her speech, Cleary was born in London (in 1978) and immigrated to Pennsylvania with her family just before she turned 16. In England she was just at the point of focusing on a single subject in preparation for taking exams, and it was to be the arts. *And then I went into high school here, into a school that was doing its very best to get rid of the art programs and encourage students to focus on the academics. They said that the art classes were full. It took a year for my mother to somehow end up in the room with an art teacher and mention, "Naomi really wanted to take art classes, but they're full." And the teacher said, "What? My classes are not full; they're half full; they're trying to cancel them." Then we realized you could actually go and make a stink and fight.*

So the very last semester of high school, when I had finally gotten into some art classes, the art teacher went on sabbatical and we had a replacement who was a professional working artist, and she basically saved me. Because I had not been encouraged to apply to art school. She helped me develop my portfolio, got me an interview at Tyler, and I was accepted there. I went there for a year and decided I need a little time, took a year out, and then went back and visited some other schools and eventually applied to University of the Arts and moved downtown into Philadelphia.

What's really funny is that as I traveled around to visit schools, I thought I wanted to draw or paint, so those were the programs I was looking at. I visited Maine College of Art and saw their ceramics program and thought how lovely it seemed, but I knew I wasn't going to do that, because I had taken a ceramics

class at Tyler and really disliked it. But, to her annoyance, Cleary was stuck taking a ceramics class at UArts. *I got hooked! We made molds of vegetables, and I thought: yes.*

My parents still have these very large wall pieces that I made. I made molds of vegetables, and I stuck them all together, a lot of zucchini, to form these wavy, moving, water/ocean wriggling things, and then I put all these patterns all over them.

The mention of foodstuffs is significant. *I love cooking. Food and dishes are obviously very connected. I like to think of my dishes as things that will bring people together, that will be used at family dinners, dinner parties, gatherings. I think I've said quite a few times in my life that I would be almost equally happy planting and growing flowers, baking bread, making dishes. Something about comfort and connections and community and people.*

At UArts *I didn't learn a lot about concept. I learned about what good craft was. I learned a little bit about the history of craft. My last year there, Linda Cordell was the tech in the ceramics program, and she was a resident artist at the Clay Studio. She recommended that I start volunteering one day a week in order to secure a working space once school finished. At the time they had an exchange program where you could volunteer one day a week at the school, loading kilns, reclaiming clay, all that stuff, and you would get a shelf space.* [Laughter] *But you would have access. I'd get a key, and I could come whenever I liked and work in the classrooms and be able to fire my work. If I hadn't done that, I think I would have left UArts and probably not continued with ceramics.*

I became the weekend tech, then three days a week loading kilns. At that time the resident artists had to pay for their space, and when they went away they wanted somebody to rent their space. So I would sublet a resident artist's studio and go and work on the fourth floor with the professionals. I got to be very friendly with a few of them. They would pay me $10 an hour to mix their glaze, wet-sand their work, whatever they needed studio help with, and I learned a huge, huge amount. I saw what it took to be a professional, working, committed studio maker.

I stayed there for three years after undergrad. I assisted with the Claymobile program, so I learned about teaching kids, and I also worked for Jason Silverman, who has a production pottery in South Philly. He wholesales to craft boutiques. I learned about packing and shipping, how to use the ram press.

Cleary began to talk to people about grad school, applied to three, and chose Ohio State because the funding was more certain. But first she went to Watershed. *I actually cooked there for the summer.* [Laughter] *I met a ton of people as they came through for summer sessions. I had just made all of that work for the grad school portfolio, and I took a little break and cooked, which felt the same.* [Laughter]

Watershed is like a magical escape of Maine and blueberries and the ocean and the farmland and cooking and campfires. It's like a summer camp for ceramic artists. I don't know that anybody going there for two weeks or being there over the summer really figures out the great problems that they have with ceramics, but I think people form relationships that maybe down the line help them find the answers. And community. You work by yourself all the time in the studio, and that can be isolating and then you go to a place like this and it's like, oh, my people!*

At Ohio State I was the only person in the art department that was making something functional. We could argue that paintings have function and all that, but there were 50 art grads and I was the only potter. The others were making sculpture. I struggled the whole time with whether I wanted to make pots. I have since realized that pottery works for me as surface. I like three-dimensional surface, and I like ceramic materials to make that surface.

I built a print table in my basement and started printing textiles while I was there, trying to make surface. I dabbled in everything. I always want to learn the next thing. I interned at an auto mechanic's shop and learned a lot about cars. [Laughter] *I don't know why I did that; I just wanted to know about it. It was really only my last two months of grad school that something clicked and I started the work that I still am making. My thesis exhibition really was the first body of work that incorporated the types of surfaces that I was trying to achieve printing on the textile and paper. Right at the last minute I figured out how to transfer that to the ceramic surface. I felt really good about that work.*

People didn't understand what I was doing. I became very friendly with a group of the grad students, and I started having people over for dinner. I realized that serving food on my personal collection of handmade pots, I was showing them, kind of convincing them. And it really worked because people started asking me to make them things. It was subtle and I'm sure I didn't convince everyone, but I think they started to understand a little bit better. And then my thesis show was well received by my peers. If I had not slowly cajoled them [Laughter], *brought them in, I don't know if they would have understood. You wouldn't think you'd have to be sneaky to get people to use handmade pottery, but I was sneaky.*

I finished school and I stayed in Columbus for almost another year. I set up a studio with another grad and started making pots. But then I came home for a visit and actually had a show at the Clay Studio and went back to Ohio and felt very lonely. My family was here; I had a lot of connections in Philadelphia. At the end of grad school, Nancy

Blum came as a visiting artist. She was really supportive and said something about there being three things that you have to consider: whether you're happy, whether it's good for your career, and whether it's financially rewarding. And you should always have two of those things. And I'm in Columbus and I'm not feeling happy, not feeling it was a good place for my career, and nothing financially rewarding was happening. [Laughter] So I thought about that and said: I gotta go.

Two people that I knew in Philadelphia were renting a warehouse space that had a live/work situation, and I moved in. I took what I had started in grad school, and I went with it, explored it, and made, I think, more pots than I will ever make over the rest of my life. I didn't really do anything else other than make pots. And I used the internet and social media things that I had learned a little bit about in order to promote myself. I used Etsy and I had a website and I emailed a million galleries and said would you like to carry my work, and the ones that said yes I made the work and sent it to them. I did craft shows, like the low end, costs $100 and you will make $600, and then I did the Philadelphia Museum of Art craft show, which is one of the higher-end craft shows—everything I could do to make the pots and get them out there.

I did keep my head above water, just about. [Laughter] Because I was really learning. So I did that for two years, and then one day I was down at the Clay Studio for First Friday and talking to Jeff Guido, the artistic director, and I said, "Jeff, I think I need a job because I spend all day by myself talking to my dog, and I need some people in my life." And he said, "There might be something for you." And then he suggested I apply for the NCECA coordinator position, because the Clay Studio was the on-site liaison for Philly NCECA. So I stepped from being isolated in my studio into a role of more emails than I will ever deal with again in my life. [Laughter] And that was amazing. I got to email so many different artists, and I learned so much from helping put on that gigantic event here. And then I went from that position into the gallery coordinator position.

As time went on, though, Cleary began to worry about her limited studio time. She has never stopped making, but of course it was far less than when she was in the studio full time. Having a baby and renovating a row house (with her partner Daniel Ricardo

Teran) also seriously cut into her time. The house is in the Brewerytown section of Philadelphia. It was maybe in the '30s a very prosperous part of the city, but the breweries all closed and a lot of people left and there's something like 40 percent vacancy in all of the properties. But I've never lived in a place where so many people will acknowledge your presence and respond to you when you say hello to them. It's nice. My neighbors know who I am. They ask about me and they ask about my baby. Our house cost $24,000 to buy. Granted it needed to be fully rehabbed, but you walk four, maybe six blocks, the houses cost $300,000 and not a single person will acknowledge you when you say hello. It's also a ceramic community, where among the residents associated with ceramics are or were Michael Connelly, Ryan Greenheck, Rob Sutherland (no longer making), Rebecca Chapel, Giselle Hicks, Peter Morgan, and Kensuke Yamada.

She reflects that what was good about her gallery coordinator role was working with all the artists and handling a great variety of work. Guido would tell her, "When you go back into the studio, you'll be surprised at the things you learned watching everybody else." And it was true. I had more time to reflect on what was good and what was maybe not so good instead of rushing toward the end, just going, going, going in the studio.

She's had to develop new work patterns. So we had the baby, and we had about two months to rest [Laughter] and meet our baby and be together. Then I needed to start making the work for Art of the Pot [the pottery tour in Austin, Texas]. When I was invited to that, I almost didn't do it, but Daniel and I talked about it and we said that would be a really great way to say, "OK, I've got to get back into the studio." So he came to the studio with me. He held the baby; I made the work. I nursed the baby [Laughter]; I handed the baby back; I made the work. And he was just super supportive because he understands, because he makes the same thing and he knows how important it is.

I had never been very good at making forms. [Laughter] When I came to the Clay Studio, I worked with Rain Harris. She would make molds of all these different things, and then she would join them together. For my portfolio for applying to grad school, I made molds, I joined things together and I handbuilt on top of them. And it worked OK, but I just wanted to get the forms over with so I could put the pattern on them. I wanted them to be good, but I didn't want to invest the time. So then I started going to thrift stores, collecting pieces of glass, lampshades, or decorative glass dishes, things like that. I would make molds of them and then I would slip-cast the pieces.

And then I would pattern it and fire it. But they weren't mine. I tried casting them and then hand-building on them the way that I had seen Kari Radasch doing it. It still didn't work. And then one day I took a plastic dish that I had, and I turned it upside down and I put it on top of a mound of clay and extended that form, like built onto the form, before I made the mold. I changed it. I could take all these different dishes that I collected, and they become the same body of work because I treat the edges the same way and they relate to each other.

That was a huge breakthrough. I make a lot of molds. I make them really thick—they're probably the worst molds in the world [Laughter], but I can cast a ton of things before the mold is too saturated with water. And then I have this table full of all of these dishes that are ready for me to spend time with surfacing, because that's really what gets me excited.

Another breakthrough was figuring out how to be a little looser. When I first was in grad school, I was patterning quite intricately, but it looked labored. I was drawing with an underglaze pencil and painting perfectly within the lines, and things were very tight and uptight really. In grad school I'd be in the studio and glazing things and watching TV at the same time. Suddenly things were a little looser because I was not so scrunched up over the pot. My focus was a little bit elsewhere. I started using a bottle with a needle tip to draw instead of underglaze pencil, and I started filling in the leaves and the flowers not with underglaze but with transparent colored glazes. I would really pile them up, and then I would purposely want them to bleed out of the flowers and leaves. And then I discovered cutting paper stencils to make the same kind of patterns that I had been screen printing.

Using stencils gave her a sharp line that played against the fluidity of the glaze. The things I'm drawing, like fruits and flowers, there's this abundance of juicy, overripe berries that are ready to burst and flowers that are dripping with their sap and pollen, all of that. That's what I'm looking at and thinking about in drawing it.

I had no problem making a piece that looks really good by itself, but I do have a problem when it comes to making a full display or table setting or collection of pieces that all relate to each other without each one kind of yelling to be the center of attention. She's been working on that. I might pattern the outside or the underneath, but the inside is just one color glaze to try to be able to make a full table that they all talk to each other; they're all related, but they consider each other.

Sometimes I forget how much I like to see other people use my work, and when they tell me how much they like it, I feel like I am part of this bigger thing; I'm part of this larger cycle and connection between people. That's important to me. I make dishes in order to feel part of that. ■

CHAPTER ELEVEN

LOOKING TO TRADITIONS

T raditions are defining factors for pottery—regarding forms, which are culturally
determined, and decoration, which has
been both the outcome of local opportunities and
materials and the result of international exchange.
Potters in America today have infinite choices in
what to make, so it's interesting that a substantial
number are attracted to traditional practices, both
local ones and those from elsewhere around the
globe.

This chapter offers the example of several
contemporary potters in the Appalachian Southeast.
In that region, traditional family potteries had not
died out when new crafts making bloomed after
World War II. So establishing a studio there provides
an immediate and apparent connection to the traditions of the place.

It bears noting that "tradition" does not equate
with copying works from a style of the past. The
word implies continuity. Tradition, in the tales that
follow, is an ongoing conversation with a still-vital
precedent. ■

MARK HEWITT

*Dovetailing with
Southern Folk Potters*

Mark Hewitt, 2016.
Photo: John Svara

It's a long way from Staffordshire, England, to Pittsboro, North Carolina. But maybe it's not
such a stretch for Mark Hewitt. For one thing, both places have a pottery tradition. Besides,
when he recounts his family history he notes that *there's been sort of a continental shift every
generation*. His mother was born in South Africa, her father in India, and her grandfather in
England. His own children have been born in America.

His father's side of the family was associated with Spode, the English pottery factory, his grandfather as CEO. Hewitt himself was born in a little town about 10 miles south of Stoke-on-Trent, Staffordshire, the pottery industry center, in 1955. His mother's uncle was a manufacturer of industrial ceramic insulators but also made Chinese-style and domestic objects. *Functional, sturdy pottery, glazed in an oatmeal glaze, using the same industrial porcelain. And it was beautiful. My mother made comfort food in those baking dishes—apple crumbles and pies and custards. And so I had a very strong association and sentiment, benevolent sentiment, towards those early pots. Moreover, my father traveled around Europe selling pots and bringing pots home, so we had Karat vases, we had Richard Ginori pieces, we had very good glass. He sold to shops that sold pottery and glass and silverware and cutlery, so we had very good tableware. White earthenware plates that were lovely, very cheerful, floral designs, pink and blue. We had bone china dinner sets, the best, for Christmas and Easter and all the rest of it.*

If you think of the middle class as being a gradation, we were a little above midway. We had good things, but in terms of money there wasn't a lot because the ceramic industry never paid a lot. And the industry was going downhill. There was increasing competition from Europe and Southeast Asia. And they didn't own the company; they were just managers. Although Hewitt had two older brothers, the first went into music and the second became an engineer who spent years in Africa, so there was some hope that he would follow the family tradition with Spode.

It's quite common for English people to have this so-called gap year between high school and university. I went to work for a company that my grandfather had set up in Hamburg, Germany, in between the wars. It was the import-export agency for Spode. I started out in the office. I was going to learn the ins and outs of the business. I hated it. [Laughter] *So then they shunted me down to the warehouse, which was the physical, menial part of the business, and I loved it.* [Laughter] *I think there's a physical, athletic component to the life of a craftsman that is not talked about. There's an element of athleticism; there's a choreography to your movements in the workshop. I feel like I'm a sort of underpaid athlete.*

After that, I went on the hippie trail to India, through Turkey, Iran, Afghanistan to India, meeting all sorts of fellow travelers. It shifted my perspective. Four months. You see how the other half lives. And then I came back to England and went straight to university. I'd already gotten my place. I went to Bristol University. Although Hewitt studied geography, he began to feel that he *wanted to get good at something,* and he thought back to the pottery class he'd had in boarding school, in which he had made some African-looking pots. *I decided I was going to go to the university student union, which had this little pottery studio, and start making pots. And about that time a friend of mine who'd been working at that studio gave me a copy of* A Potter's Book, *and that first chapter, "Towards a Standard," which was an indictment of industry, read as if it had been written for me.*

He took a pottery course at Dartington Hall, an estate / creative center. A quiz was given on general knowledge about pottery, and Hewitt got every answer right. *I knew some of the science and technology and terminology and history because I'd grown up with it. And I thought: this is the first thing I'd ever found easy.* In his final year at university, the Bristol Museum hosted the British opening of Michael Cardew's 75th-year retrospective. There, he, as a budding potter, met Cardew and also Svend Bayer, Cardew's former assistant. *The next day there was a screening of Michael's movie "Mud and Water Man," a biographical movie of his life. And all of a sudden on the silver screen, it was announced, the fact that I didn't know, that Michael worked for my grandfather back in the 1930s.*

At the end, I went over to Michael, and he said, "Oh, I remember you from last night." And I said, "But you didn't know that I was Ted Hewitt's grandson. You worked for him at Spode." And Michael just roared with laughter and thought it was the funniest thing ever. [Laughter] *That was in November, and that worked on me over the winter, so by the spring break I was wanting to be a pottery apprentice.*

His idea was to work with Bayer. *I really liked his work, and I'd seen it at a store in Bristol, and*

I'd met him again and I thought: he's the guy. That winter I was increasingly disenchanted with geography, but I hacked it through; I got my degree. But I was reading A Potter's Book, The Unknown Craftsman; *there was a book called* Potters on Pottery, *and Svend had a really nice essay in that. I liked his take on everything. So Michael was actually number two on my list. But Svend has always worked on his own. I hitchhiked down to stay with Svend, and then he drove me out to the highway and he said, "There's just one thing; don't show Michael any of your pots. He doesn't even like his own."*

I walked down to Wenford [Wenford Bridge, the Cardew pottery] *and walked in, and there was Michael drinking his coffee out of one of his big Svend cups. We ended up having this great conversation about nothing to do with pottery; it had more to do with hitchhiking. After about an hour of banter we walked out towards the workshop, and on the way out the door he said, "I suppose you want to be an apprentice here," and I said, "Oh yes."*

So Hewitt apprenticed to the brilliant but difficult Cardew for three years. It was worth the stress *because he was also incredibly passionate about pots. We sat around talking about pottery all the time. He would discuss at great detail the way that a handle felt, the way that a glaze looked. When I called to say I'd gotten an apprenticeship with Cardew, my father disowned me.* [They later reconciled.] *He was mortified because white china and brown china are opposites. Imperial pottery and folk pottery are opposites. Industrial pottery and hand pottery are opposites.*

When Hewitt left Cardew's, it was to learn more-practical skills, because the pottery *operated at the pace of a 76-year-old, and I was a young buck anxious to conquer the world. You were sort of gently suppressed at Wenford. But I knew that Svend had set up this pottery in northwest Connecticut with Todd Piker. Todd and Svend had been at Wenford at the same time and become good friends, and Todd had invited Svend to come over and help him set up his business and build a kiln. And so I wrote to Todd and asked if I could come over, and Todd had an opening, luckily. And I thought I'd just stay a year and come back to England.* At Cardew's he got room and board and toward the end a tiny weekly payment. At Piker's he was earning $10 a week plus room and board, and he actually saved money.

But he did not go back to England, because in Connecticut he met Carol, who became his wife. He also made a trip to Taiwan and Japan to see how big pots were made. *They had such architectural presence. I'd seen big pots in West Africa. In books, you see these things. And when you're a novice and you can't even make a little mug, you think: how on earth do you make big things?*

Hewitt lives in central North Carolina, not far from Seagrove (Jugtown), a traditional center of folk pottery. He distinguishes it sharply from Penland, another ceramics center but of a more experimental sort. Folk potters know how to produce rapidly and in quantity. He sees them as one model for making a living through pots. *When you look at Vernon* [Owens] *making pots, they're these simple functional pots. They're not trying to be individual expressions.* Another route is exemplified in the work of Bayer. Although he lives in England, Bayer *has a presence every year on our local public TV station, UNCTV, making pots to be sold in their annual fundraiser drive. And everybody sees Svend, as a result. He gets mainstream American exposure. He's got pots in the Smithsonian, he's got pots in all the big collections, but he's a businessman and he's figured out a very streamlined production cycle. He sells big vases to hotels; he's got relationships with designers at like the Mandarin Hotels, the Hyatt Regency Hotels. He's even got pots in Japan through these interior designers. That's a story that often gets neglected by craft writers. They don't look closely at the way some of those old-timers, very quietly, make good money, keep businesses going. They're survivors. They flourish. Svend is flourishing in this economy.*

It used to be that *you could live on the margins. Now you need mostly two incomes. When I get apprentices now, they've got cars, rent, health insurance, cell phones; they've got all of this as basic necessities. If it weren't for the fact that our business is doing well, I couldn't afford to keep them because that's like $1,000 a month right there. I'm starting people out at 10 bucks an hour here, which is good. But it's hard, even at 10 bucks an hour, when you take the taxes out and this and that and the other, to make a living. It's like if you want it you can get it. If you work your tail off and you develop your skills and you've got a nice character, you know.* Daniel Johnston (see below) is Hewitt's example of how to do it, starting from nothing.

It was kind of an easy dovetail with southern folk potters, because Michael made, at least in his prime, pots in large quantities. And unlike Leach—this is a big difference too—we never made special pieces on the weekends or evenings. Through all the variations that come, there was no standard ware like the Leach pottery's. There was nothing identical. You concentrated on each pot to try to make it as best as you could. And I pick out the very best ones that come out of the kiln to go on exhibition. The southern tradition, like this, is simple, straightforward, unpretentious. But deeply skillful. Full of pride. It's not trying to be new, it's just trying to be good.

Hewitt has developed a local clay. I came here for the clay, and the wood, deliberately. And I also had the sensibility about rising energy costs. I was a geography student learning about natural resources at the university when the oil embargo was happening, and the whole back-to-the-land thing was going on. My zeitgeist, my intellectual and aesthetic sensibilities, were: I've got to go where the clay is. And there's something to me about the quality of work.

Hewitt's home is full of pottery examples that he pulls out as he talks about his work. This is local material in the glaze. It's wood ashes, a local granite that I use, and local clay. The only thing that isn't local is this glass, and that glass came when I stuck scraps of glass into the clay. That's a treatment I first saw from the Lincoln County tradition over in the western part of the state. It's an old ash glaze tradition. [The glass melts during firing and leaves an ornamental streak on the pot.]

This is actually a hybrid form of North Carolina pottery. It's salt glaze with an ash glaze, but the ash glaze has been salted too. This shape is quite industrial, but it also goes through the Cardew thing, so I'm just synthesizing all of the ceramic elements that I know from personal experience. I've never been to Penland as a student. I've never been to art school. I've been in a production context all my life. But there's kind of restrained expression.

I was very influenced by the New England potters. I think theirs are the greatest jugs that have ever been made, although some of the southern jugs are amazing too. They're virtuoso forms. To make a jug that good, that shape, in large quantities, is incredibly difficult. They're just brilliant craftsmen.

This is an early mug, this is a Moravian earthenware decoration, so I was picking up aesthetic influence from all of the traditions around here. I basically have stolen a lot of ideas from history. I've been influenced by [Peter] Voulkos too. The lines that you put on, I love the gestural quality of it, done very quickly.

How Hewitt describes a piece of his own work tells much about his goals. I'll tell you how I read this mug. I'll turn it over and look at the glaze, I'll see how shiny and smooth and neat it is here, and then you've got this diagonal going here—this is one X; that's the other. It's like a hologram. You've got this darkened spot where the glaze is pooled. And I deliberately put . . . these are a couple of iron dots. And it just gives a nice little chocolate-y, a little break. And that little bit of blue glass, that's something that you play with, with your thumb. You know the word "haptic"? It has to do with your sense of touch. Philip Rawson has used it. It's part of what's missing in industrial ware. And you feel that, the ripples of the glaze and the ripples of the salt glaze, the stipplings, enormously tactile; it's got this great sensibility to it, a different feel, different from burlap, different from denim, but it's got a very sweet feel to it.

I make 200 of these in a day. And that's because I'm good. [Laughter] I've got good skill and I've got good material, and I want to educate my children and I go the extra hour, you know. And I can do it. I won't quit until the job is done, and I want every one of those to be good. It's like I am a performer. But it's not that the functional potter performs while the art potter composes; rather, my expression is a day's worth of mugs, okay? A mug is a canvas. And they're beautiful shapes. These are fucking awesome. [Laughter] And I love making them. And they're very different.

These are what I call my barrel mugs, and these are my straight mugs. But the most difficult pot to sell is a plain brown mug or a plain brown pot. People like ornament. People like blue. I've pleased myself, I probably use the glass more as a calling card, it's a signature thing that I do, but I'll tire of it eventually and do something else. That lizard is sort of one of my totems. A lot of the folk potters around here would scratch birds and fishes in their pots.

I have three firings a year, and two apprentices.

There are about 6,000 pounds worth of clay in each firing. There are 1,500 pots that go into each firing, more or less, and about eight to twelve really big pots (4–5 feet). It takes me two weeks to make those big pots, to make twelve of them. And then I'll have another two weeks making medium-size pots, and I'll make vases, jars, and then I'll have two weeks making flatware, plates, and bowls. Thrown and trimmed. I'll make 125 plates in a day; the second day I'll make 150 cereal bowls. The third day I trim all the plates, the fourth day I trim all the bowls, the fifth day I decorate and glaze all the plates, and the sixth day I decorate all the bowls, and there's usually a little more that I have to do on the seventh day, on the Sunday. I'll have maybe three weeks of making, ideally four weeks; I'll be making pitchers, vases, jars, mugs. I always make mugs at the end of my making cycle, when my skills are really at their very best, because they're the most intimate form. Every little nuance matters.

And the other thing I want to just say about function is, well, I invented the iced-tea ceremony. These are my iced-tea vessels. These are the most difficult things that I make. How do you get your hand inside that and make it so tall and skinny without trimming it? That is really difficult. That is well made; it's light. It's not trimmed; it's a virtuoso piece. And that matters to me. And it matters to me that the pots are light, well balanced, easy to use. And that they're sort of classic, understated, but they've got all sorts of flourishes on them. They don't hit you over the head with things straightaway. They're much quieter, even with the blue glass.

Of his iced-tea vessels, he says: I think if I tried to make them cylindrical, they'd be pretty boring. They'd be quite hard to hold. Some of them; this is quite a narrow waist. If I made them triangular, this shape, they'd have a really delicate foot that would be unstable. So these are sort of a compromise. They're a little bit like a lager glass that's got a thick bowl at the bottom and tapers a little bit and then comes out. I'll often look at industrial design and design of utensils in other media. There's something strong about the way that the pot sits on the ground. They're lovely to use. In the summertime I take them out to the workshop all the time. People use these all the time. I tried to codify the iced-tea ceremony the same way Japanese people do. ∎

MATT JONES

A Battle for Your Life

Matt Jones in his studio,
Leicester, North Carolina, 2012

Matt Jones (b. 1971) makes a range of functional pottery and is known for his large, highly decorated, history-influenced yet often current-commentary ceramic jars. He apprenticed with Mark Hewitt and has been a dedicated blog writer from his home in western North Carolina, gaining special note for his exchange with the argumentative critic/dealer Garth Clark.

Jones spent the major part of his childhood in Charleston, South Carolina. His mother was a nurse and his father a doctor; several uncles are also doctors and another is a dentist. Yet, inexplicably, he became a potter. He speculates that material comforts yet personal trauma in his early life—his father's sudden death when he was four, and the family's relocation—may have predisposed him to be a seeker. When his mother remarried, *I was always sort of craving that adult male mentor figure, and I basically got it through hanging out with my stepfather on the weekends and whenever he had time, which was when he wanted to work in his garden, work on his boat. And so I was tagging along quite a bit and learning a lot and enjoying the security in that sense, a different type of security. It was kind of an emotional bond to that work.*

His mother had a creative streak, but it had to do with cooking, especially desserts, and with entertaining. *Charleston is kind of a hoity-toity town, and she was within that upper echelon of society and enjoyed entertaining. I ended up pulling back from my parents very strongly in my teenage years and got involved in things that if I could go back and change, I would.* [Laughter] *Nothing too heavy or terribly illegal, but just spending too much time smoking dope and doing dumb stuff like that.* But he still managed to get decent grades and to take art classes. *It was considered a nerdy thing to do. I hung out with stoners and jocks.* [Laughter] *They didn't understand why I would stay after school when I didn't have to, to do art. There were potters wheels there, but nobody knew how to do it, including the teachers. So it was something I didn't do. We handbuilt pots, and I remember thinking: hey, this is cool. But it was just a passing moment in a yearlong curriculum of art. We were mostly drawing.*

I finished high school, graduated in '89. I did my first year in Memphis at Rhodes College, but then I transferred the next year to Earlham College in Richmond, Indiana, a Quaker school. At Earlham I took several art classes, and I just noticed that whenever I didn't have an art class I was a very cranky, unhappy person. There was a particular semester where pottery was the only art class I could fit in with the other classes I was taking, so

I signed up, and within three days I was completely mesmerized, transfixed, and probably hopeless from that point on. It was just a very immediate immersion, I suppose. Mike Thiedeman was a professor there, and he was somebody who had worked in some capacity with Warren MacKenzie, so that whole MacKenzie/Leach model was available to students through him. He was great; he got us right into mixing our own clay, mixing all the glazes; he just put us right into it. He also had us doing all this reading from the beginning.

Thiedeman showed that pottery was *a discipline that you could take seriously and be taken seriously if you chose to do so. And that had never even occurred to me. I think that Mike Thiedeman was the right person at the right moment for me. He kind of helped guide me onto the path, or helped me understand that there even was a path, because until that point I had no idea. South Carolina does have a long history with pottery, but I didn't discover that until after I was at school.*

I had never been moved by anything in the same way. And I remember calling my mom and stepfather and saying, "You know, I think I'm going to be an art major. [Laughter] *I'm making pottery* [Laughter] *and I really enjoy it."* [Laughter] *And this long silence on the other end of the phone.* [Laughter] Years later his mother told him that she had turned to her husband and said, "He says he's going to be an art major," and he shook his head and said, "He's never going to make it." *So very funny, but that shows you while I was up there finding something that I could take seriously, my parents' perspective was very different. Really that was not the best use, in their opinion, of the education that they had paid good money for me to have.*

My first interest was in handbuilding. I invested quite a bit of time and feeling in that, and then watched them explode in the kiln. And I was like, maybe [Laughter] *I'll put a little less energy on the pots and start getting some feedback and know a little bit more about this firing thing before I put my* [Laughter] *precious work in there. I switched over and, after some frustration on the wheel, began to enjoy turning pots. I wasn't particularly gifted at it, but I persevered. That work thing from my childhood came out, and I was just like, I can do this, and I will do this. Skill is going to come if you give it that kind of time and interest.*

Thiedeman tried not to emphasize his own leanings toward functional pottery, to make the course more general. *But a lot of us became attracted to it anyway because we were attracted to this person. He had this kind of gravitas.*

Jones met his wife at Earlham. She was two years ahead of him and went into a master's degree program in conservation biology in Madison, Wisconsin. He spent a semester in Madison with her. Checking out a ceramics production operation in Cambridge, Wisconsin, *I saw this little sign that said "wood-fired pottery," and there was a little arrow.* [Laughter] *I investigated, and I met Mark Skudlarek, one of Todd Piker's former students. And I sat there and talked to him for probably three hours. He probably had to shoo me off with a stick.* [Laughter] *But anyway, we ended up becoming friends. I'm still in touch with him. I went out and helped him for a couple of firings, and I was like, here's this dude that's actually doing this thing that I have sort of fantasized about doing. Here was a guy that was making really sturdy, big—there's something kind of rustic and earthy and just, you know . . .*

I said that I would like to work for him when I graduated, and he said that he had a student already working for him. I was like, surely there's some way; what am I going to do when I graduate? And he gave me addresses for Todd and Mark at that point. And I knew who Mark was. I had seen him in Ceramics Monthly, *and I liked his work.*

I wrote to both of them simultaneously, and I got letters back from both of them within a week. Mark Hewitt said something to the effect that "I've already got an apprentice." Todd Piker said, as luck would have it, "I'm going to need somebody in the next six months." I was like, "Definitely keep me in mind; I'll come visit you this summer." Which I did, and we had, I guess, an interview at that point, but he had pretty much already told me I could have the job. [Laughter] *Todd is a fairly open person, a really wonderful person, and just took people at their word, and it had worked out for him in many ways. So I went and worked for Todd in the fall of '94. And I stayed there through maybe the spring of '97. I lived at the pottery. There was a little apprentice shack there. And I got married there;*

Christine came with me.

I learned the demands of working within the rhythm of studio cycles, throwing, then decorating, then loading the kiln, firing, cutting the wood. It's all about repetitions of cycles and cycles within cycles. I began to adjust to that kind of living experience. Todd is a wonderful thrower and a very good teacher when it comes to throwing, but he would probably deny that.

I stayed in touch with Mark. I was still going home to Charleston occasionally, and we would drive right near there so we stopped off on Mark a couple of times. Mark's wife he met in Cornwall Bridge, and her family still lived in the area, so he would come up every Christmas and he would stop in on Todd. So I got to develop a nice cordial friendship with Mark at that point. I remember telling him, "I would really like to work for you in the future because I want to get back down to the Carolinas. That's where I'm from, and I'd like to consider the Carolinas as a place to set up. I really like your work, always have, and I would really like to see . . ." And Jesus, Mark had the kind of business, the kind of demand that most potters could only dream of. And coming from Cornwall Bridge, where we were making to some extent a tourist product that was tied to this covered-bridge idea of New England, it was exciting to be able to go to Mark's, where his clientele were not tourists at all; they were pottery collectors, enthusiasts, people who were just absolutely rabid for pottery. He's one of the most skillful potters I know of. He's also one of the most driven people around. When you work for him, he will work you like a slave, but he works himself the same way. He was pursuing an aesthetic vision that was rooted in his European background, but something that was simultaneously very contemporary and very interesting to a knowledgeable audience.

This is something that I've struggled with as a potter, which is that you're not only selling your work, you're selling yourself. You're selling your vision of what pottery is, can be, could be, should be, might be; you're selling that, and that's a very personal thing. And if you have incredible self-confidence like Hewitt does, that's a huge, huge advantage in selling. And there's a psychology of selling that I struggle with because I'm not a naturally good salesperson. I can talk with people till the cows come home [Laughter], *but I am not going to twist* your arm and say, "Oh, you should really . . . this would look great in your living room." [Laughter] In many ways I'm too modest, I should push harder to try and sell my work, but I've always felt that's so weird, almost like a conflict of interest.

Mark is a spokesman for pottery. Which I think is important. Pottery needs spokesmen. A lot of academics in North Carolina concentrate on pottery history, which is a very important aspect of the collecting climate in this state, but you also need somebody like Mark who's out there saying, "Contemporary pottery (and particularly his own brand of contemporary pottery, which is historically rooted) is a natural outgrowth of this historical tradition here. The history's not over; it's still being manufactured. And what a wonderful thing that is. You're part of something very special when you collect North Carolina pottery." So it's a really very clever [Laughter] marketing, and yet it's totally sincere as well.

After you apprentice to people, and this is an important issue, you come out, you don't even know who you are, because you have been making pots for this person. I would say it probably took three or four years before I felt that these pots are my pots. Then probably four or five years after that, I went through a whole other transformation where the decorative stuff really began to change and I converted over to using a local clay, started doing all my own local glazes. That was terribly challenging but incredibly satisfying to come through and have a body of work that seemed much more personally mine.

I was at Mark's for about six months. It was July of '97 that I went down to Mark's, and my wife followed about a month later. She was finishing up a job. So when she came down to North Carolina, we began going over to the mountains. Because she told me flat out, "I'm not living down here in this kind of climate." We have 10 acres. We have a pond, which kind of takes care of itself; the woods up that hill takes care of itself. We probably mow 2 acres. [Laughter] That's pretty serious. We've got goats that take care of portions of it, keep the kudzu and multiflora rose back.

It all came together here. A 30-minute drive from town, it's already got a house, it's a plus that it's a beautiful old farmhouse, it's got a pond, and it's got room to put buildings and so forth. This house is from the 1860s. We moved in January of '98, and my cousin [a carpenter] and I built these [out]buildings. This goes back to my dad dying at such a young age. My grandmother, his mother, passed away the year I got married, '95. So we essentially inherited money when we were in our 20s, instead of when we were in our 50s, which is more typical. This was a for-sale-by-owner situation, so I didn't have to go through the banks and have them look at my measly [Laughter] apprentice wage. We got a mortgage from the guy that owned the house. It had a balloon on it so he could call it in after five years or something like that, but by that time we had a history of paying; what bank wouldn't take it? The business was up and running; we had enough equity in the house; it was a no-brainer.

I watched Mark Skudlarek, or I heard all about working piece rate in the pottery factories in Wisconsin and then on weekends going and doing your own thing. It's hard, hard work. But the truth is, it's hard work anyway. Even if you're lucky enough to have the means to get it started, you're immediately engaged in a battle for your life [Laughter], so that you don't get foreclosed on. There was a pretty good little bit of pressure. But you know, I would say that I was going to do it anyway. I was going to find a way. That was my opinion at the time; if I didn't have this money, I would just keep working until I could figure it out. I would bounce around from Penland to Archie Bray; I would do whatever you have to do to build a portfolio. Maybe I would have gone back and gotten an MFA; I don't know. I'm sure I wouldn't have had children at age 28, 29. I will say, this is my bias, that the apprenticeships prepare you skillwise and disciplinewise in a way that residencies and MFA programs don't always do. You really do develop a confidence in your ability to throw. You learn how to execute somebody else's idea of how to decorate something and then see it sell. And that's a lesson that I think is very valuable.

I worked for three years without anybody. Todd had always said, "When you're ready for an apprentice, one will show up." [Laughter] And sure enough, this dude drove up in 2000, 2001, it was before 9/11, and said that he was out of school and between jobs and he had always liked pottery and wanted to try it out or whatever. I think he had been in touch with both Mark and Todd, and he got my name from one of them. I was like, "Listen, I'm really not ready for an apprentice. This is why. I've got a newborn baby. [Laughter] *You seem like a nice person, but I'm not going to have you live in my house, and I don't really have anywhere for you to live, and we're basically hand to mouth, and I don't know what the pay situation can even be right now."* And he just wouldn't hear no for an answer—he said he'd work it out somehow; maybe he'd work here two days a week and get an apartment in town. He made it work.

He lived in Asheville, and he got a job bartending where he could make a pretty darn good amount of money, probably more than I was making. In three or four shifts a week he covered everything, and then he could spend a couple of days out here working. An apprenticeship is a galvanizing experience. It will either tell you that yes, this is the life for me, or no, this isn't the life for me. I've seen it go both ways, both here and at other potteries. Pottery is just such a strange, strange way to make a living, because you have to be a dreamer to even think of it. [Laughter] *Then you have to have the other end, which is the discipline to make the dream turn into something that is anywhere near sustainable.*

Joe, my first apprentice, came in with a very romantic notion about the pottery life and what it might be. And he came to the rude awakening that it's just a crazy amount of work. I've seen a lot of good potters who couldn't make it work, and you start doing side jobs and then pretty soon you don't have enough energy left over for pottery.

I had three apprentices named Alex in a row. [Laughter] *The first Alex was very self-confident, capable, able to do the work, naturally artistic, etc., etc. But he couldn't stand the solitude. He was a real people person. My second Alex was Alex Matisse. He worked for me for two years and then worked with Mark Hewitt for a year and then set up his place in Marshall, about an hour from here. So he's alive and well and making pots. My third Alex was another Earlham grad. And he is living in Baltimore, not making pots. I did end up building an apprentice shack here.*

I knew that people were going to always compare me with Mark, and that has been true. I think a lot of people have looked at my work and have wanted to call me just one of Mark's students. Actually I was one of Todd's students first, and a lot of what Mark is doing came through Todd and Michael

Cardew. But you can't have that conversation. People just want to put you in a category. And I'm always grateful that people put me in a category with Mark. He's a great potter. I want to clearly delineate myself from this incredible phenomenon.

I think from the very beginning I was interested in the question of who is Matt Jones in clay. I knew who Mark was and I knew who Todd was . . . and if anywhere I was somewhat between the two in disposition and attitude. Unsurprisingly, I picked up several things from each of them that were very useful for me throughout the years. Mark has never been a brush painter; that's never been his forte, I should say. He's been a slip trailer, a very capable slip trailer. And that looks wonderful with salt.

I wasn't going to salt. What was I going to do to capture the attention of potential buyers? The glass was something that I was working on at Mark's. Curiously, I had also done that as far back as Earlham. Because I was reading [Terry Zugg's] *Turners and Burners* book, I was shoving glass in. Anyway, I did from the very beginning do some painted stuff, which I'd learned at Todd's. Todd had a fair little bit of wholesale business, and he had inventory at the store that was kind of consistent. He had three patterns—the fish, the bird, and the dragonfly, and we kept that in stock. Dave Bean was almost as important to me as Todd was in terms of developing as a creative person. Dave would come in at the end of a work cycle, and in two or three days he would paint 1,000 or more pots. It was absolutely amazing to watch because he was so calm and deliberate. Todd's shoving boards and boards of pots at him, and he's just sitting there chatting and painting, and it was the same thing over and over again, but it didn't seem to bother him; he would just whip them out. He had such a beautiful stroke with his brush.

I began experimenting with the brush, and I got to where I could do the fish, bird, and the dragonfly, and I still do those patterns. [Laughter] *They look great and I love them. And they sell well. And I'm not going to say that's not important, but what's more important is they'll teach you strokes, and you can take those strokes and put them into patterns.* Mark had brushes and he did have a white, I think it was a shino, and he did have the oxides there and encouraged us to use it because, in his words, "We need to sell it somehow, so put some blue in it and it will sell," something kind of pejorative. But I remember painting a couple of birds and dragonflies and seeing Mark just kind of groan. [Laughter]

Mark didn't make any jugs. Todd made very few jugs. They're these utilitarian pots of the past that convey some strange cultural trace memory for people. I've been interested in taking these old shapes, and even the slip trailing and the types of patterns, into a different context. So taking a bit of this and a bit of that, sticking them together and finding that it's its own new thing. I can't think anybody would look at this and not see history in it, and at the same time it's very contemporary. I've got my name written right on there with the date. [Laughter] So it's very proudly saying, "I'm not a reproduction." [Laughter] I'm taking a shape that could be right out of Jugtown, but I'm adding a painted flower that could have come right out of China 1,500 years ago. It's an interesting thing to play with.

An ordinary mug, Jones says, *communicates beyond function, to me. This communicates information about North Carolina's history and about the history of certain kinds of patterns, about the history of this glaze, about my personal journey with the history of both slip trailing and North Carolina pots.*

I have done a number of pieces now that have political commentary. And I had not done that before the discussion with Garth. My blog post was called "Rising to Garth's Bait." *I was taking it seriously on the one hand, and on another hand I was saying you know I'm playing a game here. The more serious question is, Matt Jones is a critic and a critic of himself. And he needs to learn about himself and needs to learn what it is he wants to say. Because although he's enjoyed the things that he's done, he's restless* [Laughter] *and needs stimulation. And here is a jousting partner that I could engage with. I will say that it has stimulated a lot of new thinking, and quite honestly it's opened up this whole outlet of writing, which I've found very interesting and had a lot of good feedback on. Maybe I would really actually like to write more. I wouldn't be the first potter who had done that. And I discover that I am extremely opinionated about a lot of things that I could back up with good, reasonable arguments.*

If you know what you're doing, and you can express it in words and reasoned argument, you should do so, because that communicates more than just "Wow, isn't that a nice pot? See you later." If I was going to sit here and tell you all about why I made this pot, that description is almost as important as the damn pot itself. Why do we know Michael Cardew, Mark Hewitt, Bernard Leach; why do we know about them? It's because they spoke. And through their speaking it opened their work up. ∎

DANIEL JOHNSTON

Making Your Own Work

Daniel Johnston in his studio in Randolph County, North Carolina, 2017.
Photo: Ben Michael White

Another North Carolina potter, Daniel Johnston, bridges the divide between folk potters and studio potters. He is a "local boy" of the sort that Bernard Leach sought for his pottery in England, but he operates on his own and has found a ready audience for his work, especially his large pots. They have made his reputation. He did this independently, without an art school imprimatur and without a financial benefactor.

I was born in 1977 in Randolph County here. We were essentially a modern-day version of a tenant farmer. We lived on a large, 250-acre cattle farm and exchanged rent for maintaining the farm and keeping the cows going. We all worked. I think we had close to a 2-acre garden that we worked. My mom canned the winter food over an open fire outside in the summertime. Mostly corn, okra, and tomatoes, all together, to form a base for chili or soup or anything. So we had just hundreds of quarts of that, and then pickles.

I've got a younger brother and an older sister, so we all would go down on Saturdays and pick the garden. In the winter, the first thing I did when I got home from school was to get the wood in, which is quite a big chore because the wood barn was a good ways from the house and we used a lot of wood, so just wheelbarrow load after load. At the age or six or seven I couldn't wheelbarrow that much, so it would take numerous loads to fill it up. My early fondest memories of my childhood was this sort of farm and that life. It sounds hard, but it was really beautiful.

I was probably 20 years old before I really understood the concept of an electrician or a plumber. [Laughter] I thought it was someone that worked in an apartment building in New York or something. I saw my father do all those things, so I just assumed that's what people did. One weekend we'd be working on the car to fix that, and the next weekend we'd be rewiring the barn, and if something broke we just fixed it. I think more than I learned how to do all those things, I learned that you never question your ability to do something. I was certainly really poor compared to the other kids. And this is in the '80s, so we're not talking about a time period where poverty was a popular thing, you know. Not that's ever been, but at least in some time periods it seemed easier to be poor.

I actually was really bright in school; I did

really well but would have what I now know is anxiety attacks, even as a young kid, and only recently have I actually gone and been tested and realized that I'm sort of dyslexic and had some difficulty learning in the conventional way. I was really hard working, and a conceptual thinker, which is really difficult for teachers that have a classroom of 30 people. I had a tendency to become hyperfocused on particular things. I would have a math problem that I would be wanting to figure out in the morning, and that's all I would try to figure out all day long. At 15 you have more confidence about life, and my conceptual thinking was getting bigger and more grand, and so I would question the teachers more and more; not necessarily their authority, but I would question their intellect, which is like throwing gas on a fire. You know, to question someone with authority's intellect is more dangerous than questioning their authority.

The other side of that story is that at 16 years old I bought 10 acres of land. I didn't have the money. I had a job. I was flipping through the newspaper and I saw an ad for a new Mustang, and the Mustang was like $14,900. You could have this new Mustang, and to a poor kid that seems like that would fix your problems. And so I did the math, and if I worked I could pay the payments on it. And then just beyond that there was an ad for land for sale, and it was 10 acres and it was $13,500. And it just hit me how solid land is, how permanent land is. So I called, and very luckily it was a developer who had grown up poor who had bought the land and who was developing it. He's now one of the wealthiest men in the county. He agreed to owner-finance it for me. And take responsibility until I was 18. He also sort of obligingly charged me 10 percent interest.

So I did it. $177 a month it was. And so I was working 40, 45 hours a week and going to school too. I had managed a barn for a big farmer who essentially buys cows here and then sells them out West to feed lots. The cows would come in every week, and I would have to sort them, vaccinate them, and get them ready to load. I was the one in charge of doing all that. Then I was a waiter, which I absolutely loved for a while; it was a great job. It moved so fast. But you were problem-solving constantly, so your mind was active without having to be stuck on the big questions. That was a big relief for me.

I came down to Seagrove because the land was here. On the way down I saw a pottery, J. B. Cole's pottery, and stopped in. I had always been interested in art and had always drawn and painted. I was even making sculptures in the wood pile, building big abstract sculptures out of piles of wood. So I went into J. B. Cole's and they were showing me around. There was a gentleman sitting down at a table, and they said, "Well, he's designing pots." So I thought: okay, this is pretty interesting; this could be a little bit of a future, design pots. I'm interested in art; I might could figure this out. I got a job there, and a few weeks later I figured out they said he was signing pots, not designing pots. And I quickly realized that the design element of pots in the folk pottery tradition was not, you know, not . . . I saw the powerful split between art and pots at that point, or at least the initial conception.

Johnston quit school. I was fairly naive and didn't really grow intellectually for the next couple of years. I just sort of made a lot of pots. So how the career started, I got the job putting on handles. I worked with Nell Cole Graves, and she was brilliant. She would make hundreds of mugs, and I would put handles on them. But I was being paid $5 an hour and the turners were being paid 50 cents a pound, and that was a lot of money because you could make a lot of work and it really added up. So I sort of nagged them about seeing if I could turn production. I'd never really thrown pots before, so they gave me a week and they told me I had to make 100 pie plates in one day, and then I could keep the job as a production thrower.

Half hour or so of instruction. Showed me how to center the clay. It's the beauty of being 16; your brain is a real sponge. And having grown up on the farm, I had great dexterity and I had a real sense of how things work, so I kind of understood centrifugal force just from having dealt with so many

things. So by the week's end I made 100 pie plates in a day. Which were horrible little pots, but nonetheless quite an achievement. So I went on from there. The first two years of my career as a production potter, I made 30,000 pots a year. It's not bad money at all, but I had a mortgage and I had car insurance. I had a little shack that I lived in. It's still here, just down in the woods. I was living here on my own and supporting myself and helping my family out as well, financially.

I met Mark Hewitt at a potters' conference at Asheboro when I had made pots for two years in Seagrove. It was predominantly creative ceramics. What I was doing I perceived as the unintelligent, moneymaking, no-glamour kind of grunt potter. And I perceived the other as the very fancy, intellectual, very educated, and valued work. And at that time I really was interested in the import of that world. I thought the art pottery world was where it was at. And so I met Mark there, and he wanted me to come over and help them fire a kiln, so I went over and helped, and then he asked me—which is pretty uncommon—he asked me if I wanted to work with him. Usually it's the other way around. I think he knew that I was local, and I think he had some fascination with that. I was a folk potter, that's what I was. Mark never was that, you know. And I was born that, sort of, or I'd become that through growing up on the farm, and then potting.

Probably Hewitt saw this as a kind of authenticity, but Johnston was not conscious of that at the time. I probably thought he saw like great art potential in me, you know. I was very naive. And I also had this big truck that I had built this bed for; I welded this nice dump bed for the truck, and he saw that dump bed and he was very impressed with my mechanical ability. For a pottery, someone with that kind of ability is a really great thing. So what's really funny is I told him I'd have to think about it. [Laughter]

Johnston decided that he couldn't do it, because the pay would be so much less. And so I told Mark, and he said, "How much money do you need a month to pay your bills?" I think it was about $1,100 a month, and he said OK; he would do that. So he started me there. I lived here and I would get up and drive an hour to Mark's and work for eight hours, and then I would get in the car and drive back to Seagrove, and then I had production jobs in the evening and I would work for another four hours in Seagrove, and then come here and go to bed. I did that for the first year or so. I did that constantly to just make enough money.

I love working, and I was meeting people through the jobs and got to spend time with people who were older than me and more intelligent than me. When Johnston quit school, someone told him he could repair that by being around people smarter than himself. He took it as gospel and over time has had apprentices from prestigious private liberal arts colleges like Carleton, and people who know chemical analysis of clay. Kate, his wife, has a BFA from Alfred.

Johnston says he read a book for the first time at the age of 19. It was given to him by a friend who was working at Hewitt's. *It was something like 176 pages—that's the first thing I did, look in the back to see how many pages. And it had just enough sex in it to keep a young man reading until he was hooked.* He continues to read but insists that the books be under 200 pages and be more or less historically correct fiction. He became fascinated with accounts of the Cultural Revolution in China and began to read classics such as *Catcher in the Rye. That was my education, through novels.*

His first year as an apprentice *was hell, actually, because I was working in Seagrove four hours a night. I didn't know who the hell Michael Cardew was, who Leach was; I just didn't know those people. I was around the other apprentices—college students who had grown up fairly wealthy who wanted to be folk potters. And I had grown up a poor folk potter who wanted to be a successful artist.* It involved a lot of wondering who he was and what he was doing. *We're all just these little worker bees until we die. And so my theory is to feel that work is very satisfying. If you're going to be solving problems, then find very satisfying problems to solve. And the conceptual part of life, I get all of that; I get the sort of Joseph Campbell mentality of you can, you know, watch someone eat an apple or you can eat an apple. If one goes down the sort of psychological roads that people can go down, then you just become paralyzed in life. They're right that it does not have any meaning. It has every meaning, as much meaning as you give it, also. It's both, you know.*

This is my work; this is my passion; this is me being human. I am connected with, I've always known how humid it is, not because I've watched

the news—*I don't have TV—but I can always tell by how my pots are drying out and how the kiln's firing. I always know what the temperature is because I have to deal with it in this old drafty building, and it affects how the pots dry out, how my clay dries out; it affects when I can dig clay. So I find it really gratifying that I have the ability to be in touch with nature in that capacity, by the extension of my job rather than recreationally. And again I feel like that's what it is to be human, to experience our surroundings.*

So two years out, working with Mark, I decided to go to England. I had never been overseas, never traveled, and so England seemed relatively safe. I was really interested in this earthenware potter Clive Bowen. I went over to work with Clive Bowen. I really started to be removed from Mark's situation until another sort of Cardew-esque studio made me start appreciating Mark's more. There was two of them, so it became a basis for a comparison. And there are other people in the world who eat lettuce for lunch and not meat three times a day. Or we would have intellectual conversations, which I loved, and I sort of fell in love with Clive's work, the earthenware. What I know about decoration, I really learned from Clive. What I like about my own decorations is what I learned from Clive.

The third year I worked with Mark was probably the best year. I really understood. I'd been to Cardew's old place and met Seth Cardew, his son, and he had just fired Michael's kiln so I actually got to unload Cardew's kiln. And there's a little pathway, a little route down to Cornwall that Mark had hitchhiked and Svend Bayer had hitchhiked to get to Cardew's, and I was able to take that same route. I was able to walk in their shoes. I was able to understand them as people, so I came back with a huge amount of respect for Mark and understanding. I also began to see the freedom in the life I had lived prior to that.

I was just making this up. There were no rules. I started to get a lot of confidence about my own life, how beautiful my life was, rather than thinking that it was a failure. [Laughter] *Failure for being poor, failure for not having finished school. And I started to see that it was actually amazing things that I had achieved.*

And then I started realizing that these pots I was making looked exactly the same as Mark's, but they didn't have the same power that Mark's had;

they didn't have something that Mark's had. And I couldn't understand that. Why could I still tell the difference between mine and Mark's even though they looked the same? And I realized that Mark's entire history was behind his pots, and you can't imitate that. I realized the best way was not to copy their pots, but to do what they did conceptually. So I decided that I would go to Thailand and look at these aesthetics for myself rather than to look at them through Mark's deluded reproduction of them, or Leach's deluded reproduction of them. I wanted to experience the aesthetics and make conclusions for myself. I wanted to get the fresh power for myself and then turn it into what I wanted it to be. There's something about removing yourself and being put into a situation that's so abstract to you that you become objective. And then you become objective when you come back as well.

I'd been looking at these books; I'd met Louise Cort from a couple of lectures she had given at different conferences. I would go up afterwards and ask her about classic form, ask some question that was probably just a very big conceptual question that she couldn't answer, but she would talk to me about the question more than she would answer it, which I thought was brilliant. And so several times of this we began to know each other, and then I would just give her a ring occasionally if I had some big question I was trying to figure out, and talk to her about it. And me and Mark would go up to DC to look at pots, Freer/Sackler a lot, and so we would always stop by and have dinner with her. I began to talk to her about Thailand. She made the connections. *I raised the money on my own after being rejected several times from the Asian Cultural Council for grants.*

With some advance coaching from an anthropologist on what to do and not to do, *I was there working with this family in the pottery village making these large jars. Same way I started out making pots in Seagrove, I just sat down at the wheel and started helping them. I was there for three months. And fell in love with it, fell in love with everything, and really felt at home. In England, Thailand, and here, what I realized after my travels: I had a lot in common with farming villages. It was the people in the cities that I couldn't connect with, regardless of where I was at. I had a great deal of culture shock coming back. I was broke and I had to sell pottery to make*

money, and luckily that's a recipe for work, so I just started to work.

I built the studio and the kiln shed and the kiln in six months and then had a month to make work. The studio cost $2,000 to build. The logs I cut myself; these are really old salvaged windows; the brick was salvaged. The only thing that cost was the new tin. The kiln shed was $900 because I used tin on it, and I borrowed it from Mark; I think I borrowed the $900 from Mark. I had a credit line at the gas station because I didn't have any money, and it was about a month I was by myself, so I think I ate hot dogs from the gas station because they would give you credit. If anything had gone wrong, if the kiln hadn't fired right—I was probably a month behind on bills—it would have been over. It was 2003. And the first kiln opening sold out.

This sort of concept of making your own work is a weird thing and always has been to me. If you're honest and are on your way to your true work, that will always reveal itself. The only way, for me, is to deconstruct form mathematically, deconstruct it aesthetically, intellectually. That's how I hope to arrive at work that's powerful. And that's what I'm interested in. I'm not interested in work that is "my work." It's more this human experience of figuring out how you apply your life to something and make that worthwhile.

The work ranges from very contemporary big patterns on pots that I've toyed with to very traditional shapes and ideas. I've been able to dismiss the borders that separate those things. And I've been able to see them clearer and clearer every day that I look at them, and hopefully it all transpires into my translation of that. And I think through your own translation of your questions then you become relevant. Our very existence makes us relevant. [Laughter]

I've always made big pots. After I came back from Thailand, which is where I learned how to make the big pots, I used to get about 12 or 15 in the kiln, so I'd make 12 or 15 big pots before I had to stop and make the smaller pots. I started to get ideas about how to make them, and it occurred to me that if I could make 16, 17 big pots, those would be better, and if I could make 20 that would be better. So this idea started rolling around in my head: What would happen if I could sit down and make 100 pots right in a row, and it would go where it would go? And then going back to my life, I thought, well, you know,

I have all the freedom in the world; there's nothing to stop me from doing this. So I decided to do it. I think it ended up taking about 14,000 pounds of clay; we fired five times. It was 35 cords of wood. But what I discovered from the project; firstly my technical ability exploded. It took me all day to make a big pot before the project. The last day of the project I made 10 big pots in a single day. [Laughter]

My ability to see big pots really improved, my ability to understand the scale and the weight, and the balance and the curve. I began to truly understand that. One thing that's missing in America with large ceramics is that no one makes enough of them to ever start to experience that, to understand it, for them to have that grace that understanding provides. Also, people don't have the technical ability to make the big pots in a timely fashion that makes it possible to sell them relatively inexpensively.

The other part of this project was if I make 100 pots, how will I get rid of them? I thought, if I don't give myself pressure, I give myself freedom, and one way to give myself freedom is to know that I'm only going to charge $450 for them. If I charged $450 I hopefully can sell some of them. And if I wanted to try decoration on something, I wouldn't be scared to mess the pot up. So very quickly I started trying a lot of new decorations, and a lot of new forms that I wouldn't normally try. To look back on the project and to look through the pots, I'm sort of embarrassed by a lot of them because I was going way out on different limbs trying things, but the conclusion is, what I'm making now is really the product of the large jar project.

And one thing that I thought would happen is that I would progress, and I numbered them 1 through 100. Looking very closely, I realized that my evolution is not a linear process; it's much more of a root system that expands all out at one time. So understanding that about myself has really helped me develop my work. Whenever I think two things are so unrelated, knowing that's how my brain works has really helped me to be able to maintain interest in both things.

Not only was Johnston able to sell them all, he ended up getting orders for more than 100 more, so that within the period of a couple of years, he made 250 big pots. He did, of course, raise the price. *I think one reason people responded to me is because I have passion about what I do, and I think people love that, and I think people wish they had more passion. But having passion is a lot of work. [Laughter] I've always worked hard to be my own person after I left Mark's. He cast a big shadow. And I think this really sets me apart. I've made a real statement about big pots by having done the project.*

I like to make a lot of small work. I mean, I love, you know, dinner plates. I mean it's really nice. It's so ingrained into our habits as humans and so connected; it's what we feed ourselves, what we get ourselves filled with, what connects us to our food source. It's the tool that we use to stay alive in many respects. And it's the last refined tool that the food touches. And I think that's one reason there's so much aesthetic emphasis put on ceramics, because it is the last thing that food touches before we take that into our bodies and turn it into ourselves. So I think that's important because it makes you think about the food, about yourself, about everything. Roughly 40 percent of his production is utilitarian ware.

The quality of the clay, the quality of the material, is probably where I started from. Yeah, local clay. For that to be able to expose as much of its beauty as possible, that's where I start, rather than try to transform the clay into something I'm interested in. I refine my own glazes using ash and other different clay, and in conjunction with firing them in the wood kiln, I try to make that cohesively work with the beauty of the clay, the beauty of the firing, and the beauty of the raw materials that I've refined for the glazes. I tend to like some not decorated, but if decorated I tend to like decorations that possess simplicity but that capture complexity with simplicity. ∎

DAVID STUEMPFLE
Fusion Pottery

David Stuempfle in his
studio, Seagrove,
North Carolina, 2010

David Stuempfle (pronounced *stemflee*, b. 1960) is a Seagrove, North Carolina, potter independent of linkage to Mark Hewitt, but his work also is shaped by that folk pottery locale. He's from Gettysburg, Pennsylvania, the son of a minister turned hymn writer, and a teacher. Music was a big part of growing up. *Oh yeah, it was sort of a requirement; you had to play classical music, just like you had to eat vegetables or brush your teeth.* [Laughter]

That was actually one of my early interests, before pottery. He played oboe, but also guitar and other picking instruments for traditional music. And also Irish pipes. *I thought I was going in the direction of becoming a musician until I discovered pottery in high school. The last couple of years I went to a boarding school in New Hampshire, and they had a great pottery teacher there. I started making pots the year before I went there, but it wasn't until 1977 that I had a really good teacher and started taking it seriously. So I would say by 1978 or something I was totally committed to it.*

His parents had sent him to a college preparatory school, not expecting this outcome. After that, he did an apprenticeship in Tennessee—found, as he recalls, from an ad in the back of *Ceramics Monthly. It was a two-year commitment. Responsible for basically everything: cleaning the workshop, making clay, making glazes, of course making pots. All the places that I've worked I've done functional ceramics. After my apprenticeship I became a journeyman potter. I was a journeyman all through the*

'80s, before I bought this land here in 1990.

I sort of had a rule where I wouldn't work for one place for more than two years, because after you've worked for a pottery for two years you pretty much know what they have to offer you. I think the exception for that would have been the last place I worked, here, in Jugtown Pottery, because I really wanted to learn about wood-fired pottery. I had been doing just a little through the '80s, but I didn't know enough about building the kilns and all that stuff.

The places after my apprenticeship were more-specialized jobs. Sometimes I had glazing and firing responsibilities, but for the most part I was a wheel person. So I would just use the wheel eight hours a day, making somebody else's pots to exact specifications. Exactly the same size, weight, shape. I was looking at it in the long term. I really wanted to develop those hand/eye skills. The only way you can ever get that is to do that kind of work. I was using that skill to make things exactly the same size and shape, but it's actually the same skill that allows you to make individual pots, too, because you can really articulate pots. I mean you're not just putting clay on the wheel and accepting whatever you get. You have decisive ideas about what you're going to make, and you go right to that.

I worked for about seven or eight potteries. Each one was a different situation. Here in Jugtown I actually lived right there and ate a lot of meals with them, almost like part of the family. One place I worked in Wisconsin, there were 100 people that worked there. It was a pottery factory. There's very much division of labor. That is not the kind of thing I'd be satisfied doing for a whole career. I had a lot of good teachers early on, and they sort of set me straight on how long it was going to take me to become a good potter. It takes more than just a couple of years. I really wanted that extended hands-on experience before I tried to launch my own business. Plus I was in my 20s, so I wasn't really ready to settle down and open my business anyway. So it was a nice life for a while there.

After I was at Jugtown Pottery for a year or so, Vernon [Owens] introduced me to his father, Melvin Owens, who's since passed, so I worked with his father for a couple of years as well. Even after I was building the kiln here, I would work there part time. I'd go to Jugtown in the morning and make 100 small pots, tableware, cups, and bowls, and then I'd come out here to make my own pots. I think that's a big part of the reason why I'm making what I'm making now. Because if you go to a place and make 100 cups in the morning, come the middle of the afternoon you really want to do something else. [Laughter] So it was natural to make some bigger pots. Also, since I've been here I haven't had the production line; it's more been individual pots, because most of the places I've worked at in the past I was making their pots in a production line, so I really wanted to get away from that.

In 1990 you could go to the bank in Seagrove, and if you had a reasonable business plan and reasonable experience, you could say, "I want to start a pottery," and they would loan you money, which is very unusual. Very few places in the country you could do that. But at that time there were only 20 potters in town, a different scene. I remember we questioned at that time whether there was room for more. By the mid-1990s there were 100 shops, so it sort of exploded in the '90s.

It's not easy to get started. If you notice, I've got big kilns but inside my workshop I don't have many tools. I do have my pug mill and a nice collection of wheels, but I don't have anything else. I don't have any fancy equipment. There could be slab rollers or different kinds of kilns. I don't know what tools other people have, but basically I don't like to have any extra tools, just a couple of good ones. I built the kiln shed and started building the kiln. I salvaged all the refractory for the kiln. Then I started this building. Originally I was working downstairs here and living upstairs. When Nancy moved here, we continued that for a couple of years, but it just got to be too dirty. That's when we built the workshop, 1995 or something. Then we remodeled the house.

Most of the places where I worked as a journeyman, it was all functional, tableware, all small pots, so that's definitely my background. But things change over the years. For me, making these larger pieces and vases and bottles, that's very much functional pottery too; it just has a different function. Its function is more aesthetics. People like to have beautiful things in their home. Most of the functional pots I make now, I'll make cups and bowls and mugs. Not too many plates anymore. Pitchers, just different things. It changes each year. I don't have a line here, but my customers, when they come to the kiln openings they expect something different each year. That's been good for me, a challenge really.

When setting up on his own, I was really interested in the local style of pottery. Seagrove actually has several local styles. It started earthenware, then 100 years of salt-glaze earthenware, and then after that what they call the art pottery era, back to earthenware. What really interested me was the wood-fired stoneware. I realized after I'd been here for a year or so, it's not just having a groundhog kiln and salting it, it's all about the clays. If you're not using the local clay, you're never going to get that surface to the pots. There's a number of reasons that I'm here. The clay is one of them. Informed customers are another one. Cheap or relatively cheap wood is another one.

The local clay is high in silica, so it's really great for salt glazing. There's many, many different kinds of clays here. White clay, yellow clay, red clay, blue clay, green clay. I did a lot of time digging and testing clays. It's something I enjoy doing, making clay. I know it's drudgery for many people, but I do it gradually. I might spend like 15 minutes a day making clay. I'll slick it down one day and screen it the next, then mix it, then dry it. So I don't really look at it as being grunt work. I have a more holistic idea about clay making. It's part of the whole process. For me, the main thing is, What does the clay look like when it comes out of the kiln? So I'm sacrificing some plasticity to get the surface of the pots the way I like.

When I first started, the pots I made were pretty local pots because I'm using this local material and connected to this local tradition. But I also like pots from around the world. We went to Japan and Korea and worked there, and to different pottery places in Europe. I'm interested in how they relate to what's happening here in Seagrove. So my pots are sort of a combination of all the things I've seen in my travels.

I've always been interested in history, so I spend a lot of time in libraries and museums, used bookstores, antique stores. At first it was early American pottery that I was interested in, and then it gradually expanded out from that. It got to a point where I was studying Asian pottery, so much I wanted to figure out how to get there. I wanted the influence to be more than what I saw in museums or books. So that was what the trip to Japan was about. There's an organization, Japanese American Friendship Commission, that sends artists back and forth. I was a part of that.

In the middle of the Japanese stay, he went to Korea for a conference about Onggi pottery, the large Korean food storage jars. He went back for a month the following year. Both Japanese and Korean pottery acquaintances have also come to Seagrove to work with him. I like working with interesting people, because most of the time I work here alone. I have one helper who helps cut up wood and clean up the kiln, but he only comes six or eight times a year, and other than that it's just me working, so I'll go six or seven weeks without seeing anyone except Nancy. Seagrove is great for that. Not many distractions here; you can really focus on the pottery. But it can be isolating, too, so it's been important to me to take a trip every couple of years, to get out of the country and see a different part of the world. England, France, been to the Baltic area a couple of times. We went to La Borne, which is the famous pottery town in central France. In England of course we went to museums in London but then also in Dedham,

the south of England, where there's lots of pottery made.

Stuempfle also gets away to do workshops. He first went to Penland as a teaching assistant and really had a fantastic experience there. Later they asked me back to teach. He has taught clay testing and making large pots. He also does workshops in conjunction with exhibitions a few times a year.

So all these influences. Besides the Japanese and Korean and historic North Carolina sources, mid-20th-century European potters who came to America, the Natzlers and the Wildenhains, and then in England Hans Coper and Lucie Rie; I think all these people were really influential for me. I hope it shows up in subtle ways. Basically what I'm doing here is fusion pottery. Hopefully I'm putting them together in a way that's unique to myself. That's the creative part, how you put these different things together.

I'm pretty narrowly focused on what I make. I'm making unglazed, wood-fired stoneware. Some tableware, things you would actually use plus some vases and bigger jars and bottles. Basically whatever I want to make. I'm very fortunate that way, and that's part of living in North Carolina. We have a great market here and a really informed customer base. He makes a fair number of small bowls and cups, but they sell quickly and he doesn't photograph them. He has also been handbuilding reductive abstract forms.

I'm aiming for elegant simplicity. Simple pots are a lot more complex than people think. It's difficult to make a simple pot. It really has to be just right. Otherwise it just shows up so easily if there's something wrong with it. I keep the surface pretty simple because there's a lot that happens inside my kiln. I fire for four or five days. Pots will get buried in piles of embers and moved around. I don't do any decorating with a brush on my pots at all, I don't use glazes. I'm doing this sort of like action glazing because all the ashes in the kiln are glazing the pots.

Stuempfle compares his own techniques for big jars with Daniel Johnston's: his own techniques come more from Japan and Korea and Johnston's from Thailand, but they both involve coils. So you put it on, a relatively small coil at a time, and build it up gradually. Oftentimes people think it's an exercise in machismo or something, but the truth *of it is it's just the opposite. It's all about finesse and sensitivity to your materials and just having some kind of technique.* The only part that's really physically taxing is moving the pots from the wheel into the kiln, and you can hire a young guy with a strong back for that.

As for what distinguishes his work, *partly it's the materials. I don't have anybody else make my clay. I'm always changing my recipes. It's a lot like cooking. I can make real small batches and change it. There are certain clays that work good in certain zones in my kiln. As far as the shape, I think that forms of pottery—that's really the most important part for me in a lot of ways. I'm really interested in proportions, the rhythms of the way different dimensions and proportions fit together. I like pots with clean, classical lines. My throwing style is sort of* controlled, *I think. I'm not so much interested in showing the rhythm of the wheel on my pots.*

It's sort of the potter's secret weapon: this business of functional pottery, it's how we sort of get into people's lives. [Laughter] *It's really one of a potter's great secrets as far as communicating with people, this thing with function, this sort of extra thing that pottery has.*

I hardly ever use my own pottery here. I use it just enough to make sure it's going to work, but then I made it, you know. I want to use pottery that someone else makes, so I can be part of this communication thing between maker and user. I'll go through years without reading the popular magazines, because I really want my pots to come from within me. I'm not interested in fads. I want my pots to be appreciated by people down the road. ■

CHAPTER TWELVE

TOUCHED BY JAPAN

Ceramics has been a method of cultural transmission from one country—or even continent—to another. Not only did the actual goods travel afar in trade, but techniques and even raw materials have moved across vast distances. Aesthetic exchange has been a constant in ceramics history—and in global economic and cultural history.

Japan occupies a special place in this story, first because of that nation's historical esteem for this artistic medium: ceramics may be the most exalted art form in Japan. That makes it seem like paradise to a potter. Second, just after World War II, as crafts in general were burgeoning in America, Japanese philosophy and arts were coming to widespread attention here. That's partly because of the exposure of many individuals to Japanese culture because of war and the subsequent occupation, but also because of older factors.

Zen Buddhism was introduced to the general American population during the 1893 World's Columbian Exhibition in Chicago, which included an event called the World Parliament of Religions. A young man named D. T. Suzuki was an assistant and translator for a Zen master who spoke at the conference. Suzuki married an American woman and developed superlative language skills, and he began to publish and to become a spokesman for Buddhism. His most famous book is probably *Zen and Japanese Culture* (1959). Importantly, he taught Buddhist philosophy at Columbia University in the postwar years, with such subsequently important creative people as composer John Cage sitting in on his classes and gradually spreading some of those ideas.

The English potter Bernard Leach also served as a conduit between Japan and the West. Leach lived in Japan as a young man early in the 20th century. He discovered ceramics and became close to young intellectuals, especially the philosopher Soetsu Yanagi, who was soon to become a collector of folk crafts and later founder of the Nihon Mingeikan (Japan Folk Crafts Museum) in Tokyo. In the 1920s, accompanied by the potter Shoji Hamada (another lifelong friend), Leach returned to England, where he established a pottery in Cornwall. He published *A Potter's Book* in 1940. It both described being a working potter and introduced Asian aesthetics. He spread knowledge of Japanese ceramics during his visits to America, solo in 1950 and again in 1952, accompanied by Yanagi and Hamada. The three taught workshops and lectured at several locations across the country, events that were highly influential to young American potters of the day.

Warren MacKenzie and his wife, Alix, were the first Americans to apprentice with Leach. MacKenzie subsequently taught at the University of Minnesota in Minneapolis, turning out generations of potters who saw themselves as indebted to the legacy of Leach and Hamada as well as to an ideal of an "unknown" craftsman (that is, a person not concerned with his own signature or fame) who served his community's needs with utilitarian and decorative objects reflecting a communal aesthetic rather than individual expression. A collection of Yanagi's writings, translated and adapted by Leach after Yanagi's death, was published as *The Unknown Craftsman: A Japanese Insight into Beauty* (1972) and is still influential. Hamada was later named a "Living National Treasure" by the Japanese government under a program begun in 1955 out of concern that modernization and industrialization were obliterating the country's artistic heritage.

Yanagi's Mingei was only one concept in

Japanese ceramics, although the term has become confused in recent years and is sometimes (erroneously) applied broadly to any Japanese tradition. Hamada, for example, was not a Mingei potter: he had been educated at a ceramic technical school, so in no way did he qualify as a folk potter. The Mingeikan has exhibited his work, along with that of Leach and others, under the rubric "Artist Friends of the Mingeikan."

Other famous Japanese traditional pottery came from the "six ancient kilns"—there were actually many more—each with characteristic clays and methods, many of them still being used today. Shigaraki, near Kyoto, is one of the sites most familiar to American potters now, and Bizen clay has also attracted users from the West. After World War II a few intrepid Americans began traveling in Japan, touring the potteries and meeting the potters. Some were curious because they were of Asian descent, such as Marie Woo and Toshiko Takaezu, but many others as well, and they brought back specific knowledge and a sympathy to the aesthetics they encountered.

Those who traveled, studied, or apprenticed in Japan brought back an interest in wood firing, and the first *anagama* (cave) kiln was built in the 1950s. Wood firing became a "movement" only in the 1980s. It appeals to those interested in the natural qualities of clay because the direct contact of flame and clay is recorded in color and other markings, while the wood ash is deposited on the pot and melts, all of which tells a careful observer the story of the pot's experience in the fire. Potters who choose this method see the kiln as an active participant in the almost collaborative making of the work; they embrace a far-greater degree of unpredictability than happens with the measured flow of gas or electricity. Wood firing requires constant attention over a period of two to ten days and thus is difficult, or sometimes impossible, for a person to do alone; the cooperative stoking of the fire is typically a "community" effort, which also has value to the potter who chooses this process.

Also impressing Westerners was the vivid and specific language given to clay effects in Japan. The Japanese in general seem sensitive to and appreciative of nuances that other cultures overlook.

A number of currently active potters show or acknowledge Japanese influence on their work. Some make pots that, to American eyes, resemble Japanese models, but a Japanese observer would not think so. Some potters have been entangled in long-lasting arguments about work seeming "too Japanese." There is a spectrum, and absolute judgment is difficult.

One of the most deeply entrenched Japanophiles is Jeff Shapiro (b. 1949), connected to Japan through study, technique, aesthetic, and marriage. He apprenticed in Japan and lived there for nine years (1973-81). Back in the States he established a pottery in the Hudson valley of New York State and subsequently built (and rebuilt) an anagama kiln. The knowledge was something many others wanted to share. Shapiro's practices of allowing the character of unrefined clay to distinguish the work, accepting asymmetry, and wood firing have been associated with Japan. Another significant individual is Richard Bresnahan (b. 1953), long the artist in residence at St. John's University in Minnesota, where he fires an 87-foot-long *noborigama* (climbing kiln) that is the largest wood-burning kiln in the US. Through its annual firing and, even more, through apprenticeships, he has passed along his learning from a three-and-a-half-year stay in Japan in his early 20s. While his firing preferences remain indebted to Japan, Bresnahan's forms and motifs may be Asian or Western or a mix of the two. ∎

Things for Drinking and Noshing

John Neely in the studio,
Logan, Utah, 2014

Like Jeff Shapiro, John Neely (b. 1953) studied in Japan, married a Japanese woman, and has maintained regular connections to the culture. Neely, a Kansan who has now lived and taught in Utah for three decades, had his first ceramics class as a high school sophomore who was as interested in science as he was in art. Something of a prodigy, he did his first art fair after just a year of study and plunged into teaching ceramics to a bunch of nine-year-olds at summer camp and building a wood kiln with them. Still in high school, he read Bernard Leach's *Potter's Book* and took classes with Rick St. John, an early master of salt glaze, at Wichita State University. He went to Kansas University for two years until an Alfred University professor, in town for a conference, recruited him to Alfred. In the meantime, living with several friends, including a Japanese American, he had started studying Japanese language, and he enjoyed a yearlong stay in Kyoto before he went to Alfred.

He recalls the time as *the height of the Vietnam War, and there was this kind of awareness, I think, of the other side of the world because of that, and I was really involved in political stuff in high school, and applying for conscientious-objector status. So I think it wasn't such a stretch for me to decide to go to Japan. I was still young enough that it was easy for me to acquire language, and I was, I guess, hungry or just ready to absorb stuff. It opened the world up for me. Food was probably the biggest reason I stayed there.*

What he found in clay was far more than what he knew through reading Leach and other books. *I thought it was fabulous. Blue-and-white ware I loved, and overglaze enamel, and all this light and color and pattern.*

During this first stint in Kyoto, he set up an apprenticeship that for a few days operated traditionally, with him confined to sweeping up and other menial tasks. *And then they had a big order and they needed a whole bunch of little plates, and before I knew it they had me making those plates, and within a month those things were being sold on the streets of Kyoto.* He left the apprenticeship for the opportunity of Otani University, a Buddhist institution, which he calls the single most important experience he had in Japan. In particular, painter/teacher Shimomura Ryōnosuke was both a mentor and a model for the creative life. Looking back, Neely recognizes that he would also have learned much from staying at the workshop. But he has no regrets.

When I went to Alfred, I continued to do porcelain and spent a lot of time working on surface pattern. I was really enamored with Victor Vasarelli when I was in high school, so I had this predilection for decorative division of space, and this was an outlet for it. I would take a plate, for example, and put a distorted grid on it that would make it look deeper than it actually was, or shallower than it actually was. I spent a lot of time with pattern.

After graduation Neely applied for an intensive, yearlong Japanese-language course, and at its end he was one of five "budding scholars" selected for a program examining aspects of Japanese life, so was there an additional year. He looked for a place where he could make pots, and through a woman he met at a summer job he ended up in a dilapidated traditional thatch-roof farmhouse on the Bōsō Peninsula, in the Tokyo Bay region. That woman, Atsuko, became his wife a few years later. He spent about three years there, subsidizing his pottery hobby, as he puts it, with a little English teaching, translation, and interpreting.

In the farmhouse studio he had no money to buy a gas kiln and no electricity, so he built a wood kiln. *I spent weeks doing surface decoration and I put it in this wood kiln and I obliterated it all with wood ash. So I knew that I had to find other ways to make pots that would be somehow harmonious with this firing process. I started making things that had surface design that was impressed.* Thus sensitized to wood firing in Japan, when he returned to the States for grad school and wood firing was taking off here, he had different and useful information. He did his graduate work at Ohio University, where he was offered an assistantship. When he completed that, he went back to Japan for another two years on a government fellowship. *I spent all of my 20s in Japan, basically. That's colored my worldview, I'm sure.*

Wood-firing knowledge was an advantage, but some of his Japanese learning was not. *I had a real hard time with the tea world in Japan. I really did not like the pretension and the, well, snootiness, that are part of tea culture. As much as I was intrigued and interested in the history and the origins of tea in Japan, I really resisted that. And so I went in the other direction of making things for drinking and noshing, which is another important part of Japan's culture. I got involved making pots for cold sake. This became kind of a unifying theme between all these pouring vessels I was making. Well, the irony was, when I came back to the States and started graduate school, this was a distinction that was lost on everyone. It was like, "What difference does it make?"* His adaptation was to make salt-glazed teapots in grad school; it came out of a desire to have an audience, he says.

There was yet another discovery in Japan, a way of getting gray unglazed stoneware through reduction cooling (keeping the kiln sealed and without oxygen during the long cooling process). *And that, if anything, has been the thrust of my work. It is a vitreous, glasslike surface that is colored black and reflects light in a way something like cast iron.* Another significant part of my career has been the development of this thing called the train kiln. That began after he accepted a position at Utah State University—a job that he imagined would be temporary but has now lasted 30 years. *I was convinced, having fired [anagama kilns] and visited a number of them in Japan, that there was a good reason that they disappeared. That technology was grossly inefficient. There were very interesting things that were coming out of these kilns—Bizen, Shigaraki, and those kinds of places, but I was convinced that I could do it more efficiently. And that's what gave rise to this train kiln concept, which is a high firebox, a low chamber, and a down-draft flame pattern and a big chimney on it. Typically we'll fire it in 36 hours, and you have more ash glaze buildup than you can . . . Any longer than that and you'd have to unload with a crowbar. And it cools for another 36 hours or 48 hours.*

Neely's studio time has been limited because of his teaching responsibilities, the administrative burden of being department chair for a while, and the time expended in returning to Japan every summer. His work remains primarily functional. *In my head I feel like it's all the same, dealing with the same issues. But I am enamored of things that are used for food and drink. So I continue to make those things.* The Utah program is known for its acceptance or even encouragement of functional work, something that is not true of all university ceramic programs. *I determined when I took the job that I was going to make a place for that, especially because in the '80s I think that functional pots were very much in decline compared to when I started out in the '60s.*

And also compared to Japan, where there were these kind of parallel worlds. I wanted to make sure that was possible where I was teaching. So I've always been really supportive of both potters and sculptors.

He says his form sense is more Scandinavian, his materials more Japanese. People associate him with wheel-thrown teapots. But he's clear: *My work is the stuff that goes on the table.* ∎

ROB BARNARD

Pottery as a Language

Rob Barnard in his studio, Timberville, Virginia, 2013.
Photo: Sally Lambert

Rob Barnard (b. 1949) and his wife moved to Japan after he became obsessed with understanding why Japanese pottery that to him looked rough, ungainly, even downright ugly would be regarded as important in ceramic history. Barnard enrolled at Kyoto City University of the Arts, and Kazuo Yagi became his teacher and mentor. Yagi was a significant figure in the *Sodeisha* group that had introduced avant-garde forms in Japanese ceramics after World War II, and Barnard's encounter with him was life changing. Barnard's dark pots recall Bizen pottery, but they equally allude to early American vessels in their simplicity and fullness of form.

Barnard is the eldest in a Roman Catholic family of nine children, and he spent most of his childhood in a small Kentucky town, where, he says, *you really couldn't do anything wrong because everybody knew you.* He says he was a serious child, and picky. As a kid, he and his friends played war—reliving every war America ever fought and some others as well—and they also practiced the Catholic mass. He could do the whole mass. He found it enthralling, *almost like transcendental moments. And later, when I started doing art, I had those moments with art, this sense of mysticism and transcending your ordinary self into bigger things.* He credits the nuns in his hometown for teaching him that art was important—*not because they knew or understood art, but they always had an art class. They had bunches of*

postcards of famous paintings, and they would tell you that it was important. So the imprint of that was always with me.

As a high schooler he went to seminary, and it was a trial in some senses: *I'd just got glasses; I had trouble memorizing things; I didn't know how to study. I was constantly struggling to keep up with everyone else.* But the discipline of it—rising at 5:30, periods of enforced silence, rituals of prayer—he found easy.

After the third year, I quit. I think besides the obvious things of girls and stuff, I just felt like you don't know if what people are saying really translates into what people are doing. A whole bunch of people struggling to understand God, this big thing. They want to believe and to know this, and they spend their lives struggling with it. Despite my time there, my juvenile hormones and things notwithstanding, this was of interest to me. He did his senior year in a regular high school.

Then, after an unsuccessful semester of college, he enlisted in the Marine Corps the day after his 18th birthday and was sent to Camp Pendleton, California, for basic training. The hardest part was cultural for this deferential southerner, such as guys who brought guns and switchblades with them, and meeting Hispanics for the first time. With his single term of college, he stood out from the others.

I was in the reconnaissance unit [in Vietnam], and I had a little team. It was usually about eight guys on a team. He was released from the Marine Corps on his 21st birthday. He went home and returned to the University of Kentucky, not sure what to do. He had seen some ceramics in Okinawa and thought it was interesting without knowing why, so he took a class. *Again, I was a bad student. It was just an inability to concentrate on things after the war.* But the ceramics class was blessedly physical: they built kilns. He thought it was wonderful to be *building this big box that would get really hot. Second semester was learning how to throw, and I started thinking it was really interesting. I met Lynn* [who became his wife] *at the end of that first semester, and she and I went up to Cincinnati to the museum there, and that was the first time I'd ever been to a museum.*

Production potter Byron Temple had been at the college the year before, *and I remember seeing catalogs of some of Byron's things, and Lynn remembered him. At that time nobody did pottery except for me and maybe two other people there. It was all Funk art sorts of things.* He basically taught himself, with help from a graduate student who liked to throw. *I had this feeling about pottery, but everybody else was antagonistic, and I had to defend what I was doing all the time.*

Why did clay speak to him? *I think that of all the things that I experienced at that point, it was completely raw. I had no defenses against things. That's one thing. The second thing is that my predisposition to spiritual, religious, philosophical things made me respond to pottery in a different way than it made everybody else respond. The critical aspect existed in my mind, not in the outer world. I just liked the activity, that I could create*

things by the activity of my hands. It was a concrete, physical thing.

I would go to the library, and I looked at every single book that had to do with pottery. That's how I discovered Leach. I thought, here's somebody that's writing intelligently about pottery. I wrote some quotes down. It seemed like everybody was referring to Japan; Japan was a place where they took this as a serious activity. It wasn't thought of as some retrograde thing like it was thought of in Kentucky. So I looked up schools in Japan in the library [Laughter] *and I found Kyoto University of the Fine Arts, and I thought: that's where I should go.*

Barnard was able to see and handle Asian ceramics at the Freer Gallery in Washington under the supervision of Josephine Knapp. *She took me down into the stacks, and she got all these things out, all these things I had only seen in pictures. And I was just flabbergasted by them, because it was the first time I had actually held something in my hands and felt it. There's all kinds of information. So this is what the real thing is. And I remember walking out after about two hours, walking across the Mall, and I felt as if I wasn't touching the ground. I was just so totally, completely entranced by my experience. And that's when I started working harder and harder. And I applied to the school. And every time I'd come down to Washington I'd visit Mrs. Knapp. We became kind of friends. I told her about where I wanted to go.* She knew someone there and wrote a letter of introduction.

In the meantime, Barnard found a Japanese person in Kentucky who introduced him to the rudiments of the language. That fellow soon went back to Japan, but one night *I got a call in the middle of the night, like 3 in the morning; it was February, and it was my friend who had gone back to Japan, and he turned out to be my guarantor, the person who would guarantee that I was an okay guy. And he said, "You've been accepted at school. It starts in April. You have to get here really soon." And I was going, "Holy cow!"*

He and Lynn spent all their meager savings getting there. She was the first to find a job, teaching English, and he got a job soon after. *I met Yagi and I thought he wouldn't like me because I was American, and a sculptor doesn't like anybody who does pottery. He wasn't like that at all. You would ask questions, and he would talk to you. He was kind of shy.*

An American potter staying with Barnard for a month accidentally knocked a Yagi sculpture off a pedestal in a Kyoto gallery, and it broke. Barnard was mortified and thought he'd have to leave the country. He got someone to help him write an apology letter in Japanese, and he delivered it to Yagi. *He started reading, What's this? And he's reading it and reading it. At the end of it he just slapped himself and laughed and said don't worry about it. That was kind of the beginning of us as friends.*

The separation between the sculptor and the potter was nonexistent. It was just a question about whether something had a kind of life to it. And he was looking for life; in other words, the sense that when you saw an object it made you examine everything that you knew about the world prior to seeing that object. That was the beginning of me thinking seriously. Before that I was just going to try to make a bunch of things, be a potter, make 100 mugs, and sell them. And all of a sudden I got caught up in this other thing. And after I got caught up in it, I couldn't go back to thinking about craft fairs or craft shops or anything like that.

Barnard learned to think in a new way. *When you throw dinner plates, you have to keep them always flat; you can't throw a ridge and then flatten the ridge down, because it folds back up when it dries. Well, I got mad. I came back and it had folded back up and I just took a big bat and broke it. And it just looked kind of neat. So I let it sit around and then I thought, well, we rented a big chamber at the noborigama right next to Kawai's house* [the museum of Kanjiro Kawai, an artist friend of the Mingeikan]. *I'll fire in that; that will make it really interesting. I thought it was going to be dark, but when it came out I was like, that's it? Wood firing and that's all I got?* [Laughter] *It sat around and sat around. Yagi saw it and he said, "That's very good." Then he said, "We'll put this in the student show." It was the first time that any foreign student had been in the show, so I was excited about it. It was a freeing moment to be able to think: I don't have any rules. Like when I did dinner plates in Kentucky, I would worry about the wax resist, or how a casserole lid fit. I'm not a very good craftsman, so all those things were difficult for me. But it was when I quit having to worry about technical things and only had to worry about emotional content of something that my work started to take off.*

Barnard began to take notes on Yagi's comments. *He was really direct, which I found so different from most of the Japanese. Yagi at that time wasn't that important. I mean he was important but he wasn't a Living Treasure; he wasn't the father of modern Japanese ceramics at that time.*

He still treasures Yagi's words. When Yagi learned that Barnard was moving to the country and building a wood-fire kiln, he cautioned him, saying, *"Anybody can take a piece of clay and stick it in a wood kiln and make something interesting, but until you can make something that interesting using your own intelligence and skill, you have no business playing with this because it will retard your growth as an artist."*

Before Japan, I just had a big general idea that I liked pottery. When I got to Japan, it became defined and it became a conceptual, intellectual, spiritual pursuit as opposed to an object-making, selling-of-mugs pursuit. Yagi wrote a letter for me for the NEA Fellowship and said something like I had deeply entered the philosophical world of Japanese ceramics. That was true. It was a world that I didn't know existed before I got there; it was a world that he opened up for me. And so when I came back there, that was my model. It was a model of making almost as an iconoclast. Making things, and you just demanded that people take them for what you meant them to be.

His readjustment to America was difficult. He told people he did not want to do craft shows. He wanted to exhibit his work in a gallery. *And people would look at me like, "Poor pathetic Rob, he doesn't understand the way the world is." But Gail [Enns] had just opened Anton [Gallery], and I got introduced to her. And she didn't really know that much either, so it was lucky that I could do things. People in Washington would buy things, because there was a sophisticated market. I wasn't making as much money as somebody who'd go to one of the ACC craft fairs. Just by a confluence of things, I made enough that it was viable for me to be in the gallery. So people that I met and talked to were all artists. I just naturally found my milieu, the water I swam in.*

I started going back to Japan and taking pots back there. That was a difficult thing, too, because in spite of what people here think, these things don't fit in Japan very well. Japanese have a kind of computer brain—they match all this stuff and it doesn't compute; it doesn't spit out as Bizen, as Shigaraki. Some of the shapes are maybe a little angular, some of them are Chinese, Korean, or early American, but they're done in a wood firing. So they look at them and say, "What are you doing?" His things fit in Japan *in a spiritual way, not in the right-pigeon-hole way.*

He has had the problem of Americans thinking of the work as Japanese. *The wood firing is part of it, because before myself and a few other people, it didn't exist in the US, so the only frame of reference was Japan. And just the fact that I studied there.*

I'm trying to keep it within a certain context. A pitcher is always going to be a pitcher, I'm not going to break it up, so it's not a pitcher, or I'm not going to make something that's not a pitcher and call it a pitcher. It's nuances; it's poetry; things are out of kilter a little bit. It's still within the language of pottery, but it's its own version of that language. The issue is to pick up a genre, an idiom, and work on it and work on it and work on it, so that you expand the idiom.

Barnard has continued his intransigence and ambition ever since. He settled in rural Virginia outside Washington, DC. He was far enough away to buy 9 acres with a tiny house on it for $29,000, but close enough to find an audience and a community. And he worked toward that end by writing for the *New Art Examiner*, a Chicago-based magazine that then had a bureau in Washington (he had previously written a little for one of the English-language newspapers in Japan). *I can't write about things I don't care about. I write only if I feel real passionate about something or something's interesting or I can write about it to clarify my own feelings about it. Once I wrote one thing, I started to think maybe I could write something else if I felt like it. And somebody else asked me for my opinion about something. So it wasn't a plan, just following my nose.*

He also advanced the pottery cause by advocating for his ideas at NCECA conferences. He was able, through an acquaintance, to get Philip Rawson (author of the brilliant *Ceramics*, 1971) to speak, and he participated in a panel on pottery. In a private conversation rehashing the panel, Rawson, then elderly and not in good health, patted Barnard on the knee and said, "Some people don't take it as seriously as you do." Quite!

Rawson was important to him, because *after Yagi had passed away he was the next person who pointed out the whole notion of ceramics and pottery being a language and having grammar and syntax. It doesn't change the fact that everybody uses the same words every day. Some people use them eloquently and some don't. So I don't have to change my language; I don't have to change pottery for it to be poetic; I just have to use it poetically. That made tons of sense to me.*

I look at things, and if I find something that's real, to me it's real, it resonates with me. I know the academic framework behind those things, but when I go to conferences I'm like, I wish you all would get to the damn point. [Laughter] Let's talk about this. Is this real or not? Is it going to move anybody or not? Is it going to change the world or not?

I don't see myself in the context of the field any more. When I look at it I don't see something that I understand, that has the values that I have. And what I mean by values: When somebody makes something, is it really authentic? Is it a gimmick, or something that really speaks to somebody's inner struggle? Barnard quotes a poem by Kanjiro Kawai: "In creating something one sees oneself. In choosing something one sees oneself. What kind of I should I create? What kind of I should I choose?"

I accept the fact that there are a lot of ways of speaking, but I'm doing it this way. I eat McDonald's hamburgers, but I don't mistake them for carefully made food. I can separate those things. My sense of self does not come from that world, no matter how I fit into it or don't fit into it, am liked or not liked. And that's the nice thing about living in a place like this. Nobody tells me how to feel about things. I can do what I want to.

When someone brings him food on a handmade plate that he admires artistically, he thinks: *How does it get any better than that? Somebody did it just for you, not for the whole world, in a little sacred spot just for you. It's play, and it's imagination, and it's things people do for each other. It's not a thing that you do to gain, like "I'll be in the Museum of Modern Art." [Laughter] It's just something you do for somebody else.*

I don't look at this jar and say, "Oh, you're really good, Rob, because you made that." I just feel lucky that it happened. ∎

BETSY WILLIAMS

Learning with Your Hands

Betsy Williams on a return visit to Japan, 2015, with her teacher Yutaka Ōhashi and his daughters Megumi and Tomoe (*front*), at his Ōsugi Saraya Gama studio, Kitahata village, Saga Prefecture

Betsy Williams, like Neely and others, came to know Japanese culture deeply. She mastered the language as well as undertaking a long apprenticeship. Neither she nor anyone else would have predicted this path. Exceptionally, no one says her work "looks Japanese," except that some diminutive bowls might be mistaken for sake cups, and her new brushwork is as spare as some Japanese ink painting.

Williams (b. 1964) is from Georgia and spent her early years in the kind of *rural Georgia place where everybody knows everybody; chances are they not only know everybody, they're related to each other. From my earliest memories I was always drawing. My brother and sister were at school and gone for the day, and my mother was busy with chores. I loved to draw all kinds of little people and scenes, portraits.*

Then later *I loved school. I was a great student. You know, you begin to recognize aspects of your existing self in those early-childhood things, so I was just totally into making an A+ on everything. An A made me cry.* [Laughter] *If I left my spelling in school, I would not be able to sleep at night.*

When her parents divorced, she moved to a larger town with her mother. *I was terribly shy, so I think of that time as my first experience with culture shock and learning to deal with being a stranger.*

It was still Georgia, but for me that move was a big deal.

So then I went to high school and became kind of apathetic because school was very easy for me. I could make A's on everything. Totally not challenging. I did a lot of reading on my own and still was drawing. I had one teacher who was interested in me, but by then I was kind of a lost cause as far as trusting adults, so I was not approachable, really, and I wouldn't talk. You can't get really far with a kid like that. I just wanted to get out of Georgia. I don't know what it is, I just felt like I had been born in the wrong place.

A friend received a brochure from St. John's College in Santa Fe, a Great Books school where students are not given grades. It listed in three or four columns the names of the authors—Plato, Aristotle, et al. *And that was it for me, because I loved to read. I wanted to be around people who* were nerdy like me. I didn't know where Santa Fe was; I'd never heard of it before. I asked my dad if we could go out and look at it, because it was so different that they encouraged prospective students to stay in the dorm for a few days and go to classes, listen, and see what you think. He agreed to do that, and he also took me to Vanderbilt because he wanted me to go there; that was where nice young ladies go. [Laughter] But I had already fallen in love with the whole idea of St. John's and discussing the Great Books and not getting grades. Even at that age I had a feeling that grades aren't the measure. Williams and her father got a campus tour from a student who was from the East Coast. She talked so fast I could barely understand her. [Laughter] And she's telling us all this stuff, and she leaves us alone for a while, and my dad looks around and he says, "Bunch of damn weirdos out here." [Laughter]

But he said okay. She went first to the school's Annapolis campus because he wanted her closer to home, but went to Santa Fe as a sophomore. In a school of Great Books, discussion is essential, and she still didn't talk. She tried to, but conversation is like a river; it doesn't stay in one spot. My heart would start beating so fast, and then finally I would say something but it was already not inserted in the right spot because it had taken me a few minutes to get my courage up. But some of the students were very sweet to me, and once I actually said something, because they didn't even know what I sounded like, everything would just stop. And someone would come over and say, "I thought that was a really good point you made in class."

In lieu of grades, students had to sit before a panel of tutors. You go in, you sit down on this one little lonesome chair, and one of them says, "Well, how do you think Ms. Williams is doing?" And then all of your teachers will discuss you as if you're not there. It's so hard. [Laughter] So this is my second chapter of culture shock, going to St. John's, being around non-southerners who made fun of the way I talk. They read all these books. [Laughter] I thought I was the most well-read 18-year-old, and they make me look like . . . I mean, you learn. I'm so not even close to being at this level. Plus they're very good at conversation. All that was very eye opening to me, to hear a conversation, not an argument but a conversation.

I had a French class, and that was kind of the beginning of finding out that whatever it is in a person's brain that makes them good at languages, I'm very good at languages. I had no way of knowing that as a child. (She had taken French in high school and of course earned an A+, but it gave her no measure.) Probably has something to do with why I like music. I'm a good mimic, maybe? I like to hear sounds and imitate them; it's easy for me.

So I graduated from St. John's, and at that point I was very interested in Dostoevsky. I tend to get kind of obsessed with certain things, and Dostoevsky was my obsession of that day. I didn't really know what I wanted to do. St. John's does not prepare you for a career in the real world; it prepares you for more studies in other schools. A lot of people who go there want to be academics. That's a good beginning for that. I realized that being totally in my head makes me unhappy. I need to be doing something with my hands. That took a long time for me to figure out, that part. I studied Russian for a few years, floated around here and there.

Between my junior and senior year at St. John's, I went to the Monterey Institute of International Studies. They have those intensive summer language programs, so I enrolled in one of those. That's when I realized I was good at memorizing and learning language and being able to speak with very little accent, which you wouldn't think a southern girl . . .

Later she went to Leningrad on a program for college students. On the street, people could spot a Westerner from a mile away. So young people about my age would come up, and they would say, "What time is it?," just to see if I could answer that question. Then they'd sit down and start talking. I made so many friends. That was my very late version of a high school social group. [Laughter] I think I was so used at that time to feeling odd that [Laughter] it wasn't a big deal for me. I never was popular, never really had a core group of friends, so being in a strange place and feeling uncomfortable was totally normal. [Laughter] So I would go out there after school, and people would befriend me and we'd go to the lake together and ride on a motorcycle or go out for cocktails or end up in somebody's kitchen, or whatever. That's what I did the whole time. So when I got back from there I was pretty exhausted. That was a two- or three-month program. I went back to Georgia.

On a whim, she and a Georgia friend moved

to New York City, found housing in a dorm-type residence for women only, and found jobs. Williams was hired at *a small branch of a regional Japanese bank, and I had maybe 15 or 16 coworkers. About half of them were Japanese men. Started working there, and I guess that's chapter 4 or 5 of culture shock.* [Laughter] *You see where I'm going? Culture shock's getting to be pretty old. Dealing with this Japanese culture was totally new for me, but in a weird way I felt comfortable there, because they're complete fanatics and overachievers. I began to really try to do a good job at work. I would stay, if they asked me to stay overtime to do anything; I would say yes. After about a year they asked me if I wanted to be a trainee for the money-trading desk. That was a very intensive stepping out of my comfort zone.*

At the same time, one of my coworkers invited me to go the Metropolitan Museum one weekend, and I saw this Korean pot. And that was it. I kept working at the bank but from that moment I was just . . . I saw this Korean celadon jar in a glass case. It was a little asymmetrical. It was almost 400 years old, and I felt so connected to it. It was so warm and so human and so quiet, and not about ego but so beautiful. By then I'd been working at the bank for a couple of years, and I was doing well. I knew that if I stayed there I would have a good career. But I didn't feel a sense of meaning or purpose in my life. I was really searching for something that was more meaningful than going to a job and then having leisure activities. That kind of division didn't really make sense to me. So from that moment, I began to think of ceramics and started to read books about ceramics, started to look at photos of ceramics.

That same coworker called me over to her desk one day. There was a little Japanese newspaper for Japanese businesspeople in New York. She said, "There's an ad here for a Japanese ceramics studio. Do you want to go there? Would you like to take a class there?" And I was like, "Yeah." And she said, "Do you want me to call for you?" And I said, "Would you?" It was a group of young Japanese women who were doing this little pottery studio thing. She talked to them, and when she hung up the phone she said, "Betsy, they said they don't speak a lot of English, but if you don't mind that, they don't mind if you come." So I started going over there, and they were so curious about me. *[Laughter]* I *was very curious about them. I would do that after work and Saturdays and stuff.*

What they did have was a nice library. I couldn't read Japanese, but I looked at the photos. I started getting this plan. I was just sort of hellbent on getting somehow closer to this image of being able to make things that drew me so much. So I kept working at the bank, moved to a cheaper apartment, started to save money, hatched this plan in my head about how I would make this work.

Off I went to Japan. Went to different parts of Japan to see the ceramics. The work that I was most drawn to had painting on it. That was really what it was for me, that childlike decoration done with iron oxide. She discovered a potter whose work she really admired, Yutaka Ōhashi. He was not a Living National Treasure or anything, but his work was right for her. She had to ask repeatedly, over a period of months, leaving the country to renew her visa twice. And only when someone in his family guaranteed to be "responsible" for her did he finally consent. When she began there, she could speak not much more than tourist-level Japanese. She soon realized that the people in the studio were speaking dialect. That's how she learned to speak, and she sounds most like her teacher, which means that she's using terms and pronouns that men would say, which sound bizarre coming from a woman. They also sound regional, so her way of speaking Japanese amuses people from Tokyo. She says it would be like a Japanese who learned to speak English in rural Georgia saying, "I'm fixin' to do it."

Anyway, the whole Japanese apprenticeship thing, a lot of that's pretty well known. I'd do all these mundane tasks. You're kind of like a . . . not a slave exactly [Laughter]*, but you're very low on the totem pole. It was hard. But that's why I said that I got the culture shock, because by the time I got to Japan I think I had done that enough times that I was strong enough to endure it and to say to myself, if I don't make this work, if I give up here, I'll never have this opportunity again. I'll never go through that round of asking three times and being told no and crying every day. I can't do that again. So I have to make this work, or I have to give up on this whole idea of doing this. For some reason it never occurred to me that I could come back to the US and go to school.*

I worked pretty much seven days a week. I'd go into the studio on Sundays by myself, worked late at nighttime. I took a calligraphy class—that was my social activity. Every now and then my teacher would go fishing, and I'd ride along, sit there, and look at grass while he fished. I made friends, but they were usually friends of his family who would kind of reach out to me. There was one very nice neighbor lady who would see the lights on in the studio and would bring supper over if she knew I was working late. After her family had dinner, she would pack up a little box and bring it over. That was my social life. I didn't make friends with other Americans or whatever, because I really wanted to learn what I came to learn.

On the first day, *I sat down to throw so these men could evaluate my level, and I think not even 15 seconds went by and they kind of started laughing and went outside and continued their conversation. And I was like, well, do I keep throwing?* [Laughter] *Do I stop? Basically at that point they just wiped my slate clean and they said, "OK, so this is what you do. Start making these cups." I made as many of those cups as I could, filled up my ware board* [8 inches wide by 4 feet long], *and it's the most cups I've ever made, it's like 36 cups. I don't even remember how long it took me to make them. The other employee at the studio came over, and he says, bad, bad, bad, bad, bad, bad, bad. That one's good, but I'm sure it's just a fluke. Bad, bad, bad. I had to get rid of all those except that one that was just a fluke. At that point I'm just so pissed off, but fortunately I don't know enough Japanese to say anything to him except just sit there and make some sort of pouty face. So I kept my little cup and started over.* [Laughter]

Being shy and being without an ego are two different things. I'd go home, I would cry, I would think: I hate these people; they're so mean. And then by the next day I'd go in to work and start all over again. Somehow you get better. Maybe you get better a lot faster. If I said something wrong [in Japanese], *they wouldn't say, "Oh well, this kind of ending doesn't go with that"; they would just laugh at me, and believe me, that's a very good mnemonic, being laughed at. I would think: I'm never going to make that mistake again. I think that kind of instruction, strangely enough, actually worked well for me. Not the verbal instruction method. I've noticed that so many times in the West, we think the more we talk*

about something, the more questions you ask about something, the more you'll understand it. But with something like ceramics, which is so tactile, it's the learning with your hands. So much of that is not about talk, and the talk can become a distraction. If the people around you are paying attention, when they see you do that one right thing that's a fluke, somebody in the studio would come over and say, "That one looks good; remember what that felt like."

And there were other painful ways to learn. *I would work on the thickness of the lip, trying to get the proportions right. I would struggle with that, struggle with that, struggle with that, try out every angle with my fingers. I was just not getting it, so frustrated. And at some point, two or three weeks into it, my teacher would come over and he would say, "Oh, why don't you try holding your finger like that?" And it would solve every problem that I had had. And I would sit there and I would think: What are you trying to do to me? Why didn't you just say that three weeks ago?* [Laughter] *And at one point, as I became more able to verbalize* [Laughter], *everybody started to know when Betsy's pissed off. That was the beginning of not being shy anymore. I don't understand it psychologically, but I was in a foreign culture speaking a foreign language; it was like a baby getting born all over again, and my personality was much more outgoing.*

When I was in Japan, I wasn't allowed to paint anything. My teacher gave me a try a couple of times, and after like three cups he would take away my implement and say, "Never mind." So when I came back here that was something I really struggled with a long time. How do you make a line look the way you want it to look? I've told you a little bit about the nonverbal communication. He would say to me, "Betsy, when I'm doing something, no matter what you're doing, I won't think you're slacking if you stop [and] watch me. So take whatever that is." He would use a word that in Japanese can mean to steal something. He would say, "Take it and steal it and just put it in your head. And you might not use it for years and years and years, but some day you'll be doing something and that will come out." So that was his idea. It wasn't just what he's teaching me, but a lot of it really was about what he was showing me. So I would see how he approaches an image, what kind of brushes he uses, how he switches brushes, how he turns a piece. Like when you're painting you don't turn a painting upside down so you can draw a line more easily, but with a ceramic piece you're usually holding it in one hand and can turn it every which way. All those things, even though I didn't get to do them, I got to see him doing them, so it was really helpful.

I could tell you lots of good and lots of bad things, but in Japan one of the best is that in any given social situation you know what you're supposed to say. And you say it, and the other person says what they're supposed to say, and everybody is comfortable and happy. I loved that. It's a very old culture where that has worked for a long time. The only problem for me was, you know, I'd go home and look in the mirror after being there for so many years, and I'd think: my god, I am so strange looking! [Laughter] *Because everybody around you had black hair and brown eyes. No wonder people stare at me. My teacher is barely 5 feet tall.* [Laughter] *So even though I say that there were so many things about the culture that felt so comfortable in a way that I had never felt comfortable in my life, at the same time I'm a foreigner to the very end. It doesn't matter how good my Japanese was; there were still men who would not even look at me when I was talking.*

After five years in Japan, at the age of 35, she returned to the States and chose to settle in rural New Mexico. *I wanted to live in a place where I could go outside and not hear anybody else's voice, and know that nobody else could see me, and there were trees around. I love that.* For her last two years in Japan, her recreational activity was drawing plans for a kiln and a house. She drove the countryside and finally found a piece of land to buy between Santa Fe and Taos. *It's on a steep hill, and you could drive up it, but there was no driveway. There was nothing on it, just trees and dirt. I built a little shed because I wanted to learn how to build something, just to know what a building is, you know?*

I moved back in 1999, bought the land the end of that year, built the house; it was finished by June of 2001. Built the kiln the summer of 2001. Sold my first cup or whatever it was at the studio tour in November. Fortuitously, she moved into an area having the oldest continuously operating studio tour in the state, which was a big help to her in the beginning. At first, *all my glazes were formulas that I inherited from my teacher. I had so little training in*

the US. *I didn't know the names of glaze materials, so I had to look up in reverse. Choseki, that's feldspar; kiseki, that's silica. So I learned the vocabulary in English and then went to the store and tried to figure out what I needed to get to make those things. A lot of stuff just didn't work.*

The first year of working, I made $12,000 more or less. [Laughter] *The second year, I can't remember exactly, I've got the records, but it was like twice that, maybe. And then by the third year I was starting to be able to pay off some credit card bills. I can't remember how many years that took, but at some point I didn't have any more bills that were unpaid. It took awhile. And honestly, there were days when I would think, I am an idiot. Nobody can do this right. What was I thinking?*

Williams met Mark Saxe, a stone sculptor, whom she would later marry. After she'd been working for several years, they built a gallery onto his studio, which is located beside the highway, so that *I could present my own work in a way that I envisioned it being displayed. We talked about that; almost killed each other. Once you start getting involved with finances with someone else, oh god.* [Laughter] She paid him a percentage of her sales to reimburse him over a five-year period, and then the percentage would drop. It didn't actually take that long. Each firing was selling out by the time she was invited to show at Northern Clay Center in Minneapolis, which she counts as her first national show. That affiliation meant she could stop participating in every small art fair. *At the gallery I just make whatever I want to make, and it comes out of the kiln and I take it down and try to display it nicely, and people buy it. But without that, I don't know what I'd have done.*

Changes include building a studio separate from her house (in 2018), and gradually adding more brushwork. She discovered a grid object in a Santa Fe antique store that intrigued her. It was an old attic vent. She made cups that fitted into all the holes—80 of them—and it drew a strong response on the next studio tour, although no one bought it. Later she began to make smaller grids for cups, and these have continued to be part of her work. She made enigmatic objects, such as a group of things that look like vases but don't have a hole, and they hang on the wall as presentation devices for stripe decoration. At the same time, she worked out forms as a sort of production ware, such as a squared bowl, decorated with thick and thin abstract lines. She began to work with glaze combinations in which something leaches into something else. A dark-green glaze is something she has used consistently. *That was supposed to be some version of black, and I mixed it up and it turned that strange green color, but I kind of liked it and so I've used that from the beginning and found out ways to use it in combination with other things.* She also uses a white slip, which was problematic in Japan but in New Mexico dries in no time.

That's been the biggest change, use of white slip and realizing that's the perfect technique for where I live now. I get a nice toasty clay body, which I love, and then the white slip, which is actually a little creamy and gets these blush areas in reduction. Once that's done, dried, bisqued, you have a beautiful surface to paint on. And then just a clear glaze.

So soft, right? And before, I would make sure that the foot was something I could hold on to so I wouldn't get my fingers into the white area, but now I'll purposely hold on to the area with the white slip so it has those finger marks.

About brushwork, she says suggestive is a good word, or a distillation of an image. *I don't like things that look really anal and super tight, but I'm not trying to be the next abstract expressionist. I got interested in ants just because I see them a lot, you know? And then bugs. Not me as a sort of entomologist; it's me as somebody who's dealing with bugs. Or weeds. That part of it, it's important to me that I'm not doing some Japanese imitative thing like painting bamboo with a calligraphic look. I feel like I'm a three-year-old drawing what's in my environment because it's interesting.* ■

CHAPTER THIRTEEN

DESIGN CONSIDERATIONS

S ometimes art, craft, and design are presented as a Venn diagram, each one slightly overlapping the other two. Some artists, and some designers, have nothing at all to do with crafts, but other people trained in ceramics come quite close—conceptually or actually—to being a designer or moving from the craft sphere to an art context. Conversely, some artists have turned to clay. Although most painters or sculptors working in clay, from Gauguin and Picasso to today's many dabblers, have tended to make sculptural forms, a few were committed to functional pots, such as the modern-era painter Henry Varnum Poor, who made a broad range of plates and bowls, to say nothing of doorknobs, shower enclosures, and even sinks.

There are at least two art world figures today—the painter Mary Heilmann and the sculptor Steve Keister—who have separately and sometimes collaboratively produced functional ware.

The design guru Jonathan Adler, with his chain of stores, started out as a potter. Rob Forbes, the founder of Design Within Reach (though no longer associated with it), was trained in ceramics and even taught the subject. But hewing closer to the ceramics field are those who have established small design businesses or freelanced for large companies, and those who can be associated with design through working methods (such as casting), through the reductive clarity of the forms, or through exceptional concern with ergonomics. ∎

PETER SHIRE
Social Objects

Peter Shire at his Los Angeles studio with a display of Echo Park Pottery designed and striped by him and thrown by Benigno Barron

Peter Shire (b. 1947), celebrated as the only American member of the Italian design collective Memphis, speaks in a ferocious kind of patter, a sharp-edged comic routine. He has a history like none other—Californian, Jewish, semi-Beat, pottery and design mixing together. Every conversation seems to start in the middle, with a plethora of inside references and funny stories, never short. *Yeah, I love stories; I see things in terms of stories.*

For instance, there was his high school ceramics teacher, Anthony Scaccia. *He loved Marguerite Wildenhain. And so he had me cutting pots in half forever and making footed bowls, and they looked like they came out of postwar Austria or something. We loved all that stuff, sort of Scandinavian modernist pottery, that very elegant modernist pottery. I did tons of that. I had a deal with Scaccia. By the 11th grade he'd seen that I had some aptitude and desire. He'd keep the kids at arms' length because he didn't want to clean up after them, so he put off getting working. By the 11th grade I knew his deal. I needed to get going, and I said, "Scaccia, let me work." And this went on about a week, and he'd go to his locker, pretend he was looking for something, and I'd go, "Scaccia," because that was sort of our high school style; "Scaccia, you know, let me work, c'mon, man," and he'd go, "What's your name again?"* [Laughter] *And I'd say, "Peter, you know it's Peter; let me work, man, come on, let's go." And so he let me work, and I had a very interesting view of the classroom because I'm the only one at the potter's wheel and everybody else is basically doing goofy stuff to keep them busy and out of his hair.*

But, not always an obstructionist, Scaccia arranged Shire's schedule for his senior year so that he was at the wheel five hours straight, working through lunch. Shire went back for night school with Scaccia, and then he picked up a Saturday class at Chouinard Art Institute. Shire attended Chouinard (which was becoming the California Institute of the Arts, or CalArts) from 1966 to 1970. *So I had a very intensive, pretty much a potter's beginning.* He envisioned himself *as sort of a bohemian potter with tons of free love, girls* [Laughter], *and a Citroën 2CV, you know, and I was just as cool as anything imaginable.* [Laughter] But he concedes that while that life might have been an option in the 1950s, by the '60s there were few models for pottery making. Peter Voulkos, John Mason, and others broke away from pottery to make sculpture.

He points out that *the state of California calls me a small business; they tax me and ask for paperwork accordingly. They don't say, "Well, you're an artist," or "You're a studio potter"; they think of me as a guy they can audit for sales tax if they feel like it. Being a studio potter is a hard row, but in the state of California, the statistic was nine out of ten new business starts fail within the first year. So what's so easy about being a dry cleaner, etc., you know?*

Preparing for that, his teacher at Chouinard, Ralph Bacerra, *taught us to do a ceramics sale. We had a class assignment, so we're third- and fourth-year students. Work all week on making some kind of great cup. A crit at the end of the week, and then we came back on Sunday on our own time and did a production day where we were asked to do 30 mugs or so. Every week, one of the objects of ceramics. Do, crit, produce. Wednesdays we took the morning, and everybody had a common glaze moment. And we'd all gather, you know, big pots of glaze and do them, whatever. Then we went off and fired. I was part of that twice, two years, and I was actually the so-called chairman of the sale, which meant that most of it fell on me. And I loved it.*

One complaint: *The way that we were taught was sort of a funny, redundant, hard way to do things. As a professional you can't afford to fuss in that way. [After you got out of school], you'd think about better ways to do things.* Another lament: *School teaches you to be a star, which is a very hurtful thing because not everybody's cut out for it.* Some people, Shire says, don't want to be the maestro. *The first 20 years I'd see people that I went to school with, and they'd sort of say with this hostile tone, "Are you still making pots; are you still working?" "Still" being the operative word. On the bright side, everybody I went to art school with that I still know has done something very interesting and very imaginative* that really incorporates the fact that they went to art school, and that they, if nothing else, learned, shall we say, diagonal thinking.

After graduation, Shire shared Adrian Saxe's studio for a year, worked for Franciscan Pottery for a year to save money, and then established his own studio. *And there I was, kind of mucking around and doing really weird stuff, trying this and that. I had two glazes: maiolica, and maiolica with 2 percent cobalt. That's a light-blue maiolica. And I was trying to do everything with those glazes because I ended up getting a low-fire kiln. We were taught high fire.*

Today, he says, he has a ceramics sale of the functional work that he produces under the name Echo Park Pottery *partly as a way of having fun and partly as a way of providing things for people that can't afford the other work. Which is really a big part of it for me. There was a point when I looked around and I said this work is bitchin', everybody loves it, but I couldn't afford it; my friends can't. What are we doing here?* The thought sends him off on a chain of ruminations, mostly bleak, about current conditions.

His wife sometimes tells him he's charging too little, but he goes to IKEA and sees great bowls *for 3 bucks or 6 bucks. How does that even pay for getting it on the boat? What's wrong with it? And this is getting into a very big and very dynamic political discussion. It supersedes simple ideas of craft, and of course we're part of an attitude and a movement that really came about at the advent of the Industrial Revolution. We're looking for what's real, that's the deal. And that's part of having objects that have some spirit in them. And we're entering into these questions in ways that we never imagined.*

I don't like the word "craft," because it became a word used to describe a quasi-rustic approach or a basically working in the decorative arts realm, and that permitted a lot of middle-grade things. He accepts the word "skill." *A high skill level, because it also means that it's well crafted. And we use words like value. My uncle, my dad, my grandfathers on both sides were involved in cabinetmaking. My grandfather on my dad's side was part of the Russian Revolution and fled the czar's army and all that kind of stuff.* In America he was a union shop steward, but he ended up being the in-house cabinetmaker for a rich man. *My dad, the same. There he was, a union organizer and all that stuff, and basically he worked in Bel Air.*

We're in this business, so with all the talk about whatever it is, the love of what we're doing, basically the milieu that we're operating in has to be capable of supporting it. And that's a polite way of saying that people have to be able to afford this degree of intensity of labor and materials. Echo Park Pottery makes the work available to more people. But sometimes there's *a Robin Hood thing, where we're doing commissions, and that's really paying folks that help me and then maybe even myself keeping the studio open while we sell pottery for, really, not living wages.*

As I understand it, the definition of economy is the flow and exchange of goods and services. And this is the key problem, this becomes a conversation about investment, and not about what's actually being made. It's not about the job anymore, not about the actual work. We were just talking about these phone apps where you can just wave your phone in front of the cash register and it pays, and the comment was "This further separates the consumer from the actual value of the exchange." Before they were handing them an actual card, and before it was actual money, and you felt and said, "I have so much money in my pocket, when I've spent 10 bucks on a cup of coffee, I'm out."

Shire is saying there's a disconnection between value and object, and between *participation* and *being of value.* Once there was seasonal or diurnal time for certain activities; in between *there might be something to do or maybe not, but it wasn't about hustling. There were moments when people came together.* All that has been lost.

So, back to the chronology. After he got into his own studio and paid to have a high-fire kiln rebricked—one he had scrounged from Franciscan—he began to make *the first work that I felt superseded what I developed in school, which was a group of square teapots that were based on a very constructivist idea of sculptural movement.* A friend's father introduced him to *Jan Turner, who had a gallery. And I loved this little gallery; it was a penthouse on Beverly Boulevard, a little deco penthouse; it was really perfect for my work, and she immediately liked the work and said, "Let's do a show."* She had a paid show by a woman from New Mexico coming up, and she said after that she'd have enough money to do Shire's show. He rues that the New Mexico woman unknowingly paid for his show. *So I worked for the show, which is a focus and an imperative. Gives you a push. I did that show in 1975, I believe, and we did quite a few shows after that. And I felt very good about that because I wasn't showing in one of the ceramic galleries or high-end ceramics stores. I did some shows with people in the craft milieu, to varying degrees of response. I've never felt particularly accepted by the ceramic world. That isn't where my collector base has been. There's some, obviously some of the big teapot collectors, but I've managed to have a lot of people who are art collectors accept my work.*

Way back in school, I would go in the library and they had Domus *magazine, and I was just all over that, and it was just magical. If I haven't used that word yet, and I think I haven't, maybe even better would be mystifying, because I couldn't read it and I couldn't understand half of what I was looking at, which is something that I've always responded to. To be charmed and to feel a little bit dizzy and giddy is just amazing.*

The same man who had introduced him to the gallerist *would say, "You've got to meet this guy, Ettore Sottsass; you'd love him. And he'd love you." So I'd done a number of shows, I was in my studio, and I remember I got an offer to do an article with* Wet *magazine, and I remember holding my resume for months till the thing actually came out, because that was all that was on it.* [Laughter] *And that article actually introduced me to Sottsass. These two guys, Aldo and Mateo, showed up, and that was just the best. My kind of guys, European guys with these tennis shoes; you can't buy those here. You know what I'm talking about? My model was always sort of European, I don't know how else to put it. What passed for fashion here was just not going to make it. And it always seemed like the interpretation of the size and the proportion and fineness was much more present. So here are these two guys. Mateo looks at me and says, "This is your moment." I looked behind to make sure he wasn't waving at the blonde, you know.* [Laughter] *They said, "You must come to Europe." Some of our friends were getting stipends and tickets, and getting sort of treated as grand people, and I thought: Well, send me a ticket. And then I thought: Well,*

you know, this is not a bad idea. I've never been and at least I'll know people and have a place to stay, and what could be better?

Later Sottsass shows up. We went to lunch, and I was about to sort of test the water and say, "What do you think of my coming to Italy?," and he turned to me and said, "When will you be in Italy?" And I said, "How about August?" And he said, "Not August, September. Everybody will be on vacation in August." So the upshot of it is I booked a ticket because I said, "If I don't buy a ticket and own it, and I think about how much it cost me, if I let it drop I'll never go, because there will always be a kiln to fire."

So that was my strategy, and I went, and just it was out of this world. It was just the best. That really sent me into that phase of my production and life, where my multipronged approach coincided with their rebellion. And I set out to do some work for Alchemia—because that was the company that was extant at that moment—and they sent me down to Salerno to meet with a ceramic factory and negotiated various things. They were very disorganized, real Italian, you know.

And then I guess in late '79, Barbara [Radice] *called and said, "We've broken away from Alchemia and we're starting our own; will you come with us?" And I said, "Anywhere."* [Laughter] *And that was Memphis. And so they asked me to do a vanity, which is a funny piece of furniture. But just being there, that was such a great moment because it was that transitional time when people weren't famous but they were doing things.*

Things came to me as visions. So I had drawings of those things, and of course those were the things they responded to because they were from that atmosphere, that swirling moment. I did that for seven years, and I did other shows in Europe with a glass guy, and we did pieces with glass in Venice, Murano. There's always little things. Sort of like scheduling a show and then there's a stock market crash. [Laughter] *We survived. We've been through a number of those kind of passages.*

I stopped making ceramics altogether for five years, between probably 1985 and 1990, '91. We were doing so much metal work. But at the same time we were often making tables, basically bespoke furniture. As Californians—maybe more than others—and as Chouinard graduates we were saying, "Well, this is art, and clearly there's price and value attached to that." And I'd say, "This is really a sculpture with a piece of glass on top; let's take the glass off." And so I did that, and those things seemed to survive.

I make tables and teapots. I've made chairs and cups, certainly, but I'm famous for teapots, and I veer in those two directions if left alone. And the reason, I've decided, is that those are social objects; those are hubs. People come together around a teapot and pour tea from it—it's a conduit; it's not an individual or a contemplative object in that respect. And the same with the table; people come together and it's a hub, a denominator. So that seems to be some part of my makeup.

Shire has run Echo Park Pottery from the beginning, more than 40 years now. We think we've made 40,000 mugs. Forty years, we average 1,000 a year.

The pottery moved with the abilities of a Mexican production thrower named Benigno Barron (who died in 2018 at the age of 92). He would sit here for five or six hours a day and do hundreds of pots. Two of the people that worked here really worked for him. They prepared his clay, cleaned up after him, fired the ware. So it did operate as an art pottery, with a maestro of sorts. And Benigno's strategy in life was to find someone who painted, and so Gonzalo Duran and a guy named Teddy Sandoval, who died of AIDS, and then me. I virtually didn't throw for 20 years, which I probably wouldn't have anyway. And I tell people that when I do, I really throw better just from watching him over the years. And so we just had wonderful years. He was such an amazing person. [Laughter] I would give him a general shape and I'd say, "Put some ruffles on it." And he'd do something and I'd say, "How did they turn out?" So there was sort of a fail-safe zone for him to work in. And then things like the bases; I'd sit with him and trim with him, because he didn't have the snap, the eye, to really pull the shapes.

This space is 6,500 and the attic is 2,000. Then we use the outside for glazing, so we're incorporating another 1,500 square feet outside, and kilns, and whatever space for miscellaneous storage, and then a paint booth. And then I've got easily 1,500 square feet of storage off-site. A lot of stuff for three people to manage. Shire's wife, Donna, does the bookwork but also, since she's a graphic designer, she does all the catalogs and flyers. We work all year—you know, here and there, and the last two months I was on it probably 70 percent of my time. Which is too much, because I was juggling the more substantial commissions that we have. They didn't suffer from it, but they weren't helped either. We weren't pursuing the work that really supports the studio.

The studio is set just off the street, and in front of it is a beauty shop run by Shire's daughter. So we have a close familial orbit. And then there's a yoga salon. And a Pilates salon. And a guy who does internet applications. Shire rents out those spaces. So the building is debt servicing, which is also how things get done, really, and so we don't have the same kind of pressure on us as if we didn't have that. So that finances the pottery also.

His compound is immediately recognizable because it is wildly colored, like his work. People used to say, "What's your address?" And I'd say, "Don't worry about it." [Laughter] Explaining the source of that color is not necessarily simple. One doesn't know when things start necessarily. We make certain guesses and remember things and tell our stories in a certain way, right? But with that said, I remember certain things. My mother came from Berkeley, and she was very imbued with ideals of good taste, muted colors, and so forth. I'm trying to think. I know how this story gets told all the time, and that makes good press, and there is an aspect of that—that there was a sort of a shock value and that whole idea of being so affronted by something that actually you lay down with it.

And then I realized that my dad trained in art school and painted our house with colors that were of that nature. The kitchen was salmon, chartreuse, and gray. With a pea-green counter. My room started out, I think, a sort of salmon pink and my brother's is blue, and so forth. And I think we were subject to, when you think about it, the California design milieu really responded to chartreuse and hot pink and orange. And then you come to the '60s, and there was a store called Joseph Magnin's, and they really pumped out the bright colors, very pop and very beautiful packaging, very shocking, and they were very thrilling, to use a proper word. And my mom always disliked all those colors, and that probably helped with pushing me in that direction.

And I found that the more I used them, sort of the happier I got. And everyone said, "Well, your work is whimsical," or "It's happy," or if we're being

MARK
SHAPIRO

TOP Square teapot with four cups with "U"s, 2012. Stoneware, salt glazed and wood fired, teapot H: 7".

BOTTOM Five faceted cups with markings, 2018. Porcelain, salt glazed and wood fired, each H: 3.5".

KARI
RADASCH

RIGHT Mini tulipiere, 2007.
Earthenware, glaze, 9" × 5" × 5".

BELOW Charm bowls, 2017.
Earthenware, glaze, gold luster, 5" × 5" × 5".

BRYAN
HOPKINS

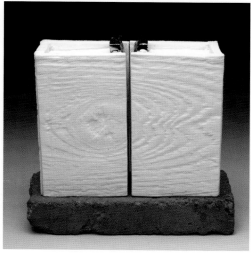

TOP Egg cups, 2014. Porcelain,
celadon glaze, each 2" × 2" × 2".

BOTTOM LEFT Salt and pepper set, 2016. Porcelain,
platinum luster, celadon glaze, concrete base, H: 6.5".

BOTTOM RIGHT Cup set, 2012. Porcelain, platinum
luster, celadon glaze, concrete base, 6.5" × 6.5" × 3.5".

NAOMI
CLEARY

RIGHT Summer Flowers
tumblers, 2016. Porcelain,
underglaze, glaze, cone 6
electric, 7" × 5".

BOTTOM LEFT Fall Leaves
plate, 2010. Porcelain, slip,
glaze, cone 6 electric, 8" dia.

BOTTOM RIGHT Wintergreen
plate, 2010. Porcelain, slip,
glaze, cone 6 electric, 8" dia.

MARK
HEWITT

TOP Rectangular platter (with watermelon slices), 2014. Wood-fired stoneware, white slip with marbled decoration, L: 22".

LEFT Pitcher, 2018. Salt-glazed, wood-fired stoneware, celadon blue neck with vertical black slip lines, 12" × 7".

RIGHT Four iced-tea-ceremony vessels, 2012. Salt-glazed, wood-fired stoneware, ash glaze with incised lines and blue glass runs, each 9" × 4".

MATT
JONES

TOP   Large jar with lid
and four handles, 2016. Wood-fired
stoneware with cobalt and iron
brush painting, 36" × 20".

RIGHT   Platter, 2014.
Wood-fired stoneware with iron
oxide brush painting, 16" dia.

ELLEN
SHANKIN

FRONT COVER Twisted pitcher, 1992. Stoneware, thrown and altered, cone 10 reduction fired, 11" × 6.5" × 6.5". *Photo: Tim Barnwell*

RIGHT Salt basket, 1974. Stoneware, thrown and altered, salt fired with slip glazes and oxide washes sprayed on, 13" × 5.5" × 5.5".

LEFT Teapot, 2005. Stoneware, thrown and altered, cone 10 reduction fired, crystal matte glaze, 5.5" × 8.5" × 6". *Photo: Tim Barnwell*

DANIEL
JOHNSTON

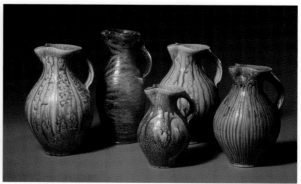

BACK COVER Fifty large jars at the studio, Randolph County, North Carolina, before installation at Peters Projects Gallery, Santa Fe, 2017. Local stoneware, wood fired, salt glazed, with black-and-white slip dots, 40" × 24" each.

LEFT Tea pot, 2014. Unrefined stoneware clay from Randolph County, North Carolina, 5.5" × 7.5".

RIGHT Pitchers, 2016. Local stoneware, red slip, tin slip, ash glaze, natural fly ash, wood fired, salt glazed, tallest 18", widest 8". *Photo: Jason Dowdle*

DAVID
STUEMPFLE

RIGHT Large pitcher, 2015. Wood-fired local clay, 21" × 10". *Photo: Jason Dowdle*

BELOW Large jar, 2010. Wood-fired local clay, 25" × 23". *Photo: Jason Dowdle*

JOHN
NEELY

RIGHT Goblets, 1985. Stoneware, thrown, faceted, and assembled, gas-fired salt kiln, 1300°C, each 5.5" × 2.5", Logan, Utah.

BOTTOM LEFT Hailstone teapot, 2017. Yellow Yixing duan-ni stoneware, thrown and assembled, Korean-style wood-fired kiln, 1200°C, 5" × 5", Yixing, China.

BOTTOM RIGHT Thrown plate, 1975. Porcelain with underglaze decoration, gas fired 1280°C, 11" dia., Alfred, New York.

ROB
BARNARD

RIGHT Dish, 2013. Stoneware, wood fired, natural ash glaze, 1.5" × 9".

BELOW Teapot, 2009. Stoneware, white slip covered with limestone glaze, oil fired, 9" × 7".

BETSY
WILLIAMS

RIGHT "Rosa Parks' Dress," 2018. Stoneware with white slip, hand painted with underglaze oxides, electric fired to cone 6, each 4.25" dia.

BOTTOM LEFT "Cupism 25," 2015. White slip on stoneware cups, wheel thrown, wood fired to cone 10, 16" × 16" × 2.5".

BOTTOM RIGHT Small lidded jar, 2017. Semiporcelain with ash glaze (lid: black glaze), wheel thrown, hand painted with underglaze oxide, wood fired to cone 10, H: 3".

PETER
SHIRE

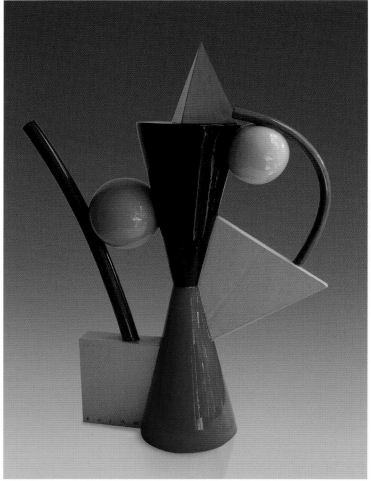

TOP Echo Park Pottery
mugs, 2018. Cone 06 clay,
underglazes and clear
glaze, H: 3".

RIGHT Hourglass,
1984. Cone 06 clay,
underglazes and clear
glaze, 24" × 14" × 5.5".

KLEINREID

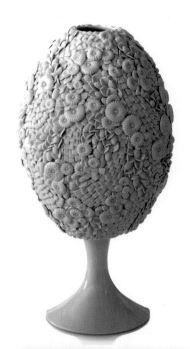

LEFT Still Life Collection, "Selfish Giant with Flowers Vase," 2004–07. Glazed porcelain, H: 24".

BELOW Prime Collection, "Painted Canyon," 2011–12. Hand-painted porcelain and turned walnut (new glaze introduced 2017), tallest 14".

BOTTOM Nimbus Collection, 2017. Glazed porcelain, tallest 18".

KATHY ERTEMAN

RIGHT 18th Street Dinnerware, 2011. Designed for Crate & Barrel.

BELOW Big knob jars, 2017. Wheel-thrown white stoneware with glaze, cone 6, 10" × 7".

RIGHT Carved tableware set, 2003. Wheel-thrown and slip-cast whiteware with slip, glaze, and carving, bowl 6" × 6" × 4", dinner plate 1" × 10.5", salad plate 1" × 7", tiny plates 1" × 4".

HIROE
HANAZONO

TOP Sundae set, 2008.
Slip-cast porcelain, cone 6 oxidation,
bowls 2.5" × 7" × 6", toppings dish
3" × 16" × 5".

BOTTOM LEFT Brunch set, 2017. Slip-cast porcelain, cone
6 oxidation, plate .75" × 13.5" × 6", mug 4.5" × 4" × 3.5",
bowl 2.5" × 6" × 5", egg cup 1" × 4.5" × 2.5".

BOTTOM RIGHT Vase, 2008. Slip-cast white stoneware,
cone 6 oxidation, 5" × 12" × 9".

S. C.
ROLF

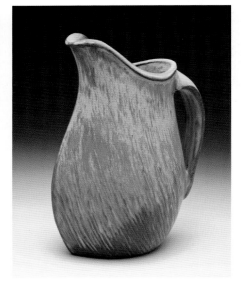

TOP Dessert bowls, 2014.
Chocolate stoneware, brown
satin glaze, 2" × 5.25".

BOTTOM LEFT Teapot, 2017. Chocolate stoneware,
cast spout and handle, blue satin glaze, 7" × 9.5" × 7".

BOTTOM RIGHT Pitcher, 2016. Chocolate stoneware,
satin matte glaze, 11" × 8" × 4.5".

sort of grand we say, "It's optimistic." And I find that no matter how upset I am, I'll get in there and I'll say, "I'll show them gravitas, I'll make it all gray and use Prussian blue to hammer it on, and I can use a little cerulean"; it's a little dull, and the next thing you know it's . . . [Laughter] *And part of it is when I work I feel really good. And then the better I feel, the more I work, and the more I work, the more chance there is to pump the colors up. And that's what happens. And then there's aspects of fashion and the world around us.*

And also you didn't see it done, and that's a big attraction. People don't tend to use color the way I did. He thinks of his approach as being exactly the reverse of what he describes as the Art Students League's practice "after Velazquez." *In his case, 95 percent of it is high major, and 3 or 4 percent of it is neutrals, and I keep them apart where I have to. And on top of that, everything has to conflict, has to either be complementary colors next to each other or values that are completely separate, so there's always these huge vibrations between them and shape differentiations. And I also don't like to put the same color on twice if I can help it. You know I don't match one thing to another.* This determined independence permeates his life.

At this moment, pottery is a weird thing, what people will buy. When we were at school, people bought a lot of covered jars and decorative boxes. People don't really do that now. You don't keep a jewelry box, a little ceramic box, on your vanity, the way people did. And so most of the time we're not supplying daily-need type of things; these are special things.

The functional pottery we do love, and often we really make it for ourselves. I say, "This is what I'd like to have," and I'll take a bunch of them home and I'll use them, and I prefer mine. It makes whatever I'm having special, no doubt about it. Echo Park Pottery continues to produce mugs and bowls, and Shire concentrates on his signature artworks, in the teapot format and others. ∎

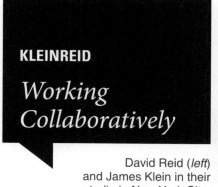

KLEINREID

Working Collaboratively

David Reid (*left*) and James Klein in their studio in New York City, 2017

James Klein and David Reid, who met in high school in Ohio, not only design and produce their own ceramics from their studio in Brooklyn but, in 1999, began working with the eminent designer Eva Zeisel to produce new designs, and continued until her death.

Klein, the youngest of four in a blue-collar family, was an arty kid who thought he'd be a fine artist. *I only discovered clay in college, and it was only because David took a class. I was in painting, and David took a class so I took a class. And that was it.* Perhaps important was that earlier he had gutted his attic bedroom and created a little oasis for himself. He grew up with *old stuff* in the house, including relics of Ohio's great 19th-century pottery industry, such as Rookwood planters and vases.

Reid is the middle of five children, whose dad owned a furniture store—*very much a Lay-Z-Boy and Broyhill kind of place. I think it somehow planted this seed about objects and interacting with things and who chooses what. His furniture store was set up with little three-walled sort of fake-room vignettes that my sisters and I used to play in as kids, and something about that stuck with me as far as the environment you create around you. I think that plays into what we make today.* He remembers a first exposure to clay in junior high school. In high school he concentrated on art in general. Then he took a ceramics class as an undergrad at the University of Akron and really gravitated toward it. At the same time he was becoming a ceramics collector. *There was a big Goodwill near the University of Akron, and when we had time we used to go thrift shop. I think everything starts with Fiesta ware, if you're in Ohio, and then spreads out to Russel Wright and lots of dinnerware. So by the time I was 19 or 20, I was collecting dinnerware. It was easy to find and it was cheap. That process was really influential when we started creating our own work together.* Klein agrees: *Putting a collection together from different places and seeing how it all worked together, that was very influential.*

Reid: *In the summer of '89 we did summer studies abroad in Italy. James and I both spent the summer in Cortona doing ceramics. That was a wonderful eye-opener as far as moving not beyond but before the 20th century. For me it was this amazing thing about seeing age. We looked at tons of maiolica and red- and black-figure ware.*

Klein: *It was realizing that everything has already been made, and it's already really, really beautiful, so I'd better step up. It pushed me to embrace the decorative quality.* It was from the Italian experience that they picked up applique and sprigging that appears in their work today.

After undergraduate college together, they went to separate graduate schools. Reid went to Cranbrook. He says, *as far as decorative art and as far as design, it further opened my eyes. Ohio and ceramics were really great for early 20th century, and this was suddenly very midcentury. That was amazing, the Eameses and Saarinen and those folks. The other thing that was great was that it was a really open school; critiques were open, departments were relatively open, so everybody kind of wandered around and gravitated towards what interested them. So things became much more mixed media for me.* As he worked in other materials, his ceramic objects became more functional than sculptural. *They became about containing and pouring and things like that.*

Both men had some exposure to mold making as undergraduates, but at that time, *slip casting was pretty verboten; it was pretty industrial, you know. It was something you didn't do if you were a real ceramic artist. And even molds were a little questionable,* Reid says.

Klein, a year younger than Reid, was accepted at Cranbrook but also at Alfred, and the latter would be free. *I chose to dig into the material. I really wanted to know more about it. So I went to Alfred because it's like a wonderland for that. There were five or six or seven faculty, you know, rotating, and a huge undergrad ceramics department. The facilities. It was a very tempting place; hard to say no to that.*

Klein: *I always felt like I was making art; it was always art to me. But to a lot of people it looked like design, and at the time people didn't quite understand what I was doing. I was slip casting figurines, but it wasn't about multiples; it was about using the mold because that's the way the thing needed to be made, and also for its aesthetics, how it ended up looking. I had a very production quality to the art I was making. Tony Hepburn actually asked me once, "I don't know who you are," he said in critique. "Are you Jeff Koons or are you the guy who makes Jeff Koons's work?" And I thought that was the greatest thing anybody had ever said to me. I wanted to be both.* Reid: Those works looked like *animals that were melting soft-serve ice cream. They were matte.* Klein: *I liked the collaboration with the mold. I feel less and less ownership over the piece by the time it's done, and it becomes more a thing separate from me. I think all art does that, but it can happen quicker if I use these tools.*

They didn't particularly know where they were going with this until, while Klein was enrolled at Alfred, they came up with the idea of starting a production line. Reid: *We want to move to New York. And we have these degrees and this knowledge. What are we going to do? The plan was: we'll start a production line, and that will give us money, and in our spare time we can make our own work. We started testing, we started working on the porcelain slip that James was working with, sort of refined it, tightened it, made it more vitreous, and we started doing glaze tests. We were living with all this thrift-store ceramics, and that's what we really looked to for glaze, so we had this palette of soft matte glaze colors.*

Klein*: We set up a studio in Williamsburg [Brooklyn] in 1993 and at that time developed these white matte glazes. Those were specifically reactions against everything that we could see that was available. Everything was painted; everything was shiny. It was a real reaction against, you know, underglaze, Duncan's Clear, not-so-thought-about craft. And we were really, really, really interested in form, making form-based work.*

Reid: *When we started our business, we wanted the work to be proudly slip cast. We wanted to make work that could only be made in a mold.* They did not want to slip-cast imitations of thrown forms. *Now I think people can understand that something can look clean and be about form and not be wonky and full of fingerprints and brush marks. People can understand that it's still handmade. But that took a while.*

Klein worked as a decorative painter in New York, which gave them entrée to trade shows, and they could walk through and see what they didn't want to do. They looked back to the 20th-century American Ohio pottery, which in turn had historical references. Reid, meanwhile, was getting a different view, working at Franklin Parrasch Gallery when it was located on Broadway in SoHo. They began figuring out how to work collaboratively. Reid: *We did a series of three-part vases. There were 10 or 12 middles, 10 or 12 tops, and 10 or 12 bottoms, and they all had the same opening so they could all*

interact. The mold parts were numbered, so I'd say, "Oh, that's a 1-7-8" combination, and I would give it to James, and he would kind of finish the piece, like sprig mold it and apply handles. That was actually a really great way to move through form quickly. It gave us really clean form; it gave us this kind of touchless feel. We both like it; I mean at the time especially, we wanted the work to look like it just appeared—it didn't look labored over, overthought, or overworked.

Klein: *You can see a lot of handwork, especially in the handles, but it's all clean; the detail comes from mold relief and sprigging. We were going for something that was hard to place as far as time period, a thing that continues through the work that we've made. We just snatch things together, cultures, time periods, and ideas, until it's something different. Our timing was really good because stores were ready for something else, and so they embraced it. There were always questions like "Is this a limited edition, is this numbered, how many do you make?" And we're like, "We make them until we're tired of them."*

Reid: *We started contacting stores directly, and we got a really big order from Bergdorf Goodman in 1994, and that let me quit my job. James still taught a couple classes a week, but it let us concentrate full time in the studio. And at that point we realized that the one-of-a-kind thing really didn't matter, and in fact buyers don't really like the idea of "well, it looks something like this, but you'll see when you open the box." They really want to know what they're buying. And we also realized that there were some shapes that we were ready to commit to. We started doing what we do today, which is like coming up with an idea for a form and making it, and what you see is what you get—and what you see is what you get in two months. [Laughter] We started putting together a collection, and that's what we took to shows.*

It was all very much about form and surface. We moved away from the applied handles and things, and we wanted the decoration to be in the mold, so we just started coming up with a shape and outfitting it with a pattern. There was a show of Dior's first collection at the Met Museum, and there were tons of pleats and patterns that kind of undulated, that got really small at the waist and then expanded over the hips and the skirt. We sucked that all up and put it on pots, a lot of undulating raised pattern. They called the series New School.

It was about this time when we realized that this work could be our art. There really wasn't a delineation between personal and production. And that's when I think the work got really good; it got honest and personal.

We try to just pretend we're in grad school again where we're coming up with new ideas. It's really just: What do we want to make? I always joke that the customer comes last when we're designing, because we can never make anything good if we're starting with the customer and working backwards, if we're thinking of, like, what's a hot color, or everybody's doing chevrons, or whatever's happening. It never works for us; it always falls flat.

Klein: *It's a privilege to do that. It's also been sort of a branding problem for us, because our work, series to series to series, can look very different. It's hard to brand that idea. Collaboration has been really good for our relationship because it forces us to be really honest with each other. We have to not take anything personally. We have to be open to stuff that we're not thinking about but maybe that's a good idea; maybe it's a better idea. It forces all these relationship issues into the workplace. But it's funny going home. We can spend all day together, and we'll need to have a date or something because it's not the same kind of time. It doesn't equal personal time.*

I'm not a very good sketch person. I make quick sketches about ideas; I write things about ideas. David's a very good sketcher. And he keeps good notebooks and things like that. We're constantly talking.

Reid: *When we began, nobody was working in matte glazes, so I think that softness was surprising for people. They were single colored, which was pretty not done at the time, like I think it took a lot of balls to make something one color and not try to decorate all the facets of these shapes with colors. They were simple and reductive in a nice way. I think people really responded to the form, although form is something people know last. You know, people get surface and color but they don't know form.*

Klein: *It's harder to brand a form; you can't copyright a form anymore really, and it's because people don't see them. So how do you try and build a company based on a curve? Eva Zeisel did that,* but I don't think a lot of people could. Our Stewardess series evolved over maybe a year and half. China was opening up and production was becoming easy for a lot of people, so suddenly there were lots of matte glaze patterns, so we wanted to move away from this. The Stewardess series was sort of the idea of smashing together Danish modern with Japanese tea bowl. We clipped out a picture from a magazine of a Marc Jacobs model on a runway where he had done these coats that ended, and maybe 3 inches of skirt showed below the coat. And that's where this little raw recessed foot came in. It's called Stewardess because the forms are also influenced by tailored uniforms and so they look tight. It was a slightly different shape, a language of curves for us, more of a midcentury Danish feel, kind of more classic.

A series they made in '98 and '99 grew out of an idea of holes, mouse holes. They called it See Through. Klein: *This was like the biggest introduction we had. It sold really well. We were really surprised by its success.* Reid: *See Through came out that same year we met Eva Zeisel and started working on shapes together. She was a big hero of ours. Actually, back at Alfred in our little funny business plan that we made as grad students, it was like "and one day we'll collaborate with people on special projects," and she was at the top of the list.* Klein: *So we met her and she said, "Do you want to reissue something?" And we said, "No, we want to make something new." We wanted to spend time with her, and we just thought she needed to make something new. So we worked over the summer and introduced six shapes. People loved it, instantly just responded to it. And we continued to expand on that. We did the pitcher set and a tea set in 2001. And then worked on the prints and things like that in 2005 and then in 2010 with her.* Zeisel died in 2011 at the age of 105.

Reid: *Travel is another big influence for our work. There is a kind of fake ash glaze that we worked on. It was trying to mimic this beach that we liked when we went to Italy. This was the next series; this was 2000. We wanted to do something really classic but stretched. These are all sort of tall, elongated shapes, just thinking about classic Italian shapes. And once we did the See Through, I kept pulling things apart, and we did this series called Hybrid. How do you put two holes through something; how do you pull something apart? And* suddenly things started turning into tubes, and we were looking into Dutch tulipiere shapes, so it really became: How do you make a vase into a bowl? There are double-wall cast shapes that hold flowers.

Another series went back to warm-looking, vaguely Scandinavian surfaces. One featured geometric flower shapes, and through Aid to Artisans they were able to have pillows that went with them. One shape was influenced by bell-bottom trousers. And on and on. They had been using porcelain all along, but it was usually covered with matte glaze. With each series they did something in gloss clear, but it was the matte glazes that everyone wanted. Reid: *And so we finally decided like this series is just going to be about porcelain. So it came in clear and it came bisque. We were talking, and we landed on this idea: "Oh, if it's a still life you can put whatever you want in it, and it makes sense because it's a grouping." So this series was a little more Victorian. The shapes are very modern, these pedestal shapes, but the detail on them is really delicate.*

It was this exploration of these objects, and it was funny what objects we knew were appropriate and which ones weren't. Like we did an oil lamp, a porcelain oil lamp that was electric and a candelabra and candlestick and an apple, and we realized James was reading a lot of Oscar Wilde at the time, and we wanted this kind of literary feel. It was just about the idea of these ghostly stand-ins for real objects. We thought about his desk. What would you find on his desk? This is a candelabra. And the candles are porcelain, but you can remove them and use real ones. So it can be sort of sculpture and functional object at the same time. The Still Life collection was also about Reid dealing with the death of his father. As they were working on it, they kept thinking, Reid says, *Nobody's going to buy this; it's too expensive; it's too weird. Those were all my worries, but we just did it because we needed to.*

Another time we were upstate at our friend's cabin, and we were staring at the fire thinking that a campfire is the greatest thing, and we pulled the logs out of the fire and let them cool and we cast them. For us it was just like this centerpiece thing, but our friend in Los Angeles was like, "Everybody has a nonworking fireplace." Duh. They have this funny life, especially in the decorator market, as a stand in for a nonworking fireplace.

Other projects have been prints derived from Klein's paintings. Reid also does drawings.

Reid: *After the still-life stuff, after a couple of years of very stark black-and-white work, we wanted to return to color, and we modified that glaze we had been working with, the sort of sugary, plasticky, sandblasted one.* Klein: *Let me just modify that statement. We worked all summer developing a new glaze* [Laughter] *that would be this new thing that we wanted it to be.* Reid: *It lets us do really great color, it breaks shiny and white but it's matte, and it moves, so when it's nice and thick you get nice drips.* Klein: *Totally stealing from Ron Nagle. We were really wanting to move back toward something that felt potteryish. This glaze is the decoration of the form. You can do these big, very simple forms and still have them be interesting.*

KleinReid has farmed out work: not only the Aid to Artisans pillows, but large print runs at the Lower East Side Print Shop, and for a time a US factory produced the log set. *We're not opposed to it,* Reid says. They traveled to Jingdezhen, China, in 2009, partly just for a break but also to see what was going on there. They did a residency and found a small factory/studio and designed shapes that were produced there in a limited run. It was a collection of lidded objects that could be functional or decorative. They were high-fired (cone 12 or 13) in *super-white porcelain that's just the prettiest stuff I've ever seen,* Reid says. However, the recession made that a one-shot deal.

The benefit of such contracts is being able to sell the work at a lower price point. Another design project was working with Dansk's design teams from about 1996 to 2001. The Dansk people saw dinnerware that KleinReid was making at the time, and contracted to redesign it so that it could be produced in a factory in Portugal. They've also designed for a glass company in Portugal, for Herman Miller, Chella, and West Elm. For about 20 years they made (in-house) custom collections for Room & Board. Reid: *We love all aspects of making, you know. I think that we're very hands-on for a designer, but we're not hands-on enough for a potter. Those appliqué pieces, James is responsible for all that. Somebody is sprigging it, but he's making all the decisions. It's not like he makes one and then we have somebody copy it, which I think certain people assume.*

One of the things that keeps us viable and functioning and around is that we can move quickly, and we can do it ourselves. And there was a point in the beginning where we said, well, even if we only sell one of these or cast two of them, it's still worth going ahead and making it. And I think that's also the thing that keeps us really agile. We're not designing something and sitting on a container of it and waiting.

Klein: *For instance, when we did the still-life pieces, they hit like so big; everybody was doing it and our pieces were getting really ripped off. We move on. We're not that invested in it. So we're artists; we function in that way, not business people. A business person would make that brand, would really go for it, would disseminate it, and would probably make a lot of money doing it. But we just move on into something else.* [Laughter]

They do a collection for fall and a collection for spring. It has to do with the trade shows, and it's the way the stores work. Reid: *Working at a gallery for a couple of years, I realized, in its own way, it's just like a store. I mean, the owner knows what his clients like, and that's what he brings in and hopes that they'll buy it. We realized that if we sold to stores, we could find great people to work with and they would buy the work outright. So stores just* seemed like a nice road that we wanted to travel. Over the years we have had exhibitions and group shows, and we've sold in design shops and museum shops. We've been able to cover a really broad spectrum of ways to get our work out in public.

From the beginning they had at least part-time help. Reid: *We've had as many as six people, and that's much too much. But overall I think people always assume that we're bigger.* Their assistants are sometimes ceramics grads, but they don't require experience. Klein: *One of the worst assistants we had was somebody just out of grad school who had lots of experience, but doing what they wanted to do and not what we wanted them to do. So it's much easier to teach somebody who has less knowledge but has the aptitude and ability. We also have interns, generally. It's nice to be able to mentor that way.*

Reid: *When you were asking about how we collaborate on things? I think that James is very much the shape guy and I'm the concept. Like I need a concept, something to hang all the work on, and James, you know, we work back and forth but he's much better at shape.*

Klein: *I'm more physical and David is less physical.*

Reid: *That's why we went to Cranbrook and Alfred. That's who we are.* ∎

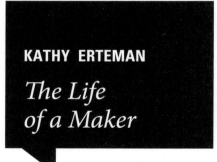

KATHY ERTEMAN

The Life of a Maker

Kathy Erteman in her Kingston, New York, studio, 2016

Kathy Erteman has not concentrated on a signature look or even a signature identity. She has worked in pottery and design, and—early in her career and again recently—she has also made sculptural work. A native Californian (b. 1952) now based in New York, she is the daughter of immigrants. Her father was from Amsterdam, where he *worked in the diamond trade, which is what almost all the Jewish young men did if they didn't have a college education. He was an industrial diamond cutter.* Her mother, from Vienna via Argentina, had been in California as a teenager and graduated from the Art Center School of Design as a commercial artist. She became a designer in a firm started by her grandmother, which manufactured women's formal high-end clothing, and her husband eventually worked for the business as well.

Although Erteman's parents encouraged her with art supplies, *they probably hoped that I wouldn't do anything that involved using your hands, making something. Jews always want their kids to do better and to aspire higher. It was always assumed that my brother and I would go to college, but my parents didn't know how to help or guide us.*

My mother also taught at Chouinard in fashion design, and occasionally she would spring me out of school if she was having an interesting speaker. And they would have a student fashion show every year. We would always go to the pottery sales. I still have some of the pots that I bought there, and they were excellent; they were part of the gold standard that kept me going for many years and inspired me until I discovered Lucy Rie and Hans Coper. I did bring up to my parents that I would like to go there, because they wouldn't pay for me to go away. But it was just at that time when Chouinard was changing over to Cal Arts, and they weren't accepting any new students—that was the party line—so I didn't pursue it. Erteman went to UCLA and hated it, because it was so big and unfriendly.

But to back up for a moment more, *growing up in Southern California in a slightly show business neighborhood that was very well heeled, having immigrant parents—in the old country this was the right social stratum for them, but they weren't really living up to that in the US—was a socially high-stakes environment, and I found it challenging. There weren't very many kids who had parents with accents. No Oreos, peanut butter sandwiches cut on an angle; we didn't have any of that. And also my mother worked and we had somebody who took care of us who was German. And the story goes that at a certain point I told my mother that I didn't* *want her to help me with my homework because she spelled with a German accent.* [Laughter] *Of course later, you know, I'm very happy that I had that background.*

Erteman went to a good public high school, and it was there that she took her first ceramics class. *I think by the time I got to high school, I already had made a certain peace with who I was, and I found my own group, the sort of smart and artistic kids. I always thought art would be for me something on the side, and that I would do something more academic. I think because family was so challenging and maybe school socially so challenging, having an inner life and the life of a maker even as a kid was a nice refuge. The minute I got to the wheel, it was like a lightbulb went on in my head, and I just couldn't get enough of it.*

I found out about a studio in West Los Angeles called Potters Studio. It was for adults. You could have a membership and go there and work. It was owned by Robert Brent of the potter's wheel—that's a brand; there's a person behind it. So it was all his prototype wheels there. It was a great place, and you could go any time of day and night; they had really good glazes, gas kiln, and wheels, so I started spending most of my free time there. My parents were so strict, I was amazed that they'd let me do that.

The summer after high school, Erteman went to a nine-week pottery workshop in Santa Cruz, California. *Big Creek Pottery. It was total community, country life; we threw pots, we went through rigors of cup-plate-bowl every day, ate really great food, drank too much wine, they had a jug band, and it was just a wonderful experience. You'd make 100 mugs. You'd decide on a shape and make 100* of them and keep 10. Then you'd go on to bowls. And after that, I was supposed to go home and start at UCLA. If I'd had the courage at the time, maybe I wouldn't have gone back and my life would have been very different. As an 18-year-old [at Big Creek], I just thought I'd died and gone to heaven. But there was something about it that wasn't quite a good fit. There was a little bit of a conflict, and I don't know if that's being an urban person at heart or being Jewish.

She started college still living at home. But it didn't work. *That was like the old-school part of them; they thought I should live at home and be under the same old rules as being in high school. It was terrible.* She ended up living with her boyfriend, from the time she was a freshman. *I did take one ceramic class there, and then the summer after the first year I took a class with Adrian Saxe. He was new there teaching. I wanted desperately to get out.* She transferred to Sonoma State. *Everybody who was teaching was also a practicing artist. Their instruction was pretty poor, but they told us about going to galleries and reminded us to pick up resumes at the front desk, and the philosophy there was that the way you learned about being an artist was to pay attention to artists, not stick your head in a book.*

I would take my general ed classes and go to San Francisco and go to a lot of galleries. It was an exciting time for ceramics with that whole Funk movement, even though I wasn't really that interested in it. I was making pots, and you weren't supposed to be making pots; you were supposed to be making sculpture. I thought I was going to pursue something like psychology or sociology. Then at a certain point when I was very close to graduating, I realized that every free moment I was still in the ceramics studio; I had my own studio where I lived. I thought: this is ridiculous; I should just take a stand.

So she talked to Adrian Saxe and told him she wanted to get a fine-arts degree. He said if she wanted formal classes and traditional training, she should go to Alfred or to Cal State Long Beach. *I think Alfred was out of the question; it seemed too far away and scary, and I didn't know how to do that. So I applied to Cal State Long Beach [for a BFA], and I went there for about a year and a half and it was really great. It was actually the opposite of my experience at Sonoma State. I really loved*

the structure because there was instruction in how to build a large-scale sculpture, figure sculpture, glaze calculations, ceramic art history. I didn't even think about going to graduate school, because I'd been in school so long at that point.

I found a studio in an industrial area of Long Beach. It was a great studio, 1,000 square feet. I barely spent any time in it because I was working all these other jobs to pay for it. At Long Beach she had learned *plaster turning, which is a way of making shapes, models, on a wheel, but carving them out of plaster. It's a popular technique in Europe, and it's associated here with industry. It's getting a little bit more popular, now that mold making and slip casting is not considered a big no-no. At that time, Alfred and Long Beach were the only two schools in the US that taught it. I spent a lot of time there learning those skills. I generated these shapes that were very reminiscent of Lucy Rie, who I had discovered on a trip to visit my relatives in Holland. It allowed you to make a very precise form and get exactly what you want. At the time I was interested in narrow-based forms that defied gravity. Happily, I had these molds and models that I'd made in school, so I had something to continue with in my new studio right away.*

It was a rude awakening that there wasn't a gas kiln. You know: How am I going to make my work with an electric kiln and without the support of school behind me? How am I going to learn how to be an artist? At that very moment, somebody told me that Judy Chicago was looking for somebody to work on her ceramic team for The Dinner Party, *and my name had come up.*

Chicago wanted a commitment of full-time working at her studio for free. I said, "Well, I can't do that; sorry." But then she yielded because she needed my skills. I would go there a couple of days a week from Long Beach, and then I did some of the work in my own studio. It was a challenging situation, but what kept me going was I knew why I was there—to observe Judy Chicago and see how she talked to the Plexiglas fabricator and got what she wanted, how she dealt with galleries and museum people and collectors. Even though she had a very different personality, it was still useful just to see her passion and her drive. Nothing stopped her. I was at a good point to learn from what was available. I did that for I think two years until The Dinner

Party *opened, all the while working in my own* studio.

I started showing my work at Dorothy Weiss's first gallery that she had with some partners in San Francisco, and at the Craft and Folk Art Museum in Los Angeles, and then other galleries found me through those, and slowly I started giving up some of my many extra jobs and spending more time in my studio. The sculpture that I was doing at the time, which I had started at school, was with neon and ceramic. It was very much influenced by the L.A. Finish Fetish movement and sort of the slick and bright colors. I was making slip-cast domes. All you would see is the ceramic disk that had some luscious surface, and then the glow of neon too. It was surface, form, color, no political statement. It was sheer, slick beauty. All the while I was making vessels as well, and they were related in their surfaces, and they had a lightness to them. I was doing a few different things trying to develop my voice. So I'd go back to the wheel and make this stoneware pottery like we were taught at Cal State Long Beach, but it didn't really hold my interest.

I saw a show at the Craft and Folk Art Museum of Gertrud and Otto Natzler. It also had black-and-white photographs around their house and of them working. And I thought: I want that life. Always in the back of my mind I was aspiring to have what I imagined their life to be. I imagined that they just went to work in their studio every day; they didn't have to commute—you know, put on a dress and perfume and drive to downtown L.A. the way my mother did, and I found very depressing. They would just roll out of bed and work in the studio towards a show, go to their opening, sell everything, and come back to an empty studio and start over again.

Dorothy Weiss asked me if my parents were subsidizing me, and I said, "No, I'm teaching, I'm doing this and that and selling my work, and I want to be like the Natzlers, that's what I'm trying to do." She basically said, "Oh, you silly girl; don't you know they have a patron—that's how they do it, Sperry Rand Corporation." I think that underwriting their living expenses was what Dorothy was inferring. The subtext was you can't expect to live from your work solely, that the reason they are able to do that is because somebody underwrites them.

There was an art community for sculpture, and painting, but there really was not a craft or ceramic community in Southern California. Feeling the lack of community, Erteman kept wanting to go back to Northern California, and finally she and her boyfriend, a sculptor, moved to Benicia, where *there was a great community. Robert Arneson, Manuel Neri, a lot of glassblowers, a friend from* The Dinner Party, *and Judy Chicago herself were there. And that's when I started doing the ACC shows, because some of the others there did it, and they showed me the ropes. And then they would do open studios twice a year; that's where I learned how to do that. There was one stoneware potter, but that wasn't the strength of that community. But then Sandy* [Simon] *and Bob* [Brady] *moved to Benicia. I invited her to join me in my open studio. There was a big ceramic community in Berkeley, which was half an hour away. And through doing the ACC shows, because the first one I did was in San Francisco, I met some of the other potters in the area. With those ACC shows, everybody I knew was working, solely, with no extra jobs, as an artisan, craftsman, artist. Working hard but living comfortably from their work.*

Yet, at the same time, Sonoma State had discouraged making pottery, and the California College of Arts & Crafts in Oakland did the same. And a major figure like Bob Arneson would disparage functional work. *It would be like, "Oh, you've got a little factory going there," you know. It made me feel bad like it was supposed to, but it wasn't in me to make the kind of work that he did. Besides, if you opened up the cupboard in their kitchen, it was full of handmade stuff. I was still thinking about doing some work that was one-of-a-kind gallery work. But making the work that I was showing at those fairs kept me busy nonstop for a number of years, so I couldn't even consider that. And I did think about going to graduate school at some point, but I never did that.*

When Erteman surveys her oldest studio work, from her Potters Studio days, she describes it as *the ultimate of a stoneware glaze; it has these speckles, just a functional bowl, very rustic.* And then there was the *very L.A. slick and shiny.* [Laughter] *It was the beginning in the '70s, maybe a reaction to stoneware glazes and pottery, of using bright colors and different kinds of surfaces. Chicago was using china paint and lusters, and I learned these techniques while I was there, applying luster. Also I* loved the work that was going on in L.A. with the spray painting of automotive paint. It was a way of expressing that in my ceramic work, using ceramic materials.

Then there's shapes with a lot of lift that I was so interested in, and they were prompted by Lucy Rie / Hans Coper work that I saw in Europe, as well as some Scandinavian glass like that of Timo Sarpaneva and Tapio Wirkkala. I loved the silhouette, the curve on it. The form was so different than my training and what was popular with functional work.

Ceramics has so much process involved, and it takes so long to see your final results. You have to wait until it comes out of the glaze firing. So I was looking for a way to work where I could see what I was doing at every step along the way. I wanted some spontaneity, some vitality in every step of the process. And one day I had some black slip and a carving tool, and I just put it on a piece and carved a spiral, those earliest markings that man makes, like drawing in sand with a stick. It was so satisfying and so direct, and I knew it would look the same even after it was glazed. I thought, this is what I've been looking for. The carving technique was the birth of this black-and-white series of work. It seemed very open ended. I could make the pieces using the potter's wheel; I could make them handbuilt or slip cast; they could be functional or sculptural. It was the beginning of a very long conversation. It became very popular, so I was very busy making, making, making.

When I was really busy, I was having people help me in the studio, and that was something that I really couldn't teach somebody about: the relationships, what to do next. So I always carved those myself. I did some abstracted botanical motifs of leaves and seed pods as well. Using different tools expanded my vocabulary. This artisan tool company started, Dolan Tools, and they made steel carving tools, all different types, and that allowed me to expand what I was doing.

It's almost like printmaking because the forms would be consistent, like a blank sheet of paper, and then each surface could be different. The form is studied and the surface is spontaneous. And that's what I liked about this series. I'd have 10 of these bowls lined up, and while I was carving one it would suggest what I was going to do next on the next

piece. So each piece is one of a kind, but they're related. And also it's the vulnerability and the unpredictability of the human hand. Sometimes your hand skips a little bit; some days are better than other days for carving; all the emotional content of your brain comes out your hand.

Always searching for how to improve, how to make it more interesting to myself, I wanted to add a third color, another neutral, and so there's some that I did black, white, and a tan color, and that added a whole other dimension and level of depth. And then sometimes I just did a white-on-white carving. She did some wax resist designs, added gray, and then I started layering the slip, doing less carving, and it was more like painted surfaces, and I started sanding away, scumbling the surface. As it got to be more painterly, it was on the same pieces, but that didn't really make sense. And that's when I started to work on flat surfaces. Most of her studio work now is wall compositions.

The carved works began in the mid-'80s, when her relationship was ending. The steady thing was the work. I really loved just sitting at my table carving all the time while chaos was going on around me. So I continued.

I thought at a certain point, okay I need to move somewhere; I need to change my life. I started looking around in Berkeley and even Mendocino but couldn't decide. She found her answer in New York City. I just felt really good when I was here. And there were some artists in this building [16 E. 18th St.] that I had met at the Rhinebeck show many years before. Those ACC shows gave me community on a national level. So I met all of these New York potters, and when I ended up moving here in '94 I already had an instant community.

This was a dirty factory space with a floor that had been unused. But everybody of my generation of ceramic artists in New York at some point in the '70s worked in this building or had something to do with it. The nice thing about this building was concrete floors, lots of power, and cheap rent, and you could live and work and have it a little bit separate. She barely got it, having leased a space and written a rent check and started fixing it, but not yet moved in, when the city seized the building for back taxes. When the new owner came in, I had a lawsuit which cost me a lot of money, but as a result I had a long lease. Still, nothing is forever, not in New York anyway. Erteman finally had to leave the building in January 2015. One by one the artists had left or were evicted, and the building turned over to a new population: young professionals with their first jobs, living five to a floor, some young doctors. In the aftermath she lived and worked in the Hudson valley, in a house she bought and rehabbed. Then, just a little late, after a 14-year wait, she got space in Westbeth, a New York City industrial complex converted in 1970 to artists' residences.

Teaching has been a supplement to the studio work—first at Parsons but most consistently at Greenwich House Pottery, where she was surprised to find deeply engaged students.

Design has also been a major focus in Erteman's career. Even in her functional studio work, *there's a lot of consideration to every curve and shift in profile, and so I guess that could be called design.*

It's interesting that I think every potter I know is a good cook and a food adventurer, and it's very important to me what I serve the food I cook on. I begin with giving the most consideration to the function and how is the food going to look on the plate. It should be in service of the food.

Food needs can overcome her misgivings about studio pottery. *It just doesn't make a lot of sense in my life and in this modern world to be making tons of functional work because of the cost to me as the maker and how much work I can make and the cost to the consumer. It's not green and sustainable. So there has to be a very good reason to make it. Like I feel like there isn't a really good ice cream bowl out there, and I'm going to design and make one. The ice cream bowls that I made, which could also be for a Thai dessert, are small, slightly shallow, tall enough so that it doesn't drip out of the sides but shallow enough so that you can see the whole scoop. It's not concealed by the sides of the bowl. I've made some wide, low bowls because I wanted a bowl for stews or curries, or an arranged salad. So it was menu-driven design.*

I know it's not a popular point of view. I think the only sustainable way of making pottery would be the way that teacups are used in India, where they're made and baked in the sun, and you drink out of them and then you throw the clay back in the pile. That would be green and sustainable. I understand we all want something that's handmade and is emotionally sustaining. I feel blessed that I have that contact every day. But in terms of resources and financial viability, it really isn't that viable to produce and sell artisan handmade pots. I mean I do it [Laughter], but that's why I'm feeling better and better about having my designs continue in the form of factory-produced as well as a very limited amount of handmade.

I also think about making functional work as a design project for prototypes. I get to work on the part of the process that I love the best, which is the problem-solving, perfecting the design in every way. And then the part I don't enjoy is having to make hundreds exactly the same. Once I've worked everything out and made about 10, I feel like I'm done with it.

The dinnerware that's now being produced by Crate and Barrel, 18th Street Dinnerware, I made for myself. It's a bit of a modernist simple design. Very pared down, also black and white, and there's a little bit of the raw clay edge showing, really meant to be a frame for the food but with a real thrown quality. I made all the first set for myself on the wheel, and also the final prototypes that Crate and Barrel sent to the factory in Thailand went right from my wheel into a box and off to north Thailand, where they were interpreted. What I like about working in this way is that it's so populist; everybody can afford it. The $60 mug, I really have a problem with that. I feel happy that there's a mug that costs $11 that has that handmade quality. And you know it gets people jobs. I feel like it's very wasteful, using up all this power and materials to make pots.

I've done some lamps for Crate and Barrel. I did another set of tableware that was black and white a few years ago. I did a collection of decorative pieces for Tiffany some years ago when they wanted to start working with artists in the spirit of Louis Comfort Tiffany and have some handmade studio pieces. The design was inspired by a Native American coiled bowl. You could use them, but I think people mainly used them to set on a table. Those actually weren't manufactured, though; I made them in the studio. And then I did some tableware for Dansk, but that never made it into production because the company got bought by Lenox. It's been one here, one there. I would like to do more.

I did one group of work where I made pieces

in Peru at this studio. They invited me down there and then they said, "Okay, now we can make these and you market them." So I tried that out, and that was kind of disastrous, I mean because I ended up like having an importing business.

Mostly these opportunities came about from doing those shows like the American Craft Council show. Some are coming to buy; some are coming to scout; some are coming to steal [Laughter]; it's all those things. Crate and Barrel, it seemed like lots of different people in the company noticed my work and said, "Oh, you should work with us," and it just took us a long time to figure out how to work together. They do work with designers, and they're doing it more now, but it's kind of hard to make that all work, especially with my pottery because it had such a handmade quality. One more thing about that; there isn't as much difference as one would think between making ceramics by hand and making it in a factory, as I learned from visiting factories in this process. No matter how you make ceramics, it is touched by human hands hundreds of times from inception to finish.

Sometimes they consider design as an unnecessary expense because they can go on the internet or do a little sketch on a cocktail napkin, and then their technicians can make the pieces. And that's been a problem in the US. I would say that in Europe the value of using a designer is understood, and from touring factories in Thailand and in China, what they said is "We're very good at copying but we're not very good at innovation, so we need you."

A company like Dansk would come to me or KleinReid, different people, and say, "Can you design some tableware for us, and you just do it your way, and then we'll go through a review" or whatever. But some of them, they don't want to do that because they follow the trend, the market, and all that. It's because of the corporate mentality.

Another of Erteman's design-related activities in recent years involves assisting others through Aid to Artisans, a private nonprofit organization that connects the artisans in developing cultures to a marketplace. *I let them know that I'd be interested in doing something, either in South America or Asia, especially Asia. I love all traveling. I think it just adds so much to expansiveness in life, not to mention the incredible visual inspiration. So I got a phone call out of the blue in 2007 saying, "Could you go to China in two weeks [Laughter] with these potters?" And I said, "Well, I don't know; that's my busiest time in the studio."*

They had a grant that was about to expire. It was a USAID-funded program, and because of the Tibetan conflicts and China, it had been very difficult to complete this grant in the cycle. A consultant had done a study, and when she came to the Nixi (pronounced *nee-shee*) potters, she recommended that a designer who was also a potter be brought in.

Somebody had known about me and just called me and said can you do this. But they didn't go into detail; they didn't tell me anything about it; they didn't tell me they were Tibetan; they didn't tell me I was going to the Tibetan Plateau. I thought I could teach them artisan to artisan to improve their existing work. As it turned out, I think the organization didn't really expect me to accomplish very much. They didn't say that, but . . . I accomplished an incredible amount; the potters accomplished an incredible amount in two weeks. I had a fantastic translator who ended up being a great studio assistant, because as I was teaching something, she would absorb the information and then help and translate it, but then she would help me teach it. We got some new designs done, talked about craftsmanship issues and some marketing ideas, just some very simple ones like getting the pots above the ground, dusting them off, display, packaging.

The Mountain Institute was another organization that had an office in the area. And so a couple of years later, that organization contacted me and said, "Would you like to continue the work? We just got a grant." And again it was last minute. We decided after a lot of back and forth that I would travel with some of the Tibetan potters—they're all men—from their village to Jingdezhen, China, and do the exchange there because that's an international city. So I flew up there, to Shangri-La, to the village, and then met with the translator and 17 men from ages 18 to 70. [Laughter] I realized, omigod, what a huge responsibility, I must be insane. Then we went to Jingdezhen and we stayed there for three weeks. Three of the potters got to come to the US, and several years later Erteman went to multiple US sites with a larger group.

So she balances all these activities. The black-and-white carved work has had the most passionate, devoted audience, and a few years ago someone pressed her to do more because something had broken. *But I had a terrible time. The materials had changed; my hand didn't do it. It was kind of a disaster. I did it and I made a little money and I learned that everything runs its course.* ■

HIROE HANAZONO

A Pedestal for Food

Hiroe Hanazono in her Philadelphia studio with Bobo, 2018

The design quality of Hiroe (pronounced *hee-ro-eh*) Hanazono's porcelain ware is its clean, orderly, nonexpressive appearance. She is interested in multiples, and she inventively looks for new purposes and forms.

Hanazono arrived at ceramics circuitously. She was born in a provincial city north of Tokyo. When she reached high school age, she moved to Tokyo and lived with an aunt so that she could get a better education, following in the footsteps of an older sister. That sister is an architect, while her eldest sister is a cook who owns a restaurant in Port Townsend, Washington. Hanazono *was always interested in making something; especially I was into cooking because my mother was a horrible cook and I didn't like anything that she made, so I studied cooking at an early age.*

Her professional path, however, was photography. She studied commercial photography for two years and was a photographer's assistant for one year. When that business closed after Japan's "bubble economy" burst in the early '90s, she freelanced, *making product photos, going to companies' facilities, taking pictures of companies. One job I did was blue background, shooting hundreds of different plastic containers, just keep taking the same photo. Commercial photography is not really interesting, not something I wanted to do at all, but I did that because I needed to make money.* When she had a nest egg, she moved to San Francisco.

Although the major motivation was a medical treatment not available in Japan, she came on a student visa and started studying English as a Second Language at City College of San Francisco. She lived with various roommates, and in one place *I saw a bunch of handmade pots in the kitchen, Japanese looking.* [I asked,] *"Who made those? Whose pots are those?"* And they said, *"Oh, Natasha made them; she takes classes,"* and I said, *"Oh, classes? I didn't know anything about."* You know, back in Japan we use so many ceramic dishes every day at mealtime, but I didn't really think there were classes in those traditional craft forms back home. If I lived in a pottery village, I might have had some sort of way to get into it seriously, but nobody knew anything about that, not me.*

I found there was a noncredit ceramics class that I was able to take at Fort Mason, City College of San Francisco. My English skill was so limited and I was so very shy I couldn't ask questions. But I knew right away that I wanted to continue. I was so frustrated I couldn't make anything very well. Then my friend told me there was a ceramic studio at UC Berkeley; anybody can go, doesn't have to be a student. So Hanazono worked at ceramics while also working (off the books) at a bistro. *I got so excited about what I can make; I had so much fun. I wanted to study more, so I decided to go to college. I took TOEFL, went to City College of San Francisco as a regular full-time student because I needed to keep my student visa, and taking other classes and ceramic classes every semester. My teacher asked me if I'm interested in being a tech.*

I learned to fire a kiln, mix glazes, go to studio when no one can use; it was really exciting. So I stayed in college for quite a long time, maybe four years. I had so many units I couldn't take any more classes, so I went to university. I didn't want to become illegal, so I needed to keep going to school. I chose Cal State U Hayward, doing ceramics. I just got my BA and then had my senior show. Then okay, what's next, what should I do? Every summer I was taking workshops at the Mendocino Art Center with different artists from all over, and especially I like to go there for soda firings or any other kinds of firings I couldn't try in the city. That was really fun. And then the summer right after I graduated from Cal State U, I took the summer class at Mendocino and met Robbie Lobell.

Hanazono had by that time applied to three graduate programs. She was rejected by two and had no reply from the third. *As I went to take this workshop with Robbie, I was putting in my portfolio and saying this is where I'm at. I didn't get into grad school, I really don't want to quit working with clay, this is my passion, and she was like, "Why don't you come and see my place, Wooster Center for Crafts?" She used to be a resident coordinator there, and they have an affiliated college to get the paperwork for you. So after the workshop I flew to Wooster, Massachusetts, to see what's possible.*

I moved to Wooster summer 2003, and then I was living in a class house right across from the studio, so I was there every day. I had 24-hour access to the studio, which I had never had, and I was

so happy. I was being a special student. I had to take some classes, so I learned some more ceramics. It was a smaller, more in-depth kind of program, and I also was a studio assistant so I was making glazes for 200 other students. I was helping them do bisque firing, unloading kilns. It was a really good experience. I didn't have a life. I was just there to make pots.

She stayed two years, the second year as resident artist. *I was learning so many new tricks. And then I wanted to try going to school again. I thought if I don't get in this time, I was going to give up. But I got into quite a few places, including Ohio University. I chose to go there. My second year when I was in Wooster I did summer assistant at the Peters Valley Craft Center. And there I met my husband* [Stephan Goetschius, who ran the wood shop there]. *So I was doing a little long-distance relationship for a while from Wooster, and then I went to school in Ohio, and my first year I was there by myself and then my second year my husband joined me.* [They are no longer together.]

My first year in grad school I found out I couldn't get any scholarship money from Ohio because they said they weren't getting paperwork from Wooster. They had not done the paperwork properly, so my visa was totally terminated. So I thought: Oh my god, what am I going to do; I'm already in grad school! So we rushed our marriage.

Grad school was amazing. I hated and loved it at the same time. It was really hard. I don't know how many times I wanted to quit, but I had amazing teachers. They really care about ideas and how I can communicate my ideas. It was real important to the program. My first crit I didn't know what to talk about. I had never been in that kind of formal situation. They helped me learn how to make a portfolio, all that stuff, provided all those classes; they made us teach, teaching assistant, course creating; we got all that training. It was torturous but it was a really good experience for me.

The more I made my work and understood about why I was making—I never made single pieces, I was always making sets, and that told me that I really like to cook for a bunch of people, having a meal with many people, interchange with people. And my work is always minimal, very simple. Food brings all the textures and colors. When foods come into the plate, they complete the images. So

I feel like the surface of the pot is almost like a canvas, a pedestal for food. That's how I feel, so keeping inside pretty simple. My work has been always like that.

I like to invent forms; how can I say . . . I'm good at copying someone's work; once I learn the technique I can copy it, but it's not my work. So I'm always struggling with what makes my work. Whenever I design my work, I hope no one is making work like this, so I don't want to look at too many magazines, do too much research, because I want my work to be original. Sometimes I was getting inspiration from architecture, furniture, modern design, and whenever I see some unique forms, sketches, not really looking at other people's pots. In my thesis work and also when I studied at grad school, it was thrown on the wheel, then handbuilt, but I was erasing all my finger lines to make it smooth.

Then I got interested in mold making. Then everything became slip-casting work. In the third year I also started making forms, and they could be very heavy, not very easy to use. I was thinking about the American culture, that everybody is living really busy life, driving and eating at the same time, eating in front of the computer. I kind of wanted to give a message about slow down, eating a meal can be very enjoyable, take a half hour. So that was my thought about making all those not very easy to use. I continued to make handmade dishes, hoping that my work would be part of those enjoyable meal experiences for anyone instead of using plastic or paper plates and bowls. Presentation of the food is super important in Japan; how you present and decorate and what you're using, not only the taste of the food but also visually pretty, aesthetically important. I'm hoping that if I keep making dishes, my work could contribute to somebody's home, to a pretty meal.

For my thesis show I made two different place settings. One was a party setting like a Japanese-style table; one was breakfast. Everything was a heavy meal with multiple people. For that show my husband made tables; the party table was 8 feet long and everything ceramic was double wall. I had a big salad bowl, appetizer bowl, a tray that looks like a sculptural form if you see it by itself, some dip bowls, a vase in that party setting; everything pretty massive. In the breakfast set everything

was double wall, almost like a peanut shape repeated. The double wall, which gives an appearance of weight, was part of her effort to slow down the experience; even if it made them harder to wash, they would be beautiful to use. She was drawing shapes on paper that she could not make any other way, but she suffered a lot of breakage in firing because air would be trapped inside the form and expand during firing. The double wall was also more time consuming to make, so she has done it less since leaving graduate school.

Her summer residency at the Archie Bray Foundation in 2008 wasn't as stressful as grad school. She exhibited and sold objects from her thesis show and developed one body of work there, although she had only two months instead of the usual three because she had to pack and move to Philadelphia, where she had been awarded a fellowship at the Clay Studio. That was for just one year, but fortunately she was able to stay on as a resident artist for four years following.

She had mixed feelings about Philadelphia. *I don't like the weather here at all. But there is such a strong artist-supportive community, I feel really fortunate to be here. I've been getting promoted by artistic directors, interior decorators; everybody has been supporting me so well. I got a solo show at Philadelphia airport; I got a grant from Independence Foundation to go to Denmark for three months.* She also found places to teach locally. So she stayed on after her residency ended in 2013.

On process: *Drawing the life-sized template, specifically drawing how high, how deep everything goes, then I draw onto wood so I've been making wood cutouts. The form I was interested in was hard to make out of clay or plaster. Plaster is very brittle. So wood was the way to go. Also my husband was very good with wood, so he taught me quite a bit.* She's thinking of drawing on a computer and sending it to a CNC router, because it's hard on her hands to make each model out of wood. She has substituted Styrofoam.

On color: *Neutral; right now I'm using a bit more pastelly color, but very light; the inside is pretty much always white.*

On purposes: *I do imagine certain things, but it's not necessary; it's very adjustable to any foods. Bowls, plates, serving dishes. I like to have a big plate with little food, so my plate could be too big* for some people, and then it could be a serving plate.

On terminology: *The thing is, you know, it's hard for me still to name some of my work. So sometimes I would go downstairs and talk to the* gallery person; *how would you call this? I know what I'm making, but if anybody asks me the title it's really hard to say it in English still. Is this dish or is this bowl; what would you say?* ■

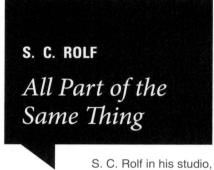

S. C. ROLF

All Part of the Same Thing

S. C. Rolf in his studio, River Falls, Wisconsin, 2016

Steve Rolf might have been a designer or an ergonomics specialist, so attentive is he to the functioning of his pots. It's part of a thoughtful, careful, orderly practice.

Rolf (b. 1965) grew up on a southern Minnesota farm because his parents decided that he and his siblings needed the farm experience. Both parents had grown up rural, and his father wanted to retire early from his job as an air traffic controller. *The three of us children could help work the farm and take care of the animals.*

Rolf had a hard time with school until seventh grade, when he *went from a very, very poor student to . . . just flipped and was an A student within a year and a half. What changed is that I figured out how to teach myself. I figured out a different way to organize my thoughts. That has really come in handy when I teach workshops. That's become one of my fortes, trying to figure out where people are stuck.*

He started college at the University of Wisconsin, River Falls, went on a student exchange for a print-making program on the East Coast, apprenticed under a painter and wood engraver well known for his book illustrations, then returned to Wisconsin and finished his degree. He took a studio in Milwaukee and was doing 8-foot drawings and paintings. *My goal was to be disciplined and work every day. But something was really missing for me.*

He had taken a few clay classes at River Falls but was not thrilled. However, he had an epiphany after his parents suggested that he come to the farm and work for a couple of months. *It was almost instant; something in my head and body connected. I started doing chores and lifting buckets, and that tiny experience I had in the clay studio was so similar to doing chores, because as a potter there's these cycles. You start out in your studio, you prepare the clay, you have this cycle of making, and then you bisque fire and glaze and high fire. And then you start all over. And it's so much like planting crops.*

You raise the crops, you harvest the crops, you prepare the soil, and it starts all over. Also the chores I was doing, feeding the animals—that's physical work, and I realized that when I touched that clay there was a medium that was pushing back at me. I really like working with my body, and that's what was missing.

He looked for schools and ended up at the Kansas City Art Institute. *KCAI was pretty intense. I needed a place where I could learn very quickly because I didn't want to spend another four years in school. I got in as a junior because of my painting/printmaking portfolio, but all of my peers were heads and shoulders above me in terms of their knowledge and skill. I did two years there and then I knew that I had a certain facility with my hands, but my work was not really my own. It lacked my fingerprint. And the sensitivity that I wanted to have in the work wasn't there. I felt I needed to go to graduate school right away.*

He went to Alfred from '92 to '94. When he finished he stayed in town and started a pottery while his wife completed graduate school in glass science. *Alfred . . . has allowed for a lot of marriages between scientists and artists.* [Laughter]

He taught some classes and worked at the ceramics museum and a little bit for a kiln builder. *And then I started the pottery with a buddy of mine. He and I built the kiln and shared costs. And a year and a half rolled around and we didn't have two cents to rub together. We literally had $300 in the bank, and that was before the expenses for the month. And we thought about it and we prayed about it and we thought what feels right; we're just going to jump. So we jumped. And I started selling pots, primarily in Pennsylvania, and a couple of galleries picked up my work. We literally had checks that would come in for the pottery that would keep our electricity on.* [Laughter] *It was really this incredible ride at that time.*

When I first started selling pots in Pennsylvania, there was some issue in recording of the studio name for tax purposes, and they wouldn't allow me to use my name as the business; they wanted a separate business name. So we said could we just say S. C. Rolf; is that change enough? And they said that will work fine.

I'm still making pots now, and the financial situation of course gets better every year. But if we just had the pottery it would have been very different. We wouldn't live where we live, and we wouldn't have children, or we probably could have children but our lifestyle would be different. With her having a job, we need two vehicles; if we were both potters we could probably get by with one. You just have to make some trade-offs. I'm so thankful that we both can pursue careers which are pretty intense, and yet the children are really important to us. We're all in this together, and this is the whole package.

My wife comes from East Germany, so half of our family is in Germany. We go see them every other year or so, and they come here every other year. We had to make the decision to either move to Germany or move here when we left Alfred. They chose River Falls, and she was subsequently hired as a materials scientist by 3M, headquartered just across the state line in Minnesota, so everything worked out surprisingly well.

Rolf is an exceptionally goal-oriented person, and one reason for that *is having such a difficult time early on in school, and only when I figured out how to focus on a target could I get any traction in school. I have a hard time with distractions, so I have to pick the goal in the distance to look at. It has helped in the pottery. It has helped in coaching young people, in having had studio assistants and apprentices, and trying to help them to imagine: Where are you going to be in five years, and where are you going to be in ten years? And how are you going to do that? What do you need to do now in order to realize those dreams?*

Rolf is also a neat person—now. *That's been a real change too.* [Laughter] *When I was in undergrad school, Ken Ferguson would give me a hard time because I walked around on an inch thick of clay on my studio floor, practically.* [Laughter] *It was when Jacky and I had children I realized that I need to kind of rein in some of these variables, like keeping my studio a little bit neater, for the health of our family but also for my sanity. That might be a little different if I had my showroom off-site and my studio off-site. I would probably be a little more relaxed. But I've had people from all over the country stop by here. Oftentimes they'll give me a call and I'll say, "Yes, that's fine; I'd love to meet you. Where are you at?" And they'll say, "I'm at your front door."* [Laughter] *So I need to be a little more in control, having a showroom here.*

They bought a house just before prices started to rise, and he was able to get a permit to build a kiln in town, which can be an issue. The house is a comfortable size, but his studio is in the basement and he foresees the possibility of outgrowing it, and also the wish not to have to carry the pots from the basement to the kiln in the backyard.

At one time I was working with only white bodies because the color response is very different on a white body. And now I'm working on a body that is almost antithetical to that. It's a chocolate stoneware. And I'm just really interested in how glazes respond on this very dark body. It's a very high-iron body. It's a pretty fine grain and it has a dense body, so in that way it has some characteristics of porcelain. You have to work the dense bodies in a certain way to give them a real sense of breath and openness and feeling because everything wants to shrink down, and I don't want to have pots that look like they're just huddled down. You're making things almost a little larger than life because you know that they'll come down to earth quickly. [Laughter]

I'm asked, "Well, you have all this painting and printmaking background; why are your pots not painterly?" I really feel like I am very, very specifically dealing with surface. A lot of my surfaces have to do with patterns in textiles. I'm trying to develop glazes that work as a veil so you see some of the information, and some of it is obscured. Those surfaces to me are really exciting.

I'm really interested in seeing this information underneath this glaze, and how these high points on the pots kind of burn through where the glaze pulls against certain areas, and there's a sense of depth and layering. On certain pots I want the eye to be able to get down into that surface. And on other parts of the pot I want you to be very aware of that surface. I've been able to find some good glazes by playing with certain bases or making up my own base and playing around and testing, testing, testing, testing.

I want my pots to be easy to grab out of the cupboard. I work with the dishwasher as a tool quite a bit because as a contemporary American potter I know that most people have dishwashers, and I don't want these pots to be separated out from other pots in the house. I want these to be daily-use pots that have an ease about them, that people don't have to worry about.

So even a little dessert bowl I designed, you can put it anywhere in the dishwasher and the water will drain out of the foot. And yet it becomes an architectural element in the pot. And a butter dish of mine, for example. How do I design a butter dish that fits in a compartment within the door of a contemporary refrigerator; how do I make a butter dish where it can still hold the whole stick of butter and yet butter will not get on the rim when you take off the lid, so you can put it on fine tablecloths without getting butter all over, and yet put it in the dishwasher so it will drain well, and everything will work? Those kinds of things for me offer this huge world of freedom to explore because it gives me something to push against, some problem to solve. I find that interesting.

Some pots—sometimes small ones because they're easy to move around—I like to be heavy because I like the sense of that clay in your hand. But I like my pitchers to be light, because they're going to hold a volume of liquid. And it's very important for me that they don't drip either. So how do I make this? When you're pouring here, the water comes out, and then when you bring it back it has to cut off at a certain point. I've had pitchers before in my collection where this is made very, very sharp to cut off the liquid, but they tend to chip in the dish rack. So I've taken this and rounded it off so you can put it down in the dish rack, and it never seems to chip because everything is tucked in and yet it has this little bit here that will help cut off that flow. And I look at commercial milk cartons and try to figure out why do they pour well when they're so ugly? [Laughter]

When I grew up on the farm, we had to make a lot of our own stuff. And in making it I wanted to use it, and in using it I wanted it to work. I think that's just kind of a part of my personality. I am very analytical, because it's a tool for me. I'm really not that engineer mind at all. Being analytical helps me to grasp all this unorganized information that's floating around in my head [Laughter], *all the visual information I'm seeing every day. It's kind of a tool that I try to use to get it to go somewhere, to become something usable.*

On color: I think the landscape could have something to do with it. Also the local history. I think Warren [MacKenzie]'s influence is huge. In my area, not terribly far from me, there was the Red Wing

Pottery, and most everybody had crocks in their house when I was growing up. Even though they weren't being used anymore, they were still on people's porches. And I remember as a youngster just loving those pots. They have two things. One, they have these very earthy colors, these browns, these beiges, and secondly they're very hardy pots. And I think that has influenced pots in this area too. I think there is this deep love of the hardy pot. I always thought of those crocks as having a softness to them. They have these big rolled big rims, big lips, sturdy feet. And oftentimes even the sound of them; sometimes the older ones are cracked, but they just had this kind of thud to them so that even the sound was soft and not this high ring.

I'm in love with food. [Laughter] I can't claim to be an excellent cook, but I love to cook. I cook the way I make pots, I get a taste in my head and I just try to figure out, follow that taste and get there. My wife is the baker in the family. I know that food looks wonderful in brightly colored pots too, but my particular palette, I am always thinking about food. And there's a lot of this brown glaze. For some foods, browns tend to be a little warm in color temperature and some tend to be a little cool, so I'm thinking about that. I'm thinking about red peppers and I'm thinking about orange juice in this, and it's wild how it just zings. My color palette is a bit subdued because I try to use the food to really push the space.

On preconceiving: I don't generally make sketches of pots and then go make them. I maybe sketch part of a pot, but most of it happens on the wheel. Most people who want dinnerware have been looking at my work for a while, and they know that I really love to just explore with whatever I'm making. The work is going to ask for a certain glaze. I have a certain intent and the clay is just telling me, no, I don't want to go that way; I want to do something else today. If I'm able to follow that, the work is much stronger. People, thankfully, have been okay with me making my work in that way. But when I'm making, it's like drawing, it's like sketching to me; all these ideas come up.

On glazes: The glazes that I use for dinnerware sets all marry together nicely, so I will even do dinnerware sets where the dinner plate is stoneware in one color, the sandwich plate is stoneware in another color, and the dessert plate might be porcelain, so even this white in it. It makes sense as a painting,

in terms of pushing and pulling space as you look at it on the table. And the depth that I talked about earlier now becomes the actual physical depth in how the plate sits.

On problem-solving: I would try to come up with glazes that don't metal mark. When you see a metal mark on a pot, the glaze is actually so hard it's taking the metal off and causing a streak of metal on the pot.

I noticed that when children first start using the spoon, it skids across the plate and so does the food, and it keeps going. [Laughter] With these bowls with this rolled rim, the food hits the rim here, or it hits the side of the bowl, rather, and the food just curls over and drops right on the spoon.

I make bowls specifically for mixing and specifically for serving certain types of things. I thought I had every size of bowl that I needed in the kitchen, and every year I find a new shape for something that I'm making that would work better—a more vertical bowl or a more open bowl, in terms of the diameter in relation to the height, particular bowls that really require a pretty wide foot for a certain stability in working. I make pots very specifically for certain types of foods. I even started making pitchers for juices in the morning, to hold a certain volume and to fit in the refrigerator.

On spirituality: Our spirituality underlies every other decision that we make. You know, if we believe in generosity, if we believe in forgiveness, then we'd better get at it and do it, and not just say it. I really believe in generosity with pots, and giving. In regard to making work, I guess my spirituality relates to the pottery in that we tend to be a little bit slower than some families, and that's probably due to my wife more than anything; she's really good at slowing us down. Like if we really believe that having dinner together, that using pots, talking with each other, talking with other people, is important, then we had better do it. So that has been great, and that all makes sense in the world of pottery and spirituality. They're similar. All that works together.

That's one thing I loved about the farm. It's the same way with spirituality and career and everything. If they're separate, they don't work well. Every day on the farm was just living, and there was an ease about that. And then of course we always ate together. A lot of what we ate in the summertime came from our farm. It was all part of the same thing. ∎

ACKNOWLEDGMENTS

Such a lengthy project inevitably accrues debt to many, many helpers. I was housed, fed, advised, and otherwise assisted by many individuals and institutions. With all thanks to the following, as well as to others whom I will be mortified to have forgotten to name.

Mary Barringer, Pat Burns & Andy Balmer, Stefano Catalani, John Chapin, Rebecca & Kim Chapin, Linda Christianson, Brian Compton, Guillermo Cuellar & Laurie MacGregor, Kira & Mike Donnelly, Cary Esser, Leslie Ferrin, Emily Galusha, Beth Gerstein, Jeff Guido, Sherman Hall, Robert Harrison, Peter Held, Giselle Hicks, Michael Hunt & Naomi Dalglish, Lissa Hunter, Randy & Jan McKeachie Johnston, Stuart Kestenbaum (Haystack), Jo Lauria, Nora Leet, Suze Lindsay & Kent McLaughlin, Jane and David Maynard, Jean McLaughlin (Penland), Rick & Liz Newby, Shawn O'Connor (Robert McNamara Foundation), Jeff Oestreich, Scott Parady, Chris & John Roberts, Randy Shull & Hedy Fischer, Sandy Simon & Bob Brady, Richard Swanson, Deb Schwartzkopf, Sam & Dianne Scott, Akio & Vicki Takamori, Emily Free Wilson, Mardi Wood, and Jennifer Zwilling.

I must especially thank the transcribers, both paid and volunteer, without whom this book of interviews could not have been realized: Clovy, Emily DuBois, Joshua Green, Jeff Guido, Lissa Hunter, Kim Keyworth, Annie Markovich, Kathryn O'Halloran, Dandee Pattee, and Deb Schwartzkopf.

And clearly, I am indebted to the potters, whose wisdom and charm made the interviews richer than I had dreamed. There were many more wonderful interviews than could be accommodated in this single book.

INDEX

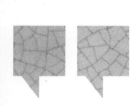